THE PRESIDENCY

THE PRESIDENCY

AN INTRODUCTION

Robert J. Sickels

University of New Mexico

Prentice-Hall, Inc.
Englewood Cliffs, New Jersey   07632

Library of Congress Cataloging in Publication Data

Sickels, Robert J
  The presidency.

  Bibliography: p.
  Includes index.
  1. Presidents—United States. I. Title.
JK516.S48   353.03'13   79-20606
ISBN 0-13-697433-3

Printed in the United States of America

10 9 8 7 6 5 4 3 2 1

Material from *St. George and the Godfather* used by
permission of the author and the author's agents,
Scott Meredith Literary Agency, Inc., 845 Third Avenue,
New York, New York 10022.

PRENTICE-HALL INTERNATIONAL, INC., *London*
PRENTICE-HALL OF AUSTRALIA PTY. LIMITED, *Sydney*
PRENTICE-HALL OF CANADA, LTD., *Toronto*
PRENTICE-HALL OF INDIA PRIVATE LIMITED, *New Delhi*
PRENTICE-HALL OF JAPAN, INC., *Tokyo*
PRENTICE-HALL OF SOUTHEAST ASIA PTE. LTD., *Singapore*
WHITEHALL BOOKS LIMITED, *Wellington, New Zealand*

CONTENTS

v

PREFACE

This book is intended to provide a general introduction to the American presidency in the 1980s. It differs from other books on the subject in one or more of the following respects. First, it examines the modern presidents broadly—their selection, politics, administrative problems, domestic affairs, foreign affairs, personality, popularity, and so on,— along with the more important contributions of their predecessors. Second, it reviews a good many judgments about what is right and wrong with the presidency and what should be done to make it better, but makes no special case for any one point of view. Third, it puts together the products of all major approaches to the study of the presidency, noting the strengths and weaknesses of each. It does not take a single approach, such as historical, behavioral, or public policy analysis, to the exclusion of others. This book is, in other words, comprehensive, ideologically neutral (some irrepressible Madisonianism aside), and methodologically eclectic.

□ □ □

My thanks go to Alice and Wendy for aid, comfort, and patience, to Sally Farr for kind assistance, and to Stan Wakefield, Greg Hubit, and three anonymous reviewers for editorial improvements.

R.J.S.

INTRODUCTION

If men were angels, no government would be necessary. If angels were to govern men, neither external nor internal controls on government would be necessary. In framing a government which is to be administered by men over men, the great difficulty lies in this: you must first enable the government to control the governed; and in the next place oblige it to control itself.

James Madison, *Federalist* No. 51

The purpose of the framers of the U.S. Constitution was to design an effective national government with ample powers and, equally, to erect safeguards against the abuse of those powers by any branch of the government. To that end, they made the three branches independent of each other by separate election or life tenure and in addition gave them powers that might be used defensively if one branch attempted to enlarge its authority at the expense of another.

It has worked, against all odds. The framers knew from history that democratic government was not easily established or maintained—as we know well today, in a world littered with failed democracies. Writing a constitution that would sustain a democracy into the dim future was a rare feat. But not only has the government survived; it has also kept reasonably well to the framers' intent through war, civil disruption, and the assassination and impeachment of presidents. By contrast, the *policies* of succeeding administrations have fared less well. Considering our experience with federal efforts gone awry in the last generation—the war in Vietnam and the programs to eliminate poverty, conserve energy, and curb inflation, to name a few—it is all the more remarkable that the underlying system has run so predictably.

The branches have remained in fair balance from the beginning, checking one another when constitutional bounds seem to have been overstepped. There are many illustrations at hand from the Nixon era, which was a time of unusual tension among the branches. Displeased with the wide-ranging liberal activism of the Supreme Court from the 1954 school desegregation decision on, for example, President Nixon appointed a succession of conservatives to turn the Court rightward, and partially succeeded. Yet when the president authorized domestic wiretaps without warrants—without judicial supervision, therefore— the Court, in an opinion written by one of his appointees, lectured him on his responsibility to adhere to the Fourth Amendment. It was much the same with Congress. In 1971 it passed a measure urging the president to set an early date for the withdrawal of American forces from Indochina. President Nixon said he would ignore this measure because it encroached on his authority as commander in chief. In 1974, on the other hand, as evidence accumulated that the president had participated in obstructing justice in the Watergate affair, Congress set the machinery of impeachment in motion and, when the evidence was overwhelming, forced Nixon's resignation from office. Even the public took part as an independent force in curbing presidential excesses: The "firestorm" of outraged telephone calls, letters, and telegrams that swept Washington after the president removed Special Watergate Prosecutor Archibald Cox for doing his job encouraged investigators in Congress and the Department of Justice to renew their efforts. The framers of the Constitution knew that governmental decisions would often be made by people of no great intellectual or moral strength. They designed a government that could put weakness to good use. "Ambition," said Madison, "must be made to counteract ambition."

The Nixon years thus demonstrate the tendency of the three branches to return to some kind of balance after disturbances have occurred. During the history of the United States, each branch has experienced periods of strength and impotence. The presidency has had hard times: For much of the nineteenth century, and occasionally in the twentieth, it has lived in the shadow of Congress. But it has recovered each time, so well that the other branches have before long fallen into its shadow and have themselves taken measures to restore the balance. There are cycles in public attitudes, too: fairly regular fluctuations from active to passive moods and back, favoring strong political leadership for a time, next relaxing with an Eisenhower, a Ford, or a Carter, then giving signs of need for boldness in government again. Thus in the long run the system works.

But long-run stability is cold comfort in the short run. A president may—for better or worse—make fateful decisions on economic, diplomatic, or military questions without concurrent action by other parts of the government and before they can undertake effective countermeasures. In time of crisis, presidents tend to act largely on their own. In the extreme case of nuclear confrontation, where consultation and checks might be of greatest value, they are least likely. In 1962, during the showdown between John Kennedy and Nikita Khrushchev over the placement of Soviet missiles in Cuba, the world was on the verge of nuclear war. We came to understand our utter dependence on the judgment of a chief executive who was young, inexperienced, and, in this case, lucky.

As Theodore Lowi of Cornell has shown, the ability of presidents to act alone depends on the policy in question as well as the era. His theory that "policies determine politics" leads to the conclusion that institutional constraints overwhelm presidents in some areas of policy and not in others. There are some matters in which the president must accept a nominal role at most, and some in which the president may have his way if he chooses. In still others, the role of the president is moderate or ambiguous.

Lowi classifies public policy as distributive, regulatory, or redistributive.[1] Under distributive (or patronage or pork-barrel) policies, government benefits are broken up into the smallest possible units and distributed to a few people or a single person at a time: Nineteenth-century land policy, tariffs, subsidies, rivers and harbors projects, defense procurement, and services for labor and agriculture are examples. Those most likely to be involved in making distributive policies are congressional committees or subcommittees, bureaus in executive agencies, and private individuals or corporations. The president is generally excluded. If he intercedes other than as a facilitator, he may be rebuffed, as was Jimmy Carter when he tried to force Congress to economize on water projects.

Regulatory policies are more general. Typically they affect whole sectors of the economy—those reached by the regulations of the Federal Communications Commission, for example, or the Federal Trade Commission. They are likely to be made by Congress acting as a whole rather than merely ratifying the decisions of its committees and subcommittees, and by interest groups representing those affected by the policies. The president may be involved, as an equal, along with Congress.

Redistributive policies have the broadest impact of all. They affect—or at least at the time of passage seem destined to affect—whole classes of people such as the affluent or the poor, by taking possessions or rights from one group and giving them to another. Examples are progressive income taxes, civil rights legislation, and the social security legislation of 1935. It is these policies in which the president is most likely to play a part and in which his support and political skills make the greatest difference. Success in enacting redistributive legislation depends on his influence over Congress and key executive officials, on the manipulation of appropriate symbols for public support, and on the assistance of "peak" outside associations representing broad coalitions of interests. The process resembles the making of foreign policy in time of crisis; in both, the president has a leading role.

The business of the federal government in the nineteenth century was overwhelmingly distributive—land disposal, shipping subsidies, internal improvements, tariffs, and the like. Presidents were relatively weak, and even those with qualities of leadership tended toward passivity on matters of policy, rare questions of redistribution aside. The states, by contrast, were heavily engaged in regulatory and redistributive policy making in this period, on everything from slavery to public health, and enjoyed a more controversial and ideological political life. With the passage of the Interstate Commerce Act of 1887, however, the federal government entered an era of regulatory policy making.

During Franklin Roosevelt's administration a mixture of distributive, regulatory, and redistributive policy was initiated at the federal level. Roosevelt's leadership was most evident in redistributive policy. Lowi sees him as responding creatively to pressures, fashioning new programs and selling them to Congress and the people. On other matters, even Roosevelt played a more modest role.

Activist presidents since have taken less advantage of the opportunity for redistributive policy making than did Roosevelt, Lowi contends. Like any president, Roosevelt faced the institutional constraints of his era, but he made the most of the space left for maneuvering. Others since have given in to the ideology of government through organized interests, downgrading potentially redistributive policies—for example, Lyndon Johnson's War on Poverty—into heavily distributive or pork-barrel and thus, in Lowi's view, unworkable programs. The boundaries between policy types therefore are not inflexible. A president may widen his influence by gathering issues together into one large redistributive policy or by adding provisions to pork-barrel legislation to give it a redistributive cast, as Roosevelt did with the Tennessee Valley Authority. Or he may relinquish his influence by allowing a potentially redistributive question to be broken down into regulatory or distributive components.

How the president cooperates and competes with other components of the political system, and at times engages in a Madisonian struggle of action and reaction on questions of basic authority, is the subject of this book. In Chapter 2, "Presidential Personality," we begin with the psyche—what is known about presidents' deeper motives and what the motives have to do with success or failure in office.

Next, the exchanges of presidents, and of candidates for the presidency, with the public generally and with party members and the electorate in particular. A central question is how presidents win popular support: This is dealt with in Chapter 3, "The President and the Public"; Chapter 4, "Presidential Nominations"; and Chapter 5, "Presidential Elections."

The relations of president and Congress in domestic and foreign affairs follow. The actual power of the two branches bears only a passing resemblance to the provisions of the Constitution: See Chapters 6, "Congress: Legislation and Confirmation" and 7, "Congress: Foreign and Military Affairs."

Then we examine the interaction of the president and his own executive branch, which is on the whole as troublesome as Congress, in Chapter 8, "The Cabinet"; Chapter 9, "The White House Staff'; Chapter 10, "The Civilian Bureaucracy"; Chapter 11, "The Military Bureaucracy."

Next (Chapter 12, "The Supreme Court") the cold war of the executive and the judiciary. which once in a while breaks out in spectacular public fighting.

And the involvement of various parts of the government in filling in during a president's disability, removing him for misbehavior, and providing successors is discussed in Chapter 13, "Succession."

Finally, an assessment of the difference presidents make—their impact on policy making and, more broadly, on society—is given in Chapter 14, "Presidents and Policy."

The characters in this story—presidents, members of Congress, judges, bureaucrats, voters, and others—at times behave admirably and about equally often do not. Madison would find them, on balance, to be about the same kind of people he and his fellow delegates had in mind when they convened in Philadelphia in 1787.

PRESIDENTIAL PERSONALITY

Much of the presidency's appeal is, simply, the presidents themselves, a diverse and interesting lot. Some are pushers, some wait to be pushed; some are honest and reasonably truthful, some not. They come old and young, religious and agnostic, fun loving and dour, highbrow and lowbrow, rich and self-supporting, a grand and gaudy show of saints and sinners (although we seldom agree on which is which). We are amused and angered by their conduct in office—and now and then, it is true, lulled to sleep by a president who lacks his predecessors' sense of theater. We keep time, historically, by wars and the coming and going of presidents. We are convinced that presidents affect the course of history.

Style

How much the surface qualities of presidents have affected their work in office is a live question. There was no doubt from the outset that the gregarious and magisterial Franklin Roosevelt was more of a leader than had been, let us say, the quiet and less forceful Calvin Coolidge. There was a special match of manner and performance in each. But another apparently contrasting pair, Theodore Roosevelt and his successor, William Howard Taft, were less different in fact. Roosevelt was impetuous, an adventurer and showman—a "wild man," in the opinion of boss

Mark Hanna; a hero to many. Taft, an enormous, genial, and gentle man, Roosevelt's friend and vice president, was uncomfortable in politics and the presidency and later was to find the more sheltered office of chief justice more suited to his temperament. The contrast in demeanor is reflected in their somewhat overstated positions on presidential authority, written after they had left office. Roosevelt's was the classic statement of the strong and active presidency:

> I did . . . many things not previously done by the President. . . . I did not usurp power, but I did greatly broaden the use of executive power. . . . I acted for the public welfare, I acted for the common well-being of all our people, whenever and in whatever manner was necessary, unless prevented by direct constitutional or legislative prohibition. . . . The course I followed, of regarding the executive as subject only to the people, and, under the Constitution, bound to serve the people affirmatively in cases where the Constitution does not explicitly forbid him to render the service, was substantially the course followed by both Andrew Jackson and Abraham Lincoln.[1]

Taft had a more passive interpretation of the presidential role:

> The true view of the Executive functions is, as I conceive it, that the President can exercise no power which cannot be fairly and reasonably traced to some specific grant of power or justly implied and included within such express grant as proper and necessary to its exercise. Such specific grant must be either in the federal Constitution or in an act of Congress passed in pursuance thereof. There is no undefined residuum of power which he can exercise because it seems to him to be in the public interest.

He went on to twit his old political comrade and competitor:

> Mr. Roosevelt, by way of illustrating his meaning as to the differing usefulness of Presidents, divides the Presidents into two classes, and designates them as "Lincoln Presidents" and "Buchanan Presidents." In order more fully to illustrate his division of Presidents on the merits, he places himself in the Lincoln class of Presidents and me in the Buchanan class. The identification of Mr. Roosevelt and Mr. Lincoln might otherwise have escaped notice.[2]

The two differed in political ideology as well: Roosevelt leaned toward progressivism; Taft considered himself a conservative.

Yet for all the contrasts, their performance in office was not dissimilar. Indeed, a good case can be made that Taft, in an unobtrusive way, was the stronger president. Roosevelt made a display of trust busting and deserves credit for getting the campaign against monopolies under way, but Taft instituted almost twice as many antitrust prosecutions in his single term as had Roosevelt in two. And under Taft's leadership, Congress passed important reform legislation expanding the authority of the Interstate Commerce Commission, requiring candidates for Congress to make their campaign receipts and expenditures public, enlarging the role of the federal government in the conservation of natural resources, creating a Children's Bureau and a Department of Labor, and proposing two amendments to the Constitution, for a federal income tax and the direct election of senators.[3] "A conservative by temperament," wrote Arthur M. Schlesinger, "he found it impossible to resist the liberal spirit of his day, and the statute book of his administration actually recorded greater victories for progressivism than had been won in the seven years of his predecessor, the first Roosevelt."[4]

Taft, especially, is an example of a *mis*match between promise and performance: His personal style and conception of the office were a poor basis for predicting what he would accomplish in office. There are other examples—enough to suggest the risks of forecasting. Who could have guessed that Harry Truman, minor politician from Missouri, overwhelmed by sudden elevation to the presidency and unprepared for momentous decisions on war and peace, before long would be known for his leadership and decisiveness; that John Kennedy, who came into office breathing fire, would be reduced to near passivity in domestic affairs by the time of his assassination; or that Richard Nixon, master politician and mover of mass opinion, would undo himself by misjudging Congress, the courts, and the people at every one of a long series of turns in 1973 and 1974?

There are all too many examples of presidents whose style of operation changed in office. It cannot be said that presidents do more or less what is expected of them, as a rule. Sometimes they exceed expectations built on style and manner, and sometimes they fall short.

Character

There are those who argue, however, that there is a better basis for understanding and predicting presidential behavior, namely, underlying motivational patterns—character, for short. It may be that knowing the shape of a candidate's or an incumbent's character is more useful than knowing his public self; it is certainly more difficult.

Two general approaches have been attempted: One is to diagnose motivation by observing what a president or candidate says and does; the more common approach is to employ biographical information to trace the development of character from childhood onward. Both require inferences about what is really going on inside the person in question, rather than simple projections of surface behavior.

A good example of the first approach is the application of David McClelland's concepts of the need for power, the need for achievement, and the need for affiliation to presidential candidates and presidents. In the laboratory, what are called, interchangeably, *needs* or *motives* are seen in responses to projective tests in which a subject is asked to tell a story about each of a series of ambiguous photographs of people in various configurations and settings. Need for power is defined broadly as "a thought about someone *having impact*"—"about establishing, maintaining, or restoring . . . prestige or power." Each time a person responds with a story about aggression, giving help or advice, or producing emotion in others, he or she is credited with expression of a power need. The achievement motive appears in thoughts about doing something better than it has been done before. Achievement, as McClelland and his associates view it, is a "one-man game that need never involve other people," in contrast with power. The affiliation motive involves concern about making friends. It is the motive "that leads people to care about the happiness of particular others."[5]*

Richard Donley and David Winter have analyzed presidential inaugural addresses from 1905 to 1969 for the frequency of two such themes, power and achievement. Inaugural addresses are hardly an ideal source of information about inner urges, to be sure: They constitute a pathetically small sample of a president's formal utterances, which typically are written with the help of others. And they are purposeful and contrived, unlike the less controlled responses to projective tests in other studies. Still, it is a provocative first step. What we know intuitively about strong presidents, that they are concerned about *both* power and achievement and conversely that weaker presidents such as Taft, Harding, Coolidge, and Eisenhower, score low on both motives is borne out by the study.[6]

In 1976, Winter did a similar content analysis of all official announcements of candidacy for the presidency, this time scoring the affiliation motive as well as the power and achievement motives. Many of the scores were unexciting, in the middle ranges, but two are worth noting. Gerald Ford had the highest achievement score of any candidate (or president, when the data from the earlier study are included) and the lowest power score. His affiliation score was near the top. Jimmy Carter gave evidence of a similar pattern of motives, but the frequency of his use of each of the three themes was much nearer the average than was Ford's. Their studies of both politicians and corporate managers lead McClelland and Winter to regard this as an unpromising configuration for a leader. High achievement motivation is often found in leaders, but

*David C. McClelland. *Power*: The Inner Experience © 1975 by Irvington Publishers, Inc. Reprinted by permission of the publisher.

it is not required. Achievement-motivated presidents are not the most honored and best remembered. People high in achievement motivation aspire to moderate gains and prefer moderate risks. They are efficiency-minded and tend to modify their behavior on the basis of feedback and rely on expert advice. What seems to be required is high power motivation rather than need for achievement or affiliation. The affiliation motive may even be associated with a degree of corruption in office, minor in the case of the Truman administration and major in Harding's, if friendship and loyalties keep a president from firing scoundrels among his entourage.[7]

Power motivation has many manifestations, McClelland and Winter believe. Its form varies according to one's emotional maturity, for example, and to some extent one's sex. And it can be directed at social ends or mere personal gain. It can be benign or cruel. For better or worse, though, it is the basis of leadership as we know it in the United States. And since power in our culture is viewed with some suspicion, while achievement and friendship are more openly valued, care must be taken to use subtle measures such as projective tests (or sometimes, for want of a better expedient, content analyses). Given literal choices on a questionnaire, most respondents would disparage power seeking and vote for apple pie and achievement.[8]

Another example, of personality assessment from what a president does or says, is Lloyd S. Etheredge's study of American foreign policy makers between 1898 and 1968. His general theory is that personality differences affected foreign policy decisions. Specifically, he felt there was reason to believe that observations of a person's behavior in interpersonal relations could be generalized to international situations. Thus, "an American who believes children should be subjected to strict discipline might be more likely to favor use of nuclear weapons internationally." Etheredge chose to measure two personality dimensions—dominance over subordinates and extroversion—by coding historical descriptions of policy makers' interpersonal relations. The scoring criteria for dominance were

> *Highest scoring*: Recorded as regularly intervening at lower levels *or* ignoring subordinates completely *while setting policy himself*. May berate subordinates, seeks to impose will forcefully. He runs the show. Complex, variegated information-acquisition system.
>
> *Mod. High*: In command of situation, may by-pass channels. Some power sharing and flexibility;
>
> *Mod.*: Sets guidelines and makes final decisions himself. Fair amount of autonomy to subordinates. Tends to work through channels.
>
> *Mod. Low*: Often takes a stand, primarily to check excesses. Generally grants large amount of autonomy to subordinates. Appoints people and tends to stay out of their way.

Low: Seldom interferes, defers to others, almost welcomes initiatives of others as a relief. Doesn't as much share power as abdicates it.

And for extroversion-introversion:

High Ext.: Emotionally outgoing, loves crowds. Enjoys contacts with many kinds of people. Leisure time spent with people.

Mod. High: Warm, outgoing, affable, possibly not drawn to crowds. Likes to socialize in his leisure time.

Mod.: Mixed—usually warm and considerate, especially with a moderate number of friends, is sometimes seen as a bit withdrawn.

Mod. Low: Reticent, shy, self-controlled, unemotional, spends leisure time in relative isolation.

Low: Cold, icy, or aloof, or actually shy. Few or no close friends, leisure time spent away from people.[9]

Etheredge's hypotheses for the differences among presidents and advisers on a long series of policy questions from the Spanish-American War to the possible responses to the Soviet invasion of Czechoslovakia were, first,

In cases of disagreement on the following aspects of the use of force those scoring *higher* on dominance will be *advocating* the threat or use of military force, military intervention, ultimata, and the military occupation of other countries and *opposing* moves toward disarmament and arbitration agreements when compared with those scoring lower on dominance.

And, second,

In cases involving disagreement about policy toward the Soviet Union or the Soviet Bloc, those scored as *more extroverted* will advocate cooperative, inclusive policies—recognition, more trade, summit conferences, negotiations to resolve differences—when compared with those scored as more introverted.[10]

Both hypotheses were amply supported by the data. Presidents such as the two Roosevelts, Woodrow Wilson, and Lyndon Johnson who dominated their subordinates *did* favor coercion and threat in foreign affairs. Extroverts such as Harding, Eisenhower, Kennedy, and Johnson favored inclusionary policies toward the Soviet Union—over the doubts of their more introverted advisers such as Secretary of State Dean Rusk.

Both studies—of the need for power, achievement, and affiliation and of dominance and extroversion—arrive at significant conclusions about presidents on the basis of straightforward analysis of readily obtainable material, notably public statements and information about face-to-face relations with other people. Both provide a basis for predicting the behavior of would-be presidents as well as helping to explain why incumbents acted as they did.

The alternative approach is to examine early family relationships and childhood experiences in a search for the development of more or less permanent attitudes toward oneself, other people, and social institutions. The emphasis is on antecedents rather than on current indicators, and the information is more difficult to acquire and use. Two questions underlie these studies: How easily and firmly instilled are attitudes affecting performance, and to what extent do they allow or inhibit adaptive behavior?

There have been some useful studies of single dimensions of character development. Doris Faber, for example, concludes that most presidents have been, in her words, "mama's boys." They have been the first sons of strong, religious mothers, and—it was noted well before the 1976 election—"a rather startling number of presidents seem to have had younger brothers who became serious drinkers." Few presidents' fathers achieved distinction—the exceptions are the fathers of John Quincy Adams, William Henry Harrison, John Tyler, Theodore Roosevelt, William Howard Taft, and John Kennedy. Faber speculates that the indifferent success of fathers spurred the mothers to be unusually ambitious for their first-born sons. She regards this family configuration, revolving about a demanding mother, as the price of success.[11]

In a less sanguine study of British political leaders, Lucille Iremonger links childhood deprivation through illegitimacy or the death of a parent to a drive for political power. A great majority of prime ministers, compared with only a small fraction of the general public, she finds, have suffered the loss of a parent before their fifteenth year. As a result, she argues, these men felt unloved and inferior and were likely to be depressed, recklessly ambitious, and desperate for love and acceptance throughout their lives. In her view, they are "the loveless products of their loveless childhoods."[12] It is a point not entirely distinct from the "mama's boy" argument, since the loss—or by extension the eclipse—of a father may be accompanied by the emergence of a powerful mother. But, as we shall see, there are more general theories.

Insecurity and Power

Harold Lasswell, a pathfinder in American political science, raised questions about the rationality of politicians: Are they the product of their upbringing or its victim? Are they fully capable of rational, adaptive behavior? Can they learn from their mistakes, or are they programmed to fail? Lasswell's pessimism is suggested by the title of one of his early works, *Psychopathology and Politics*, in which he describes politics as "the arena of the irrational." He added, "But a more accurate description would be that politics is the process by which the irrational bases of society are brought out into the open." He described political man with the general formula $p \rightarrow d \rightarrow r$, which signifies that private (p) motives are displaced (d) from family objects to public objects and rationalized (r) in terms of public interests. Political man is a power seeker working out his personal problems on society and justifying his behavior with appeals to principle. The political arena is irrational and unlovely: "The prominence of hate in politics suggests that we may find that the most important private motive is a repressed and powerful hatred of authority, a hatred which has come to partial expression and repression in relation to the father."[13]

But despite some initial oversimplifications, there has been no neat matching of childhood and adult behavior in political leaders and no agreement on the relative importance of compulsive and adaptive activity. The problems—and the prospects—of psychobiography can be seen in the case of Woodrow Wilson. He was a man of exceptional ability and regarded by many as a great president. But he was given to pettiness and rigidity, and because of these shortcomings ended his presidency of Princeton, his governorship of New Jersey, and his presidency of the United States in failure. Why it should have been so has been the subject of many books and articles, which generally suggest psychic damage in childhood.

The bare outline of Wilson's family life and later successes and defeats is well known.[14] His father, a robust Presbyterian minister, was a powerful influence, regularly leading the closely knit family in prayer, songs, and reading and demanding perfection of young Wilson in speaking and writing. But the writing—and reading—came slowly. Tommy, as he was known, was a poor student, the worst in his class at ten and unable to read even passably well until he was eleven. He admired the skilled use of words, but may have fallen behind because of the pressure to excel and his father's practice of teasing him for his mistakes.

In college, Wilson was active and successful. An essay of his entitled "Cabinet Government in the United States" was published in a leading journal. He went to law school, had no success in the practice of law, entered Johns Hopkins University for graduate study in political science, and there wrote *Congressional Government*, which brought him to national attention as a scholar at the age of twenty-eight. Instead of enjoying his success, he soon fell into depression and looked about for new challenges, including the possibility of running for office.

A few years later, with a growing reputation as a writer, lecturer, and teacher, Wilson joined the political science department at Princeton University. It is a measure of his success that within a short time he had been offered the presidency of several universities, but he stayed on at Princeton and in 1902 was named its president. He was a reformer from the outset, bursting with ideas for the improvement of the intellectual life of the university. In time, though, more and more of his energy was devoted to personal disputes, particularly with Dean Andrew Fleming West of the graduate school. The two men disagreed over the proper degree of autonomy for the graduate school and even its physical location. Wilson fought West at every turn uncompromisingly, often deviously, losing much of his original support among trustees, faculty, and alumni along the way. When his dear friend John Hibben disagreed on a point of dispute with West, Wilson broke the friendship. At last a large bequest to the university settled the graduate school controversy in West's favor.

Wilson, who had long dreamed of becoming a "statesman," turned to politics. His eyes were on the governorship of New Jersey and the presidency of the United States. He became the Democratic candidate for governor after giving written assurance to the state party leaders, in response to their expressions of concern, that he would not work against the machine if he were given the nomination. Then he repudiated the bosses who had made the nomination possible. As governor, he changed into a progressive, fought the machine, and became an effective and popular governor. In the next legislative election, however, his party was divided, and the Republicans took control of the legislature.

Soon after, with the help of his newfound friend, Colonel Edward M. House, he began a campaign for the Democratic nomination for president. The nomination was a struggle; the election, in 1912, was easier, because the Republicans were divided. The oratorical skills he had developed in academia and in New Jersey politics had made him a winning national figure. With a Democratic Congress, he went on to enact a legislative program as he had in the first months of the governorship. As always, he went relentlessly from one task to another without pausing to enjoy the satisfaction of a job well done. He shunned the company of those who could not offer ready approval and agreement on all questions. Until their falling out Hibben had been for a time the only man who enjoyed Wilson's full trust and confidence. Colonel House became another, artfully suppressing his own opinions and deluging the president with flattery, which he rightly suspected the president needed to shore up his self-confidence.

Woodrow Wilson's two terms in office were marked by periods of successful leadership of his party, of Congress, and of national and world opinion. He and Franklin Roosevelt share much of the responsibility for establishing the strong modern presidency. It is all the more intriguing, then, that he should have ended his second term in defeat. In 1919 he got into a fight with the Senate over the terms of the Covenant of the League of Nations contained in the Treaty of Versailles. The Senate, which he had not consulted during negotiations leading to the signing of the treaty, learned of its final provisions in the press. When certain reservations to the treaty designed to protect American sovereignty were proposed by the chairman of the Senate Foreign Relations Committee, Henry Cabot Lodge, Wilson refused to consider them. He would not compromise, although the reservations were not unreasonable. When it became clear that his support in the Senate was insufficient to secure ratification without reservations, Wilson went on a national speaking tour to win popular backing and turn the Senate around. In late September, 1919, he suffered a disabling stroke from which he never recovered. The Senate rejected the treaty, and the United States never joined the League.

One of the first to try to explain the personality underlying this remarkable combination of successful and unsuccessful behavior was Sigmund Freud, in collaboration with William Bullitt, later American ambassador to the Soviet Union and France but at the time a disaffected former member of the Peace Commission in Paris in 1919. Together Freud and Bullitt brought a blend of malice, professional expertise, and limited acquaintance with Wilson to the task. Their study was completed in 1932 but for various reasons not published until 1967.[15]

They argued that the adult Wilson had trouble dealing with other men because of unresolved conflicts in his youthful relationship with his father. The senior Wilson was an overpowering father, hugging and kissing, instructing, and relentlessly dominating his son, often humiliating him. One response to such an onslaught might have been open hostility. Young Wilson's was love and submission. He was never known to have said or done anything overtly hostile to his father. On the contrary, rather than maturing normally and asserting his independence, Wilson paid his father the ultimate compliment of identifying with him wholly—or, rather, with an idealized conception of him. In Freud's symbolic language, the father became God and Woodrow the son of God.

Having a divine father has its good side and its bad side. The good side is that the child may be infused with feelings of power and righteousness and like Wilson be driven to accomplish extraordinary things for mankind. The bad is that it becomes very difficult to engage in the give-and-take of social and political life. Freud and Bullitt suggest a specific disability in the form of Christ-like self-sacrifice in which Wilson would have his way by submitting rather than fighting. More generally, they see Wilson as knowing only two ways to treat other men: submitting as he had with a mixture of pleasure and anxiety to his father or, in reaction to the shame of submission, asserting himself forcefully and belligerently in a display of exaggerated masculinity. All men were threatening to him. He was passive toward some, as toward his father, and may in this role have conceded too much in the peace negotiations in Paris. More often he avoided the threat of submission: He preferred the company of women, and had few friends and advisers, dropping Hibben and House when they showed first signs of disapproval. Presented with a confrontation he could not easily avoid, however, as with West and Lodge, he was tough and uncompromising, even when neutral observers could see compromise as a winning strategy. He would go down to defeat in an all-out fight rather than show weakness. Thus he was reduced to either repeating or reacting to one narrow childhood role.

Alexander and Juliette George's *Woodrow Wilson and Colonel House*, published in 1957, is a more careful and sensitive analysis of Wilson's life and personality. It agrees in many particulars with the Freud-Bullitt account, which was not in print when the Georges wrote, but its general argument differs somewhat.

The Georges stress the damage done Wilson as a child. The exactions and ridicule he suffered, reinforced by a religion that taught the immorality of man (and boys), made young Wilson feel helpless and inadequate. As an adult he struggled compulsively against these feelings by exercising power and authority. When his self-esteem was at stake, he fought to win with dogged inflexibility and masked his drive for power with appeals to principle, which convinced much of the world and often Wilson himself.[16]

His continuing weakness was not hidden from everyone, however. Two men understood Wilson well enough to manipulate him successfully. The first, Colonel House, a confidant and along with Wilson the subject of the Georges' book, sensed that special care would be required to stay in Wilson's good graces. He fawned, kept criticisms to himself, remained in the background, and so buoyed the president's sagging self-esteem that for years he was the one person outside the family with whom Wilson felt at ease and was willing to relax his protective reserve. Senator Lodge with equal facility taunted Wilson with criticisms of the League of Nations and drove him to a rigid strategy on reservations that very likely was the only way Wilson could have lost the vote on the covenant. He was a father figure for Wilson. He had to be resisted, since the young Wilson had failed to resist his real father, and his disapproval was particularly galling. Lodge, counting on Wilson's opposition, was able to maneuver him into a losing position.

In 1977 Princeton political scientist Robert C. Tucker offered still another interpretation of Wilson's successes and failures. Tucker regards the Georges' view of power—as a way of trying to overcome low self-esteem—as a plausible explanation of Wilson's drive to win high office, but deficient as theory in two respects. First, it does not account for power seeking by people who do not lack self-esteem or for the failure of many with low self-esteem to seek power. Second, it does not explain Wilson's failures. Tucker prefers Karen Horney's theory of the neurotic personality, which holds that childhood anxiety typically leads to an idealized image of oneself which, if it persists, becomes real in the unhappy sense that the neurotic feels compelled to prove to himself and the world that he is the ideal. Horney characterizes this as an endless "search for glory." Wilson was not after power for its own sake, Tucker believes, but glory. In office, he worked ceaselessly for new things to bring greater personal glory, and sooner or later he met enough opposition to bring him to defeat.[17] According to Horney, the neurotic is dissatisfied with his accomplishments no matter how great, is hungry for approval, and is often perfectionistic, arrogant, or vindictive—all of which fits Wilson as we know him to have been.

(Still another view was cogently argued by Edwin A. Weinstein, James W. Anderson, and Arthur S. Link recently: that major difficulties experienced by Wilson throughout his life can be explained *organically*. They present evidence that his slowness in learning to read was caused by dyslexia and that his troubles at Princeton were precipitated by a series of strokes beginning in 1896, long before the better-known stroke of 1919. They believe the Georges and others have jumped to the wrong conclusions with inadequate psychological theory.)[18]

In his book, *The Presidential Character*, James David Barber takes essentially the same position as the Georges on Wilson's drive for power and achievement as compensation for feelings of inadequacy developed in childhood. Barber's analysis is more comprehensive, however. It builds from Wilson to a general theory of presidential personality. Wilson is described as primarily an active-negative type, along with Herbert Hoover, Lyndon Johnson, and Richard Nixon—all of whom were energetic in office but did not enjoy being president.

> The activity has a compulsive quality, as if the man were trying to make up for something or to escape from anxiety into hard work. He seems ambitious, striving upward, power-seeking. His stance toward the environment is aggressive and he has a persistent problem in managing his aggressive feelings. His self-image is vague and discontinuous. Life is a

hard struggle to achieve and hold power, hampered by the condemnations of a perfectionistic conscience. Active-negative types pour energy into the political system, but it is an energy distorted from within.[19] *

Each of the active-negative presidents, according to Barber, exhibits the same pattern of behavior: "a process of rigidification, a movement from political dexterity to narrow insistence on a failing course of action despite abundant evidence of the failure. Each . . . helped arrange his own defeat and in the course of doing that, left the nation worse off than it might have been."[20]

How a president behaves in office depends heavily, in Barber's view, on the interactions of three psychological and two environmental variables. The first, largely determined in childhood, is character, which is a "stance toward life," an "orientation toward experience" and toward oneself. Second is what Barber calls "world view," composed of "primary, politically relevant beliefs, particularly . . . conceptions of social causality, human nature, and the central moral conflicts of our time," which develop mainly in adolescence. The third is "style," a "President's habitual way, acquired in early adulthood, of performing his three political roles: rhetoric, personal relations, and homework." The environmental variables are (1) the "power situation," the support or resistance a president receives from the public, interest groups, Congress, and the Supreme Court; and (2) the "climate of expectations," the "predominant needs thrust up to him by the people."[21]

Of these, the most important to Barber is character. There are four basic types, defined by levels of activity and enjoyment in the life of politics. The most effective of the four is the active-positive type, an active president who likes his work, exemplified by Franklin Roosevelt. He is productive and capable of learning and adapting in office, a well-put-together person who sets goals and stands a good chance of meeting them. The active-negative type, the most interesting and in Barber's view the most dangerous type, is a compulsive worker, incapable of deriving lasting satisfaction from his efforts. Active-negative presidents are aggressive, hungry for power, and driven to fail in the long run. The other two types are less interesting and far less likely to be elected these days. A passive-positive type such as Warren Harding is a compliant seeker of affection; a passive-negative such as Calvin Coolidge is in politics unwillingly, out of a sense of duty, and is more withdrawn in office than the others. In today's demanding world, the choice may tend to be between active-positives and active-negatives.[22]

*19, 20, 21, 22, 24, 26, 27, 28, 29, from the book, *The Presidential Character: Predicting Performance in the White House,* 2nd Edition, by James David Barber. © 1977 by James David Barber. Published by Prentice-Hall, Inc., Englewood Cliffs, N.J. 07632

The most common theme in these studies is that the quest for power or glory in Woodrow Wilson and other political leaders of similar nature can be understood as the product of a lifelong search for the self-esteem that was missing in childhood. Their power drive seems to stem from weakness and insecurity, paradoxically, rather than from strength. A person so driven may perform extraordinary feats of leadership, but also may be less able to learn and adapt than someone with greater emotional maturity.

Is it worth having such leaders? Do their abilities outweigh their disabilities? One of the more thoughtful students of the presidency, Erwin Hargrove, building on Lasswell, argued in 1966 that the best presidents were precisely those whose insecurity drove them to a life of persuading and dominating others—"men especially in need of attention and power." He cited Wilson and the Roosevelts as examples. By contrast, Hargrove contended, Taft, Hoover, and Eisenhower were ineffective presidents with healthy personalities.[23] (His view of Hoover—and, as we shall see, of Franklin Roosevelt—is different from Barber's.)

Hargrove's assumption as of 1966 was that such men would be constrained by the checks and balances of the constitutional system and by their own strong moral purpose. The country stood to gain a great deal from their rule. He could not predict the excesses of the later Johnson years and of Watergate. But looking back almost a decade later, Hargrove confessed a change of mind and called for presidents who combined the political skills of a Franklin Roosevelt and the self-respect and emotional stability of a Dwight Eisenhower—a combination of qualities he knew would not be easy to find.

Barber's active-positive president, who is energetic in office and enjoys being president, offers a resolution of this problem. He has "high esteem and relative success in relating to the environment." Barber says of him:

> The man shows an orientation toward productiveness as a value and an ability to use his styles flexibly, adaptively, suiting the dance to the music. He sees himself as developing over time toward relatively well-defined personal goals—growing toward his image of himself as he might yet be. The emphasis is on rational mastery.[24]

This category includes Franklin Roosevelt—though no president is a pure type. Whether Roosevelt was secure and adaptable, or, as Hargrove believes, a compulsive power seeker is something scholars may never agree on, partly because there are episodes that seem to favor each view and partly because he never let his guard down in public and rarely did so in private. Disagreements are also possible on each of Barber's other active-positives: Harry Truman, John Kennedy, Gerald Ford, and Jimmy Carter.

The democratic ideal would seem to be having both the leaders and the led equally open to new experiences and adaptation. But there is abundant evidence that some people, including some presidents and many ordinary citizens, are programmed to respond endlessly to problems of their youth and to that extent are programmed *not* to learn and adapt.

Consequences of Personality

Students of presidential character tend to believe that early life experiences significantly affect the behavior of adults, including presidents, and that what presidents do significantly affects the world about them. It is a deterministic system in which the adequacy of the senior Wilsons or Nixons as parents matters very much for the country. It is an important theory, but not to be taken without qualification.

For one thing, not all presidents are "determined" to the same extent by the conditions of their childhood and adolescence. According to Barber, for example, active-positives, the relatively productive and happy presidents, are less constrained by their upbringing than are the rest, all of whom have suffered low self-esteem in childhood and in one way or another are destined to spend their adult lives trying—vainly—to make up for early deprivations. The active-positives are self-actualizers, unburdened by neurosis, autonomous people who were lucky enough to be valued for themselves as youngsters, felt secure, and later set out on their own as free adults. In office, they are capable of growth and adaptation. They are less predictable than active-negatives, passive-positives, and passive negatives.

Another caveat is that what one person explains psychologically, another may explain as well or better politically. Alexander George, who has used the psychological study of presidents to advantage, as we have noted, nevertheless criticizes Barber for relying too heavily on character variables to the neglect of others—notably, of world view. For example, Barber attributes Herbert Hoover's inability to cope with the Depression to the rigidification of an active-negative under stress; George prefers the more direct explanation that Hoover's long-standing philosophy of individualism was not up to the task. "Certainly Hoover was stubborn on the matter of a public dole, but he appears to have been strongly opposed to it from the beginning—before attacks on his politics posed threats to his power and rectitude—because he found the idea peculiarly antithetical to his political philosophy."[25] Nor does George feel that Lyndon Johnson's Vietnam policy should be ascribed more to character flaws than to world view. In the case of Woodrow Wilson and the League of Nations, however, George is content to let the psychological explanation carry the weight.

Barber's theory of presidential character and his specific concern about the problem of the active-negative gained wide notice when his prediction of disaster for Richard Nixon came true. Writing in late 1971, when even most of the president's critics acknowledged his successes, Barber noted an ominous pattern:

> For the active-negative character is, as I have argued, an accumulative personality, one which tends to experience compromise as an erosion of the ego, and achievement as a reason for escalating the demands of a perfectionistic conscience. The process takes time; the frustrations of power pile up slowly but steadily, until the temptation to reassert one's integrity and manhood by some adamant stand becomes irresistible.
>
> The primary danger of the Nixon Presidency is that the frustrations and erosions of self he experiences will accumulate and that the process of rigidification, triggered by a serious threat to his power and his moral confidence, will show him a way to rescue, as he sees it, his Presidential heroism.[26]

And looking ahead to the possibility of defeat, Barber noted, "The loss of power to forces beyond his control would constitute a severe threat. That would be a time to go down, if go down one must, in flames."[27] One reasonably good prediction, it must be said, does not prove a theory. Perhaps we should see it as a logical deduction and a lucky guess and wait for more data.

Barber is certain that presidents, for better or worse, make a difference. The man is more important than the office. "Shuffle the system as you will, there is still at the center the person, and it is his initiatives and responses that steer the ship."[28]

> Who the President is at a given time can make a profound difference in the whole thrust and direction of national politics. Since we have only one President at a time, we can never prove this by comparison, but even the most superficial speculation confirms the commonsense view that the man himself weighs heavily among other historical factors. A Wilson re-elected in 1920, a Hoover in 1932, a John F. Kennedy in 1964 would, it seems very likely, have guided the body politic along rather different paths from those their actual successors chose. . . . Only someone mesmerized by the lures of historical inevitability can suppose that it would have made little or no difference to government policy had Alf Landon replaced FDR in 1936, had Dewey beaten Truman in 1948, or Adlai Stevenson reigned through the 1950's. Not only would these alternative Presidents have advocated different policies—they would have approached the office from very different psychological angles.[29]

Perhaps.

THE PRESIDENT AND
THE PUBLIC

Presidents spend a good deal of their time trying to please the public, with legislation, popular appointments, military excursions, summit meetings, and other tangible and symbolic offerings, taking care to make the most of successes in the administration of government programs and as little as possible of failures. It is, by popular demand, part substance and part theater. Presidents are assisted by specialists in each program and, increasingly, by a staff of press aides and professional image builders in the White House, whose job is all the more difficult because the public knows about them and is on guard against their excesses.

Public response is usually a disappointment to presidents. Some start out with higher ratings in the polls than others, but their nearly universal experience is to witness an erosion of their popularity year by year in office. Only the children—a large bloc 'of nonvoters—tend to respond warmly, and even they are less enthusiastic than their parents were a generation ago. But, mindful of forthcoming elections and the judgment of history, presidents keep trying.

Direct Contact

Presidents used to depend on the press to convey their verbal and visual messages to the public. (Though the press has been favorable to presidents, on the whole, inflating more often than deflating their public image, there was always the chance that what presidents wanted to say would be ignored, underplayed, edited, taken out of context, or criticized.) Then came radio, the fireside chat, and direct transmission of presidential messages to the public without intervention by members of the press. (Television allowed a more complex message, but hardly a more powerful one than Franklin Roosevelt could transmit by radio.)

One of the most adept at direct communication with the public was Richard Nixon, though it did not help him in the end. During the 1952 presidential campaign he was discovered to have an $18,000 fund provided by wealthy political friends for noncampaign uses. His detractors hoped the revelation might drive him from the ticket, given the importance Eisenhower placed on rectitude in public life. But Nixon went on television with a winning appeal for support. It was a masterful presentation. He argued that the fund was not unethical: "Let me point out, and I want to make this particularly clear, that no contributor to this fund . . . has ever received any consideration that he would not have received as an ordinary constituent." Indeed, it was a boon to the taxpayers: "Every penny of it was used to pay for political expenses that I did not think should be charged to the taxpayers of the United States." He had no family fortune, as Adlai Stevenson had. ("I don't happen to be a rich man.") Nor would he put Pat on the Senate payroll. "Let me say, incidentally, my opponent, my opposite number on the Democratic ticket, does have his wife on the payroll." In fact, he had decided against employing his wife because there were so many other deserving women looking for jobs.

There was a dog story, patterned after one told by Franklin Roosevelt:

> One other thing I probably should tell you, because if I don't they'll probably be saying this about me too, we did get something—a gift—after the election. A man down in Texas heard Pat on the radio mention the fact that our two youngsters would like to have a dog. And, believe it or not, the day before we left on this campaign trip we got a message from Union Station in Baltimore saying they had a package for us. We went down to get it. You know what it was?
>
> It was a little cocker spaniel dog in a crate that he sent all the way from Texas. Black and white spotted. And our little girl—Tricia, the six-year-old—named it Checkers. And you know the kids love that dog and I just want to say this right now, that regardless of what they say about it, we're going to keep it.

And then the knockdown argument:

> The purpose of the smears, I know, is this—to silence me, to make me let up. Well, they just don't know who they're dealing with. I'm going

to tell you this: I remember in the dark days of the Hiss case some of the same columnists, some of the same radio commentators who are attacking me now and misrepresenting my position were violently opposing me at the time I was after Alger Hiss.

He concluded with the promise that he would go on working nevertheless, to "drive the crooks and Communists and those that defend them out of Washington."[1]

The Checkers Speech turned a serious attack to his advantage and left Nixon with an enduring faith in his ability to bring the public to his side with a well-staged television appearance. As he noted in his book *Six Crises* in 1962, the response to the speech was immediate, massive, and favorable. "Thousands of people went out of their homes that night and lined up at Western Union offices. It was recorded as the greatest immediate response to any radio or television speech in history. . . . The effect was to lift my name to national prominence and to give me a national political following. . . . I emerged with far greater political and personal stature."[2] *

When Nixon learned of the Watergate break-in in 1972, he might well have maintained his popularity, won reelection, and served out his second term had he gone before the people immediately to condemn the burglars and announce the dismissal of their superiors in the Committee for the Re-elect of the President. He chose instead to cover up. Later, as the truth came out bit by bit he went on television with talks reminiscent of the Checkers Speech—full of untruths, we were in time to learn—to convince the public of his innocence. On April 30, 1973, the president spoke from his desk, flanked by a bust of Lincoln and a photograph of his family. An effort had been made, he said, to conceal the facts from him and from the public.

> Last June 17 while I was in Florida trying to get a few days' rest after my visit to Moscow, I first learned from news reports of the Watergate break-in. I was appalled at this senseless, illegal action, and I was shocked to learn that employees of the re-election committee were apparently among those guilty. I immediately ordered an investigation by appropriate government authorities. . . .
>
> As the investigation went forward, I repeatedly asked those conducting the investigation whether there was any reason to believe that members of my administration were in any way involved. I received repeated assurances that there were not. Because of these continuing reassurances, because I believed the reports I was getting, because I had faith in the persons from whom I was getting them, I discounted the stories in the press that appeared to implicate members of my administration. . . .
>
> However, new information then came to me which persuaded me

*Excerpts from *Six Crises* by Richard M. Nixon. Copyright © 1962 by Richard M. Nixon. Used by permission of Doubleday & Company, Inc.

that there was a real possibility that some of these charges were true and suggesting further that there had been an effort to conceal the facts from the public—from you—and from me. . . .

I was determined that we should get to the bottom of the matter, and that the truth should be fully brought out no matter who was involved. . . .

I wanted to be fair, but I knew that in the final analysis the integrity of this office—public faith in the integrity of this office—would have to take priority over all personal considerations. Today, in one of the most difficult decisions of my presidency, I accepted the resignations of two of my closest associates in the White House, Bob Haldeman and John Ehrlichman, two of the finest public servants it has been my privilege to know. . . .

This office is a sacred trust, and I am determined to be worthy of that trust!

I will not place the blame on subordinates, on people whose zeal exceeded their judgment and who may have done wrong in a cause they deeply believed to be right. In any organization, the man at the top must bear the responsibility.

That responsibility, therefore, belongs here in this office. I accept it.

And I pledge to you tonight from this office that I will do everything in my power to insure that the guilty are brought to justice. . . .

There can be no whitewash at the White House.[3]

A year later, on April 29, 1974, under pressure to release crucial tapes, Nixon again tried to turn the tide. He kept the tapes themselves but released edited transcripts, which he displayed on television in two tall stacks of binders. (They turned out to amount to about 200,000 words, or the contents of one good-sized book. Some of the binders had only one page of transcript. And of course the most damning material had been left out.) To his surprise, public reaction was unfavorable. The moral tone of the Oval Office was shown to be so low, even by edited transcripts with many "expletives deleted," that he lost ground rapidly and failed in his attempt to stifle the demands for the tapes themselves. Checkers, in the end, had let him down.

Jimmy Carter also favored direct communication with the people, but in contrast with Richard Nixon was most comfortable in informal settings. He won nomination with the help of a quiet, moralistic style of speaking. He was warm and effective in small gatherings, and a good listener. His theme: "I want a government that is good, and honest, and decent, and truthful, and fair, and competent, and idealistic, and compassionate, and as filled with love as are the American people." In simpler form for schoolchildren: "I want a government always to tell the truth." Perhaps the most unusual statement, widely broadcast in television advertisements, was "I'll never tell a lie, I'll never make a misleading statement, I'll never avoid a controversial issue. . . . If I ever do any of those things, don't support me."[4] It was powerful medicine. But in formal speeches and on television he was considerably less effective.

Carter is reported to have chosen a low-key style in reaction to what he considered to be the overblown, sometimes racist, political oratory of the traditional South and the hell-fire and damnation sermons he had endured in church.[5] Whatever the reason, there was no music in him, as one commentator put it. Former Senator Eugene McCarthy was less charitable: "He's an oratorical mortician. He inters his words and ideas beneath piles of syntactical mush." He was justly accused of being fuzzy on issues, and he mumbled—not enough to be incomprehensible, but enough to be unexciting. Once in office he learned to pace his speech and emphasize important words, but the White House pulpit did not suit his talents the way Iowa living rooms and New Hampshire sidewalks had in 1976.

There are other dimensions of the presidential presentation of self than the verbal: Appearance, for example, is more important than ever in the age of television. Some presidents seem big, strong, and handsome. Harding was one, as were Franklin Roosevelt and John Kennedy, both jaunty and confident. (Roosevelt was not depicted as crippled. Newsmen united in friendly conspiracy to avert their cameras when he was sitting in a wheelchair or struggling with his heavy leg braces. Cartoonists drew him standing firm, striding, and otherwise acting in ways in fact he could not.) And Dwight Eisenhower and Jimmy Carter had their smiles.

Some visual effects for television and the other media are staged. Carter was much photographed during the 1976 campaign and in his first year in the White House in blue jeans, carrying his own suit bag, and otherwise displaying a lack of pretentiousness that may have been genuine enough to begin with but that after a time bordered on affectation. Gerald Ford once staged a "photo opportunity" in the White House kitchen toasting English muffins, apparently to show his common touch and, perhaps, his manual dexterity. President Nixon was by nature more formal. During his first term, he ordered new uniforms for White House guards and musicians: Revolutionary War garb with knee breeches and three-cornered hats for some occasions, red and white comic-opera suits for others, and long horns festooned with banners for the honor guard to tara-tara the comings and goings of the president and other dignitaries—all of which produced so many guffaws around the land that they were soon withdrawn.

Of all recent presidents, John Kennedy was most at ease on camera and required the least primping and direction. Gerald Ford, because of his woodenness, required the most attention. To reinforce his image as an informal and unpretentious person, for example, he would appear at a conference table with reporters or sitting in the White House library (by a fire of special noncrackling, pressed sawdust logs) in preference to the more formal Oval Office, which Richard Nixon favored. Ford used the latest-model teleprompter, allowing him to look directly into the camera, with cues such as "stand up," "sit down," and "change cameras" interspersed in the text.[6] Because he was a word botcher, he sometimes taped and retaped broadcasts for days to attain what H. R. Haldeman might have called "zero-error performance."

Jimmy Carter's advisers were similarly concerned to overcome his deficiencies as a performer. When he did poorly in television appearances during his first year in office and declined in the polls, his advisers debated what to do to restore his popularity. As in the Nixon White House, the emphasis was on image and technique rather than on substance. "We haven't clearly enough articulated that overarching, unifying theme or presentation of what we're about or the way we're approaching things," said his press secretary. One of Carter's advisers, Barry Jagoda, argued for news conferences and other live appearances: "People watched the spaceshots because they knew each time something could go wrong and the astronauts could be burned up before their eyes. We want that kind of authenticity, that sense of natural vulnerability and of being on top of things." Another, Jerry Rafshoon, starting with the twin assumptions that "The public is not getting enough clear symbols from the White House" and that "All politics is marketing," urged controlled presentations in controlled environments, in which the president would explain complex problems to the nation informally.[7] In fact, the president kept trying both approaches: regular news conferences supplemented by appearances in a cardigan by the fire (with real crackling logs) in the library. And as time went on it was clear neither was working. It took some spectacular summit diplomacy at Camp David to change public opinion, and even then the effect was short-lived.

The President and the Press

In general, modern presidents have made the most of radio and television when they felt the press was distorting their image—if there were to be distortions, in other words, they would be provided by the White House. And presidents have tried both to control or intimidate the press and to bring it around with friendly persuasion.

The feeling that the press is unfair comes to every president sooner or later. It is natural for the president to present good news about his administration and to suppress bad news, and for the press to prefer a mixture of the two. Even the most open and successful president is stung now and then. It is not that the press is hostile: Even in the Nixon administration, it was not until a good deal of evidence of wrongdoing in high places had been gathered by Carl Bernstein and Bob Woodward of the *Washington Post* that the rest of the corps homed in on the Watergate story. The press was not accustomed to making a case against a president.

> Washington in the 1970s had to reinvent the old-time police reporter. . . . The best of them have mysterious sources, they threaten, they flatter, they trade information, they deal with an underground of rumor and gossip as they follow one thread after another to catch the crooks. . . . Without them, the stories that began the process of disclosure of the Watergate scandals by the prosecutors, the courts, and Congress would never have appeared.[8]

In normal times, the press, and the White House press corps in particular, with notable exceptions such as John Osborne of the *New Republic* and John Herbers of the *New York Times* during the Nixon years, has been passive and accepting, for two reasons. First, unless a reporter is unusually enterprising, his flow of information depends on the continuing goodwill of the White House. The press and the White House have an incentive to be cooperative with one another in the production of news favorable to the administration. "There is a strong tendency for White House reporters to become part of the court," says one who worked there, "to depict the President as larger than life, to assume an air of self-importance, and to view the White House as the center of the Universe."[9] Second, there is usually little ideological distance between the two—presidents and reporters tend to be middle-of-the road politically. The result is that reporting about the president and his subordinates is based very heavily on handouts, press conferences, briefings, and friendly interviews. Investigative reporting is arduous, risky, and infrequent.

Press conferences are not particularly informative. They are not often the scene of unintended admissions by the president. Tough questions can be turned aside with a cliché or a jest. Follow-up questions are infrequent, and even they can be answered with finesse: Reporters may play cat and mouse with a president, but he determines who is the cat and who is the mouse. To take one example among hundreds: President Eisenhower unleashed Richard Nixon to conduct a no-holds-barred campaign against the Democrats in 1954 and then in a news conference refused either to take responsibility for his vice president's attacks or to disclaim them.

> *Reporter:* Mr. President, Vice President Nixon made a speech the other day. His thesis, as I understand it, was that the Acheson foreign policy was to blame for the loss of China, and from that flowed the war in Korea and the difficulty in Indochina. The Democrats didn't like it very much. I wondered if you had any observations to make about it?

The President: First of all, let's recognize this: each individual in this country is entitled to his own opinions and convictions.

The next thing is, I admire and respect and like the vice president. I think he is a very splendid American.

Thirdly, I think my own job is to look at America today and to look ahead. I carry administrative and executive responsibilities and planning responsibilities that don't fall on some of the other individuals; so I just simply haven't time to go back.

My belief is this: we must seek agreements among ourselves, with respect to foreign policy, that are not confined to any party. We must get every American to studying these things and reaching conclusions regardless of party, because they are too important. Regardless of what party takes over, there must be a stability or there is no foreign policy.

Now, as to exactly what he said or what this was, taken in context, I don't know; I have never seen his speech. But as I say, everybody is entitled, I think, to his own opinion.

Reporter: Do your remarks about the vice president mean that from now on members of the cabinet do not have to clear with you any speeches they may make in the public forum?

The President: I think you have been here long enough to know that the vice president is not a member of the cabinet; I invite him to all meetings.

Reporter: Yes, sir.

The President: No member of the cabinet, I believe, would make a foreign policy speech without consulting with the State Department, and if there is any question in the mind of the secretary of state, certainly they would clear with me.

In this case, I don't know; but I assume whatever the talk was, it was made on an individual responsibility. As I say, if he made the speech, I know this: he believes what he said. But I didn't see the speech.

Reporter: Rightly or wrongly, sir, we are in the habit of saying that a vice president speaks for the administration. If he makes a speech of that kind we say that is the administration viewpoint. Now, perhaps we have been wrong in saying that. Should we make a distinction?

The President: Well, are you trying to make one swallow a summer? [*Laughter*]

I am saying that normally I think that the vice president is kept in such close contact with everything that is going on that he would know and would reflect what is administration thinking. Certainly neither I nor anyone else is ready to say that any other individual is always going to state exactly the things the way I would state them, and exactly as I believe.

Now, you are not going to get me in a position of condemning my vice president, because I repeat, I like and admire and respect him.

The mere fact that I might not have said it doesn't make it something that I am going to be disturbed about too much. But I would say this: you can normally take it, when he talks, he is talking pretty much the language of this administration. I thoroughly have this belief: no president has the right to go through his career here without keeping the next in line thoroughly informed of what are the big problems, so he would know how to take over if misfortune would overtake the chief executive. So he stays so close in, and normally we find our minds running so closely the same that I wouldn't try to excommunicate him from this party if I were you. [*Laughter*] . . .

Reporter: Mr. President, back to the Nixon speech, Mr. Sam Rayburn, who comes from Sherman Democrat territory, told the House yesterday, he said in so many words, the bipartisan foreign policy you want was threatened by the Nixon speech, and he sort of warned that if any more speeches came out like that, that hurt the Democrats' feelings very deeply, that there might not be any bipartisan foreign policy. Under those circumstances, would you consider asking Mr. Nixon to apologize? [*Laughter*]

The President: I told you that I liked and respected him, and I think if Dick Nixon ever finds any reason for apologizing for his own actions, he will do it without any advice from me.

Now, I am working for a proper, long-range, commonly supported foreign policy, and I am not going to give up just because someone may hurt my feelings or threaten me or anything else. I am going to continue working.[10]

It was the performance of a professional. He had parried every thrust. He had no intention of giving the reporters what they wanted.

The modern White House has clearance systems to coordinate publicity as well as to suppress embarrassing information and guard against the disclosure of military and diplomatic secrets. Any administration likes to speak with one voice on matters of any importance, simply to be effective. In the Carter administration, when United Nations ambassador Andrew Young and presidential assistant Midge Costanza made headlines with uncleared statements, they were disciplined—Young was publicly corrected; Costanza lost most of her staff and her large office near the president, and before long was gone. In a secretive administration, clearance is even tighter. The Nixon White House allowed key officials to be interviewed by designated friendly reporters; all others were warned against contact with the press. Henry Kissinger was the only high official in the administration to whom reporters had relatively free access throughout the Nixon years. In the final year, presidential assistant Alexander Haig was available also. When Gerald Ford succeeded to the presidency, he made a point of permitting his subordinates to talk freely with reporters.

Despite secrecy and clearance systems—one might say, *because* of them—a large amount of information is leaked to the press by officials at all levels. During the Watergate period, Washington was awash in leaks: leaks made in the public interest, and leaks to destroy political adversaries. The notorious "plumbers" unit was intended, of course, to fix leaks made in the public interest, and leaks to destroy political adversaries. The notorious "plumbers" unit was intended, of course, to fix leaks. The Justice Department went to court to try to prevent publication of the leaked Pentagon Papers. And so on. On balance, leaks have proven a boon to democracy.

But there was more than the publication of embarrassing leaks behind Richard Nixon's resentment of the press. David Halberstam sums it up:

> He brought his capacity for suspicion and innate hostility to the Washington press corps and turned that body—so readily manipulated by chief executives in the past, so given by nature to governmental status quo—into a press corps deeply hostile to Richard Nixon, deeply suspicious, disliking him on all grounds. A press corps in his own image.[11]

His distrust of the press was in the last analysis no different from his distrust of the American people, which too was repaid.

For a time during Watergate, President Nixon simply shut himself off from the press—no interviews, no news conferences. But a more general strategy before and after was to talk directly to the people on television. Breaking tradition, he chose not to release advance copies of his talks to the press, which meant that television commentators could not editorialize before he went on the air. But the networks retaliated. From 1970 on, commentators watched the broadcasts along with everyone else and went on the air to review and criticize the moment the president was done. On top of that, the Democrats demanded equal time to answer the president.

The White House was infuriated. Said presidential assistant Patrick Buchanan, "My primary concern is that the President have the right of untrammeled communication with the American people. When that communication is completed, what he has had to say should not be immediately torn apart or broken down even before the American people have had a chance to make their own judgment about what he said."[12] Another assistant, Charles Colson, called on senior executives of the three major networks to pressure them into resisting the Democrats' request and to be more positive toward the president in their own reporting and commentary. "The harder I pressed them" Colson wrote in a memorandum that came to light in the Senate Watergate hearings, "the more accommodating, cordial, and almost apologetic they became." He found them "very much afraid of us" and "anxious to prove they are good guys." Other White House memoranda of the period contained such language as "get the networks" and "what we are trying to do here is to tear down the institution [of broadcast journalism]." Presidential assistant Jeb Stuart Magruder wrote of pointing the "rifle" of government agencies at the media: The "possible threat of antitrust violations," he said, "would be effective in changing their views." Even the Internal Revenue Service could be set to work: "Just a threat of IRS investigation will probably turn their approach." In 1972 the networks were indeed harder on George McGovern, who campaigned, than on Richard Nixon, who played the role of president instead. All three networks were guarded in their White House reporting, and CBS management barred newsmen from analyzing or commenting on presidential speeches immediately after their delivery, a gag not removed until well into the Watergate period when the president was in retreat. [13]

Public television was even more vulnerable to White House pressure because it depended heavily on public financing through a government corporation. For a time there was only a short life expectancy for public affairs programs that annoyed the White House ("You've got Sander Vanocur and Robin MacNeil, the first of whom, Sander Vanocur, is a notorious Kennedy psychopath, in my judgment, and Robin Mac-Neil, who is anti-administration," said Patrick Buchanan. "You have Elizabeth Drew—she personally is definitely not pro-administration: I would say anti-administration.")[14]

The Nixon White House was equally critical of the written press. It loosed Vice President Agnew on the *New York Times* and the *Washington Post*. It harassed reporters with court orders for notes bearing on criminal investigations, backed by jail sentences for noncompliance, with the evident purpose of drying up their confidential sources. And the president proposed new laws that at first glance seemed reasonable but that would have curbed criticism of presidents and other officials. One was a libel law meant to undo the Supreme Court decision in *New York Times* v. *Sullivan* giving constitutional protection even to "erroneous statements honestly made" about public officials. [15] In President Nixon's view the decision amounted to "a license to lie." He wanted to limit constitutional protection to statements that could be proven true. But the infamous Sedition Act of 1798 had allowed the defense of truth and had been no less effective a means of locking up critics of the government for it. The fact is no newspaper can print ordinary news day to day under the threat of having either to prove every critical statement in court or to pay heavy damages to the public official criticized. The Supreme Court required only good faith—that newspapers not knowingly print falsehoods or print statements with reckless disregard of whether they were true or false. President Nixon's other proposal was a federal right-to-reply law for newspapers similar to the fairness doctrine for broadcasting. Again, an apparently reasonable idea: a public official or candidate would have the right to have his or her side of an issue printed in response to an adverse news story or editorial. But here, too, the intent was to harass the press and induce editors not to print critical items in the first place.[16] The Supreme Court declared the right-to-reply principle unconstitutional with respect to newspapers later that year in a case arising under a Florida statute.[17]

President Nixon and his people were bitterest of all toward the *Washington Post* for its Watergate stories. "Using innuendo, third-person hearsay, unsubstantiated sources, and huge scare headlines, the *Post* has maliciously sought to give the appearance of a direct connection between the White House and the Watergate—a charge which the *Post* knows and half a dozen investigations have found to be false." Presidential assistant Charles Colson is quoted as saying, early in November 1972, "As soon as the election is behind us, we're going to really shove it to the *Post*. . . . We're really going to get rough." The administration did indeed make a move against ownership of some television stations by the *Post*, but before long it had been too weakened by Watergate revelations to continue.[18]

The attacks on television were sharper and more effective than those on newspapers for both practical and legal reasons. Television was more feared by the Nixon administration because of the size of its audience—an angry editorial in the *New York Times* might be read by a few thousand people at most, but a barbed analysis of White House behavior by Dan Rather on CBS would be viewed by millions. As Patrick Buchanan said,

> You can yell and holler about the newspapers, but you can't say they have to change because that's their prerogative to print what they want. But in terms of power over the American people, you can't compare newspapers to those pictures on television. They can make or break a politician. It's all over if you get chopped up on the networks. You never recover. The newspapers can beat the hell out of you, and you've got no problem. But you sit there and see somebody take you apart before 20 million people.[19]

And television was more vulnerable to pressure. Legally, the written press enjoys the full protection of the First Amendment. But, some recent rumblings for deregulation notwithstanding, Congress and the courts have allowed comprehensive regulation of radio and television on the premise that "where there are substantially more individuals who want to broadcast than there are frequencies to allocate, it is idle to posit an unabridgeable First Amendment right to broadcast comparable to the right of every individual to speak, write, or publish."[20]

Weighing the attacks on all the media together, it is clear that the Nixon administration wanted to make the press uniformly docile and compliant. No other president has ever been so angry with the press and so vindictive—with the possible exception of Thomas Jefferson. In his second inaugural address, Jefferson complained that in "this course of administration, and in order to disturb it, the artillery of the press has been levelled against us, charged with whatsoever its licentiousness could devise or dare." His remedy?

> This is a dangerous state of things, and the press ought to be restored to its credibility if possible. The restraints provided by the laws of the states are sufficient for this if applied. And I have therefore long thought that a few prosecutions of the most prominent offenders would have a wholesome effect in restoring the integrity of the presses. Not a general prosecution, for that would look like persecution; but a selected one.[21]

Even the best could slip from grace after a time in office.

John Kennedy had a different way of managing the press. He was willing to spend time cultivating the goodwill of its members. He came to office with a genuine regard for the press corps and a good understanding of its work. The reporters liked Kennedy, too. In all respects, from their perspective, he was an improvement over President Eisenhower: friendly, charming, photogenic, and above all an activist. And he read what they wrote about him—his regular fare included many newspapers and more than a dozen magazines, foreign and domestic.

There were two sides to Kennedy's strategy, one the encouragement of favorable stories, the other the suppression of unfavorable ones. As his closest assistant wrote, he was sensitive to criticism and at heart wanted the press to be a cheering squad. He curried the favor of reporters, gave exclusive interviews to those who were good to him, planted questions in press conferences, and expressed his appreciation of friendly reporting. His press conferences were full of facts and fun ("He either overwhelmed you with decimal points or disarmed you with a smile and a wisecrack," remarked James Reston), and they made news.[22]

Suppression was brought about by persuasion rather than by the threats characteristic of the Nixon administration. Sometimes it was minor. When headline writers tried calling him Jack, he suggested that they use JFK and JFK it was thereafter. He and his family objected to stories about their private life. (Sent a note asking what she planned to feed her new dog, Jacqueline Kennedy responded, "Reporters.") On the whole, the press respected their wishes, and years later wondered whether it had been right not to report the comings and goings of a young woman who, it turned out, was having an affair with the president and a Mafia leader simultaneously. Some of the suppressions were major. Like most presidents, he tried to prevent publication of stories that might jeopardize the national security as he understood it. His assistant secretary of defense, Arthur Sylvester, described news as "part of the weaponry" of government, which, he asserted, had "the right, if necessary, to lie to save itself" from nuclear war and other grave threats. When the press got wind of the impending invasion of Cuba in 1961, the White House called editors, appealed to their patriotism, and had the stories killed. In this case too there were second thoughts later on, when the invasion failed.

Most people would agree that there are some stories the government ought to suppress. The Supreme Court once offered the movement of troop transports in time of war as a hypothetical case.[23] The Ford administration urged the *New York Times* not to publish a report that American submarines were tapping underwater cables off the coast of the Soviet Union, fearing the capture or destruction of a submarine it knew to be there at the time. The *Times* is said to have delayed publication until the submarine had left.[24] But beyond that, what the government should ask and the press concede is a difficult question. In an effort to be responsible, the press may defer too easily, particularly to a president who is liked and trusted.

It is the president's role to be at least mildly annoyed with the press, to try to bring it in line with favors and threats, and to bypass it occasionally by speaking directly to the people. Some presidents get their messages across, some not quite—and the latter do what they can to make up for their natural deficiencies by hiring pollsters, advertising and television specialists, and others to improve what has come to be called the "presidential image." The press, for its part, is torn between its formal role of full and fearless reporting on the presidency and its social and economic self-interest in reporting what the White House wants known and not probing for whatever the White House has swept under the rug. Normally the press is kind and cooperative. The president's annoyance is due more to oversensitivity than to ill treatment by the press.

The Public's Response

We know from what we read about politics and see on television, from conversations with friends and acquaintances, and from other signs, that presidential popularity varies greatly from year to year. Elections show us the relative popularity of presidential candidates, including some running for reelection. But best of all are the public opinion polls, and of these the most useful has been the question regularly asked by the Gallup Poll since 1945: "Do you approve or disapprove of the way (the incumbent) is handling his job as president?" The responses give an accurate reading of presidential popularity decade after decade. From it we know that presidents enter office with very different levels of support, none as high as Harry Truman enjoyed when he succeeded Franklin Roosevelt; that popularity is greater at the start of the term than at the end, Eisenhower's first term excepted; and that the ratings of Harry Truman, Richard Nixon, and Jimmy Carter fell the lowest of any in this period, below 30 percent.

What underlies the larger patterns and shorter-term variations in presidential popularity is not entirely understood, though some provocative exploratory studies have been done in recent years. Whether popularity is largely a reflection of the words and deeds of the president or of other forces remains unclear. What is known and not known can be seen in the work of John Mueller, James Stimson, Henry Kenski, and Richard Brody and Benjamin Page, all of whom are concerned with the rise and fall, rather than the initial levels, of presidential popularity.[25]

The findings are, first, the familiar one we have noted, that popularity tends to decline in each term. Mueller characterizes the decline as linear (a steady decline) and Stimson as parabolic (some recovery by the end of the term). In Mueller's model, the decline in popularity through time is the most important phenomenon; in Stimson's, it is the *only* one—the predictive power of his other variables is negligible.

Mueller and Stimson both proceed to speculate about the reasons for the decline. Mueller finds a "coalition of minorities" at work: "a general downward trend" as the president "is forced on a variety of issues to act and thus create intense, unforgiving opponents of former supporters. . . . The decline is assumed to start over again for second terms because the president is expected to have spent the campaign rebuilding his popular coalition by soothing the disaffected, re-deluding the disillusioned, and putting on a show for the bored." As for the exceptional case, Eisenhower's first term, Mueller concludes that aside from being a likeable amateur who ended the Korean War "*he didn't do anything*" and thus alienated relatively few people.[26]

Stimson argues somewhat differently that the causes of declining popularity lie more "in the misperceptions of the electorate than in the president's actions. It would therefore occur no matter what he did. New presidents pick up the support of many who did not prefer them, much less vote for them at election time. This easily acquired approval, based as it is on unrealistic expectations unaccompanied by commitment to the man or his policies, is then regularly lost over the early years of the term." A bottoming out occurs "as the president's support is reduced to (very roughly) the plurality which elected him." And, finally, the president takes on "a more active role in rebuilding his support at the end of the term." Although the two explanations are not altogether inconsistent, Mueller ties declining popularity more closely to the president's actions and points the way—citing Eisenhower—for a canny conservative to protect his popularity; while Stimson, more fatalistically, regards the president as "largely a passive observer of his downsliding popularity."[27]

The second important finding is what Mueller calls the "rally-round-the-flag" effect: an improvement in popularity associated with specific, sharply focused international events directly involving the United States and particularly the president, such as American military interventions, major military developments in ongoing wars, major diplomatic developments, including important summit meetings, and dramatic technological developments (e.g., Sputnik). Other things being equal, the longer it has been since the last event the lower the president's popularity. It does not matter, generally, whether the event is "good" or "bad." John Kennedy's popularity went up at the time of both the Bay of Pigs invasion and the Cuban missile crisis, though one was generally regarded as a fiasco and the other a victory for the United States. Jimmy Carter's ratings rose sharply after the Camp David summit in 1978 but soon went into decline—again—and continued to fall despite the dramatic normalization of relations with China later in the year.[28]

Richard Nixon's career offers a series of illustrations of the deliberate use of foreign travel for its rally-round-the-flag effect. As vice president he toured South America and was attacked and spat on by a mob in Venezuela. The lesson: "Just one month after my return from South America, the Gallup Poll showed me leading Adlai Stevenson for the first time and running neck-and-neck against John F. Kennedy. It was the high point of my political popularity up to that time." After the the Kitchen Debate with Khrushchev in Moscow the following year, "my personal standing rose the critial five to six points above Republican strength in general." The Gallup Poll had shown him far behind Kennedy. "After the trip, the gap closed to 52 percent for Kennedy, 48 percent for Nixon."[29] As a private citizen, during the 1960s, Nixon traveled frequently and paid well-publicized visits to heads of state in all corners of the globe. There was no doubt that he understood the publicity value of foreign travel and summit meetings long before he became president.

In his first term, President Nixon made eleven major foreign trips, culminating in historic visits to the People's Republic of China and the Soviet Union in the election year of 1972. The year 1973, after reelection by a wide margin, was his first as a president without foreign tours. But as Watergate unraveled, his popularity fell. On October 20, 1973, he fired Special Prosecutor Archibald Cox and to his surprise suffered in the polls for it. A few days later, the armed forces were placed on alert to deter the Soviet Union from introducing troops into the Middle East as a peace-keeping force, a move some observers felt had been undertaken for domestic political purposes. In 1974, as his political condition worsened, President Nixon was off again—to Europe, to the Soviet Union, and a long tour of the Middle East. A visit to Japan was planned for late in the year, but by August 9 he was out of office.

A third variable associated with presidential popularity is the state of the economy—price increases, specifically, which affect many people, but not changes in the unemployment rate, which affect relatively few directly. Those who have focused on these variables believe that in varying combinations they are helpful in explaining the results of presidential popularity polls.[30] (As we shall see in the final chapter, presidents manipulate the economy in election years, on the assumption that short-run improvements win votes.)

A new explanation with different implications, however, has been proposed by Richard Brody and Benjamin Page. They believe that presidential popularity rises when the news is good and falls when it is bad: Public opinion about a president remains stable until a different balance of good and bad news occurs and sends it up or down. Brody and Page studied two periods, June 1965 through April 1968 and January 1969 through October 1971, analyzing the content of the most important story in each day's news from one poll to the next. The results were so striking that they suggest abandoning the "coalition of minorities" explanation entirely.[31]

Whether the relative goodness or badness of the news explains presidential popularity in other years will not be known until more content analysis has been done. But at least for nearly six years in the Johnson and Nixon administrations it seems to be established. What is particularly interesting about the findings of Brody and Page is that they indicate a higher degree of popular rationality than have other studies, particularly Stimson's. The public seems to pay attention to the news and judge the president accordingly. (In so doing, of course, they may praise or blame a president for things for which he is not responsible.)

Finally, a recent study by Samuel Kernell, Peter Sperlich, and Aaron Wildavsky demonstrates that support for presidents is strongly associated with one's personal characteristics and attitudes about the American governmental and social systems. One of the findings is that there is a group of people—less educated, conservative in religion, older, and personally inflexible—who tend to be particularly supportive of presidents and at the same time less open to new information about presidents and politics ("The incidence of strong presidential support is greatest among the least knowledgeable and nonparticipant segments of the population.") Another is that those most supportive of presidents are a declining proportion of the population ("The population is becoming younger, less likely to belong to fundamentalist sects, possessing additional years of formal education, and is more likely to be psychologically flexible.") Kernell, Sperlich, and Wildavsky's conclusion, which links their findings to those in studies already noted, is that "Short-term levels of presidential support would have to rise to compensate for the long-term decline, merely to produce the same current support level as before. The American people are now requiring more performance from their political system."[32] This remains to be seen. It is by no means clear now that the population, in the years ahead, will move in the direction they predict.

Children's Response

The attitudes of children toward presidents and the presidency have always been warmer than those of adults, although Vietnam and Watergate resulted in some cooling of childish ardor. It is interesting to compare the earlier studies, made in happier times, with those from the mid-1960s on.

Three major studies, published between 1965 and 1969 but based on surveys between 1958 and 1962, were *Children and Politics*, by Fred Greenstein; *The Development of Political Attitudes in Children*, by Robert Hess and Judith Torney; and *Children in the Political System*, by David Easton and Jack Dennis.[33] They agree on the nature and lasting importance of early childhood political attitudes. Greenstein asked boys and girls in grade school in New Haven, Connecticut, their opinions about public officials in the three branches of government at the national, state, and local levels. He found that the children idealized all political authority and were particularly interested in and attracted to the president. Of the second-graders, 60 percent said the president, then Dwight Eisenhower, was "the best person in the world." Greenstein noted less idealization among students in higher grades, but they still held a generally warm and favorable view of the president and political authority.[34]

Greenstein found that older children had far better information about political figures than did younger ones. But even without much information, the younger children expressed great attachment to the president. It was Greenstein's view that a large load of favorable sentiment remains in most people, perhaps alongside unfavorable views in the form of ambivalence or vacillation.

The early development of positive attitudes toward authority, Greenstein speculated, leads to generous support for the political system among adults and therefore to stability for the system. And the early

attachment of American children to the presidency, he further speculated, creates adults who favor the national government over the states
and the president over Congress.

Not long after, during the presidency of John Kennedy, Hess and
Torney sampled the opinions of children in the Chicago metropolitan
area and in four large and four middle-sized cities around the country.
Their findings matched those of Greenstein:

> The child's first relationship with his government is with the presi-
> dent, whom he sees in highly positive terms. This indicates his basic trust
> in the benevolence of government. Young children relate to the president
> as they do to figures they know personally, expressing strong emotional
> attachment to him and expecting protection from him. They believe that
> the president is intimately involved not only in momentous decisions con-
> cerning the fate of the country but also in more mundane decisions that
> affect them and their neighborhood. . . . A strong sense of trust is evident
> in their responses; they think that the president is personally responsive to
> children's wishes and believe that they could even go to the White House
> and talk to him.[35]

Confidence in the government, Hess and Torney concluded, as did
Greenstein, stabilizes the political system. Similarly, they found a dramatic increase in information in the higher grades. For example, to the
question "Who makes the laws?" 76 percent of the second-graders
named the president—and although one might argue that that was not
entirely untrue of certain other presidents, it surely was untrue of John
Kennedy—but that response diminished grade by grade down to 5 percent in the eighth grade. The older the child, the more realistic the
response.[36]

Hess and Torney and Greenstein alike found sex differences in
their samples. Greenstein noted that boys were more politically inclined
than girls at every age studied, and had more political information. Hess
and Torney found girls to be more attached than boys to presidents and
other political figures, whom the girls saw as protective, while boys put
more emphasis on impersonal institutions of government. Hess and
Torney also speculated about the reasons for the idealization of the
president as an authority figure: they concluded it was to some extent a
fantasy in which children indulged to counteract their feelings of power-
lessness and helplessness in family and society.[37]

Easton and Dennis, drawing on the same surveys analyzed by
Hess and Torney, found idealization of authority which they attributed
in part, similarly, to children's vulnerability and in part to the tendency
of adults to teach young children the ideal, formal side of government
and shield them from the realities of the informal side: The child "learns

to like the government before he really knows what it is." And they too found the focus of idealization to be the president: "In all our testing and interviewing, we were unable to find a child who did not express the highest esteem for the President." He was seen as powerful, likeable, benevolent, trustworthy and reliable. Further, children personalize the complex institutions of government through him. "What the child sees are warm, palpable characteristics, much like those of human beings with whom he already has developed primordial ties." But "most younger children at any rate are not able to distinguish consciously between the presidency and the role occupant. . . . The general symbolism of the role overpowers the particular characteristics of the occupant."[38] The child's sentiments ought to transfer readily from one president to the next, therefore. Loyalty to a new president should be automatic.

Easton and Dennis supposed that some of this childish feeling about presidents—in effect about the presidency—lingers on in adults and helps them respect the office even when they are displeased with the incumbent. "In party politics, the specific qualities of the man as a negotiator, arbiter, leader, strategist, and policy maker may be paramount for judging an incumbent. But for most adults, regardless of the degree of competence of the President, the office as a symbol of the whole regime continues unimpaired. . . . Without the capacity to make the distinction between men and role, it is unlikely that a sense of structural legitimacy could be maintained."[39]

Despite some differences of interpretation, then, the three early studies were agreed that young children are warmly attached to the president and that this attachment has profound, lasting effects on their political thinking and their loyalty to the political system.

We now know that things are not as simple as these studies indicated. For one thing, each drew conclusions about children in general from much less than a proper sample of the national population of schoolchildren: Only urban white children were studied, Fred Greenstein's in one city, the others' (with the help of a federal grant) in eight.

Another problem appears in the way questions were posed. Hess, Torney, Easton, and Dennis used fixed-choice questions that may have induced children to give answers they might not have given on their own. Some questions indeed seem to have leaned heavily toward a predetermined response. For example, the fantasy of the president as a caring, nurturing, personal friend was built into the question, "Would the president always want to help me if I needed it?" And the imbalance between positive and negative choices in some items may have contributed to the rosiness of the president's image. "I like him (1) more than anyone, (2) more than most people, (3) more than many people, (4) more than some people, (5) more than a few people, (6) less than almost anyone."[40] For example, would someone hypothesizing that presidents nowadays are less well liked be justified in posing the question, "I dislike him (1) more than anyone, (2) more than most people, (3) more than many people, (4) more than some people, (5) more than a few people, (6) less than almost anyone"? Even balanced questions might have skewed the responses. From the same period, for example, projective tests such as telling stories about a set of ambiguous pictures gave a much less favorable impression of authority than the three studies we have examined.

Still another limitation inherent in these and other studies is that they give us information about second- or fourth- through eighth-graders at one time, but profess to show the dynamics of development through grade school into adulthood. But today's second-graders may not turn out to be like today's eighth-graders. A sounder approach would be to follow one or more groups of students through grade school and on into adulthood or at least, if that is impracticable, to test similar samples of a given age group as it grows older. One-time studies are less difficult and expensive to administer than longitudinal studies and require far less patience, but a researcher who takes a short-cut must be cautious about reading dynamics into static observations.

Since the three pioneer studies appeared, new surveys have shown that in other times, places, and circumstances, children's attitudes are different. The findings of Greenstein, Hess, Torney, Easton, and Dennis have far less general application than once supposed. Many studies made at the time of John Kennedy's assassination were largely consistent with the earlier ones. But then came studies of other presidencies and of the impact of Vietnam and Watergate on the attitudes of children and adults. The result was a fuller understanding of political socialization and the role of the president in that process.

The death of John Kennedy left much of the population shocked and grieving. Adults on the whole displayed more grief than children. ("While children contend against their impulses and feelings, adults have gained the sense that under appropriate circumstances they may give free expression to their emotions.") But to the surprise of many adults, even children seemed hard hit—perhaps, some thought, because the president and his wife were about the same age as their parents, unusually attractive, and possessed of two photogenic children, but also because of the importance to children of the presidency in a general way, as the growing literature on socialization suggested.[41]

What the studies could not prove, however, was that the outpouring of emotion gave any insight into the relation between the public, young and old, and a living president. The grief may have been more a reaction to the death of a young president than a measure of public sentiment about a president or the presidency. If some of the assassination studies assumed that the president's death allowed a rare insight into an ongoing emotional relationship, it could equally be argued that it had abruptly become the worst of all possible times to sample public opinion on the matter.

Another group of studies did show conclusively that the original generalizations at best were only partly correct. Foremost among them was a survey of poor, rural Kentucky schoolchildren in 1967 by Dean Jaros, Herbert Hirsch, and Frederick J. Fleron, Jr. They asked a sample of fifth- through twelfth-graders a number of questions used by Hess and Easton in one of the earlier Chicago area surveys: whether they thought the president was a good person, whether he was honest, whether he knew more than most men, and so on. The responses were considerably less favorable than in the urban survey. The president appeared as a very ordinary person—not bad, as in some of the Watergate surveys, but not the superior being found in the early studies, either. In Kentucky, 26 percent thought he was "not a good person," for example, contrasted with 8 percent in the Chicago area. Since, as Greenstein and others have noted, people in the lower social strata tend to be particularly respectful of authority, the Kentucky survey showing less respect in a lower-class sample is particularly interesting.[42]

This one survey upset some of the generalizations in the literature of socialization, but it was not clear why. The responses of the Kentucky children might have been related to the peculiarities of a poor and remote region. Or they might have been a result of Lyndon Johnson's desperate problems with Vietnam and the public opinion polls in 1967—the other surveys had been done during the administrations of well-liked presidents whose popularity in the polls never dropped near the low point reached by Johnson in 1967.

From about 1967, when it was fairly clear that American involvement in Vietnam had become a liability, until the resignation of Richard Nixon in 1974, public confidence in the president went down and down. At the end, polls showed that most Americans believed the president was guilty of criminal conduct. This was bound to affect the attitudes of children, and if Greenstein, Hess, and others were right, an early loss of idealism might mean lasting alienation from the political system.

Some partial answers can be found in surveys taken in the Watergate and post-Watergate periods, although the samples continue to be too spotty for broad generalization, and certainly the long-range effects of Watergate will not be clear for some time.

Early in 1974 Jack Dennis and Carol Webster returned to Tacoma, Washington, one of the eight cities he and others had studied in 1962, to find out how much the thinking of grade-school children on the presidency and the political system had changed. In 1962, 51 percent of the sixth-graders had called the president "my favorite of all" or "almost my favorite of all," but in 1974 it was 7 percent. The percentage of those who felt the president "would always want to help me if I needed it" or "almost always" fell from 63 to 9.[43]

Dean Jaros and John Shoemaker polled a second group of poor Kentucky schoolchildren in December 1974, several months after Nixon's resignation, asking a variety of questions about Richard Nixon, Gerald Ford, and simply "the president." They found, as one might expect, distinctly negative views of Nixon. More than one-third thought he was "not a good person" and more than half thought him "less honest than most men," for example. But the judgments were selective. More of the children gave favorable responses to the question whether Nixon knew more than most men than had the earlier Kentucky sample with respect to "the president." He was bad, that is, but not ignorant. And there was little spillover of unfavorable attitudes onto other men and institutions. To take two examples, a greater share of this sample than the earlier one regarded "the president" as a good person, and a greater share in 1974 regarded Gerald Ford as honest than had thought that of "the president" in 1967.[44]

F. Christopher Arterton conducted two surveys of affluent suburban schoolchildren in Massachusetts late in 1973 when Nixon was under heavy attack and early in 1975 after he had left office.[45] His findings in the first poll are consistent with those of Jaros and Shoemaker. The children's attitudes were overwhelmingly negative toward the president, though not in every respect: to the question "Does the president give up when things are hard to do?" the response was, realistically, about as favorable as in previous polls, and they believed, also realistically, about as favorable as inn previous polls, and they believed, also realistically, that the president was powerful. Arterton wondered about the effects of negativism. The dramatic shift to unfavorable attitudes, he thought, could be explained by the tendency of young children to see things as all good or all bad, with nothing between. If so, those with bad attitudes about the presidency might change back some day.[46]

Whatever the answer to that question, Arterton's findings did contradict the standard model of political socialization. The notion that children do not distinguish between the president as a person and as a role is inconsistent with his evidence that this group could distinguish Nixon's various qualities with some precision. The idea that children are vulnerable and tend defensively to idealize authority conflicts with the general negativism of the responses. And that feelings about the president are a reflection of feelings about the father is contradicted by the fact that responses about fathers did not change noticeably, while those about the president did.

The second survey by Arterton, of a similar group of schoolchildren in 1975, found that views of the president were still negative, but less so than in the last year of the Nixon administration. The "all- good or all- bad" hypothesis had to be rejected. Arterton concluded that attitudes of the children he had studied were simply following the ups and downs of politics, apparently stimulated more by ephemeral external events than by inner developmental forces. Long-run effects, if any, Arterton could not predict.[47]

Conclusions

Watergate had shown, as had the first Kentucky survey, that children's attitudes about presidents were anything but uniform. The early surveys had been done in the days of Eisenhower and Kennedy, men regarded as heroes by a large share of the population and most of all by children. Presidents since have enjoyed far less public esteem and affection. And their administrations have been attended by foreign and domestic strife. That children's judgments of the presidency were different under different conditions suggests more rationality than was earlier suspected. Their highly favorable views in the 1958–1962 surveys now must be understood in good part as a reflection of favorable *adult* views. Young children's views may not be as simple-minded as some supposed, or as immutable, although in the absence of good longitudinal studies that remains to be seen. We now have enough information to be skeptical of any simple model of political socialization.

Similarly, we should be wary of any explanation of the political attitudes of adults that relies exclusively either on the determinism of nonrational factors or on rational response to current events. It often seems to be a mixture of the two. Much of the respect people have for presidents seems to hinge on their performance, as the study by Richard Brody and Benjamin Page, described earlier, suggests. But it goes beyond that: In 1945 a Gallup Poll revealed that 28 percent of Americans thought Franklin Roosevelt was "the greatest person living or dead in world history," compared with 15 percent for Jesus.[48] A study by Samuel Kernell, Peter W. Sperlich, and Aaron Wildavsky, also noted earlier, published in 1975 but based on 1966 data, shows support for presidents in some parts of the adult population resembling that found among white, urban children in pre-Vietnam, pre-Watergate days. It is worth describing in some detail.

Kernell, Sperlich, and Wildavsky measure support for presidents on three scales—"I like presidents," "Our presidents right or wrong," and "Rally round presidents in a crisis"—each consisting of statements ranging from those with whom most could agree (e.g., "More nearly than any other person the president stands for our country") to those to which only the most ardent could subscribe (e.g., "Although he may have been an ordinary citizen before, when he becomes president he should be considered the wisest man in the world"). The responses describe, among other things, what has been called the Caligula Quotient—the 20 to 25 percent of the public who will stand by a chief executive, particularly of their party, no matter how monstrous he is.

Next the authors correlate the level of support shown on each index with the political knowledge and activity of the respondents, their demographic and psychological characteristics, and their attitudes about the political and social system. Those who know the least about the political system and participate the least tend to be most supportive of the president. Among all the other variables tested, a number proved to be moderately or strongly associated with presidential support: lower educational attainment, greater age, more conservative religious affiliation, being black rather than white, and, among the psychological variables, inflexibility. Inflexibility, which is not very different from authoritarianism, is measured by responses to two sets of statements, concerning behavior (e.g., "A job should not be done at all unless it is absolutely perfect") and beliefs (e.g., "No matter what happens in the world, my beliefs will always be the same"). They conclude that the psychologically disadvantaged are most supportive, by and large. Attitudes about the political and social system are measured by agreement or disagreement with statements such as "Despite some faults, our form of government is the best in the world," and "In this country, there is no limit to how high a person can rise if he has the ability." Putting all the data together in a multiple correlation, they find they can explain about two-thirds of the variation in presidential support.[49]

Generalized support for presidents among adults and children may be a disappointment to those who believe that democracy is better served by informed consent. Others, however, favor the stability such support lends the political system by providing a floor below which a president's popularity is unlikely to fall.

PRESIDENTIAL
NOMINATIONS

The inauguration of a new president is more than an orderly transfer of power; it is in the minds of many citizens a renewal of the office itself, a fresh beginning for better or worse. And we know more about that office when we know which kinds of candidates are favored or discouraged by the procedures of nomination and election leading to that renewal. No electoral process is more complex. It is the result of compromises in the Philadelphia Convention and of generations of political reform. Basic legal mechanisms apart, there is only modest agreement on the forces that have been at work within it in the past, shaping outcomes, and even less on what is likely to occur in the future.

Most of the winnowing now falls into a sequence of self-selection or draft → state primaries and conventions → the national convention → the November election → and, if the electoral college fails to elect, balloting in the House of Representatives. For different candidates, these steps have different importance—presidential primaries may be crucial for one candidate and not another, for example. And of course the work of the electoral college is usually both perfunctory and final, and the relegation of the election to the House is a rarity. In this chapter and the next, we shall trace these steps and note where key decisions have been made in different years and circumstances. Thanks to survey research, we can go further and examine the interests and motives of the decision makers and can piece together a partial explanation of why certain kinds of people have been chosen president in the past.

In 1960, in one of the best known studies of the presidency, Clinton Rossiter of Cornell University drew up a list of formal and informal qualifications for the presidency. The formal ones are in the Constitution: "No person except a natural born citizen, or a citizen of the United States at the time of the adoption of this Constitution, shall be eligible to the office of President; neither shall any person be eligible to that office who shall not have attained to the age of thirty-five years, and been fourteen years a resident within the United States."[1] The informal ones, reflecting the likes and dislikes of those who help select presidents, are much more restrictive. For example, "He must be, according to unwritten law: a man, white, a Christian. . . . He almost certainly must be: a Northerner or Westerner, of Northern European stock. . . . He ought to be: more than forty-five years old, a veteran, a Protestant."[2] Some people would not presume to put themselves in contention, or care to; some would fail to win the support of delegates and voters if they did. But the fact that John Kennedy upset the religious qualification (and stretched the lower age limit to forty-three) and Jimmy Carter the regional qualification indicates how readily the informal rules of the game change from decade to decade.

Whether the selection process works or not, on the whole, is a matter of personal judgment. Different answers, one cool and one warm, were given some time ago by two Englishmen, James Bryce and Harold Laski. Bryce, writing at the end of the nineteenth century, evinced the low confidence in the presidency typical of that era. He believed mediocrity to be one of the qualifications of office.

> Europeans often ask, and Americans do not always explain, how it happens that this great office, the greatest in the world, unless we except the Papacy, to which any man can rise by his own merits, is not more frequently filled by great and striking men? . . .
>
> Eminent men make more enemies, and give those enemies more assailable points, than obscure men do. They are therefore in so far less desirable candidates. It is true that the eminent man has also made more friends, that his name is more widely known, and may be greeted with louder cheers. Other things being equal, the famous man is preferable. But other things never are equal. The famous man has probably attacked some leaders in his own party . . . has perhaps committed errors which are capable of being magnified into offences. No man stands long before the public and bears a part in great affairs without giving openings to serious criticism. Fiercer far than the light which beats upon a throne is the light which beats upon a presidential candidate, searching out the recesses of his past life. Hence, when the choice lies between a brilliant man and a safe man, the safe man is preferred. . . .
>
> It must also be remembered that the merits of a President are one

thing and those of a candidate another thing. An eminent American is reported to have said to friends who wished to put him forward, "Gentlemen, let there be no mistake. I should make a good President, but a very bad candidate." Now to a party it is more important that its nominee should be a good candidate than that he should turn out to be a good President. . . . It will be a misfortune to the party, as well as to the country, if the candidate elected should prove a bad President. But it is a greater misfortune to the party that it should be beaten in the impending election, for the evil of losing national patronage will have come four years sooner.[3]

Laski wrote during the presidency of Franklin Roosevelt, when the office was more highly regarded. "All in all, I doubt whether the methods of the system are very different from those of other countries," he said of presidential nominating conventions.

They are, perhaps, more open and crude than in Great Britain. There is no generosity in the fight for power. There is a passionate determination on the part of organized interests to get the "safe" man who can be relied upon to live up to the commitments exacted from him. There is the fierce conflict of rival ambitions. There is the organization of every sort of cabal to win a victory for its man. Press and radio and platform are vigorously manipulated to this end. Immense promises are made, pretty ugly deals are effected. Yet I suggest that anyone who knows the life of a political party from within Great Britain will not feel inclined to cast a stone at the American system. It fits, well enough, the medium in which it has to work. It achieves the results that the needs of the people require.

For there is at least one test of the system that is, I think, decisive. There have been five considerable crises in American history. There was the need to start the new republic adequately in 1789; it gave the American people its natural leader in George Washington. The crisis of 1800 brought Jefferson to the presidency; that of 1861 brought Abraham Lincoln. The War of 1914 found Woodrow Wilson in office; the great depression resulted in the election of Franklin Roosevelt. So far, it is clear, the hour has brought forth the man. It is of course true, as Bagehot said, that "Success in the lottery is no argument for lotteries." . . . The issue is whether, when a crisis comes, the system can discover the man to handle it. On the evidence, this has so far been very remarkably the case.[4]

Neither Bryce nor Laski, it should be noted, had much praise for the selection process. Bryce considered it pernicious. Laski was pleasantly surprised that good people were sometimes chosen despite it.

Nomination and Election

First we may note the distinction between nomination and election. Nomination is the designation of candidates for office. It is the next-to-last elimination of contenders. It is the semifinals, and the election is the final match. Nominations now occur within political parties, but it was not always so. In the Philadelphia Convention of 1787, before parties, the supposition was that most presidents after George Washington would be chosen by the House of Representatives after the electoral college had failed to give anyone a majority. In the absence of political parties, there was no reason to think that electors in the several states would be able to coordinate their efforts sufficiently to produce such a majority. The House would then choose a president from the top five candidates. Without the criterion of intra- versus interparty competition, one might say that the electoral college was to function as a nominating body, performing the next-to-last elimination later performed by political parties.

Soon there were parties, however. By 1800, a pattern of two-party politics had been established in the United States, greatly increasing the odds that the electoral college would produce majorities. "Nomination" by the electoral college and election by the House of Representatives became the exception rather than the rule. The remaining ambiguities in the process have to do with the stage at which crucial decisions are made, not whether they are nominations or elections.

In the United States, nomination and election (whatever they may be called) occur in close sequence: Nomination is a preliminary to election to the presidency and other offices. But that need not be so. In the British parliamentary system, the selection of a party leader, who becomes prime minister when his party is in power, is typically unrelated to the timing of elections. Also, the selection of a party leader tends to be less a search for the most likely electoral success than it is in the United States. The evidence for this is that there is less reluctance in Great Britain than here to choose someone who has already led the party to defeat in a general election. In Great Britain, leaders whose parties have lost elections have commonly been retained.[5] The British case reminds us that in a democracy the nomination and election of a chief executive need not be linked in time and purpose the way they are in the United States. In fact, the American system of nomination is unique. According to Austin Ranney, "The United States is the only democratic nation in the world that provides institutional mechanisms for widespread popular participation in the selection of party nominees for high elective office."[6]

From here on let us focus on American nominations, as they have developed since 1800: conventions, primaries, and preprimary maneuvers.

National Conventions

Conventions for the nomination of presidential candidates date from 1831–1832. Long after candidates for most other public offices in the country have come to be selected by primary, conventions remain the formal site of presidential nomination. Now more than ever, however, the real choice of candidates is likely to come earlier, during or even before the primary season.

Before 1831, each party normally made nominations in a legislative caucus consisting of its members in Congress, very much as the parliamentary parties select party leaders in Great Britain today. But the Federalist party died out, and then in 1824 the Democratic-Republican party fell apart, nominations were made by state legislatures instead, and ultimately the House of Representatives gave the presidency to John Quincy Adams. Four years later the presidency went to Andrew Jackson, also nominated by state legislatures. In 1831, however, the National Republican party and a lesser party, the Anti-Masonic, experimented with national nominating conventions, and Jackson adopted the convention as the vehicle of his own renomination. His tightly run Democratic convention of 1832 became the model for presidential nominations thereafter.

A national party convention is, in bare outline, a meeting of delegates from each state held before each presidential election to nominate presidential and vice-presidential candidates, to adopt a platform and new party rules, to fire up the faithful for the ensuing campaign, and more than incidentally to have a good time—all in all, as H. L. Mencken saw it, "a show so gaudy and hilarious, so melodramatic and obscene, so unimaginatively exhilarating and preposterous that one lives a gorgeous year in an hour."[7]

Party rules, not federal statutes, determine the structure and operations of the convention. The similarity of the Democratic and Republican conventions is a result of mutual imitation. Delegates and votes are apportioned to the states by each party more or less on the basis of its recent voting strength. From Andrew Jackson's time into this century, convention apportionment followed that of the electoral college, but changes were triggered by the Republicans' troubles of 1912. Much of President William Howard Taft's support in his bid for renomination by the Republicans was in the South, where the party was notoriously weak. At the convention, he defeated Theodore Roosevelt, the popular favorite, with the help of delegates representing empty constituencies; Roosevelt bolted the party and ran as a Progressive. The upshot of the split among the Republicans was the election of a Democrat, Woodrow Wilson. Since then Republican party rules—and Democratic, too, starting later on—have progressed bit by bit from apportionment by population, which is what the electoral college approximates, toward apportionment by party strength, making a mistake as grand as the Republicans' in 1912 less likely.

The way delegates are selected has until recently been largely a matter of state discretion, controlled by party rules or by statute. Each state has used the convention, the primary, appointment by party committee, or some combination of these devices. In 1968, the Democratic party, divided and demoralized by the primary battles of incumbent Lyndon Johnson and insurgents Eugene McCarthy and Robert Kennedy and by the assassination of Kennedy after his primary victory in California, met in convention in Chicago with antiwar demonstrations outside and arguments about bossism inside and unenthusiastically chose Hubert Humphrey as its candidate. With more hope for 1972 than for 1968, the convention took steps to assure more open democratic procedures, more participation, and more representativeness in delegate selection for the next convention. Afterwards, Democratic National Committee chairman Fred Harris appointed a Commission on Party Structure and Delegate Selection, with Senator George McGovern (and later Representative Donald Fraser) as chairman to draw up specific guidelines. As the McGovern-Fraser Commission saw it, the problem was that

> In at least twenty states, there were no (or inadequate) rules for the selection of convention delegates, leaving the entire process to the discretion of a handful of party leaders.
>
> More than a third of the convention delegates had, in effect, already been selected prior to 1968—before either the major issues or the possible presidential candidates were known. By the time President Johnson announced his withdrawal from the nominating contest, the delegate selection process had begun in all but twelve states.
>
> Unrestrained use or application of majority rule was the cause of much strain among Democrats in 1968. The imposition of the unit rule from the first to the final stage of the nominating process, the enforcement of binding instructions on delegates, and favorite-son candidates were all devices used to force Democrats to vote against their stated presidential preferences. Additionally, in primary, convention, and committee systems, majorities used their numerical superiority to deny delegate representation to the supporters of minority presidential candidates.
>
> Secret caucuses, closed slate-making, widespread proxy voting—and a host of other procedural irregularities—were all too common at precinct, county, district, and state conventions.
>
> In many states, the costs of participation in the process of delegate selection were clearly discriminatory. . . . Not surprisingly, only 13% of the delegates to the national convention had incomes under $10,000 (whereas 70% of the population have annual incomes under that amount).
>
> Representation of blacks, women, and youth at the convention was substantially below the proportion of each group in the population.[8]

The commission drew up a long list of requirements for 1972. It prohibited proxy voting, the unit rule, mandatory assessment of delegates, selection processes beginning before election year, and selection of more than 10 percent of a delegation by the state committee. It required affirmative action to encourage the representation of "minorities, women, and young people in reasonable relationship to their presence in the population of the state." And more.[9] (The Republicans undertook similar reforms. They exhibited less reformist zeal, but they also had fewer irregularities in their selection processes.)

The result was a far more representative Democratic convention in 1972, by some standards: The percentage of women delegates increased from 13 in 1968 to 40 in 1972, of blacks from 5.5 to 15, and of delegates aged thirty or under from 4 to 21.[10] A survey of delegates at the 1968 and 1972 Democratic conventions gave evidence of another dramatic change: The proportion of "amateur-minded" delegates rose from 23 to 51 percent. Amateurs were distinguished in the survey from those who put party first—the professional-minded delegates—by a series of statements with which delegates were asked to agree or disagree:

> "Party organization and unity is more important than permitting free and total discussion which may divide the party."
>
> "A good party worker must support any candidate nominated by that convention even if he disagrees with him."
>
> "Controversial positions should be avoided in the party platform in order to insure party unity."
>
> "Would you characterize yourself as someone who (a) works for the party year after year, win or lose, whether or not you like the candidate or issues; or (b) works for the party only when there is a particularly worthwhile candidate or issue?"[11]

The convention's choice, George McGovern, was the prime beneficiary of the new rules. He was heavily supported by amateurs who were more attached to their issues and their man than to the party. Politically, the convention was *un*representative of the rank and file. McGovern went down to bloody defeat in November. Once again there was cause for reflection within the party. A new commission chaired by Barbara Mikulski softened the controversial "reasonable relationship" language of the rule of representativeness, which had been widely understood as a quota requirement; renounced mandatory quotas; and required state parties only to seek the participation of women and minorities "as indicated by their presence in the Democratic electorate." The party thus fell back to a middle position likely to have broader appeal than the rules of either 1968 or 1972. As anticipated, there was less amateurism in the 1976 convention,[12] and the percentages of women (33), blacks (11), and young people (14) dropped below 1972 levels. But there would be no return to the old prereform ways: All three groups remained far better represented than in 1968, and by rules adopted in 1978 women were assured nearly half the seats in 1980.

Writing new rules about delegate selection, it should be noted, is only half the battle. They are not always fully obeyed, and contests arise, therefore, that must be resolved by vote of the convention. Now and then the very outcome of a convention depends on which delegates are seated in a dispute over credentials. In the Republican convention of 1952 and the Democratic convention of 1972, the nominations of Dwight Eisenhower and George McGovern, respectively, remained uncertain until they had won key credentials fights. In McGovern's convention there was an unusually large number of contests stemming from problems of interpreting the guidelines introduced by McGovern's own commission.[13]

Once the losing contestants have been turned away and the delegates are officially in place, the convention can proceed with its main business. Foremost is the selection of a presidential candidate, accomplished by a simple majority of the delegates voting individually. Until 1936 the Democratic party required a two-thirds majority for nomination in the interests of consensus. Woodrow Wilson secured the nomination by the required two-thirds in 1912 after forty-six ballots, even though someone else had a simple majority in early ballots. Until 1968 the Democrats allowed unit voting, by which the entire vote of a state delegation could be cast by a majority, or in practice by the delegation's leader.[14] (By 1972, in accordance with McGovern-Fraser Commission guidelines, the unit rule had been prohibited in the delegate selection process as well.) With these changes, voting in the two major-party conventions became essentially the same.

Two other convention activities, the selection of a vice-presidential candidate and the adoption of a platform, traditionally have the common purpose of broadening the party's appeal in the general election. Vice presidents tend to be chosen to balance the ticket: If the Democratic presidential candidate is a liberal Catholic easterner, to take a particularly clear example, an appropriate running mate is a conservative Protestant southerner. While he was coming to a decision on the vice-presidential candidate in 1976, Jimmy Carter announced that geographic balance would be a lesser consideration than compatibility and potential ability as a president. His choice of Walter Mondale pleased most Democrats on all three counts. A southerner would have been the least likely choice, whatever his or her other qualities. President Ford's selection of Senator Robert Dole stressed compatibility—the Michigan-Kansas coalition of Ford and Dole amounted to a rejection of geographic balance.

In 1972, George McGovern had hurriedly chosen Senator Thomas Eagleton as his running mate, more to balance the ticket than to strengthen it. The disclosure soon after that Eagleton had a history of mental illness reflected badly on Eagleton (not for having been ill but for jeopardizing the ticket by concealing the fact of his illness) and on McGovern first for his uninformed choice and then for his indecision and delay in removing Eagleton from the ticket. Jimmy Carter was more deliberate. His seven possible candidates—Senators Frank Church, John Glenn, Henry Jackson, Walter Mondale, Edmund Muskie, and Adlai Stevenson III, and Representative Peter Rodino—were required to answer a detailed questionnaire about their mental health and other potential problems, including taxes, tax investigations, questionable contributions, arrests, the results of physical examinations, and "anything in your personal life which you feel, if known, may be of embarrassment in the presidential election." Carter was taking no chances.[15]

Platforms are statements of party policy for the next two to four years (together with accounts of the party's accomplishments and alleged errors of the opposition, plus some obligatory symbol rattling). Usually party factions and major organized interests outside the party are invited to present their views in the hearings of the platform and are to some extent recognized in the provisions of the document. Once in a while, however, those in control of the convention are zealous and impolitic enough to resist compromise on key planks. Barry Goldwater in 1964 imposed his anti-civil rights views on the Republican convention, to the dismay of Republican liberals, moderates, and—particularly—professionals, as defined in the study we have cited. Similarly, Lyndon Johnson, not himself a candidate for renomination, dictated a plank supportive of his Vietnam policy in the 1968 Democratic platform, although it seemed certain to be hurtful at the polls.[16] In most conventions, the leadership and delegates are too urgently concerned with electoral victory to allow one faction to humiliate another.

At that 1964 Republican convention, conservative Goldwater and moderate Nelson Rockefeller lashed out at one another's policies; and Rockefeller was drowned out by the boos of Goldwater supporters, a clear indication, if one needed signs, that the party was in trouble that year. But perhaps some years a party is so divided that the vice-presidential selection, platform writing, and conviviality of a convention cannot heal the differences. The next two Republican conventions were more harmonious. Everything that could be done was done to please factions of the party and the electorate.[17] Norman Mailer evokes the spirit of the occasion:

> For representation of all the American groups watching TV, the Jeannette Weiss Principle (discovered during Worship Service) was employed—wherever possible use a black lady with a German Jewish name doing a patriotic bit. Thus Ray Bloch, the Music Director of the Convention Orchestra, had a name which at once might please Jews and Germans as he

played music which satisfied every gamut which ran from Dixieland through Lawrence Welk to Lombardo. Chad Everett, of *Medical Center*, the Special Guest, pleased TV fans, doctors, and Californians; the United States Naval Sea Cadet Corps satisfied the military, the young, the patriotic, and Senior Citizens who remembered John Philip Sousa. The Pledge of Allegiance was given by Thomas Joiner of Rock Hill, South Carolina, winner of the 1972 American Legion Oratorical Contest, a choice which pleased Legionnaires, high-school debating teams, citizens with the first name of Rocky, or the surname of Hill, the state of South Carolina, and all the many Southern families for whom a name like Joiner was well regarded. . . . By Tuesday afternoon, the Jeanette Weiss Principle was being employed in full swing. Not only did Philip Luther Hansen of the American Lutheran Church give the invocation, but he was also Director of Alcohol and Chemical Dependency in a unit of Northwestern Hospital, Minneapolis, a lock thus on Scandinavians, Scandinavian Lutherans, Alcoholic Lutherans, Senior Lutherans on pills, and the formidable number of voters in America named Hansen or Hanson. . . .

Through the five sessions of Monday afternoon and evening, Tuesday afternoon and evening, and Wednesday night did the Jewish Rabbis, the Catholic Bishops, and the Greek Orthodox Reverends give Invocations and Benedictions, so too did the Lutherans and the Methodists, and the Baptists. . . . Indeed all the Protestant sects, including the A.M.E. Zion Church were brought in but for Episcopalians, Presbyterians, Congregationalists and Unitarians. The Episcopalians and Congregationalists were bound to be so completely for Nixon that they could take a snobbish pride in not being called to a gang demonstration, the Presbyterians were so stubbornly divided that no one could unify them and not worth the effort to try. The Unitarians were long gone to McGovern.[18]

In the 1976 Republican convention, despite a close and hard fight for the nomination, the contenders were gracious in victory and defeat; but the Democrats, too, had closed ranks that year, and they won the election.

Conciliatory behavior at a convention is more likely when there is no serious contest for the presidential nomination than when it is most needed, in a wide-open convention. William Keech and Donald R. Matthews differentiate consensual, semiconsensual, and nonconsensual nominations.[19] According to this analysis, consensual nominations are those in which "a single provisional leader appeared before the formal process of choice began and held on to his lead, advantages intact, until he was officially chosen by the convention." Franklin Roosevelt's renominations in 1936 and 1944 fall into this category (although not his third-term renomination in 1940, to which there was some opposition), as do the bids of Dwight Eisenhower in 1956, Lyndon Johnson in 1964, and Richard Nixon in 1972 for continuation in office. From 1936 on, only two nominations by parties out of power were consensual: Alf Landon's and Thomas E. Dewey's in 1944.[20]

Semiconsensual nominations are described as having the same characteristics except that they are "marked by factional cleavage within the party during the process of choice. Thus while there was a single early leader who survived the convention with enough support to win, he was opposed by one or more of the party's factions." Roosevelt in 1940, Harry Truman in 1948, Adlai Stevenson in 1956, John Kennedy in 1960, and Richard Nixon in 1968 are examples. Jimmy Carter's nomination in 1976 does not fit exactly because he was not the preprimary leader.[21]

Nonconsensual nominations, the remainder, involve more divisiveness, usually amateurs pitted against professionals. Wendell Willkie in 1940, Dewey in 1948, Eisenhower and Stevenson in 1952, Goldwater in 1964, Humphrey in 1968, McGovern in 1972, and Gerald Ford in 1976 were all nominated only after preconvention campaigns in which there was no single front-runner from start to finish. In most cases, nonconsensual nominations are found in parties that are out of power.[22]

Thus in fewer than half of the conventions in the last four decades or so have the delegates made a real choice—in the rest, the selection to be made by the convention has been in little or no doubt, and the actual choice has occurred during or before the period of delegate selection.

Presidential Primaries

Unlike other primaries, presidential primaries are not nominating elections; they are preliminaries to the nomination and, like conventions, of varying importance in the selection process. Not all states have presidential primaries, and not all presidential primaries are the same: They are a means of expressing a preference among some of the candidates or of selecting delegates to the national convention or both in combination.

In some states each presidential election year, the names of all genuine candidates are placed on the ballot by the state; in the rest, presidential primaries are optional for the candidates, who may decline to enter contests they fear will hurt their chances of nomination. In contests they do enter, candidates usually play a game of stressing the odds against winning and, when the votes are counted, of declaring that the returns have exceeded all expectation. And thus to the extent the prognoses of the candidates, and of the press, are taken seriously by the public, the outcome of a primary is not a simple win or loss. In 1976 Ronald Reagan, who won ten primaries to Gerald Ford's seventeen (which included four unopposed), cheerfully characterized each loss to Ford as a greater show of support than he and his advisers had reason to expect—as a victory of sorts—with a studied optimism that probably helped sustain his campaign down to the wire. (At the outset, shortly before the New Hampshire primary, however, Reagan's staff had blundered by leaking a poll that showed their man comfortably ahead of Ford. When Ford won the primary by a small margin, it was widely interpreted as a good showing. Without the Reagan poll, a 51 percent vote for an incumbent president might have seemed embarrassingly small.)[23] In 1968 Eugene McCarthy challenged the renomination of incumbent Lyndon Johnson in the first primary of the year in New Hampshire. The president had not filed for the primary, but when McCarthy did, Johnson's supporters responded with a write-in campaign. McCarthy lost in absolute terms, with 42.4 percent of the vote compared to Johnson's 49.5. But relative to the general expectation that he would lose by a wide margin, McCarthy's vote was enough to put him in contention for the nomination. It was a blow to Johnson and contributed to his decision shortly thereafter not to seek or accept the nomination.

It used to be thought that presidential primaries could break a candidate but not make one. But the power of primaries to put an end to a candidacy was exaggerated. President Truman in 1952, like Lyndon Johnson in 1968, decided against trying for another term in office in the wake of a primary defeat in New Hampshire. The president had lost to Senator Estes Kefauver by 45 to 55 percent, which by anyone's interpretation was a clear victory for the insurgent. (As in the case of McCarthy in 1968, Kefauver himself did not go on to win the nomination after helping to remove the incumbent.) Both Truman and Johnson bowed out early, however, and might well have won the nomination if they had tried. Wendell Willkie hoped for renomination by the Republicans in 1944, but he was not the front-runner: Thomas E. Dewey had become the favorite by the start of the primary season. Willkie, an internationalist, filed in isolationist Wisconsin in an unusual move to prove himself in a difficult contest. He lost to Dewey, who had not campaigned in the state, and had no choice but to retire from the race. Edmund Muskie in 1972, in fact, is the only unambiguous case of a front-runner knocked out by primaries.[24] Before the New Hampshire primary, Muskie was well ahead in the polls and press reports. Then his campaign faltered, notably when he wept in public over attacks on his wife, and although he won comfortably in New Hampshire he soon fell behind McGovern. (The media sometimes have a decisive part in setting the expectations by which primary results are judged. They designated Edmund Muskie the front-runner and built so much confidence in Muskie's ability to win 50 percent of the vote that his 46 percent, over McGovern's 37 percent, was viewed as a failure of sorts and marked the beginning of the end of his drive for the nomination. Four years later, the media greatly *helped* Jimmy Carter by giving him a generous amount of publicity in the race for the nomination and by not overestimating the votes he might expect to win in the primaries.)[25]

In the past, the primaries at most gave a helping hand to someone leading the field before the primaries. John Kennedy's preprimary lead was shaky in 1960. There were a number of rivals, active and passive, and uneasiness in the party about running a Catholic for the presidency—the previous attempt in 1928 had failed. The primaries were an opportunity for Kennedy to overcome doubts.[26] He won every one he entered. His victory over Hubert Humphrey in heavily Protestant West Virginia was a sign that one's religion was no longer decisive.

That small and peculiarly unrepresentative states like New Hampshire and West Virginia should have an important role in presidential nominations, New Hampshire by little more than scheduling its primary ahead of the pack in February, has bothered many observers. The attention paid to primaries, particularly early ones, which are generally in small states, is out of proportion to the delegates actually selected or instructed. Also, the results of primary elections are no easier to interpret than the results of any other election. The most popular assessments may prove wrong when the results of careful sample surveys of voters' intentions are made known. Eugene McCarthy's coup in New Hampshire was not, as virtually everyone believed at the time, an antiwar vote against President Johnson. A group at the University of Michigan, in an article published more than a year after the election, demonstrated that McCarthy's vote, far from being a peace vote, came from people who by a margin of three to two favored a *tougher* stand in Vietnam. More of those who originally supported McCarthy defected to George Wallace than to any other contender. Their vote for McCarthy had indeed been a protest against Johnson's conduct of the war, but a protest more of hawks than of doves.[27] Had he known, Johnson might not have withdrawn.

It has been suggested that the problems of unrepresentative primaries, not to mention unrepresentative conventions, might be corrected by a national primary established by Congress, perhaps with a run-off election if no candidate should receive as much as 40 percent of the vote. It would focus national attention on all of the candidates at once and encourage more uniform popular participation than the present mixed system. Still, say the critics, no primary could neatly break a deadlock between first choices by turning to a candidate who is most people's second choice, as a convention could.[28] Nor would a national primary allow a poor candidate such as Eugene McCarthy in 1968 to make a showing in early primaries and entertain the hope of becoming established and attracting support to contest the larger states later on. A halfway reform suggested by Representative (and presidential hopeful)

Morris Udall, a series of regional primaries, might still permit an occasional low-budget candidacy. But even with public financing of national or regional primaries, an expensive private nationwide head start might well determine who would qualify for financing and likely win the primaries.

All of the arguments for and against primaries had to be recast, however, in light of the nomination of Jimmy Carter in 1976. Carter's candidacy overturned the rule that primaries cannot make a candidate. He was the first to come from far behind by means of primaries and wrap up the nomination before convention time. The sheer number of primaries had made it possible. In 1968 seventeen states selected delegates in presidential primaries; in 1972, twenty-three; and in 1976, thirty (and more still in 1980). Some 76 percent of the Democratic and 71 percent of the Republican delegates were chosen in primaries in 1976, compared with about 40 percent in 1968.[29] And because it was possible under the new rules to win at least some delegates in any primary, candidates were less reluctant to run in states in which they might place second or third. In 1976 Jimmy Carter ran in twenty-six primaries. He won seventeen and came in second in eight others.

Carter's success in the primaries was partly a matter of momentum—of establishing himself as the man to beat early in the process. Indeed, he had started rolling before the others by coming in first in the earliest round of all, the Democratic precinct caucuses in Iowa in January 1976. Intensive work by the candidate, his family, and his staff in 1975 paid off in 27.6 percent of the vote, compared with 13.1 percent for Birch Bayh, 9.9 percent for Fred Harris, and 5.9 percent for Morris Udall. Carter's people moved in early and missed no opportunity to promote their candidate, and Carter himself made frequent visits to speak and stump the state. Typically he would drop in on farm families and perhaps stay for a meal or leave a note on the door if no one was at home. It worked. Carter rightly supposed that the Iowa caucuses would have some of the publicity value usually reserved for the first primary in New Hampshire. The man whose name could not be guessed by panelists on the television show "What's My Line" in 1973—even after he had identified himself as the governor of Georgia—had come to national attention.[30]

One cause of the proliferation of primaries was the rule adopted by the Democratic party for 1976 requiring proportional representation in delegate selection but allowing what came to be called "loophole primaries," in which delegates could be chosen on a winner-take-all basis by congressional districts. Statewide winner-take-all primaries were no longer permitted. The expectation was that nonprimary selection by caucus and convention would predominate. But instead party leaders supported the enactment of district primary laws in a number of states, considering this alternative less disruptive than proportional representation—most likely, that is, to serve their traditional interest in massing a state delegation behind one candidate and freezing out insurgents such as George Wallace.[31] The 1976 Democratic convention ruled against loophole primaries for the future, and presidential primaries therefore would be based on proportional representation henceforth. (If there should be a conflict between a state law and national party rules governing the qualifications and eligibility of delegates, the convention may settle the question by deciding which delegates to seat, according to the Supreme Court.)[32] In any event, as long as most delegates are chosen in primaries, the effective choice of presidential candidates is less likely to occur at the convention now than before 1976.

The primaries, further, always leave the door open to candidates who can establish person-to-person ties with the people in the course of campaigning and overcome the more businesslike plans of professional party kingmakers. In his drive for the nomination and the presidency in 1976, Jimmy Carter was most effective in small gatherings where he could talk quietly about love, faith, and honesty, and talk with, not simply to, the voters. Jules Witcover notes that Carter in 1976 and John Kennedy in 1960 both learned from the people they met on the primary trail—Kennedy of poverty and disease in the coal fields of West Virginia, for example. By contrast, Richard Nixon in his bid for the presidency in 1968 (and as incumbent in 1972) remained aloof from those whose support he courted, relying instead on staged appearances, without spontaneity and without feedback.[33]

Preprimary Maneuvers

Whether one dates the coming of age of the presidential primary from Carter's nomination in 1976 or, as some do, from John Kennedy's in 1960, it is now clear that primaries can determine the outcome of national conventions. It was not Jimmy Carter, however, who proved that conventions can be anticlimactic, legitimizing and celebrating decisions already made, as Donald Matthews put it. They have been no more than that, more often than not, for some time, with or without primaries. Usually there is some consensus on a candidate early in election year, even before the primaries.[34] And when there is, that candidate is likely to win the nomination. There have been few exceptions, counting from Franklin Roosevelt's time onward, the period for which we have the evidence of public opinion polls: Harry Truman in 1952, Lyndon Johnson in 1968, and Edmund Muskie in 1972.

Of course, it all begins with a consensus that people from most walks of life are unsuited to the presidency. Traditionally the choice has been from among presidents seeking renomination and vice presidents, governors, senators, an occasional military hero, and, until Herbert Hoover's departure from office, federal administrators. The only exception in modern times was Wendell Willkie, the businessman who won the Republican nomination in 1940.

Presidents who seek renomination get it. Franklin Roosevelt was renominated in 1940 even though custom had established a firm two-term limit; and Harry Truman and Lyndon Johnson probably could have survived their setbacks in New Hampshire. We have to go back as far as 1884 for an unambiguous denial of renomination to an incumbent.[35]

Of the sources of presidents in recent times, the vice presidency is favored: Presidents Johnson, Nixon, and Ford were former vice presidents. Walter Mondale became heir presumptive when he became vice president in 1977, although later the apparent willingness of Ted Kennedy to run dimmed his chances. People who occupy the vice presidency become presidential timber ex officio, whether or not previously thought worthy of consideration: John N. Garner, Alben Barkley, Spiro Agnew (until he ran afoul of the law), and Gerald Ford are clear examples of those who had not been so considered.[36]

The further reduction of the field occurs in ways less easily defined. In general, it has come from the interaction of at least three forces: the desires of the potential candidate (or of his supporters in the case of a genuine draft such as Adlai Stevenson's in 1952), money, and media coverage. The enthusiasm of the would-be candidate and his friends, of contributors, and of the press either catches on or dies, and it is not always clear why. It is known that media effects are most likely to be greatest in the early stages of the campaign. Jimmy Carter, for example, was given a big boost in Iowa in October 1975 by an article in the *New York Times* that turned the attention of the press, and in time the public, on this candidate.[37]

Currently a number of influences are pulling the nomination of presidential candidates away from party leaders and party organizations. Gerald Pomper suggests there is a trend toward the capture of the nominating process by people without strong party support. They decide on their own to seek the presidency, recruit a group of loyal followers—"candidate organizations" instead of party organizations—and rely on nonparty funds, now including the federal subsidies that became available in 1976.[38] John Kennedy is an example. Although a traditional candidate in the limited sense of being a senator and avowed party loyalist, Kennedy's drive for the presidency was essentially personal: He counted heavily on his personality, manner, and attractiveness, on his family fortune to finance himself in politics, and on his own band of faithfuls, nearly all amateurs, mainly Boston Irish Catholics—the Irish Mafia or, better, the Murphia—many of whom followed him to the White House in 1961. Jimmy Carter and his Georgia carpetbaggers are another example. Compare Hubert Humphrey, a presidential aspirant in the same era who was a party regular by temperament, less prepossessing and perpetually short of money. He required organizational support at every step.

In the past, strong party organizations in the larger states controlled presidential nominations. Governors or senators led their delegations in the national conventions, controlled their votes, and sometimes ran as favorite son candidates for nomination—to contend, or more often to hold the delegation together until the moment came to throw the votes to someone who could go on to win the nomination. No longer, argues Pomper. Favorite sons are about gone. Adlai Stevenson was the last sitting governor to be nominated—Jimmy Carter was a *former* governor, not from a large state or in any sense operating from a state party base, as was Stevenson.[39] State parties have lost control with the adoption of presidential primaries and proportional representation. And the Federal Election Campaign Act Amendments of 1974 as interpreted by the Supreme Court have further reduced their influence: Federal financing has been made available to candidates for nomination (as well as to the nominees later on) rather than to the party organizations, and that gives the candidates an extraordinary measure of autonomy; a wealthy candidate may spend an unlimited amount of his own money, a loophole created by the Court on the basis of the First Amendment; and unlimited expenditures may be made on behalf of candidates by people unconnected with them or their parties. In sum, there are powerful incentives for candidates and their backers to stay free of party organizations. The campaign finance law seems already to have increased the number of candidates for nomination and to have encouraged factionalism in the parties.[40]

Let us review the forces at work in the nominating process. The formal procedures of delegate selection and national conventions in the great majority of cases serve only to anoint the early front-runner: Whoever is ahead in the public opinion polls before the first primary will probably become the nominee. In the past, it has almost always been someone with a national reputation in politics: an incumbent president, a vice president, a governor from a populous state, or a senator, typically, who has a well-known name and face and entrée to the mass media, party ties, and party financing. But now, under the new rules about delegate selection and campaign financing, it may be that some public figures on the fringes of politics or even outside of politics—from sports, entertainment, the military, perhaps—fortunate enough to be taken seriously by the press early in the campaign will have the strength to launch national campaigns without the help of state organizations or factions of the major parties.

We shall then have diverged even more from the British. Their system of selecting leaders has been characterized as one of apprenticeship, ours as entrepreneurial.[41] The way to the top is more carefully defined in Great Britain, and when time comes for a choice the field is smaller. Those put under consideration are politicians, invariably, and beyond that have enjoyed a special combination of legislative and executive experience as members of Parliament and participants in the councils of government and opposition. There is none of the American practice of sending strangers to the management of national executive or legislative affairs. And, too, there is a difference in the kind of personality felt to be suited to the chief executive office in the two countries: An American must in some sense be popular in order to become president, but need not be adept at dealing with other politicians at close hand. A British prime minister must have proven his or her collegiality as a requisite of office. Hugh Heclo comments,

> From the nature of the group struggle, it also seems reasonable to suppose that upon entering office a president will have learned an individualistic rather than a prime minister's collegial perspective. The future prime minister has advanced through a muted, nonzero-sum struggle requiring cooperation with sponsors and colleagues; his fate has been inextricably tied to the collective fate of his selectorate, both as government and opposition. Even if the working political life of the future president has been spent in an interdependent group, his selection for the highest office has probably taken place through a zero-sum struggle with other political entrepreneurs trying to mold winning alliances in a disorganized party. The formal constitutional separation of powers is of course consistent with such a view, but even without this separation, the president would have been predisposed by the real-life recruitment struggle to view his actions and those of his staff as independently justified and legitimate rather than as requiring agreement of his colleagues or party. This perspective goes beyond a simple lack of rapport with Congress, which, without the British parliamentary locus of selection, is natural enough. By the time of his arrival in office, a president is likely to have undergone one of the most unusual learning experiences in the world. He is likely to have absorbed not simply an individualistic but a tribunal perspective—a psychological terrain in which the outstanding features are the all-powerful but indeterminate people and himself as their chosen leader. This is a strange and heroic world, an illimitable, misty sea on which the president is the sole argonaut. As he enters the White House, the new president has already gone a long way toward learning to be "the loneliest man in the world."[42]

The Impact of Reform

Americans tinker with their political parties and electoral systems, as with everything else. It is remarkable that, constant repairs notwithstanding, theirs is the oldest written constitution and the most stable two-party system in the world, and it is even more remarkable that the system should have survived so long when all evidence suggests that reformers—probably the Founding Fathers excepted—have guessed wrong about most of the consequences of their reforms. Murphy's law reminds us that if something can go wrong, it will.

It is not a new complaint. Consider John C. Calhoun's view in 1844 that the presidential nominating convention had turned out badly in little more than a decade:

> The Convention should be so constituted, as to utter fully and clearly the voice of the people, and not that of political managers, or office holders and office seekers; and for that purpose, I hold it indispensable that the delegates should be appointed directly by the people, or to use the language of General Jackson, should be "fresh from the people." I also hold, that the the only possible mode to effect this, is for the people to choose the delegates by districts, and that they should vote per capita. Every other mode of appointing would be controlled by political machinery, and place the appointments in the hands of those who work it.

(So far, this might almost have been written by the McGovern-Fraser Commission.)

> Instead, then, of being directly, or fresh from the people, the delegates to the Baltimore Convention will be the delegates of delegates; and, of course, removed, in all cases at least three, if not four degrees from the people. At each successive remove, the voice of the people will become less full and distinct, until, at last it will be so faint and imperfect as not to be audible. To drop metaphor, I hold it impossible to form a scheme more perfectly calculated to annihilate the control of the people over the Presidential election, and vest it in those who make politics a trade, and who live, or expect to live on the Government.[43]

A reform instituted in the name of popular democracy, said Calhoun, had become an instrument of dictation.

More recently, well into the primary season in 1976 it was believed that the Democrats would have a "brokered" convention, with bargaining among factions spawned by new rules for proportional representation in delegate selection. It was also assumed that the Republicans would have an uneventful convention to nominate Gerald Ford. It was the Democratic convention that turned out to be anticlimactic, of course;

the Republicans had a free-for-all. The rules did not have their anticipated effect.

There are invariably two sets of arguments for or against changes
in electoral rules: appeals to principle, which are played up, and calculations of self-interest, which are played down. Appeals to principle are
concerned with questions of fairness, equality, honesty, improving the
representativeness of elected bodies, increased popular participation,
and the like. Self- or group-interest requires politicians and reformers to
ask, however, "Will the changes help me? My party? My friends?" There
are no neutral electoral reforms, helping or hurting no one or everyone
equally. All but a few of those for or against reforms will to some extent
be interested in short-term gains. Those who introduced the national
nominating convention, the presidential primary, and the recent reforms in the Democratic party all were concerned to improve the chances
of their kind—and even their own chances, quite specifically—to gain
the nomination.[44]

But when broad changes are made in institutions as complex as the
presidential nominating system, unexpected results are commonplace.
A good indication of the unpredictability of the McGovern-Fraser Commission reforms, for example, is given by James Lengle and Byron
Shafer, who recalculated the returns of the first fifteen Democratic
primaries in 1972 as they would have been under (1) winner-take-all
rules, (2) proportional representation, and (3) the congressional district
plan, had each of those prevailed uniformly in the states with primaries—that is, respectively, the old system, the reform, and the loophole. Then they compared actual and hypothetical delegate totals.[45]
These fifteen primaries set the stage for the winner-take-all California
primary. McGovern took it by a margin of 44 to 39 percent over Humphrey and successfully defended his victory in a credentials fight at the
convention. Had McGovern not approached the California primary with
a substantial lead, it is quite possible the results would have been
different. As Lengle and Shafer demonstrate, Hubert Humphrey would
have led under a winner-take-all plan and George Wallace under either
a proportional or a districted plan. Whether or not different rules would

	Actual	Winner-Take-All	Proportional	Districted
McGovern	401.5	249	319	343
Humphrey	284	446	314	324
Wallace	291	379	350	367
Muskie	56.5	18	82	52
Others	59	0	27	6

in fact have produced different results, something that cannot be proven, theirs is a persuasive illustration of unanticipated bias in electoral rules.

Still, party leaders continue to adjust the rules—and to load the dice. In 1978 the Democratic National Committee, under White House guidance, adopted rules for the 1980 campaign designed to reduce the representation of fringe or single-issue candidates in the national convention. The president's critics saw the new rules as a way for the incumbent to improve his chances of renomination by squeezing out any future Jimmy Carters.[46]

PRESIDENTIAL ELECTIONS

So much happens in a presidential election, that time and patience are needed to sort it out after the votes have been counted. Mixed motives—including some hypocrisy on the part of candidates and voters alike, incomplete information, and the difficulty of discovering "why" any one person voted as he or she did, much less explaining the vote of tens of millions—make the task of interpretation enormous. Most of us fall back on hunch and rumor for want of something better.

Actually, though, modern sample surveys offer good insights, all the richer with the accumulation of each new set of data. We can, for example, tell whether voters are on the whole more interested in issues in one election than in another, or what kind of people (young, old, poor, wealthy, and so forth) were most likely to vote, and to some extent why. With this kind of information, we can also see great changes taking place in the way we elect our presidents. The constitutional basis of presidential elections remains the same, but the dialogue of candidates and voters is not what it was a quarter of a century ago.

Electoral Coalitions

Traditionally it has been possible to characterize presidential elections as the work of major-party coalitions, often of quite dissimilar groups. In our political system the coalescence occurs before elections, in contrast to some parliamentary democracies in which the parties each expect and win only a minority of the votes and must form parliamentary coalitions after elections in order to govern. Ours has been a stable system with long-lived coalitions.

Every three or three and a half decades, there has tended to be a reshuffling of the component groups in the major parties in this country. The party with the larger coalition has won most of the elections until the next shuffle. This happened in and about the years 1896 and 1932—there is less agreement about dates before that, but the development of a party system in the 1790s, the coming to power of Andrew Jackson, and the struggle over slavery were clearly periods of realignment.[1] These were times of crisis and ferment. There have been accurate surveys of public attitudes only since the 1940s, but even the crude polls of the 1930s support the common understanding that in that realignment people were taking sides on the main issues of the New Deal: the size of government, welfare, and the redistribution of wealth.[2]

More recent polls also confirm our intuition that differences on issues are not of the same importance from one election to the next. Sometimes likes and dislikes about competing presidential candidates and at other times loyalties to parties predominate. One can draw the profile of an election as perceived by the voters as a mixture of attitudes about issues, candidates, and parties.[3] Patterns of voting established during an issue-conscious period of realignment, for example, may be sustained for decades by tenacious partisan identification after the debate over issues has cooled or new issues have arisen.

One question about the dimensions of major realignments of the past remains unanswered: To what extent did they represent conversions and to what extent new generations of voters replacing old? Was the Democratic New Deal coalition laden with former Republicans? Some recent reworking of old data suggests, without proof, that switching was as infrequent then as now—that the popular theory of massive defections to the Democratic party was incorrect. An unusually large pool of potential voters was created in the 1920s by the enfranchisement of women in 1920 and, more crucially, by the effects of previous immigration—people becoming citizens and their children coming of age. Voting was light in the 1920s. Most who became eligible waited several years to vote. Then the Depression of 1929 and Franklin Roosevelt's candidacy in 1932 brought many of them to the polls. Of those twenty-eight or younger who voted for the first time in 1932, about 80 percent were for Roosevelt. In 1936, it was 85 percent.[4] New young voters gave the New Deal coalition lasting strength: Harry Truman's Fair Deal and to some extent John Kennedy's New Frontier and Lyndon Johnson's Great Society were a continuation of the Roosevelt coalition.

But even while one coalition prevails, another party may win the presidency in what has come to be called a "deviating election."[5] The diagnosis is not easily made: Some of the best evidence is what happens four or eight years later. The Eisenhower presidency is our best illustration. Concern about issues was fairly low in 1952 and 1956, but interest in the candidates—Eisenhower versus Stevenson both years—was intense and on balance clearly favorable to Eisenhower. Polls showed that people liked Eisenhower and regarded him as a man of integrity. In his first campaign, his most serious disability was felt to be his military background; by the second, that concern had faded, although by then some regarded him as too old and infirm. Stevenson was appreciated for his experience and education, and was criticized above all for cracking jokes and talking over the heads of the common people.[6] The vote for Eisenhower was for the man. It was not for the Republican party: Many people split their vote, giving Eisenhower a Democratic Congress for the last six of his eight years in office. Also, the electorate continued overwhelmingly to identify with the Democratic party and went on to return Democrats to the White House in two ensuing elections.[7]

There was speculation in the Eisenhower years, however, that a new alignment was forming—"modern" Republicanism, a new middle-of-the-road coalition. How little came of this movement can be seen in the party's selection of an extreme conservative, Barry Goldwater, as its presidential candidate in 1964.

Still, it is common for a president's supporters to hope (and his opponents to fear) that a new era has begun—and in most cases to find out sooner or later that it has not. After the election of Richard Nixon in 1968, one of his young supporters, Kevin Phillips, wrote a popular book entitled *The Emerging Republican Majority* to herald a realignment in the making.[8] He contended that Nixon's narrow victory was the equivalent of a landslide of the proportions of Roosevelt's in 1936 because those who voted for George Wallace were Republicans ideologically and would vote Republican in the future. The realignment, as Phillips saw it, shifted both regional and group loyalties. Regionally it was the heartland overcoming the Northeast, reviving forces once led by Jefferson, Jackson, and Franklin Roosevelt; but while in the past it had been a victory of liberalism over a northeastern conservative establishment, in 1968 it was a conservative South, Midwest, and West against a northeastern liberal establishment. The most important line of demarcation was that separating the Northeast from the rest of the country, not North from South any longer. And since the Northeast had a dwindling share of the population, its political influence was waning ineluctably.

Phillips noted changes in the voting habits of certain groups, too. Americans of Irish extraction, once a vital component of the Democratic party, were now found increasingly on the side of conservative Republicanism—Senator Joseph McCarthy, a former Democrat, for example, and Richard Nixon. The Democratic party was losing its blue-collar and lower-middle-class support and its traditional hold on southern whites, which had been tenuous since 1948, and would be left with blacks and other residents of the central city, liberals, and a pathetic scattering of others. In short, the realignment as Phillips conceived it was enough to bring joy to Republicans and despair to Democrats. Richard Nixon won reelection by a genuine landslide in 1972—although against a weak opponent and without gaining control of Congress. Had Watergate not handicapped the party, it is hard to say whether a substantial part of Phillips' dream might not have come true. We now know that it failed. The elections of 1968 and 1972 were, if anything, deviating rather than realigning.

A different view, that the emerging majority is on the left rather than the right has been held by a number of political theorists and activists in the recent past. There has been no more empirical support for this position than for Phillips', but this says nothing against it for the future. Indeed, it can be argued that realignment and deviation have less meaning today, with fewer party indentifiers and fewer straight-ticket voters.

Short of staging a realignment, the general strategy of both parties as they approach an election is to hold on to their core groups and to appeal to enough others to win.[9] The challenge is to attract new groups without alienating the old. The largest components are likely to be given recognition in the selection of a balanced presidential and vice-presidential ticket, in the Democratic party maintaining a coalition of the urban and ethnic North with the South and West. For example, in 1952:

> The convention had not quite ended with Stevenson's acceptance speech. After delivering it late Friday night, he had met in a small room behind the speakers' platform with President Truman, Sam Rayburn, and Chairman McKinney to decide who should run for Vice President. Stevenson was leaning toward Kefauver. Truman proposed Senator John Sparkman of Alabama. The question was: Which defeated wing of the party needed to be conciliated—Kefauver's Northern liberals or Russell's Southerners? Stevenson's liberal credentials seemed better than his Southern credentials. Hence the South must be conciliated. Senator Russell had no broad base, would be unacceptable to Northern liberals, and probably wouldn't take it anyway. Kefauver, though from Tennessee, was anathema to Southerners. The conferees decided to eliminate anybody who had been a presidential contender. Thus they turned to Senator John Sparkman of Alabama who, though he had in the Senate voted as a Southerner on civil rights, had built up a record on other issues as a liberal and had few enemies in the party. On Saturday morning he was nominated by acclamation.[10]

In the Republican party, the emphasis is more on keeping a balance of moderates and conservatives. When either party fails to adopt this kind of strategy, it can expect trouble at the polls. The Goldwater coalition in the Republican party is instructive. It was ideologically exclusive—conservative ideologues, hawks, states rights southerners, and some regulars sufficiently loyal to the party to support a Republican whatever his policies. Goldwater's candidacy threatened only the southern component of the Democratic coalition, but its identification with the far right more than compensated the Democrats by driving moderate Republicans across party lines into Lyndon Johnson's camp.[11] The candidacy of a southern Democrat, Jimmy Carter, was by contrast an example of successful strategy, reasserting the Democratic party's winning North-South coalition.

In the course of a campaign, lesser appeals must be made routinely to sundry groups: women, farmers, veterans, old people, young people, manufacturers, importers, exporters, and so on ad infinitum. The daily round of playing up to such interests was so tedious to Adlai Stevenson's writers that they toyed privately with a new approach. On the ownership of offshore oil:

> Good morning, my friends in Dallas:
> I come before you to tell you plainly my position on the question of the tidelands—the title, that is, to oil which is thought to lie beneath the submerged lands along your seacoast. It has been called to my attention that some of you have been asserting a claim to those lands.
> Well, I tell you in all candor that if I am elected I will make it my business to see to it that any such dream you may entertain will come to nothing. Why, you seceded from the Union in 1860, we whipped the bejesus out of you and dragged you back into the Union; and I intend to treat you like a conquered province, an occupied territory, which in truth is precisely what you are. You prate of you rights. Well, don't you come whining to me about your so-called rights. You deserve nothing, and from me you'll get nothing. So far as I am concerned you have no right to anything, not to the tidelands nor to anything else.

Or a talk to farmers, which was to begin:

> Good afternoon, peasants:
> I have during this campaign traveled the length and breadth of this broad land, looking upon the smiling faces of Americans everywhere, and I can tell you in all sincerity that I have never seen anywhere such a bunch of ignorant, shiftless, selfish, greedy people as you farmers.[12]

If no special benefits can be promised some of these groups, the substance of the speeches can at least be neutral. The door need not be shut in anyone's face. Even members of the other party are welcome. Presidential candidates tend to think that whatever might be gained by stressing party identification and attacking the opposition by party name would be more than lost in offending potential defectors from that party. An interesting exception to the rule of trying to be pleasing or at least cordial to as many interests as possible is that of meeting one's strongest critics head on. Both Stevenson and Carter chose American Legion conventions to contradict Legion policies on "Americanism" and the treatment of Vietnam draft evaders, respectively. It is a spectacle certain to draw national attention. When the catcalls subside, some sympathy may go out to the candidate for his courage and forthrightness. John Kennedy's talk to the Greater Houston Ministerial Association in 1960 was similarly conceived as a way of dealing bluntly with the question whether a Catholic was fit to serve as president, although he, unlike Stevenson and Carter, was trying his best to please his critics.

> I believe in an America where the separation of church and state is absolute—where no Catholic prelate would tell the president (should he be Catholic) how to act, and no Protestant minister would tell his parishioners for whom to vote—where no church or church school is granted any public funds or political preference. . . . An America that is officially neither Catholic, Protestant, nor Jewish—where no public official either requests or accepts instructions on public policy from . . . any . . . ecclesiastical source. . . . Where there is no Catholic vote, no anti-Catholic vote, no bloc voting of any kind. [13]

"Today," he continued, "I may be the victim, but tomorrow it may be you." The response of the assembled clergy and of the public was, on the whole, favorable.

Competition for the Center

Along with taking care to build and maintain a proper coalition, there is a second set of considerations in American presidential electoral strategy: the concreteness and ideological direction of campaign statements. We well know that candidates for the presidency and other offices are sometimes vague, and that when they are not they often aim for the middle of the road. Voters may be hard pressed to tell what competing candidates stand for and what the differences are between them.

Why should this be so? For most politicians, a numbing discreetness in public statements is a reflex action learned in give-and-take with the public. The rule of thumb seems to be that a specific statement will alienate some voters and that the safest course is a studied ambiguity on most issues and heavy reliance on nonsense statements or Fourth-of-July rhetoric on which everyone can agree.[14] Some are better at this than others. Nearly all of Nelson Rockefeller's public statements had a high nonsense content. He was a master of the politics of buncombe. For example, in 1968 he decided to enter the race for the presidency; the press and public hungrily awaited his statement of position on the key issue of the war in Vietnam. After a suspenseful delay, he announced, "My position on Vietnam is very simple. And I feel this way. . . . I think that our concepts as a nation and that our actions have not kept pace with the changing conditions. And therefore our actions are not completely relevant today to the realities of the magnitude and the complexity of the problems we face in this co.,flict." Asked what he might mean by this, he said he would stand by his statement. He lost the fight for the Republican nomination to Richard Nixon, another master at the game.

In 1929, an economist named Harold Hotelling constructed an explanation of why, in a town formed along one main street, two competing businesses, each deciding rationally where best to set up shop, would converge in the center of town. Not to do so would mean, among other things, giving up customers who lived there, in the center. Hotelling suggested that two political parties might similarly compete for position on a left-to-right ideological scale. The party of the right, knowing its members on the far right had nowhere else to go, would concentrate on wooing the middle-of-the-roaders; and the party of the left, assuming it could count on the allegiance of the far left, would also aim for the center.[15]

Another economist, Arthur Smithies, modified the model in 1941 with more realistic assumptions and concluded that the competing stores (or political parties) might not end up side by side in the middle. At some point in their convergence, they would risk losing more in the hinterlands than they gained in the center and would therefore place themselves most profitably somewhat to their respective sides of center.[16]

A third economist, Anthony Downs, refined these theories in *An Economic Theory of Democracy* in 1957, distinguishing situations in which the voters lie in a normal bell-shaped distribution on the ideological continuum from those with a bimodal distribution with the voters clustered at each end. In the former, convergence is rational for parties bent on maximizing votes, and loss of extremist voters at the fringes is an acceptable risk. But a bimodal distribution of the electorate holds the parties apart ideologically, and then there is more to lose than to gain by convergence. A flat, even distribution of the population produces limited convergence as described by Smithies.[17]

Accordingly, vote-minded party leaders at times must suppress their personal preferences in pursuit of the center. A study of the issue positions of Democratic and Republican activists and rank and file in the Eisenhower years indicated that, while the latter were grouped near the center, the activists (in this case national convention delegates) were more polarized. Democratic leaders were somewhat more liberal than the rank and file; Republican leaders were well to the right of their membership.[18] The study helps explain what went wrong with the Republican party in 1964 when it nominated Barry Goldwater, who was unattractive to the center.

Not only have American voters in the past been found crowding the center of the political spectrum in a near-normal distribution; they have also been found to be shallow. The first national surveys to deal systematically with the question, in 1956, asked open-ended questions about what respondents liked or disliked in the two candidates and their parties. The answers were placed in four categories from most to least sophisticated. Level A, "ideology and near-ideology," included those with "any suggestion of the abstract conception one would associate with ideology." For example:

([Is there anything you] *like about Democrats?*) "Well, I like their liberalness over the years. They certainly have passed beneficial legislation like social security and unemployment insurance, which the average man needs today."

([Is there anything you] *dislike about Democrats?*) "The Communists linked to Roosevelt and Truman. Corruption. Tax scandals. I don't like any of those things."

([Is there anything you] *like about Republicans?*) "I also like the conservative element in the Republican Party." (Anything else?) "No."

([Is there anything you] *dislike about Republicans?*) "No, not at present."[19]

Level B, "group benefits," consisted of responses describing "fairly concrete and short-term group interest." Level C was "the 'goodness' and 'badness' of the times." Level D was responses devoid of issue content. An almost pure case:

([Is there anything you] *like about Democrats?*) "No—I don't know as there is."

([Is there anything you] *dislike about Democrats?*) "No."

([Is there anything you] *like about Republicans?*) "No, it's the same way I am about the other party."

([Is there anything you] *dislike about Republicans?*) "No, parties are all about the same to me."

([Is there anything you] *like about Stevenson?*) No.

([Is there anything you] *like about Eisenhower?*) I really don't care which man is best or otherwise. I don't know about either one of the men enough to give an opinion.

([Is there anything you] *dislike about Eisenhower?*) No.[20]

Only 15.5 percent of the voters were found to qualify for Level A. Another 45 percent were classed as Level B.[21]

The authors of this study concluded that there was, on the whole, a low level of conceptualization among the voters. Few of the responses would do in an examination in introductory American government. It is equally fair to conclude, however, that a large share of the voters—six out of ten (A plus B)—had some grasp of either the ideology of liberalism or conservatism or of how politics might help the groups to which they belong, and should not be disparaged. Still, the study of ideology among voters was only a small part of the survey work of the period tending to show factual and conceptual weakness in the electorate. A study of the 1960 election showed similarly that the basic concepts of liberalism and conservatism were well understood by only a sixth of the people.[22] One had only to ask a sample of voters to name key officials or describe important constitutional principles or legislative issues to begin wondering about the future of democracy. Politicians could point to the polls as reason enough not to burden the electorate with issues.

But there is a chicken-and-egg problem. Is the level of information and conceptualization in the electorate the reason for issue avoidance and issue convergence in campaigns; or is it the other way around, that simple-minded campaigning by Tweedledums and Tweedledees fails to enlighten the public; or is it both? Benjamin Page and Richard Brody address this question in a study of the 1968 presidential election, an unusually bland campaign conducted in the midst of chaos at home and abroad.[23] Hubert Humphrey and Richard Nixon, two canny politicians, chose to say as little and to disagree as little as possible about the central issue that year: the war in Vietnam. Humphrey as vice president was, for one thing, under the traditional constraint of loyalty to the president, but even when at last he spoke out for himself on the war he was still remarkably uninformative.

Page and Brody analyzed all of the two candidates' major speeches and many of the minor ones word by word for issue content, and came to the following conclusions:

> Both Nixon and Humphrey avoided the Vietnam issue when they could; when they did discuss it, they talked in vague generalities; and only on very rare occasions did they mention specific policy proposals. It is

possible for scholars, after reading all their speeches and statements, to arrive at judgments of what their "real" positions were; but the ordinary citizen may be forgiven if he failed to penetrate the haze of vague hints which alternated with total silence about Vietnam in most of the candidates' rhetoric.

Nixon was a master of ambiguity on Vietnam. Early in the campaign he promised that new leadership "will end the war and win the peace in the Pacific. . . ." Again and again he declared, "The war must be ended. It must be ended honorably. . . ." Few Americans could disagree with that, or with his insistence that the South Vietnamese should replace American troops. But Nixon refused to explain *how* he would end the war, on the grounds that an explanation might interfere with the efforts of the Johnson administration to achieve a settlement and would weaken his own bargaining position if he became president.[24]

Secondly, Page and Brody commissioned a series of national opinion surveys to learn the public's views of the war in Vietnam and of the candidates' positions on the war. On a scale of 1 (immediate withdrawal) to 7 (complete military victory), the median position taken by the public was 4.15, and median scores of their perceptions of Humphrey's and Nixon's positions were 4.05 and 4.39, respectively. Most respondents correctly saw the candidates' positions as similar. Eugene McCarthy and George Wallace were viewed, also correctly, as much closer to the two ends of the scale.[25]

It is not surprising, therefore, that the Vietnam issue did not become a crucial one for most voters. It had been defused by the candidates. A cross tabulation of the policy preferences of voters with the way they voted showed that there was little connection. Opinions on Vietnam accounted for less than 2 percent of the variation in voting behavior, even though nearly all the voters had strong views on the war.[26]

For the most part, the voters can be seen as having responded reasonably to the meager fare served up by candidates Humphrey and Nixon. As an aside, however, it is interesting that some of the voters responded in another way: Among the minority who incorrectly perceived the candidates' stands as substantially different, there was a tendency to project personal positions onto the candidate of one's party and the reverse onto the opposing candidate.

Among Republicans, who mostly favored Nixon, extreme hawks thought that Nixon was an extreme hawk; extreme doves thought he was an extreme dove; and those in the middle thought Nixon stood in the middle! The relationship between opinion and perception were quite strong. Similarly, among Democrats, extreme hawks tended to think Humphrey was an extreme hawk; extreme doves thought Humphrey was an extreme dove; and those in the middle thought he stood in the middle. . . .

Many of those who saw a big difference between Nixon and Humphrey, in other words, were responding to their own wishes. Their perceptions were the result of intended vote, not the cause. These people were not engaged in policy voting.[27]

In sum, while the dullness and ambiguity of the candidates' treatment of the war prevented most voters from taking the issue seriously as a basis for choosing between the candidates, it had the odd effect, which has been noted in other campaigns, of inducing some voters to fill in the blanks.

A subsequent study by Page, however, shows that there were real differences in the positions taken by Humphrey and Nixon on some issues, notably social welfare questions such as federal assistance for medical care and aid to education. He found that in most but not all cases the differences between the candidates paralleled differences between the rank and file of their respective parties, as indicated by public opinion polls.[28]

Candidates who avoid issues are tempted to substitute showmanship and hucksterism. It is no accident that one of the best accounts of political theater and fakery came out of the same election that Page and Brody found wanting intellectually. In *The Selling of the President 1968*, reporter Joe McGinnis exposed the inner workings of Richard Nixon's expensive television campaign with its behind-the-scenes cynicism (customarily understood to be off the record), contrived spontaneity, and exaltation of form over issues. It is a documentary of the planning and execution of panel interview programs and other public relations efforts starring candidate Nixon, with asides such as "I can't do that sincerity bit with the camera if he's sweating." No one who has read the scripts for sixty-second spot commercials in McGinnis's appendix will ever be able to sit through another with equanimity.

FLAMING APT. HOUSE DISSOLVING TO POLICE PATROLLING DESERTED STREETS IN AFTERMATH OF VIOLENCE. R. N.: It is time for some honest talk about the problem of order in the United States.

PERPLEXED FACES OF AMERICANS. R. N.: Dissent is a necessary ingredient of change. But in a system of government that provides for peaceful change—

SEQUENCE OF SHOTS OF PEOPLE MOVING THROUGH BATTERED STREETS BORDERED BY DESTROYED SHOPS AND HOMES. R. N.: —there is no cause that justifies resort to violence. There is no cause that justifies rule by mob instead of by reason.

ELOQUENT FACES OF AMERICANS WHO HAVE LIVED THROUGH SUCH EXPERIENCES, CLIMAXED BY SINGLE SHOT OF CHARRED CROSSBEAMS FRAMING A RIOT RUIN. IN CENTER OF PICTURE IS BATTERED MACHINE ON WHICH CAN STILL BE SEEN IN RED LETTERS THE WORD "CHANGE." FADEOUT. MUSIC UP AND OUT.[29]

Some years later, another work on presidential campaign strategy excited a new round of cynical commentary. Patrick Caddell, a young pollster and political adviser in Jimmy Carter's inner circle, prepared a fifty-six page private memorandum in 1976 at the request of the then president-elect on the subject of a continuing strategy for the next election, four years hence. Portions were leaked to the press the following May.[30] The memo first analyzed the Carter coalition as it would need to be in 1980. Blacks, the poor, union families, and urban Catholics were crucial for a Carter victory, it said, but strongly favored Democratic candidates anyway and might be taken for granted. The South, however, had to be courted. "President Carter must use regional sentiment, regional appointments, and his own personal leadership—through visits and political contacts—to maintain the base in the South." Secondly, Caddell advocated a centrist strategy to attract independents, moderates, and—edging over the center line—conservatives. He saw the center as a large and burgeoning part of the electorate, more important than the liberals to Carter. He complimented Carter for having turned toward the center in the final weeks of the campaign.

Third, and most interestingly, Caddell called for a first term in which style would predominate over substance. The result was to be an image of Carter as a "strong leader with vision" giving the government "a new sense of doing business," an image sufficiently ambiguous to allow the voters to "project their own desires" onto Carter. Specific suggestions included fireside chats, town hall meetings, and simple gestures such as reducing the number of White House limousines. It was obvious at the time of the leak that the president had been taking the advice. The isolation and royal splendor of the White House under Nixon had been succeeded by a touch of informality in the Ford administration and a campaign of thrift and down-home folksiness under Carter. On all points—the maintenance of a basic coalition, the courting of the center with generalities, and the concern for appearances—the memo was politics as usual; that it was revealed to the public was not.

The tendency of candidates to win and hold office by obscuring issues and manipulating images has periodically led to proposals for reforming the party system and making campaigns more meaningful. Woodrow Wilson was one president who was interested in party reform most of his adult life. In 1950, the American Political Science Association, an organization of which Wilson was once president, issued a report, "Toward a More Responsible Two-Party System," which called for parties willing to present distinct programs to the electorate through their presidential and congressional candidates and prepared to enact them if elected. The political scientists who wrote the report felt the major parties were heading for collapse for want of popular trust and support and that presidents might appeal demogogically and destructively for the direct support of the people. The solution they saw was to strengthen the parties, involving both branches of government and the rank and file in the development of policy, and to bind elected officials to promote party policy once in office.

> An effective party system requires, first, that the parties are able to bring forth programs to which they commit themselves and, second, that the parties possess sufficient internal cohesion to carry out these programs. Such a degree of unity within the parties cannot be brought about without party procedures that give a large body of people an opportunity to share in the development of the party program.
>
> The fundamental requirement of accountability is a two-party system in which the opposition party acts as the critic of the party in power, developing, defining and presenting the policy alternatives which are necessary for a true choice in reaching public decisions. The opposition most conducive to responsible party government is an organized party opposition.
>
> There is little to suggest that the phenomenal growth of interest organizations in recent decades has come to an end. The whole development makes necessary a reinforced party system that can cope with the multiplied organized pressures. . . .
>
> Needed clarification of party policy will not cause the parties to differ more fundamentally or more sharply than they have in the past. Nor is it to be assumed that increasing concern with their programs will cause the parties to erect between themselves an ideological wall. Parties have the right and the duty to announce the terms to govern participation in the common enterprise. The emphasis in all consideration of party discipline must be on positive measures to create a strong and general agreement on policies. . . .
>
> Party responsibility means the responsibility of both parties to the general public, as enforced in elections. Party responsibility to the public, enforced in elections, implies that there be more than one party, for the public can hold a party responsible only if it has a choice. As a means of achieving responsibility, the clarification of party policy also tends to keep public debate on a more realistic level, restraining the inclination of party spokesmen to make unsubstantiated statements and charges.[31]

The committee concluded, "The president can probably be more influential than any other single individual in attaining a better organized majority party, and thus also prompting the minority party to follow suit. With greater party responsibility, the president's position as party leader would correspond in strength to the greater strength of his party."[32] But still, on balance, the report was a design for the *subordination* of elected officials to party influence, particularly in shaping policy.

As one of its authors confessed in 1971, "The report was neither universally acclaimed by the American people, who—as might have been predicted—ignored it, nor by politicians, most of whom ignored it, nor by students of political parties, who have given it a great, perhaps inordinate, amount of attention. In the two decades since its publication it has more often served as a foil than as a model."[33] A survey by Austin Ranney indicates that some progress has been made toward the goals of the report, "but not much."[34] Yet now, in the wake of popular discontent with the presidential nominating process and with the excesses of presidential power in the era of Vietnam and Watergate, there has remained at least some interest in the idea of a responsible party that aims both at strengthening the hand of the president by ensuring him a like-minded Congress and at subordinating his will to that of the party.[35] It was the party that made the legislative work of great presidents like Wilson and the Roosevelts possible; an active party might also have curbed a Nixon in time.

The Decline of Party?

Looking back on the period between 1964 and 1972, we can see that, with the exception of the uninformative major-party campaigns in 1968, presidential candidates were in fact providing choices for the voters and that a change was under way in American politics. But it did not spring from a revival of popular interest in parties, as the proponents of responsible parties had hoped; on the contrary, there was evidence that the Democratic and Republican parties were more than ever in disarray.

The first step in that direction was the candidacy of Barry Goldwater in 1964. Goldwater promised—and gave—"a choice, not an echo" to the voters. During both the nomination and the election campaigns, he distinguished his positions from those of the other candidates and from the center. At the convention, goaded by criticism of his conservatism, he struck out at moderate Republicanism in a way that could only lose him votes. His refusal to disavow the support of the far-right John Birch Society frightened moderates. (It was the head of the John Birch Society who once described Republican demigod Dwight Eisenhower as a conscious, dedicated agent of the Communist party. It was understandable that most Republicans wanted to be free of any association with that organization.) Goldwater was advised to allay the moderates' fears. In answer, he said to the convention, "Extremism in the defense of liberty is no vice! Moderation in the pursuit of justice is no virtue!"— spurning the advice as forcefully as he could.[36] In the general election campaign, he opened a gulf between himself and Lyndon Johnson on issues. He was belligerent about Vietnam, while Johnson was restrained. (It is another matter that Johnson was later shown to have secretly embarked on a course of escalation at the time.) He was opposed

to most federal civil rights legislation. He was opposed to big government and wanted to make social security voluntary, whereas Johnson
promised to use the power of government freely to right wrongs and aid
the disadvantaged.[37] Johnson won the election by a record margin, as
the Hotelling-Downs theory would predict.

The Goldwater candidacy was generally regarded as a massive
miscalculation by the Republican party, brought about by a zealous
conservative and loyal followers who had some vain hope of a realignment and by the acquiescence and disorganization of moderate Republicans who gauged his strength too late and launched a stop-Goldwater
movement only when the nomination was effectively his. Goldwater
went on to break all the rules about campaigning, and he paid for it; he
also at times gave the impression that he preferred defending principles
to doing what was necessary to win the presidency.

Then came the issue-laden candidacies of George Wallace for the
American Independent party in 1968 and George McGovern for the
Democrats in 1972. McGovern had the image of a Goldwater of the left,
which he did not entirely deserve: Benjamin Page's content analysis
indicates that McGovern was roughly as close to the average positions of
the public on issues of the campaign as Nixon and Humphrey had been
in 1968.[38] Even though they lost their elections, Goldwater, Wallace, and
McGovern helped clarify the issues of the day—notably war and civil
rights—by their forthrightness. The blandness of the major-party candidates on key issues in 1968 was no longer the norm. It was becoming the
exception.

Whether, under the stimulus of more informative campaigns and
events as harrowing as civil disorder and war, the public became more
alert to issues and more polarized left and right in this period is a much-
debated question. One major study, by Norman Nie, Sidney Verba, and
John Petrocik, *The Changing American Voter* (1976), concludes that from
1956, a year in which *The American Voter* (1960) and other studies found
strong centrist tendencies in American politics, down to 1973, by which
time both major parties had experimented with noncentrist strategies,
the adult public became less comfortable with centrism on issues.[39]
Similarly, according to *The Changing American Voter*, the members of
each of the two parties had changed. In 1956, 41 percent of each could be
called centrist on issues, but by the early 1970s only 26 percent of the

	Leftist	Moderate Leftist	Centrist	Moderate Rightist	Rightist
1956	12	19	41	15	13
1973	21	12	27	17	23

Democrats and 30 percent of the Republicans so qualified. The Republicans had moved generally from center rightward; the Democrats had become more evenly distributed between left, right, and center.[40]

Also, according to this study, changes occurred in the relative ideological position of Democratic activists and rank and file in this period. It had been discovered in 1956 that Democratic followers were a little left of center, on the average, and that their leaders were a little to the left of them. Republican followers were right of center, as noted earlier, but Republican leaders were considerably to their right. In 1972, it seemed that the relative position of activists and ordinary members in the Republican party was not much changed, but that Democratic activists had moved well to the left of the average position of the rank and file, so that the party configurations became mirror images of one another. It was interesting, though, that as the Democratic activists were developing a left or liberal consensus, the membership of the party appeared to be dispersing ideologically to the left, the right, and the center.[41]

By 1972 each party had come to need the self-discipline not to select extreme candidates, given a choice in convention, but to go for someone with broad appeal. In other words, trying to win the presidency with an ideological purist had become a tempting though still losing strategy for both parties. At the same time, 1968-like campaigns seemed unsatisfying to the voters who now were interested in issues. New sample surveys showed some increase from the Eisenhower years in ideological thinking in the electorate.[42]

Furthermore, voters seemed to be more consistent in their thinking about issues since the 1950s, at least in terms of left and right. In the 1950s, the fact that a person had liberal views on one issue did not mean he or she was liberal on other issues, but by the mid-1960s correlations developed among the issues raised in polls, such as the cold war, racial integration, the appropriate size of the government, and civil liberties.[43]

But two years after *The Changing American Voter* appeared, George F. Bishop and others presented evidence that most of the apparent shift toward ideological thinking and issue consistency among the voters could be explained by changes that had been made in the wording and format of the questions they had been asked!

The first of these changes took place at the time of the 1964 national election when the Survey Research Center (SRC) converted the issue questions used by Nie and other researchers from a five-point Likert format (i.e., strongly agree—strongly disagree) to a dichotomous choice between relatively well-defined substantive alternatives. Interestingly, this is also the point at which the trend line for issue consistency (and issue voting) takes a sharp upward turn. In 1968 the SRC began to experiment with still another format, a seven-point semantic differential type of scale anchored at each end by opposing policy statements of the kind used in dichotomous questions. And by 1972 almost all of the issue questions that have figured so prominently in the secondary analyses of the Michigan Electoral Series appear in this form. But however desirable these modifications might have been from a technical standpoint . . . they have also confounded the trend analysis of changes in the structure of mass political attitudes.[44]

It was a dramatic demonstration of the methodological trickiness of public opinion analysis.

An analysis of the 1972 election indicated sharp differences of opinion between McGovern and Nixon supporters on the war, amnesty for draft dodgers, the legalization of marijuana, campus unrest, government aid to minorities, and school busing—and comparable differences between Democrats supporting McGovern and those defecting to Nixon.[45] A comparison of the 1950s with the period 1964 through 1972 shows that, while references to personal attributes of candidates remain frequent throughout in survey responses about presidential candidates, there was an increase in the frequency of references to issue positions—and a decline in references to party ties. Issue positions had to a great extent become independent of party.[46]

There are several indicators of the importance or unimportance of party in elections in addition to the relatively frequent references in survey responses about candidates. They include the willingness of voters to identify themselves with a party and to cross party lines, either by voting for presidential candidates of different parties in different years or by splitting tickets in any one year.

In explaining the voting behavior of the 1950s, *The American Voter* (the 1960 work) relied more heavily on party identification than any other factor. Voters' feelings about candidates and issues were less weighty and less stable, on the whole, than their loyalty to a party. Most voters had a strong and apparently lasting party affiliation, inherited very much like church membership.

> For the citizen, his sense of identification with a party was a guide to behavior; citizens voted for their party's candidates. It was a guide to understanding the political universe; candidates and issues were evaluated in party terms. Parties were objects of affective attachment; citizens expressed positive feelings about their parties. And those citizens with partisan affiliation were the most active and involved citizens; partisanship appeared to be a force mobilizing citizens into political life. Partisanship gave continuity and direction to the political behavior of citizens and to American electoral life.[47]

But things changed.

Given the five options of calling themselves strongly or weakly Democratic or Republican, or independent, more than a third of the population proved to be strong partisans, about four-tenths weak partisans, and between a fifth and a fourth independents in the years from 1952 to 1964. From 1964 on, however, the proportion of strong partisans fell sharply and that of independents rose—to 38 percent by the mid-1970s. What party identification remained had less impact on elections, because people had become more willing to vote for a presidential candidate of a party other than their own. It turns out that 1956 and 1960 were years with an unusual amount of straight-ticket voting compared with both 1952 and the years after 1960. In 1960, about two-thirds of the electorate voted for Democrats only or for Republicans only. By 1972, two-thirds were casting a split ticket. Also by then a growing number reported having voted for presidential candidates of different parties in different years—from one-third in 1952 to well over half in 1972.[48]

The 1976 election gave evidence of a slowing of the trends of the 1964–1972 period. In 1976 the major-party candidates were more moderate than Goldwater or McGovern, and there was no ideological third-party candidate like Wallace. There had been some speculation that primaries, now increasingly important in presidential nominations, had encouraged the selection of strongly issue-oriented candidates with intensely dedicated followers, but in 1976 the primaries seemed if anything to have the opposite effect. On the Republican side, the more moderate candidate, Gerald Ford, came in ahead of the more ideological Ronald Reagan (although it was a close race from start to finish); and in the Democratic primaries moderate Jimmy Carter eliminated a field which included issue-oriented candidates Fred Harris and Morris Udall. As Leon Epstein notes, "It is a broader category of outsiders, not just ideological outsiders, who are currently favored" by the present nominating system.[49]

The results of the national election survey conducted by the University of Michigan's Institute for Social Research help put 1976 in perspective. Issues were crucial in 1972. In 1976, too, the voters were issue conscious and the Democrats, particularly, deeply divided. For example, 42 percent of the Democrats favored government aid to minorities, 38 percent opposed. But issues in general, with some exceptions such as President Ford's pardon of Richard Nixon, had less impact on the vote than they had in 1972.[50] According to Arthur H. Miller:

> In 1976 the Democratic candidate, Jimmy Carter, appeared to adopt a strategy of de-emphasizing those issues that had polarized the Democrats in 1972. Instead of articulating major policy differences between himself

and Ford, Carter concentrated on issues that promised to reunite Democrats—issues such as unemployment, inflation, the Nixon pardon, and the
restoration of confidence in government. He avoided the so-called "social"
issues that had divided the Democrats four years earlier.[51]

People did vote according to their general ideological position to a substantial degree, liberals for Carter and conservatives for Ford, but voted
far less than in 1972 on specific issues.

In 1972, issues had more impact on the vote than either party
identification or evaluations of the candidates, the University of Michigan survey showed. Party identification had less to do with the outcome
of the election than it had had in twenty years. But in 1976 party identification was more important than either issues or candidates. It did not
seem to mean a return to party loyalty as it had been observed in earlier
decades, however. The level of positive feeling that Democrats and
Republicans expressed for their parties continued to fall in 1976. And the
number of independents remained about the same as in 1972, well above
previous election years. Party voting in 1976 may in fact have been largely
due to the decision of Jimmy Carter to campaign as a partisan, identifying
with his party and his Democratic predecessors and hoping the voters
would identify Gerald Ford with his party and *his* predecessor.[52]

The way Jimmy Carter won the presidential nomination was anything but traditional. The way he won the election, however, was more
in keeping with tradition than the McGovern campaign had been in
1972: Carter refused to be specific on questions that posed a threat to
party unity and brought many errant Democrats who had voted Republican in 1972 back to the fold.

Let us review the changes that took place in the 1960s and 1970s in
the role of party, particularly in presidential elections, and then speculate briefly about the future. Apart from the disruptions created by the
communist-hunting of Senator Joseph McCarthy, the 1950s were years
of relative stability and good feeling in American politics. Most people
considered themselves members of one of the major parties and voted
accordingly—others, enough to give Dwight Eisenhower two terms in
the White House, voted on the basis of the personal characteristics of the
candidates. Issues were not much on the minds of the people or in the
air. Popular trust in government and contentment with the political
process were high. Interest in politics and voting was moderate at best.
It was an unexciting time. Party organizations had much to say about the
selection of candidates and the management of campaigns.[53]

In the next two decades, many people became more involved in a
politics of issues, causes, and confrontation; others became alienated.
Campaigns were more interesting, and voters were more aroused and

better able to conceptualize. But increasingly they rejected parties as the medium of their expression, or as newcomers to the electorate started out as independents, partly because of distrust in politics and partly because parties and candidates were finding it harder to bridge the new spectrum of political beliefs in the electorate. All told, it was little wonder some students of political parties were concerned about the future. It seemed as if the two-party system might no longer serve the electorate. The old strategy of insipidness and centrism was in doubt. Voters seemed to be demanding more intelligent campaigns. But they were also so diverse in their points of view that candidates who made specific appeals were more certain than ever to lose ground. Jimmy Carter's centrist, partisan appeal to the voters proved far more effective than the ideological campaign of George McGovern in 1972, but there was no evidence that it had established a pattern for the years ahead.

What, then, of the future? The most that honestly can be said is that thoughtful people see a number of very different possibilities and that we shall have to wait and see who is right. One view is that the New Deal coalition remains more or less intact: The election and reelection of Dwight Eisenhower and Richard Nixon failed to disturb the underlying liberal Democratic consensus; the divisions of the 1960s—over war, race, and social issues such as marijuana, law and order, and abortion—subsided after a while; and the election of Jimmy Carter reaffirmed the North-South-urban-black majority. On the basis of data from the 1976 University of Michigan survey, Robert Axelrod concludes that "For the Democrats, the New Deal coalition made a comeback in 1976. For the first time since the Johnson landslide of 1964, the Democrats got a majority of the votes from each of the six diverse minorities which make up their traditional coalition: the poor, blacks, union families, Catholics, southerners, and city dwellers."[54]

A second view is that a realignment has been in the making for some years, eroding the support of key groups in Roosevelt's coalition, some drifting toward the Republicans and many becoming independent of both parties. The commitment of blacks to the Democratic party has increased meanwhile, but ethnic groups, blue-collar workers, Catholics, and white southerners have become less Democratic.[55] (The composition of the southern Democratic vote has changed since FDR's day. It was a white vote then; few blacks were permitted to vote. In 1976, Carter's victory in the South depended on blacks; a majority of southern whites voted against him, for Ford.[56])

A third view is that the disruptions of the 1960s and 1970s pushed the American political system beyond realignment, deep into crisis. Walter Dean Burnham has argued that realignments are a sign of the failure of existing party coalitions to represent the needs of the people—

new coalitions form as a result, and for a time the tensions of the political system are resolved. But we have suffered a disruption, he believes, far more serious than those of the past, a disintegration of the social fabric from the strains of war, blacks versus whites, poor versus near poor. All of the hopes raised and broken in foreign and domestic policy in the Kennedy and Johnson years and all the ravages of Watergate created a crisis of legitimacy in which many Americans came to believe they "had lost control over their own lives, that they had no leverage over the political process, and that they were victims of the illegitimate exercise of raw power." Defection from parties and mistrust of politicians have been only a part of a larger societal crisis, if Burnham is right. He considers realignments hazardous because their centrifugal forces may not be resolved. He has not been optimistic that the nation under President Carter's leadership could rise to the challenge. Carter fitted the public mood with echoes of the antipolitics of Goldwater, Wallace, and Reagan; he promised uplift; but if he failed, said Burnham, there would be more disaffection than ever and the danger of a turn toward demogogic leadership and worse.[57]

Certainly, as we have seen, campaigns for nomination and election are now more a contest of personalities and personal organizations than they once were. Party leaders are losing their grip on nominations, the financing and management of campaigns, and on patronage and legislation. Whether they, presidential candidates, presidents, and the voters can pull together again is speculative.

The Electoral College

In addition to building a coalition and courting the center, presidential candidates must cope with the eccentricities of the electoral college, an institution that makes presidential elections the most complex of any in the country. The bare bones of the electoral college are easily understood; its impact on American politicians and politics over the years is less obvious. The only point of agreement in the continuing debate on the college is that it does not work the way the framers of the Constitution intended.

The electoral college was the product of two concerns in the Philadelphia Convention: to devise a workable plan of government and to mollify each of the major interests whose support was needed for ratification. There was early agreement on a reasonably strong executive—not too strong and not too weak, Alexander Hamilton assured the nation in the *Federalist Papers*—but whether the executive should be one person or several and whether it should be selected by Congress, by the people, or by the state governments were questions not easily resolved.[58] The convention decided on an office to be held by a single individual chosen by a system in which the people (to some undefined extent), Congress, and the states would have a hand. It was a system as complex as the forces playing on the men who devised it.

> Each State shall appoint, in such manner as the legislature thereof may direct, a number of electors, equal to the whole number of senators and representatives to which the State may be entitled in the Congress: but no senator or representative, or person holding an office of trust or profit under the United States, shall be appointed an elector.
>
> The electors shall meet in their respective States, and vote by ballot for two persons, of whom one at least shall not be an inhabitant of the same State with themselves. And they shall make a list of all the persons voted for, and of the number of votes for each; which list they shall sign and certify, and transmit sealed to the seat of the government of the United States, directed to the president of the Senate. The president of the Senate shall, in the presence of the Senate and House of Representatives, open all the certificates, and the votes shall then be counted. The person having the greatest number of votes shall be the President, if such number be a majority of the whole number of electors appointed; and if there be more than one who have such majority, and have an equal number of votes, then the House of Representatives shall immediately choose by ballot one of them for President; and if no person have a majority, then from the five highest on the list the said House shall in like manner choose the President. But in choosing the President, the votes shall be taken by States, the representation from each State having one vote; a quorum for this purpose shall consist of a member or members from two thirds of the States, and a majority of all the States shall be necessary to a choice. In every case, after the choice of the President, the person having the greatest number of votes of the electors shall be the Vice-President. But if there should remain two or more who have equal votes, the Senate shall choose from them by ballot the Vice-President. [59]

Thus Congress was to certify the results of balloting in the electoral college and make the final choice of president on most occasions, although with recognition to the states in the voting by state delegations in the House, the states large and small counting the same. The college was to be a state affair in apportionment, choice of method of selecting electors, and place of balloting. The people were given an indirect role through their state legislatures and more directly if their respective state legislatures ordained.

If the people were slighted, it was no oversight. The delegates were divided on the question of democracy, some ambivalent and some plainly fearful of direct popular participation in the selection of a president. George Mason said, "It would be as unnatural to refer the choice of a proper character for chief magistrate to the people, as it would be to refer a trial of colors to a blind man." "The people should have as little to do as may be with the government," Roger Sherman said.[60] (And we should recall that the Constitution hedged on who might vote in congressional elections as well, leaving it to the states.) Better that the people choose men of quality to make the selection of president for them. Hamilton praised the mixed system:

> The process of election affords a moral certainty, that the office of president will never fall to the lot of any man who is not in an eminent degree endowed with the requisite qualifications. Talents for low intrigue, and the little arts of popularity, may alone suffice to elevate a man to the first honors of a single state; but it will require other talents, and a different kind of merit, to establish him in the esteem and confidence of the whole Union.[61]

Very shortly the selection process began to work in unanticipated ways. From the beginning, electors were expected to vote as pledged. It caused a stir in 1796 when an elector in Pennsylvania who was pledged to support John Adams voted for Thomas Jefferson instead.[62] That election marked the beginning of a two-party system, too, and that was a change of great moment. Narrowing the field to two contenders meant that a final majority decision could be made in the electoral college in most years.

In the short run, the presence of parties resulted in complications that had to be resolved by constitutional amendment. Since under the original constitutional provisions the winner in the electoral college became president and the runner-up vice president, the system soon produced the team of John Adams and Thomas Jefferson, leaders of competing parties. More problematic still, in 1800, with electors casting votes for two-man tickets along party lines, the two members of the winning ticket tied, and since under the original Constitution there was no designation of one as president and other as vice president in the electoral vote, the election had to be resolved by the House of Representatives. Jefferson was intended by the electors to be president and Aaron Burr to be vice president, but with factional maneuvering in the House it took thirty-six ballots to give Jefferson the presidency.[63] The Twelfth Amendment adopted in 1804 to prevent a recurrence provided separate voting for president and vice president.

> The electors shall meet in their respective States and vote by ballot for President and Vice-President, one of whom, at least, shall not be an inhabitant of the same State with themselves; they shall name in their ballots the person voted for as President, and in distinct ballots the person voted for as

Vice-President, and they shall make distinct lists of all persons voted for as President, and of all persons voted for as Vice-President, and of the number of votes for each, which lists they shall sign and certify, and transmit sealed to the seat of the government of the United States, directed to the president of the Senate;—The president of the Senate shall, in the presence of the Senate and House of Representatives, open all the certificates and the votes shall then be counted;—The person having the greatest number of votes for President, shall be the President, if such number be a majority of the whole number of electors appointed; and if no person have such majority, then from the persons having the highest numbers not exceeding three on the list of those voted for as President, the House of Representatives shall choose immediately, by ballot, the President. But in choosing the President, the votes shall be taken by States, the representation from each State having one vote; a quorum for this purpose shall consist of a member or members from two thirds of the States, and a majority of all States shall be necessary to a choice. And if the House of Representatives shall not choose a President whenever the right of choice shall devolve upon them, before the fourth day of March next following, then the Vice-President shall act as President, as in the case of the death or other constitutional disability of the President.—The person having the greatest number of votes as Vice-President, shall be the Vice-President, if such number be a majority of the whole number of electors appointed, and if no person have a majority, then from the two highest numbers on the list, the Senate shall choose the Vice-President; a quorum for the purpose shall consist of two thirds of the whole number of Senators, and a majority of the whole number shall be necessary to a choice. But no person constitutionally ineligible to the office of President shall be eligible to that of Vice-President of the United States.

The other major change in the presidential electoral system was the adoption of the general-ticket plan in all of the states except South Carolina by 1836. South Carolina joined the rest in 1860, and with occasional exceptions the states have kept the general-ticket system intact.[64] Thus while the Constitution leaves the mode of choosing electors to the states—they might legally revert to the less democratic appointment of electors by the legislature, which was common at the outset—a nearly uniform system of popular election has evolved with each state's entire electoral vote cast for the ticket winning the greatest number of votes statewide, a winner-take-all election state by state.

Within half a century, then, a system designed to elect most presidents by vote of Congress, from a list of names supplied by electors chosen by state legislatures, had in effect become one of direct partisan election. But it involved a peculiar way of tabulating votes by states that seemed to favor some states over others and even posed the occasional threat of denying election to the winner of the popular vote. It is these biases that have kept alive the controversy over reform or abolition of the college. We shall look at the problems first and then at the proposed solutions.

An unlikely but nevertheless disturbing possibility is that the wrong person may be elected, in the sense that the electoral vote may go to someone other than the winner of a majority or plurality of the popular vote nationally. This could happen in two ways legally. One, which has never occurred, is that in a close vote in the electoral college a few defectors voting for people other than the candidates who have won pluralities in their states could elect the second-place candidate or throw the election into the House of Representatives. In practice such miscast votes amount to no more than a footnote in our electoral history—only seven electors have defected since 1789. For example, in 1960 a Republican elector in Oklahoma refused to cast his vote for Richard Nixon, whom he "could not stomach," and instead announced he would vote for conservative Democratic Senator Harry F. Byrd of Virginia, and for Senator Barry Goldwater as vice president. He hoped to persuade enough Republicans and Southern Democrats to switch their votes to elect Senator Byrd president, but then, as before, the defection did not affect the outcome.[65] The fear is, however, that sometime it may.

Another way is by the capricious mathematics of the winner-take-all electoral system. The clearest illustration is the election of 1888, in which Grover Cleveland, seeking reelection, won a plurality of the popular vote (48.6 percent, compared with Benjamin Harrison's 47.8 percent) but lost in the electoral college 168 to 233.[66] Cleveland and the country accepted the result, and four years afterwards he tried again and won. The election of 1876 is another example, perhaps, Democrat Samuel J. Tilden winning the popular vote and Republican Rutherford B. Hayes the presidency. But it was an unusually corrupt election, ultimately decided along party lines by Congress and a special commission it had appointed, and is not obviously a case of different results in the popular and electoral vote, because neither vote was honest that year. And 1824 is another case, of sorts, in which Andrew Jackson, winner of a plurality in the college lost in the House to John Quincy Adams; but it was a four-way race, and for the second-place man to win in the run-off in the House was not as clear a violation of the public will as Harrison's victory in 1888 was to be.

In 1976, Jimmy Carter won the popular vote by 50.1 percent to Gerald Ford's 48.0, and he won the electoral vote 297 to 240 (one electoral vote going to Ronald Reagan); yet a shift of only 6,000 votes in each of two states, Hawaii and Ohio, would have given Ford the election. The mechanics of this defect in the electoral system are no mystery. Under the winner-take-all rules of the general-ticket system, the candidate with a plurality in a state—who has at least one vote more than anyone else—

wins the state's electoral vote. But if he wins by more than one vote, the extra votes in his favor are "wasted," as are all the votes of the losers. The trick is not to waste many more votes than one's opponent, as Carter nearly did by winning heavy majorities in his native South. To put it another way, in order to make the most of his popular vote, a candidate should win bare pluralities in a combination of states sufficient to give him a simple majority in the electoral college. Obviously candidates cannot cut strategy that fine. If the wrong person is elected again, as in 1888, it will likely be a matter of luck rather than premeditation. But it will still raise questions about the legitimacy of the electoral process and, if it comes at a time of political polarization and national unrest, about the stability of the political system.

There are other biases in the system that could in theory produce or help produce the selection of the wrong person but seem less likely to do so. Each has the effect of giving voters in some states more weight than those in others. For example, the electoral college rewards states according to population, not election-day turnout, and since the level of participation varies from one state to another, voters in low-turnout states each have more power. Similarly, because the electoral college is apportioned according to census returns, there is a lag of as much as ten years—the 1980 election based on 1970 population figures, for example—and states that have made gains in the interim suffer. With just the right combination of favored states supporting him, a candidate who loses the popular vote can win in the electoral college.

Still another problem in the operation of the present system is that if the election should devolve on the House of Representatives, as in 1824, the outcome would not necessarily be either predictable or fair. The leading candidate might well be a member of the opposition party in Congress (Richard Nixon, it will be remembered, was elected with a Democratic Congress each time) and might be rejected in favor of someone with less popular support. Problems of predictability stem from the constitutional requirement that each state cast one vote. The small states would have a decided advantage. And a tie vote within a state delegation, which is not unlikely, would keep that state from voting for president. In a three-way race, this could have surprising consequences.

And finally, among the quirks of the electoral college, there is what may be called the Wallace problem. Before Governor Strom Thurmond's Dixiecratic splinter party in 1948 and then Governor George Wallace's American Independent party campaign for the presidency in 1968, it was widely assumed that the electoral college, together with general-ticket elections common in the states, had demonstrated a strong bias in favor of the two-party system. Third parties were effectively crowded out of the presidential contest by the winner-take-all plurality rules. Third-party candidacies would be limited to those without serious interest in electoral victory. Rational folk with complaints about the way things were going would tend instead to work within the two major parties. (A parliamentary system with proportional representation, by contrast, *encourages* lesser parties.)

Wallace, however, like the less popular Thurmond, was a regional candidate. He enjoyed considerable support among conservatives, ethnic groups, and working- and lower-middle-class Amerians nationwide, but what set him apart from other third-party candidates was that he stood a chance of winning a large bloc of electoral votes in the South. His avowed strategy was to win enough electoral votes to keep either of the major-party candidates from winning a majority of the electoral votes. He then would have been in a position to bargain for appointments, programs, and other concessions with the Democrat and the Republican and to elect the one who offered the most (by having his supporters vote accordingly either in the electoral college in December or by waiting for the House to take up the question and to arrange the payoff there). It did not happen, of course. The electoral vote was 301 for Nixon and 191 for Humphrey, but until the returns were counted it was a fair guess that Wallace, running third, would control the outcome of the election. Some efforts were made to prevent this: A bipartisan petition circulated in the House of Representatives pledged members to vote for the candidate with the popular plurality, if it came to that, and the Democratic and Republican candidates promised not to bargain with Wallace.[67] But many remained uneasy, particularly Democrats concerned about a Nixon-Wallace coalition. The rise of Wallace as a presidential contender reminded the country of a grave defect in the electoral system.

The faults of the electoral college, real and hypothetical, have led to recurrent proposals of reform. Details aside, there are four basic plans. All would require constitutional amendments.

Plan One, the least radical, is simply to abolish presidential electors and to award a state's electoral votes automatically to the winner of the popular plurality. It has enjoyed broad support among politicians and ordinary citizens alike—indeed the only imaginable opposition would have to come from would-be electors, often aging party retainers contemplating the modest honor of casting a vote in the electoral college or perhaps the mischief and notoriety of voting for the wrong candidate in a close election. The reason it has not been enacted, apart from normal institutional inertia, is that many of those who favor it also favor various extensive electoral reforms as well and cannot agree on a suitable amendment.

Plan Two also entails a limited alteration of the electoral college. It is to choose presidential electors by districts, a system in use in some states in the last century and in one state, Maine, from 1972 on. The electors allotted to match a state's seats in the House of Representatives would be chosen by pluralities in the several congressional districts, and the two equaling its Senate seats would be chosen statewide, as now. This amendment would override state laws that now require statewide balloting for all electors. This plan, espoused for many years by Senator Karl Mundt of South Dakota and Representative Frederic R. Coudert of New York would have had a far greater impact before the Supreme Court's 1965 ruling in *Wesberry* v. *Sanders* than after.[68] Until that decision, rural congressional districts were often considerably smaller in population than urban districts. Rural voters therefore had more influence in Congress. The district plan would have lent the same bias to the presidency. *Wesberry* v. *Sanders* and subsequent cases required districts to be of more or less equal population. Still, the district plan would make some difference even now. For one thing, minor-party candidates could win electoral votes with pluralities in districts rather than states. And it would make a serious difference in removing the present bias in favor of large states—but so would Plan Three, so we may postpone consideration of that point.

Plan Three would retain the present distribution of electoral votes but award them in exact proportion to the popular vote, to three decimal places. If a state's popular vote were cast for party tickets in a ratio of 3 to 2, its electoral vote would be divided in that ratio. It too would probably favor third parties; therefore its sponsors have proposed lowering the requirement for election in the college from an absolute majority to 40 percent. The proportional plan was promoted by Senator Henry Cabot Lodge, Jr., of Massachusetts and Representative Ed Gossett of Texas. It was passed by the Senate in 1950 but died in the House. Representative Gossett was frank about his opposition to the existing system:

> Is it fair, is it honest, is it democratic, is it to the best interests of anyone in fact to place such a premium on a few thousand labor votes or Italian votes or Irish votes or Negro votes or Jewish votes or Polish votes, or Communist votes or big city machine votes, simply because they happen to be located in two or three industrial pivotal states? Can anything but evil come from placing such temptation and power in the hands of political parties and political bosses? Both said groups and said politicians are corrupted as a nation suffers.[69]

It is generally believed that the winner-take-all system favors the large competitive states. Since the presidency can be won with a bare plurality in as few as eleven large states currently, parties are tempted to give them special attention in selecting a ticket and framing campaign issues, and more specifically to try for a coalition of party loyalists and more volatile issue-oriented groups. In the final two months of the 1976 campaign, the Democratic and Republican presidential and vice-presidential candidates made stops in the populous states of California, New York, Ohio, and Illinois 160 times, but visited the 15 states with four or fewer electoral votes only 15 times.[70] Thus Gossett's caricature of an election decided by swing groups in swing states is not all myth. The general-ticket system has had a tendency to give presidential elections, and thus the presidency, a bias toward urban liberalism—in both parties. The proportional and district plans alike would reduce or eliminate this bias. The proportional plan would probably favor safe states, and the district plan, before 1965, would have replaced the liberal tendency with a powerful rural conservative bias.

It had been supposed by most supporters of the two plans that either would also make the election of the wrong person considerably less likely. It was a surprise, therefore, to learn that the 1960 election would have gone to Richard Nixon rather than John Kennedy had the vote been tallied either proportionally or by districts.[71] This is not to say that the campaign or the vote would have been the same under another electoral system, but it does suggest the enormous difficulty of making even educated guesses about the way reforms will turn out. We have a tradition of unpredictability in the operation of the electoral college and its appendages, beginning in the first decade of the new republic.

Plan Four is direct election, typically tied to a run-off if no candidate wins 40 percent of the popular vote the first time around. It is familiar, well understood, and broadly appealing. It disposes of all concerns associated with the college and the general ticket. It has been supported by recent presidents and, according to opinion polls, by a solid majority of the people. Yet it has not made the first full step toward enactment as a constitutional amendment: Passed by the House in 1969, it was scuttled by a filibuster conducted by a coalition of southern and small-state senators. They were concerned their states would lose influence under direct election. Southern states might suffer because of low turnout, an inability to play the Wallace game again, and possibly an imposition of additional federal voting regulations, a painful prospect to those cherishing states rights. Small states unrealistically tend to believe they have an advantage in the apportionment of the electoral college. In fact, the Wallace phenomenon apart, southern and small states probably stand to gain by direct election.[72] But uncertainty about consequences dampens enthusiasm for reform.

CONGRESS: LEGISLATION AND CONFIRMATION

No test of presidential leadership is greater than that provided by Congress. In domestic affairs, most basic policy is made through legislation. Therefore a strong president with aspirations beyond the maintenance of the status quo must approach Congress with legislation and work for its passage. But Congress does not welcome leadership except in time of crisis: Most presidents suffer consistently at its hands. Even the few who could claim significant legislative victories had times of trouble; when Congress is cooperative with a president, it is not so for long. If it has been passive for a while, by enacting a major presidential program or witnessing a display of presidential power apart from legislation, as in the Watergate period, it becomes abnormally sensitive to any suggestion that its role is any less than that of an equal among the branches of government.

In this chapter we shall examine cases of successful leadership of Congress, the conditions that have made Congress unreceptive to presidential leadership on other occasions, some of the ways lawful and unlawful that presidents impose their will on the country in the absence of legislation, and, lastly, the confirmation of presidential appointments by the Senate.

Presidential Leadership in Legislation

The great presidential legislators are of the twentieth century, when the time seemed right—to many—for massive federal intervention in the nation's economic and social life. And they built on one another, not only in inheriting evolving presidential institutions but also in modeling their behavior on their more capable predecessors. They are indebted to two men of the nineteenth century, however: Abraham Lincoln, whose work as a wartime leader is considered in the next chapter, and Thomas Jefferson.

President Jefferson asserted such effective control over the members of his party in Congress that the opposition honored him with the title of "despot." This control was no more than the kind of party discipline observed regularly in many state legislatures and occasionally in Congress since, but it was a new and controversial regimen in the national legislature then. Unlike the strong presidents of the present century, Jefferson made little use of public opinion to pressure Congress, nor of course was it easy to do so in those days of slow and indirect communication. He relied instead almost entirely on patronage and personal contact with legislators and their leaders. In making appointments before the long-delayed convening of the new Congress, he consulted local party leaders. After Congress met, he took his advice from members of the House and Senate, which helped both him and them and solidified their relationship.[1]

Because he was an indifferent speaker and also anxious not to seem forward with Congress, Jefferson began a tradition, which was to last until Wilson's presidency, of delivering messages to Congress in writing rather than in person. But he more than made it up by inviting a flow of legislators to the President's House and to Monticello, his splendid retreat in the hills of Virginia. He entertained without ceremony, in contrast to his predecessors, and conducted business at the dinner table. He also kept his party in repair by encouraging good men to run for Congress when vacancies occurred. To intervene in state and local politics in this manner has always been dangerous for presidents, and Jefferson took care to do it quietly and sparingly. All told, by persistence and force of personality he developed a loyalty among fellow Republicans that stood him well when the votes were taken.[2]

The three outstanding presidential legislators of this century were Woodrow Wilson, Franklin Roosevelt, and Lyndon Johnson. Wilson came to office with plans laid for a strong, plebiscitary presidency. He had been thinking and writing about government for decades, particularly about the evils of weak executive leadership.

Washington and his cabinet commanded the ear of Congress, and gave shape to its deliberations; Adams, though often crossed and thwarted, gave character to the government; and Jefferson, as president no less than as secretary of state, was the real leader of his party. But the prestige of the presidential office has declined with the character of presidents. . . .

I am disposed to think. . . that the decline in the character of the presidents is not the cause, but only the accompanying manifestation, of the declining prestige of the presidential office. That high office has fallen from its first estate of dignity because its power has waned; and its power has waned because the power of Congress has become predominant.[3]

In his early years, Wilson the anglophile believed the only way the United States could be rescued was to import cabinet government to guarantee a working relationship between the executive and the legislature.

When the Convention of 1787. . . came to consider the respective duties and privileges of the legislative and executive departments, and the relations which these two branches of the Government should sustain towards each other, many serious questions presented themselves for solution. One of the gravest of these was, whether or not the interests of the public service would be furthered by *allowing some of the higher officers of State to occupy seats in the legislature*. The propriety and practical advantage of such a course were obviously suggested by a similar arrangement under the British Constitution, to which our political fathers often and wisely looked for useful hints. But since the spheres of the several departments were in the end defined with all the clearness, strictness, and care possible to a written instrument, the opinion prevailed among the members of the Convention that it would be unadvisable to establish any such connection between the Executive and Congress. They thought, in their own fervor of patriotism and intensity of respect for written law, that paper barriers would prove sufficient to prevent the encroachments of any one department upon the prerogatives of any other; that these vaguely broad laws— or principles of law—would be capable of securing and maintaining the harmonious and mutually helpful co-operation of the several branches; that the exhibition of these general views of government would be adequate to the stupendous task of preventing the legislature from rising to the predominance of influence, which, nevertheless, constantly lay within its reach. But, in spite of constitutional barriers, the legislature has become the imperial power of the state. . . .

What, then, is Cabinet government? What is the change proposed? Simply to give to the heads of the Executive departments—the members of the Cabinet—seats in Congress, with the privilege of the initiative in legislation and some part of the unbounded privileges now commanded by the Standing Committees. But the advocates of such a change—and they are now not a few—deceive themselves when they maintain that it would not necessarily involve the principle of ministerial responsibility,—that is, the resignation of the Cabinet upon the defeat of any important part of their plans. For, if Cabinet officers sit in Congress as official representatives of the Executive, this principle of responsibility must of necessity come sooner or later to be recognized. Experience would soon demonstrate the practical impossibility of their holding their seats, and continuing to represent the Administration, after they had found themselves unable to gain the consent of a majority to their policy. Their functions would be peculiar. They would constitute a link between the legislative and executive branches of the general Government, and, as representatives of the Executive, must hold the right of initiative in legislation. . . . In arguing . . . for the admission of Cabinet officers into the legislature, we are logically brought to favor *responsible Cabinet government* in the United States. . . .

    The highest order of responsible government could . . . be established in the United States only by laying upon the President the necessity of selecting his Cabinet from among the number of representatives already chosen by the people, or by the legislatures of the States.[4]

But in time, with the maturing of his thought and the resurgence of the presidency under Theodore Roosevelt, Wilson came to the view that constitutional reform was not necessary: A strong chief executive could bridge the separated powers with the support of his party and the people. In 1908 a series of his lectures were published in which he said;

    He cannot escape being the leader of his party except by incapacity and lack of personal force, because he is at once the choice of the party and of the nation. He is the party nominee, and the only party nominee for whom the whole nation votes. . . .

    He is . . . the political leader of the nation, or has it in his choice to be. The nation as a whole has chosen him, and is conscious that it has no other political spokesman. His is the only national voice in affairs. Let him once win the admiration and confidence of the country, and no other single force can withstand him, no combination of forces will easily overpower him. His position takes the imagination of the country. He is the representative of no constituency, but of the whole people. When he speaks in his true character, he speaks for no special interest. If he rightly interpret the national thought and boldly insist upon it, he is irresistible; and the country never feels the zest of action so much as when its President is of such insight and calibre. Its instinct is for unified action, and it craves a single leader. It is for this reason that it will often prefer to choose a man rather than a party. A President whom it trusts can not only lead it, but form it to his own views.

    It is extraordinary isolation imposed upon the President by our system that makes the character and opportunity of his office so extraordinary. In him are centered both opinion and party. He may stand, if he will, a little outside party and insist as if it were upon the general opinion. It is with the instinctive feeling that it is upon occasion such a man that the country wants that nominating conventions will often nominate men who are not their acknowledged leaders, but only such men as the country would like to see lead both its parties. The President may also, if he will, stand within the party counsels and use the advantage of his power and personal force to control its actual programs. He may be both the leader of his party and the leader of the nation, or he may be one or the other. If he lead the nation, his party can hardly resist him. His office is anything he has the sagacity and force to make it. . . .

The President is at liberty, both in law and conscience, to be as big a man as he can.[5]

Wilson led Congress by every means at hand: proposing legislation, closely following its progress, conferring with the leaders and members of Congress, promoting the use of the caucus to commit party members to common positions on legislation, and employing his patronage power to reward his supporters. It was of both symbolic and practical importance that he went to the Capitol regularly to meet with legislators in the President's Room and that he revived the practice of delivering important messages in person. He was an accomplished rhetorician. He found he could indeed reinforce his leadership of Congress by talking to the people in the country in person and through the press, aiming at the Republicans and the special interests rather than at his own party, which he firmly controlled. Thus when his tariff legislation bogged down in the Senate in the spring of 1913 he accused lobbyists of swarming so thickly in town that "a brick couldn't be thrown without hitting one of them."[6]

I think that the public ought to know the extraordinary exertions being made by the lobby in Washington to gain recognition for certain alterations of the tariff bill. Washington has seldom seen so numerous, so industrious, or so insidious a lobby. The newspapers are being filled with paid advertisements calculated to mislead the judgment of public men not only, but also the public opinion of the country itself. There is every evidence that money without limit is being spent to sustain this lobby, and to create an appearance of a pressure of public opinion antagonistic to some of the chief items of the tariff bill.

It is of serious interest to the country that the people at large should have no lobby and be voiceless in these matters, while great bodies of astute men seek to create an artificial opinion and to overcome the interests of the public for their private profit. It is thoroughly worth the while of the people of this country to take knowledge of this matter. Only public opinion can check and destroy it.

The Government in all its branches ought to be relieved from this intolerable burden and this constant interruption to the calm progress of debate. I know that in this I am speaking for the members of the two houses, who would rejoice as much as I would, to be released from this unbearable situation.[7]

In addition to tariff reform, Congress passed the Federal Reserve Act, the Child Labor Act, the Clayton Antitrust Act, and other important legislation in the first years of Wilson's administration.

Franklin Roosevelt engineered the passage of the largest and most significant bloc of legislation in the nation's history, most of it in his first hundred days in office. Although not a student of the presidency in the bookish, Wilsonian sense, he came to office well prepared for an active role, having observed "Uncle Ted" at close hand and served Wilson as assistant secretary of the navy. With the governorship of New York to complete his training, Roosevelt was as ready as anyone could be to meet the nation's vast problems of poverty, unemployment, and social disorganization in 1933. What he did not have, however, was any clear idea of how he would go about it. He was an opportunist then, and he remained so in office.

In his campaign of 1932, Roosevelt was vague and platitudinous. "He left everything fluid, general, and discursive. He said as little as he could in controversial situations and left to the ministrations of time and his own mediating talents the issues remaining unresolved," said Rex Tugwell.[8] To the extent he was definite, he wavered between conservatism and liberalism, testing the waters. He had less guidance from public opinion than Wilson had enjoyed in 1912, in the era of progressivism. His ambivalence on fiscal policy could be observed in campaign speeches variously advocating budget balancing, in keeping with the Democratic platform, and government spending. After the election, he drew advisers and appointees around him who represented these disparate positions. The person he chose to become his budget director, Lewis Douglas, an economizer, worked on legislation to reorganize the executive branch and cut expenditures. Others laid plans to make the federal government more complex and expensive.

Sworn into office on March 4, 1933, Roosevelt gave Congress until March 9 to assemble for an emergency session, and in the interim issued an executive order of questionable constitutionality to close the country's banks and forbid the export of gold. Banks were failing fast as frightened depositors sought their money in cash. The executive order stopped banking operations until Congress could impose regulations to assure an orderly reopening. Then Congress met and within hours approved the Emergency Banking Act.

During that first week the president had heartening meetings with the nation's governors, with members of the press, and with his advisers. He went on the air with his first "fireside chat" from the White House, on bank matters, and received a warm response. The government and the people both gave signs of falling in behind their new leader. So Roosevelt decided to send Congress legislation that had been scheduled for the regular session months later. His advisers willingly readied bills, and Congress enacted them. Will Rogers described it in a radio broadcast: "Now Mr. Hoover didn't get results because he asked Congress to do something. There's where he made a mistake. . . . This fellow Mr. Roosevelt, he just sends a thing up every morning, says, 'Here, here's your menu, you guys sign it . . . right here.' "[9] In the 100 days of the session, Congress passed, among other laws, the Economy Act to cut government salaries and other expenses, over the objection of his liberal advisers; the Agricultural Adjustment Act, to raise farm prices by regulating production; the National Industrial Recovery Act, for industrial self-regulation to limit competition; acts creating the Tennessee Valley Authority for the stimulation of a seriously depressed area, the Civilian Conservation Corps to put young people to work in parks and forests, and Federal Deposit Insurance Corporations to protect people against the consequences of bank failure; the Truth-in-Securities Act, to eliminate misrepresentation in the selling of stocks and bonds; and the Emergency Farm Mortgage Act, for the relief of farmers who could not keep up payments on their property.

After the Emergency Banking Act, which was an administration bill passed in toto, Congress participated more and more in the formulation of legislation, pushing Roosevelt gently to the left. Some legislation of the 100 days was genuinely cooperative, and in the next three years Congress at times took the lead, as in the National Labor Relations Act, a measure guaranteeing unions the right to organize and bargain collectively, which was forced on Roosevelt by Senator Robert Wagner of New York; in the Soil Conservation Act of 1936; and in banking legislation in 1935 and 1936.[10] By the beginning of his second term, control of domestic policy had passed to Congress. The conditions of the 100 days never returned.

One measure of Roosevelt's success was the amount of discretionary authority Congess handed him to fill in the gaps in their legislation. Congress has always had some freedom to write legislation of great specificity in order to bind the president and his agents or, on the contrary, to use general terms in order to allow the president room for experimentation. Because he was rushed into sending proposals to Congress, and because he worked by trial and error, it suited Roosevelt to have terse legislation. For example, on March 31, 1933, Congress passed an act saying;

> That for the purpose of relieving the acute condition of widespread distress and unemployment now existing in the United States, and in order

to provide for the restoration of the country's depleted natural resources and the advancement of an orderly program of useful public works, *The President is authorized, under such rules and regulations as he may prescribe and by utilizing such existing departments or agencies as he may designate,* to provide for employing citizens of the United States who are unemployed, in the construction, maintenance and carrying on of works of a public nature in connection with the forestation of lands belonging to the United States or to the several States which are suitable for timber production, the prevention of forest fires, floods and soil erosion, plant pest and disease control, the construction, maintenance, or repair of paths, trails and fire-lanes in the national parks and national forests, and such other work in the public domain, national and State, and Government reservations incidental to or necessary in connection with any projects of the character enumerated.[11]

What later came to be called the Civilian Conservation Corps was created by executive order under this broad mandate a few days later, and shortly thereafter Congress gave the president a lump-sum appropriation that permitted him to allocate money within the program entirely at his discretion.[12]

It is true that some delegations of legislative authority to the president in that period were contested in the Supreme Court as violating the basic constitutional principle of the separation of powers. The Court had always allowed Congress to give executive agencies discretion to "fill up the details" of a statute, but in 1935 it decided that Congress had gone too far in the National Industrial Recovery Act—it had transferred regulatory authority to the executive without attaching an intelligible standard. The key phrase, "fair competition," was too vague, the Court felt. It found the act unconstitutional.[13] But the Court soon lost interest in curbing excessive delegation, and strong presidents since Roosevelt have requested and sometimes received unfettered grants of authority.[14]

Supporting his dominance of public opinion, as a lever under Congress, were Roosevelt's use of legislative clearance, liaison, and the veto. In the 1920s, clearing legislative proposals through the Bureau of the Budget was mainly a way of holding down expenditures. Under Roosevelt, it was turned from negative to positive uses and became a way of shaping the president's legislative program. Administration bills, the bills that survived the clearance process and gained White House approval, were promoted on Capitol Hill by his energetic and often brash assistants. And at the other end of the legislative process the president lay in wait with his veto. Roosevelt cast more vetoes than any other president, an average of a bill a week during his twelve years in the White House. With vetoes he forced Congress into line; with veto messages he appealed to the people to support his leadership of Congress. In one notable case his veto message was so biting the majority leader of the Senate resigned in protest. Congress had delayed passage of the administration tax proposal in 1943 and early 1944 and then produced a measure that raised too little and in Roosevelt's opinion contained too many inequities. "It is not a tax bill but a tax relief bill providing relief not for the needy but for the greedy," the president wrote Congress.

> It has been suggested by some that I should give my approval to this bill on the ground that having asked the Congress for a loaf of bread to take care of this war for the sake of this and succeeding generations, I should be content with a small piece of crust. I might have done so if I had not noted that the small crust contained so many extraneous and inedible materials.

Alben Barkley, the majority leader, who had been under criticism for playing the president's servant, retorted that the veto message was a "calculated and deliberate assault upon the legislative integrity of every member of Congress. Other members of Congress may do as they please," he continued, "but, as for me, I do not propose to take this unjustifiable assault lying down. . . . If the Congress of the United States has any self-respect left it will override the veto of the President and enact this tax bill into law, his objections to the contrary notwithstanding." He threatened to resign. Roosevelt wrote Barkley, "I sincerely hope you will not persist in your announced intention to resign as majority leader of the Senate. If you do, however, I hope that your colleagues will not accept your resignation; but if they do I hope that they will immediately and unanimously re-elect you." Barkley resigned amid tears, and was reelected to the cheers of his colleagues shortly after. By then the two houses were sufficiently incensed to override the president's veto. Roosevelt was unperturbed.[15]

Lyndon Johnson enjoyed a period of cooperation with Congress. He carried on the fight begun by President Kennedy for legislation on civil rights, Medicare for the elderly, and massive federal aid to education, all highly controversial measures requiring careful guidance through Congress. The Civil Rights Act of 1964 was the first serious piece of legislation on the subject in nearly a century; Medicare, in 1965, though short of the general health insurance program some sought, was a foot in that door; federal aid to education, also enacted in 1965, came only after fears of federal dictatorship of local schools had been allayed and some of the differences between Catholics and Protestants had been settled.

President Johnson also pushed major proposals of his own through Congress. Although thought had been given to antipoverty and voting rights legislation in the Kennedy administration, the Equal Opportunity

Act of 1964, the Voting Rights Act of 1965, and a string of lesser laws clearly were Lyndon Johnson's accomplishments, as much as any legislation can be credited to a president. Soon he turned his attention to running the war in Vietnam, however, and his stint as a domestic policy maker was over.

Rating the legislative leadership of presidents is subjective. It depends on judging the impact of legislation long after its passage. While some of their policies were blunted by events or in Roosevelt's case overturned by the Supreme Court, there is a consensus that Woodrow Wilson, Franklin Roosevelt, and Lyndon Johnson presided over the adoption of extraordinary legislative programs. More objective measures of the number or proportion of bills passed tend to miss the point by counting all presidential proposals equally: They give too much credit to an Eisenhower who asks Congress for almost no important domestic legislation in his eight years of office, and perhaps too little to a president such as Kennedy who asks a great deal and is given only a fraction by Congress. That, too, is subjective. If we judge presidents by how well they attain *their* goals, John Kennedy was a failure and Warren Harding a moderate success.

A measure of the relative power of president and Congress based on the frequency of vetoes from one administration to the next and the frequency with which vetoes have been overridden was devised by Jong Lee in 1975. Vetoes are at best an uncertain index of presidential power, since it may be argued that the president who arranges never to be sent unwanted legislation has as much control over Congress as the one who regularly puts Congress in its place with vetoes. And the overriding of vetoes is infrequent enough to be a questionable basis for statistical analysis. Still, Lee is able to distinguish between two-year periods with a higher and lower than average rate of vetoes of public bills, and between those with a higher and lower than average rate of vetoes overridden. The result is a four-cell classification: (1) presidential authority, characterized by a high veto and a low override rate; (2) cooperation, with few vetoes and no overriding; (3) conflict, with high rates of vetoing and overriding; and (4) congressional authority, with few vetoes but a good proportion of them overridden. Franklin Roosevelt was in the first category for a time, vetoing frequently and successfully. But other strong presidents have gotten along with little use of the veto power: Jackson, Lincoln, Theodore Roosevelt, Wilson, and Lyndon Johnson exhibited the cooperative pattern during some or all of their years in office.[16]

The weaker presidents have suffered conflict, as in the cases of Franklin Pierce and Andrew Johnson, or submission to congressional authority, as in the cases of Chester A. Arthur, Rutherford B. Hayes, and, interestingly, Richard Nixon during part of his tenure in office—all of these presidents saw a substantial share of their vetoes overridden, whether they vetoed frequently or sparingly.

It is not enough that a president have the desire to lead Congress to the enactment of major legislation: Motive is a necessary but not a sufficient condition of leadership. He must have a proper party and ideological balance in Congress, cooperative congressional leaders, and the support of public opinion. Lee's study also showed a greater tendency for presidents to veto when Congress is in the hands of the opposition party, as one might suspect, and for an opposition-controlled Congress to override vetoes. Congress overrides more after mid-term elections than before, and in times of economic instability—although in times of military crisis it rallies behind the president and overrides less frequently. There is also a tendency of presidents who have not served in Congress to veto more than those who have.[17]

Woodrow Wilson had sizable majorities composed of members of his party and sympathetic progressives among the Republicans in both houses. Of the 190 Democrats in the House in 1913, 114 were freshman, eager to follow the president. Congressional leadership was at its weakest in many years: In 1910, a revolt against an autocratic speaker, Joseph Cannon, had decentralized control over legislation in the House of Representatives and in effect made way for Wilson. Public opinion favored progressive legislation, as the three-way election in 1912 had indicated: Wilson and Theodore Roosevelt together won three times as many popular votes as the reputedly more conservative candidate, William Howard Taft. And Wilson had no trouble keeping public opinion on his side for several years.

Franklin Roosevelt was elected with a large majority of Democrats in Congress: 313 Democrats to 117 Republicans in the House of Representatives, 59 Democrats to 36 Republicans in the House. Unfortunately for the president, the leaders of Congress consisted heavily of southern Democrats who had risen to committee chairmanships and leadership posts by seniority. But his strong, fatherly leadership of public opinion overcame Congress. In his second election, he won 60.8 percent of the popular vote, compared with 57.4 in 1932, and swept in a congressional majority of 333 Democrats to 89 Republicans in the House and 75 to 17 in the Senate. By this time, though, rebellion had set in and Roosevelt lost his grip on domestic policy making.

Lyndon Johnson was buoyed by public opinion in his legislative effort in 1964. In the minds of some, the Civil Rights Act was a memorial to John Kennedy (though Kennedy alive probably could not have induced Congress to pass what it did for him dead). Johnson also obtained the passage of legislation that had little identification with Kennedy. And then in 1964 he had the good fortune to run against Barry Goldwater, whom he beat in a landslide that brought in a friendly Congress: The Democratic majority in the House was boosted to 295, to 140 Republicans. A comfortable majority of 68 Democrats to 32 Republicans remained in the Senate during the legislative years 1964–1965. With that support, Johnson moved on to Medicare, education, and voting rights legislation. Johnson's case, like Franklin Roosevelt's, shows that large congressional majorities are a great help to a strong president, but that his legislative record is by no means a simple function of his party's margin in Congress. One lesson seems to be that legislative leadership is most effective in the early years of a presidency, though not necessarily, as in Roosevelt's extraordinary case, in the first few weeks.

Congressional Resistance to Leadership

Congress, though, usually has the upper hand in domestic affairs. Except when presidential, legislative, and public attitudes coalesce to promote bold legislation, policy making is centered in the bureaus of the executive branch and the subcommittees of Congress and remains more distributive than regulatory or redistributive.

The guardian of the status quo in modern times has been the conservative coalition of Republicans and southern Democrats in Congress. A conservative president with sights set low may be untroubled by its presence, but a liberal president with plans for new legislation finds it a source of unending frustration. As Franklin Roosevelt discovered after a time, a large Democratic majority in Congress may be so badly split as to be useless to the president. By the end of his first term, Roosevelt could no longer rely on the loyalty of his fellow Democrats, particularly from the South. In 1937, after his reelection, he tried and failed to obtain legislation to enlarge and neutralize the Supreme Court, which by then had declared much of his New Deal program unconstitutional. By mid-term election time in 1938 the president's displeasure with Congress was so great that he intervened in several state primaries to ask voters to refuse renomination to conservative Democrats. The purge failed, by and large, and only reaffirmed the tradition of localism in legislative nominations.

A running tabulation of the activity of the conservation coalition is kept by the *Congressional Quarterly*, which counts any vote in which a majority of southern Democrats and a majority of Republicans join in opposition to a majority of northern Democrats. Such an alignment occurs year after year in about one-fourth of the votes in the House and Senate. When it does, it is generally victorious. Only in Lyndon Johnson's peak legislative years was its influence weakened, but by the end of his tenure in office the coalition had returned to power. The *Congressional Quarterly* analyses of voting by region show that both parties have their internal problems: Among Democrats, southerners tend to vote differently from their fellow partisans, while among Republicans, easterners are most unlike the rest. [18]

Sometimes, however, congressional leaders help a president overcome the natural resistance of Congress to direction. They often feel an obligation to speak for the president in Congress, and to speak for Congress in the White House. They work for the passage of the president's program and assist him in formulating a program Congress will accept. But they must maintain a balance: Congress prefers speakers and majority and minority leaders who honor the independence of committees, subcommittees, and individual members and who stop short of attempting strict party discipline.

In the late 1950s the Democrats, with majorities in the House and Senate, had leaders of unusual force and ability: House Speaker Sam Rayburn and Senate Majority Leader Lyndon Johnson. But the presidency was in the hands of a Republican, Dwight Eisenhower, and quiescent for the time. So, necessarily, was Congress. After the election of an activist Democratic president in 1960, when the party most needed guidance in Congress, the leadership ebbed. Rayburn sent President Kennedy off to a good start by inducing the House to enlarge the Rules Committee, thus breaking the power of conservative coalition leaders to use it as a means of keeping liberal legislation from reaching the floor. But Rayburn was nearly eighty and died within the year. He was replaced by John McCormack; Johnson, now vice president, was succeeded by Mike Mansfield. Leadership weakened in both houses. When Johnson tried to retain some of his old power over Senate Democrats from his position as presiding officer, he was rebuffed. One can only speculate whether Kennedy might have had more luck with Congress if he had had strong legislative lieutenants throughout his term.

President Carter's successes in the House and frustrations in the Senate during his first year are attributable in part to differences in the leadership of House Speaker Thomas P. O'Neill, Jr., and Senate Majority Leader Robert Byrd. It was the traditional time for testing a president, and in a bicameral system getting along with one chamber is not enough. The speaker was a good middleman, educating the president in the ways and prerogatives of Congress and advising him on policy and at the same time reviving the powers of the speakership to enact major portions of the new president's program. O'Neill opened the session by inducing the House to adopt, in a single hour, twenty-four rule changes designed to forestall delay and obstruction by the Republican minority. Then, by a combination of pressure, geniality, and favor trading, he pushed legislation through the House. He gave the energy bill to an ad hoc committee rather than farm it out to several standing committees with subject matter jurisdiction over its parts. Democratic members of the ad hoc committee were persuaded to caucus on key items and to be governed by majority vote. The Rules Committee was induced to limit amendments to the energy package, to force one final vote for or against the whole program, and to limit debate. The result was that the bill survived nearly intact. Other administration bills did well, too.[19]

But in the Senate the president's program fared badly. Majority Leader Byrd, selected by the Democrats to succeed Mike Mansfield, was a more ordinary congressional leader. He was in the mold of Gerald Ford and Carl Albert, chosen by their respective parties to provide minimal leadership in the House—arranging calendars, counting votes, performing housekeeping functions for the members, representing them before the public but not dominating them. Senator Byrd allowed the program to be broken into six bills and given to different standing committees. The separate interests affected by President Carter's energy proposal had full play. By the end of 1977, the senators could not agree among themselves or with the House and the energy proposals stalled.[20] Even though the rules of the Senate make leadership more difficult than in the House, a Lyndon Johnson in place of Robert Byrd might have made a difference.

The following year President Carter again pressed the Senate to pass his energy measures, this time with more success. He knew more about legislative strategy than he had in his first year. And he was aided by the steady decline of the dollar in the world market, which caused inflation at home and could be attributed in part to the failure of the United States to reduce oil imports. It was weaker legislation than the president had proposed. Some important provisions such as taxes on crude oil and on utility and industrial use of oil and natural gas were missing entirely, and others were watered down. But at least they passed a bill.[21]

One of Jimmy Carter's boldest moves when he took office was to intervene in the pork-barrel politics of water projects. In the name of economy, he picked out thirty-two existing projects for review and possible cancellation, such as a 250-mile waterway connecting the Tennessee and Tombigbee Rivers in Alabama and Mississippi, the Applegate Lake Dam for flood control in Oregon, and—the largest—the Central Arizona Project to pump Colorado River water 400 miles through aqueducts to the Phoenix and Tucson areas. That the distributive policies of dam building have served the parochial interests of legislators and their constituents more than those of the nation had long been recognized, but the public has been generally unconcerned as long as each part of the country was allowed to reach into the barrel now and then. But concern about preserving the environment had been increasing, and in opposing dams-for-the-sake-of-dams Carter may have felt he had the support of environmentalists as well as economy-minded critics of congressional spending.[22]

The president used the threat of a veto to induce Congress to drop some of the projects. A veto is a strong inducement. When a president presents a legislation program to Congress, the veto in effect belongs to Congress. But when Congress initiates a program, as in the case of the water projects, the president has the veto in both name and fact. But members of Congress did not submit docilely to this assault on their interests. Through their leaders they let President Carter know he might expect his veto to be overriden, something that had not occurred in recent Democratic administrations. Thus, with threat and counterthreat, the stage was set for compromise. The president reduced his list of projects to eighteen, and in conference committee it was further reduced to nine, amidst predictions that even some of those would be restored another year. Neither president nor Congress could be said to have won. The president waded into the fight with signs that he meant business. Congress responded, to the president's surprise, that it did too. Public works are important to members of Congress and are not lightly given over to the president's discretion.[23]

The president was advised to be more politic with Congress in this and other matters next time around:

> Given the importance of "favor" as the crucial strategic background for presidential-congressional relations, some of the early actions of the Carter Administration seem dubious in the extreme. Imperial presidents might be able to afford amateurish mistakes by [White House] lobbyists, make patronage appointments without consulting the Speaker of the House, and announce wholesale cutoffs of public works projects without prior consultations with interested congressmen. But for a president without imperial power who must deal with a Congress that is both more assertive and more decentralized than at any time in recent memory, Jefferson's advice seems apropos: Great innovations should not be (and cannot be) forced on slender majorities.[24]

The next year, Congress sent President Carter a public works bill containing six expensive projects that had been deleted in the compromise of 1977, perhaps encouraged by his low standing in the public opinion polls in mid-1978. But by the time the bill reached his desk, the president had made a comeback as a result of the Camp David meetings. ("My esteem in the country has gone up substantially. It is very nice now that when people wave at me, they use all their fingers.") And he was about to embark on a new campaign to reduce government expenditures. He vetoed the bill and over the opposition of the Democratic leaders of the House won a vote sustaining his veto, 223 to 190, far short of the two-thirds required to override a veto. A new bill without the objectionable items was then sent to the president for his signature. It was a clear victory for the president. He had established a tough style of dealing with Congress that included a willingness to veto and to mobilize public opinion to overcome resistance on Capitol Hill.[25] (What he had not done, even late in the term, however, was make any good friends or confidants on Capitol Hill. He was the first president in congressional memory to remain entirely aloof.)

Questions about where to build dams and waterways may be among the most sensitive decisions Congress must face, but they are not the only kind of administrative detail in which legislators are interested. That the involvement of Congress in administrative decisions goes well beyond public works can be seen in the rise of the so-called legislative veto.[26] In its negative form it is a statutory provision that certain proposed administrative decisions or regulations may be disapproved by one or both houses or by a specified standing committee within a stated time. In its positive form, it is a requirement of one-house, two-house, or committee approval before administrative actions may take effect. Legislative vetoes are found in public works legislation, not surprisingly, but in many other areas as well. For example, appropriations to build new postal service buildings are available only for sites approved by the House and the Senate committees on public works[27] while some of the best-known legislative vetoes are found in the War Powers Act of 1973 and in the reorganization acts passed from time to time.

There are hundreds of such statutes on the books now, the great majority enacted since 1968. By 1976 the device had become so common that extensive hearings were held in both houses on legislation to extend the principle of the legislative veto to actions of the executive branch generally. The House of Representatives voted 265 to 135 in favor of the measure, which lost nonetheless because the vote happened to have been taken under suspension of the rules requiring a two-thirds majority. A similar act may be attempted again. Meanwhile, legislative vetoes continue to be built into specific subject matter measures.[28]

Presidents have objected to legislative vetoes on constitutional grounds. They have vetoed some acts containing them. But they have accepted others rather than lose otherwise desirable measures: Franklin Roosevelt and his attorney general agreed that a veto provision of the Lend-Lease Act was unconstitutional, for example, but signed the measure without public comment. In a memorandum that was not to be released until many years after, Roosevelt wrote, "In effect, this provision is an attempt by Congress to authorize a repeal by means of a concurrent resolution of the two Houses, of certain provisions of an Act of Congress. . . . The Constitution contains no provision whereby the Congress may legislate by concurrent resolution without the approval of the President."[29] He felt that the legislative veto violated the Constitution because it allowed Congress to act without the possibility of a presidential veto. Others have made the broader point that the legislative veto deranges the system of separate powers in putting executive authority into the hands of Congress, which is nearly the reverse of the old argument against the delegation of legislative authority to the executive. Defenders of the legislative veto see it as a reasonable accommodation to modern conditions: Congress is forced to delegate because of the sheer complexity of matters to be regulated, they say, and the Supreme Court approves; Congress should therefore be allowed to supervise the use that is made of its delegated authority and to disapprove whatever is inconsistent with the intent of its legislation. Whether the Supreme Court will agree remains to be seen. Perhaps the most vulnerable of all the arrangements is the one-house veto, which, in addition to everything else, seems to be in conflict with the principle of bicameralism.

In a series of case studies, Harold Bruff and Ernest Gellhorn have found that the legislative veto, or rather the threat of the veto, has the effect of bringing legislative committees into negotiation with administrative agencies in the rule-making process. "The legislative veto power significantly alters the working relations between Congress and the agencies."[30] To protect themselves from the veto, agencies bargain with Congress in drafting their decisions. Since in practice the negotiation is with a committee rather than the full House or Senate, and even more likely with a subcommittee or its chairman alone, the upshot is that agencies become beholden to ever-narrower interests. Bruff and Gellhorn conclude that "a general veto provision will increase the power of interest groups to block or deflect agency policy initiatives through pressure on congressional committees."[31] In Lowi's terms, the legislative veto is a device to further enlarge the access of special interests to the policy-making process and postpone a return to majoritarian democracy.

A final note on congressional resistance to presidential leadership in policy making: It is not always unwelcome to the president. In one notable case, a Democratic president presented a Republican Congress a list of demands in full confidence that nothing would happen, then castigated it for inaction in his successful bid for reelection that same year. Harry Truman became president in 1945; in 1946, control of Congress went to the Republicans for the first time since Hoover, and relations between the two branches fell into disrepair. To President Truman's chagrin, Congress in 1947 passed and then over his veto repassed the Taft-Hartley Labor-Management Relations Act, which was bitterly opposed by organized labor and most Democrats. Next year, his popularity sagging, Truman convened the Republican Congress in special session and asked it for legislation on housing, national health insurance, and civil rights. He was following the advice of his assistant, Clark Clifford:

> The Administration should select the issues upon which there will be conflict with the majority of Congress. It can assume that it will get no major part of its own program approved. Its tactics must, therefore, be entirely different than if there were any real point to bargaining and compromise. Its recommendations—in the State of the Union message and elsewhere—must be tailored for the voter, not the Congressman; they must display a label which reads "no compromise."[32]

Truman campaigned against the "do-nothing" Republican 80th Congress, won, and in the process gained a reputation as a champion of liberal causes. "Of course I knew that the special session would produce no results in the way of legislation," he later wrote.[33] In fact, he would have been keenly disappointed if it had.

Bypassing the Legislative Authority of Congress

If one way, a difficult way, for presidents to overcome Congress is to lead it in passing legislation, another is to make policy without asking the consent of Congress. As Woodrow Wilson warned before assuming office, the president may "overbear Congress by arbitrary acts which ignore the laws or virtually override them. He may even substitute his own orders for acts of Congress which he wants but cannot get. Such things are not only deeply immoral, they are destructive of the fundamental understandings of constitutional government and, therefore, of constitutional government itself."[34] Theodore Roosevelt took a different position, *after* his time in office:

> The most important factor in getting the right spirit in my Administration, next to the insistence upon courage, honesty, and a genuine democracy of desire to serve the plain people, was my insistence upon the theory that the executive power was limited only by specific restriction and prohibitions appearing in the Constitution or imposed by the Congress under its Constitutional powers. My view was that every executive officer, and above all every executive officer in high position, was a steward of the people bound actively and affirmatively to do all he could for the people, and not to content himself with the negative merit of keeping his talents undamaged in a napkin. I declined to adopt the view that what was

imperatively necessary for the Nation could not be done by the President unless he could find some specific authorization to do it. My belief was that it was not only his right but his duty to do anything that the needs of the Nation demanded unless such action was forbidden by the Constitution or by the laws.[35]

In 1942, when Congress proved reluctant to pass price control legislation, Franklin Roosevelt had the choice of acting alone by executive order, which was his own inclination, or of putting pressure on Congress and risking further inaction. On the advice of Harry Hopkins and Leon Henderson, Roosevelt chose a middle course that made the best of both alternatives. In a Labor Day speech on September 7, he gave Congress an ultimatum: It must act by October 1 or he would impose controls himself.

> Four months ago, on April 27, 1942, I laid before the Congress a seven-point national economic policy designed to stabilize the domestic economy of the United States for the period of the war. The objective of that program was to prevent any substantial further rise in the cost of living.
> It is not necessary for me to enumerate again the disastrous results of a runaway cost of living—disastrous to all of us, farmers, laborers, businessmen, the Nation itself. When the cost of living spirals upward, everybody becomes poorer, because the money he has and the money he earns buys so much less. At the same time the cost of the war, paid ultimately from taxes of the people, is needlessly increased by many billions of dollars. The national debt, at the end of the war, would become unnecessarily greater. Indeed, the prevention of a spiraling domestic economy is a vital part of the winning of the war itself.

The threat worked.[36]

Presidents frequently issue executive orders under the specific authority of acts of Congress. But at times they make policy by executive order in the absence of legislation. Then their appeal must be to the Constitution directly. The area of civil rights is an example. Presidents from Franklin Roosevelt to John Kennedy made civil rights policy—"presidential legislation," in the words of one critic—but it was not until the Civil Rights Act of 1964 that general legislation that might have provided a legal footing was passed. In 1941 Roosevelt declared a national policy of nondiscrimination in government and defense industry hiring. Harry Truman ordered the desegregation of the armed forces in 1948. In 1961 John Kennedy established the Presidential Committee on Equal Employment Opportunity to enforce a policy of nondiscrimination and affirmative action in federal employment and in businesses under contract with the government. In 1962 he did roughly the same for equal opportunity in federally assisted housing. (During the 1960 campaign he had criticized the Republican administration for failure to take this action—with a "stroke of the executive pen." Once elected, Kennedy found one reason after another to delay. First, he awaited Senate confirmation of a black civil rights leader as housing and home finance administrator; next he marked time while Congress debated a housing bill; then he awaited passage of a measure creating the Department of Housing and Urban Development. He signed the order late in 1962, at the moment of the successful resolution of the Cuban missile crisis, when the country was least disposed to criticize or even pay attention.)[37]

Several other important executive orders on civil rights were issued in this period. Congress had amply demonstrated its unwillingness to pass meaningful civil rights legislation, so it was up to the other branches to act if the government was to curb discrimination in its various forms. Both did, drawing their mandate from the Constitution. Whether the Constitution was intended to allow presidents that authority is questionable, but they have assumed it nevertheless.[38]

These examples are of presidents making policy or in one case threatening to make policy in the absence of action by Congress. But there is another side of it. Presidents have ways of thwarting the will of Congress when it *has* acted. Most of these ways are quiet and subtle, such as delay, inattention, and covert orders not to obey overt orders. But one, impoundment, became the object of an open controversy involving all three branches of government in the early 1970s.

Impoundment of appropriated funds by the president is functionally similar to an item veto, a power the governors of most states enjoy to disapprove parts of measures passed by their legislatures and in a few states to reduce appropriations. The difference is that the item veto is a part of the legislative process, while impoundment comes after: An item veto can be overridden by the legislature, an impoundment cannot. Louis Fisher distinguishes four basic kinds:

1. Routine actions taken for purposes of efficient management,
2. Withholdings that have statutory support,
3. Withholdings that depend on constitutional arguments, particularly the commander-in-chief clause, and
4. The impoundment of domestic funds as part of policy-making and priority-setting by the administration.

The first two are not controversial. The other two bring the president in conflict with policies adopted by Congress. In 1949 Harry Truman impounded military appropriations in excess of the amount he had requested of Congress. A debate ensued on the lawfulness of the president's action. Truman pointed to his responsibility as commander in chief to maintain a balance between the services and, more generally, between defense spending and the demands of a sound economy.[39]

Richard Nixon created even more controversy by impounding large sums of money for the fourth purpose: to substitute his judgment in domestic policy for that of Congress. It was his unprecedented view that the president had a constitutional responsibility to impound in order to combat inflation and avoid the necessity of a tax increase. In 1970 he reported the impoundment of $12 billion in highway, urban, and other programs. Late in 1972, after winning reelection, he started terminating whole programs: the rural environmental assistance program, the water bank program, disaster loans from the Farmers Home Administration, the rural electrification program, and the water and sewer grant program, all in the Department of Agriculture. After Congress overrode his veto of the Federal Water Pollution Control Act Amendments of 1972, he ordered the withholding of half of the funds for waste treatment, amounting to $9 billion over a period of three years. Large sums were impounded in programs of the Department of Housing and Urban Development, including community development, water and sewer grants, open space grants, and public facility loans.[40]

Then court decisions began to run against the administration. In a test of the water pollution impoundment, for example, a lower court held that "Any such exercise of discretion must be consistent with the policy and provisions included in the Act itself. Congress has clearly given the highest priority to the cleaning up of the nation's waters. Nothing in the Act grants the Administrator the authority to substitute his sense of national priorities for that of Congress." And a unanimous Supreme Court later agreed that Congress had never meant to provide "limitless" power to the executive to withhold funds under the Clean Water Act.[41]

In the Impoundment Control Act of 1974, Congress took steps to prevent a recurrence of the uncontrolled withholding of the Nixon years. The act allowed the deferral of funds by the president, subject to the veto of either house, and "rescission" or cancellation of budget authority only by affirmative vote of both houses.[42] Presidential authority of doubtful constitutionality had been countered by a legislative veto of equally questionable constitutionality, and the debate subsided.

Confirmation of Appointments

The president and Congress share the power to make appointments to the more important executive and judicial positions, much as they share the power to legislate:

> He shall nominate, and by and with the advice and consent of the Senate, shall appoint ambassadors, other public ministers and consuls, judges of the supreme court, and all other officers of the United States, whose appointments are not herein otherwise provided for, and which shall

be established by law: but the Congress may by law vest the appointment of such inferior officers, as they think proper, in the president alone, in the courts of law, or in the heads of departments.[43]

Also, the twenty-fifth Amendment provides for confirmation of a vice president if a vacancy occurs in that office. As in the case of legislation, however, the bare words of the Constitution tell little about the ways the president and Congress actually divide the power. Nor is it clear even when we have batting averages—nominations submitted, rejected, and withdrawn (the counterpart of legislation proposed, passed, vetoed, and repassed)—because in both nomination and legislation the "rule of anticipated reactions" applies. The White House may decide not to submit a nomination (or piece of legislation) if it anticipates rejection, and may clear nomination and legislative proposals informally to avoid public rejection. A resulting rejection-free score obscures the fact that in clearing or tailoring its requests the executive has bowed to Congress, not led it.

On the surface, the president usually seems to have his way with the Senate. In a typical year some 60,000 names are submitted, a few dozen are withdrawn by the president when opposition develops or unfavorable information is brought out in Senate investigations or hearings, and few or no names are rejected. All but about 2,000 of the nominations are military appointments and promotions, which are not closely reviewed. Most of the 2,000 civilian appointments also are routine, in such units as the Coast Guard and the Public Health Service. That leaves about 200 policy-level posts to which the Senate and its committees give varying degrees of attention.[44]

Whether the Senate defers to the president or gives the nominee careful inspection depends largely on the nature of the office. Cabinet offices by tradition are considered the president's to fill—with people the president must trust and with whom he must work. (Members of the White House staff, by extension, are not even subject to Senate confirmation.) Cabinet nominees are almost never rejected. In 1959 Lewis L. Strauss, President Eisenhower's choice for secretary of commerce, was disapproved by the Senate by a vote of 46 to 49, the first cabinet nominee to be turned down since 1925, in part because of his demeanor. As head of the Atomic Energy Commission, he had been known for arrogance and unresponsiveness before Senate committees. He had also been involved in controversial decisions on public versus private power and on the denial of security clearance to atomic scientist J. Robert Oppenheimer. A coalition of senators with different complaints against Strauss, some serious and some not, defeated his confirmation by a narrow margin. But the rule seems still to be that the Senate will not oppose, on personal or ideological grounds, nominees to positions close to the president.

President Carter's nominee for attorney general, Judge Griffin Bell, was subjected to long, detailed, and often hostile questioning in his confirmation hearing, partly because of concern about his record as a judge in school desegregation cases. More importantly, there was a feeling that the time had come for the Department of Justice to be more independent of the president. Two of Richard Nixon's attorneys general had proven corrupt, and the department had been used in illegal surveillance and in the Watergate cover-up. Proposals to detach it from presidential control had failed. But the Senate was determined at least to share control with the president. It confirmed the appointment only after securing pledges from Judge Bell on every point of concern.

Similarly, some of the opposition to President Carter's nomination of Theodore Sorenson to be director of central intelligence could be traced to a desire to keep the CIA, which also had been involved in Watergate and in other abuses of power, as far away from partisan politics as possible. Sorenson's background in government was entirely political, in the Kennedy White House. There were other complaints, including uneasiness about his Straussian arrogance and the weakness of his attitudes on national security. When rejection seemed certain, the nominee withdrew. It was unclear whether these cases indicated a new seriousness in the Senate about confirmations or simply special precautions for agencies that had caused widespread public anxiety.[45]

It *was* clear, however, that in reaction to Nixonian excesses the Senate had taken a greater interest in the honesty and integrity of nominees. Thus when Bert Lance, President Carter's director of the Office of Management and Budget, resigned under fire for alleged improprieties in his personal finances and banking practices before coming to Washington, Senators were chagrined that they had failed to turn up adverse information in the confirmation hearings, which had indeed been perfunctory. Vows to do better next time were heard, and a brief effort was made to create a Senate nominations office to collect information from nominees and witnesses and whatever could be extracted from the FBI and other investigative agencies.[46]

Unlike the cabinet and the White House Office, which are presidential territory, the regulatory commissions and the Supreme Court are regarded as independent institutions. The Senate is less deferential in its confirmation hearings, therefore. It is particularly interested in detecting conflicts of interest between a nominee's financial holdings or business associations and the maintenance of neutrality toward those who are likely to come before the court or commission in question. Allegations of conflict of interest were crucial in the defeat of Abe Fortas's promotion from associate justice to chief justice in 1965 and Clement Haynsworth's promotion from appellate judge to associate justice in 1969—the one was withdrawn and the other voted down.

Regulatory commissions have been plagued from the start by conflicts of interest and the threat of capture by the industries they are meant to regulate. In the 1970s the Senate became tougher about such conflicts. Isabel A. Burgess, for example, was refused a second term on the National Transportation Safety Board when the Senate Commerce Committee discovered that she owned stock in Allegheny Airlines, which had been under investigation by the board, and had not reported her holdings as required by federal law. Robert H. Morris was refused a place on the Federal Power Commission (FPC) when it was disclosed in his confirmation hearing that more than half his work as a lawyer had for a decade and a half been for Standard Oil of California, a company he would have to regulate as commissioner.

One of the problems had been that the White House has not taken its responsibility to find suitable people as seriously as it might. President Nixon never met some of the people he appointed to chair regulatory commissions. President Eisenhower's staff apparently mixed up the files of nominees of the FPC and the FCC (Federal Communications Commission) and sent the wrong names to the Hill for confirmation. Questioned on the lapse, the White House insisted they were equally qualified and refused to correct the error. The Senate confirmed, but probably would not do so now.[47]

The Senate's new sense of responsibility can be seen in its rejection of a former congressman, Benjamin Blackburn of Georgia, for the Federal Home Loan Bank Board in 1975. In the past, a president could assume that a former member of Congress would be confirmed for any post without question, regardless of qualifications. But Blackburn had advocated the public hanging of public housing tenants who did not pay their rent. His was the only rejection of a former congressman anyone could recall.

Still another collection of appointments, consisting largely of federal appellate district judges and district attorneys, has been governed by "senatorial courtesy": The Senate agrees not to vote for confirmation if the senators of the president's party in the states to which the appointments are to be made object. In effect, senatorial courtesy gives the Senate the power of appointment. In his campaign, Jimmy Carter promised that judicial appointments would be made solely on the basis of merit if he were elected president, but Senator James Eastland of Mississippi, chairman of the Judiciary Committee, met with Carter before he took office and successfully asserted the Senate's patronage power over the positions of district judge and district attorney, leaving the appellate judgeships to Carter to fill as he saw fit.[48] He named a commission to recommend appellate judges to him; senators in half of the states appointed similar commissions to help *them*.

Some presidential appointments are in practice Senate appointments; therefore, some are virtually joint appointments; and some, such as to the cabinet, are the president's alone, at least under normal circumstances. The informal lines of jurisdiction are neither sharp nor fixed, but they represent a comfortable, traditional arrangement between the president and the Senate. Despite the provisions of the Constitution, some appointments are far more important to senators, than to presidents and some far more important to presidents than to senators, and each therefore is content to look the other way at appropriate times.

In the 1970s there was brief experimentation with forms of appointment other than presidential nomination and Senate confirmation. President Nixon attempted to appoint a man to head—and dismantle—the Office of Economic Opportunity (OEO) without Senate confirmation, knowing the Senate would balk at approving a bitter opponent of the agency for the post. Howard J. Phillips was given the title of "acting" director, partly to provide a plausible reason for ignoring the Senate and partly to symbolize the agency's short life expectancy. It was a sign of his eagerness to destroy the poverty program that he issued orders terminating the Community Action Agency, a key unit of the OEO, on January 29, 1973, two full days before he took office. Four senators who were convinced of the unconstitutionality of the appointment (not to mention the appointee's actions) brought suit in federal court and had Phillips removed. The court held that in the absence of legislation providing for an interim head of the agency the constitutional procedure of advice and consent must be followed. The president was rebuffed.[49]

Then in 1974 it was Congress's turn to try to short-cut the Constitution. It established the Federal Election Commission, consisting of six voting members (plus the secretary of the Senate and the clerk of the House of Representatives ex officio, without vote), two to be appointed by the president pro tempore of the Senate on the recommendations of the majority and minority leaders, two by the speaker of the House similarly, and two by the president, all six subject to confirmation by majorities in both houses. The Supreme Court, in a suit brought by Senator James Buckley, held that "officers of the United States" had to be appointed as the Constitution specified. Nothing in the Constitution suggested the president pro tempore or the speaker could name "officers of the United States" or that confirmation of both houses could be invoked to confirm their appointment.[50] Congress reconstituted the commission along proper lines with presidential nomination and Senate advice and consent.

Congress usually is not helpful to presidents who ask for the passage of major domestic legislation. The result, more often than not, is stalemate. Periods of concentrated legislative activity at the behest of presidents are few and memorable. Appointments, by contrast, are not a source of great conflict. The Senate asserts its power to guide the president's choice for many posts and to reject an occasional nominee but usually defers to the president's judgment on key executive appointees. It is a sharing of power by the two branches—not quite what the framers of the Constitution anticipated, but a sharing nonetheless.

CONGRESS: FOREIGN
AND MILITARY AFFAIRS

Presidents must be freer of Congress in the conduct of war and diplomacy than in domestic affairs, it is argued, because dealing with
other countries requires speed, secrecy, and a focused effort not often
needed at home. The Constitution, to be sure, gives presidents no more
discretion in one arena than another. As Alexander Hamilton wrote in
the *Federalist*, attempting to allay fears of an imperial presidency:

> The President will have only the occasional command of such part of
> the militia of the nation as by legislative provision may be called into the
> actual service of the Union. The king of Great Britain and the governor of
> New York have at all times the entire command of all the militia within
> their several jurisdictions. In this article, therefore, the power of the Pres-
> ident would be inferior to that of either the monarch or the governor. . . .
> The President is to be commander-in-chief of the army and navy of the
> United States. In this respect his authority would be nominally the same
> with that of the king of Great Britain, but in substance much inferior to it. It
> would amount to nothing more than the supreme command and direction
> of the military and naval forces, as first General and admiral of the Con-
> federacy; while that of the British king extends to the *declaring* of war and to
> the *raising* and *regulating* of fleets and armies,—all which, by the Constitu-
> tion under consideration, would appertain to the legislature.[1]

Even so, Congress has tended to defer to the president and not to use its full legal authority to curb and guide his military and foreign policy making.

The War Powers

The power of the United States to wage war was carefully divided between the executive and legislative branches by the Constitution:

> The Congress shall have the power . . . To declare war, grant letters of marque and reprisal, and make rules concerning captures on land and water; To raise and support armies, but no appropriation of money to that use shall be for a longer term than two years; To provide and maintain a navy; To make rules for the government and regulation of the land and naval forces; To provide for calling forth the militia to execute the laws of the Union, suppress insurrections and repel invasions; To provide for organizing, arming, and disciplining the militia, and for governing such part of them as may be employed in the service of the United States, reserving to the States respectively, the appointment of officers, and the authority of training the militia according to the discipline prescribed by Congress. . . .
>
> To make all laws which shall be necessary and proper for carrying into execution the foregoing powers, and all other powers vested by the Constitution in the government of the United States, or in any department or office thereof. . . .
>
> The President shall be commander in chief of the army and navy of the United States, and of the militia of the several States, when called into the actual service of the United States.[2]

Of these powers, the most important was to be the declaration of war. The authority to decide if and when the country would go to war was given to Congress. The powers of the president as commander in chief and of Congress to raise and support armies were to be instrumental— the means to the end of making war.

Congress has declared war five times: the War of 1812, the Mexican War in 1846, the Spanish-American War in 1898, and, in this century, World Wars I and II. The country has engaged in numerous military operations without a formal declaration, however, including three major conflicts: the Civil War and the wars in Korea and Vietnam. In each of these three, the government contended that it was in full compliance with the Constitution. Some legal justification for Lincoln's prosecution of the Civil War without a declaration, for example, could be found in the record of the Constitutional Convention, where Madison recorded that he and Elbridge Gerry had moved the adoption of the language to "declare" rather than "make" war in order to leave the executive the power to repel sudden attacks. The motion carried.[3] "Must a government, of necessity, be too strong for the liberties of its own people, or too weak to maintain its own existence?" Lincoln asked Congress in 1861. "So viewing the issue, no choice was left but to call out the power of the government; and so to resist force employed by force for its preservation. . . . It was with the deepest regret that the executive found the duty of the war power in defense of the government forced upon him."[4] In the 1960s, in support of its participation in the war in Vietnam, the government extended this principle of defensive war to the protection of American interests—as conceived by the president—in other parts of the world. "An attack on a country far from our shores can impinge directly on the nation's security," said the State Department. "The Constitution leaves to the president the judgment to determine whether the circumstances of a particular armed attack are so urgent and the potential consequences so threatening to the security of the United States that he should act without formally consulting the Congress."[5] This fanciful interpretation of the Constitution did away with the need for declarations of war.

Lincoln also provided precedent for broad use of the commander-in-chief clause. He felt that the clause underlay the "war power" and allowed the president to direct a war with a minimum of congressional approval. More recently, in the undeclared wars in Korea and Vietnam, it was said that the president as commander in chief might use the armed forces "in the broad interests of American foreign policy" at his sole discretion. "Under the Constitution, the President, in addition to being Chief Executive, is Commander in Chief of the Army and Navy. He holds the prime responsibility for the conduct of United States foreign relations," said the government. "These duties carry very broad powers, including the power to deploy American forces abroad and commit them to military operations when the President deems such action necessary to maintain the security and defense of the United States."[6]

"I shall meet my responsibility as Commander in Chief of our armed forces to take the action necessary to defend the security of our American men," said President Nixon in extending the war to Cambodia in 1970. "The legal justification . . . is the right of the President of the United States under the Constitution to protect the lives of American men." He added, "As Commander in Chief, I had no choice but to act to defend those men. And as Commander in Chief, if I am faced with that decision again, I will exercise that power to defend those men."[7]

In recent conflicts, the executive also contended that the United States had been invited to come to the assistance of an ally; that it was fulfilling a treaty obligation; and that, in any event, actions taken by Congress short of a declaration of war amounted to a declaration.[8] On the latter point, Lyndon Johnson could cite the Gulf of Tonkin Resolution (of which more later) and a succession of appropriations measures, some with funds earmarked for the Vietnam conflict. Had he asked, President Johnson very likely would have been given a declaration of war in Vietnam. But in the absence of such requests, Congress slowly grew restive under the barrage of questionable legalisms, and finally resisted.

Several times during the war, Congress considered legislation to end some or all American involvement. In 1970 the Senate passed the Cooper-Church amendment denying funds for ground forces in Cambodia. A modified version ultimately cleared both houses. In 1971 another Cooper-Church amendment for withdrawal of troops from Indochina generally was offered in the Senate but did not pass. It would have required that all funds authorized for military activities in Indochina be used for withdrawal and that fighting be limited to protecting American troops from "imminent danger" during the withdrawal. Twice that year, however, Congress passed the Mansfield amendment as a rider on a larger bill. The first version stated that it was the "sense of Congress" that American fighting end "at the earliest practicable date" and that a "date certain" be set for withdrawal. The second asserted more strongly that this was the "policy of the United States." President Nixon, in signing the measure to which the latter was attached, said he planned to disregard the provision:

> To avoid any possible misconceptions, I wish to emphasize that Section 601 of this Act—the so-called Mansfield amendment—does not represent the policies of this administration. Section 601 urges that the President establish a "final date" for the withdrawal of all U.S. forces from Indochina, subject only to the release of U.S. prisoners of war and an accounting for the missing in action. Section 601 expresses a judgment about the manner in which the American involvement in the war should be ended.
>
> However, it is without binding force or effect and it does not reflect my judgment about the way in which the war should be brought to a conclusion. My signing of the bill that contains this section, therefore, will not change the policies I have pursued and that I shall continue to pursue toward this end.[9]

The power of appropriation was used to place some limits on American actions in Cambodia, Laos, and Thailand, but not in Vietnam. The Tonkin Gulf Resolution was repealed in 1971, but by then President

Nixon was relying on his powers as commander in chief as sufficient foundation for his actions. Only in 1973, when American participation in the war was winding down—and the Watergate investigation was weakening the executive—did Congress pass and the president accept a date, August 15, 1973, to end all U.S. military involvement in Indochina.[10]

Later in 1973 Congress passed the War Powers Resolution and, in so doing, gave legitimacy to the view that Congress could authorize war by means other than a formal declaration. The resolution was framed as a response to the invasion of Cambodia, which President Nixon had ordered without consulting Congress or, for that matter, informing the leadership of his intentions. The invasion was the ultimate arrogation of the war power, leaving nothing to Congress. It was also one of the more questionable strategic decisions of the war in Indochina. In the office of Senator Jacob Javits of New York, one of many to which protesting students flocked in the spring of 1970, a plan had been conceived that offered hope of bringing the president under the control of Congress and public opinion. It passed with some revision three and a half years later.

> The constitutional powers of the President as Commander in Chief to introduce United States Armed Forces into hostilities, or into situations where imminent involvement in hostilities is clearly indicated by the circumstances, are exercised only pursuant to (1) a declaration of war, (2) specific statutory authorization, or (3) a national emergency created by attack upon the United States, its territories or possessions, or its armed forces.
>
> The President in every possible instance shall consult with Congress before introducing United States Armed Forces into hostilities or into situations where imminent involvement in hostilities is clearly indicated by the circumstances, and after every such introduction shall consult regularly with the Congress until United States Forces are no longer engaged in hostilities or have been removed from such situations. . . .
>
> The President shall submit within 48 hours . . . a report, in writing . . . .
>
> The President shall provide such other information as the Congress may request. . . .
>
> Within sixty calendar days . . . the President shall terminate any use of United States Armed Forces . . . unless the Congress (1) has declared war or has enacted a specific authorization for such use of United States Armed Forces, (2) has extended by law such sixty-day period, or (3) is physically unable to meet as a result of armed attack upon the United States. Such sixty-day period shall be extended for not more than an additional thirty days if the President determines and certifies to the Congress in writing that unavoidable military necessity respecting the safety of the United States Armed Forces requires the continued use of such armed forces in the course of bringing about a removal of such forces.

> At any time that United States Armed Forces are engaged in hostilities outside the territory of the United States, its possessions and territories without a declaration of war or specific statutory authorization, such forces shall be removed by the President if the Congress so directs by concurrent resolution. . . .
>
> Nothing in this joint resolution (1) is intended to alter the constitutional authority of the Congress or the President . . . or (2) shall be construed as granting any authority to the President . . . which authority he would not have had in the absence of this joint resolution.[11]

In his veto message to Congress, President Nixon said,

> The restrictions which this resolution would impose upon the authority of the President are both unconstitutional and dangerous to the best interests of our nation. . . .
>
> This resolution . . . would seriously undermine the nation's ability to act decisively and convincingly in time of international crisis. As a result, the confidence of our allies in our ability to assist them could be diminished and the respect of our adversaries for our deterrent posture could decline. A permanent and substantial element of unpredictability would be injected into the world's assessment of American behavior, further increasing the likelihood of miscalculation and war. . . .
>
> The joint resolution . . . would give every future Congress the ability to handcuff every future President merely by doing nothing and sitting still. In my view, one cannot become a responsible partner unless one is prepared to take responsible action.

It was repassed by Congress and became law.[12]

Some of the most interesting debate over the merits of the measure as it made its slow progress toward enactment occurred among those who were equally committed to keeping the United States out of future Vietnams and Cambodias but disagreed on means. Proponents saw it as a way of restoring the original intent of the Constitution to leave basic decisions about war and peace to Congress. Conceding that formal declarations were out of fashion and that the refusal of Congress to make them would not inhibit presidents henceforth and conceding, too, that American troops and private citizens around the world would require protection and evacuation in emergencies, supporters saw the War Powers Resolution as a fair compromise with reality. Presidents would expect to have some discretionary authority and the country would want them to have it, but the measure would encourage Congress to assert its supervisory powers rather than stand abjectly by as it had during the wars in Korea and—until near the end—in Vietnam. "A war powers bill has proven necessary," said Yale law professor Alexander Bickel, "because it is apparent that Congress must declare its own responsibilities to itself and assume them in principle before the country, if it is ever to exercise them in particular situations."[13]

Opponents of the War Powers Resolution thought it allowed the president both too little and too much. Too little in emergencies of the sort to which presidents had appropriately responded in the past: Franklin Roosevelt's military maneuvers in the Atlantic in 1941 and John Kennedy's naval quarantine of Cuba in 1962, for example, would not have been permitted. Too much, in conceding the president the right to start a war on his own, something the Constitution clearly did not, and, as a practical matter, in giving him the power to continue such a war, since Congress seems unlikely to leave American forces overseas in the lurch, however ill advised the initial action.

A more flexible alternative, proposed by Representative Jonathan Bingham, would have let the president take action at his discretion rather than specifying categories of emergencies, and allowed continuation of the military action without time limit, subject only to the veto of either house rather than both. The reporting requirement would have been retained. The thought was that presidents could go on with their undeclared military actions without rigid restrictions and that Congress would not be pushed into giving its consent, but that hostilities would cease when the president no longer had the tacit consent of Congress.[14]

The resolution as passed was specific, however, and it remained to be seen if that was a strength or a weakness.

On the parallel question, the power of the president or Congress to declare the neutrality of the United States when others have gone to war, the Constitution is silent. In 1793, within days of learning of war between England and France, George Washington issued a proclamation of neutrality. "The duty and interest of the United States require that they should with sincerity and good faith adopt and pursue a conduct friendly and impartial toward belligerent powers," he said. One reason Washington acted alone on this occasion was that it would have taken the members of Congress six or eight weeks to gather, and he wished to act without delay to prevent the involvement of American citizens in a naval conflict.[15] Whether he had the constitutional authority to do so was a matter of debate.

Writing under pen names, Alexander Hamilton defended the president's action and James Madison attacked it. The question was whether a proclamation of neutrality was by its nature an executive or a legislative power. Said Hamilton,

> What department of our government is the proper one to make a declaration of neutrality, when the engagements of the nation permit, and its interests require that it should be done?

A correct mind will discern at once, that it can belong neither to the legislative nor judicial department; of course it must belong to the executive.

The legislative department is not the organ of intercourse between the United States and foreign nations. It is charged neither with making nor interpreting treaties. It is therefore not naturally that member of the government, which is to pronounce the existing condition of the nation, with regard to foreign powers, or to admonish the citizens of their obligations and duties in consequence; still less is it charged with enforcing the observance of those obligations and duties.

It is equally obvious, that the act in question is foreign to the judiciary department. The province of that department is to decide litigations in particular cases. It is indeed charged with the interpretation of treaties, but it exercises this function only where contending parties bring before it a specific controversy. It has no concern with pronouncing upon the external political relations of treaties between government and government. This position is too plain to need being insisted upon.

It must then of necessity belong to the executive department to exercise the function in question, when a proper case for it occurs. . . .

The general doctrine of our Constitution . . . is, that the *executive power* of the nation is vested in the President; subject only to the *exceptions* and *qualifications,* which are expressed in the instrument.

Two of these have been already noticed; the participation of the Senate in the appointment of officers, and in the making of treaties. A third remains to be mentioned; the right of the legislature "to declare war, and grant letters of marque and reprisal."

With these exceptions, the executive power of the United States is completely lodged in the President. . . .

The proclamation has been represented as enacting some new law. This is a view of it entirely erroneous. It only proclaims a fact, with regard to the existing state of the nation: informs the citizens of what the laws previously established require of them in that state, and notifies them that these laws will be put in execution against the infractors of them.[16]

Madison retorted,

The basis of the reasoning is, we perceive, the extraordinary doctrine, that the powers of making war, and treaties, are in their nature executive; and therefore comprehended in the general grant of executive power, where not especially and strictly expected out of the grant. . . .

If we consult for a moment, the nature and operation of the two powers to declare war and to make treaties, it will be impossible not to see that they can never fall within a proper definition of executive powers. The natural province of the executive magistrate is to execute laws, as that of the legislature is to make laws. All his acts, therefore, properly executive, must presuppose the existence of the laws to be executed. A treaty is not an execution of laws: it does not presuppose the existence of laws. It is, on the contrary, to have itself the force of a law, and to be carried into execution, like all other laws by the executive magistrate. To say then that the power of making treaties, which are confessedly laws, belongs naturally to the department which is to execute laws, is to say, that the executive department naturally includes a legislative power. In theory this is an absurdity—in practice a tyranny.

The power to declare war is subject to similar reasoning. A declaration that there shall be war, is not an execution of laws: it does not suppose pre-existing laws to be executed: it is not, in any respect, an act merely executive. It is, on the contrary, one of the most deliberative acts that can be performed; and when performed, has the effect of repealing all the laws operating in a state of peace, so far as they are inconsistent with a state of war; and of enacting, as a rule for the executive, a new code adapted to the relation between the society and its foreign enemy. In like manner, a conclusion of peace annuls all the laws peculiar to a state of war, and revives the general laws incident to a state of peace. . . .

From this view of the subject it must be evident, that although the executive may be a convenient organ of preliminary communications with foreign governments, on the subjects of treaty or war; and the proper agent for carrying into execution the final determinations of the competent authority; yet it can have no pretensions, from the nature of the powers in question compared with the nature of the executive trust, to that essential agency which gives validity to such determinations. It must be further evident, that if these powers be not in their nature purely legislative, they partake so much more of that, than of any other quality, that under a Constitution leaving them to result to their most natural department, the legislature would be without a rival in its claim.[17]

Madison ended by quoting Hamilton's *Federalist* No. 75 against him. (The treaty-making power, he had said, "will be found to partake more of the legislative than of the executive character.")

Long after, in 1935, as fear of involvement in still another European war grew on this side of the Atlantic, Congress passed a Neutrality Act that kept the United States from providing arms for belligerents. President Roosevelt signed the legislation, but not without complaining that it improperly limited the freedom of the executive to meet changing conditions. Since the act had passed Congress by a nearly unanimous vote, however, the president felt he could not resist.[18]

Who will win out in the next struggle over the proclamation of neutrality may depend on where the votes lie, as in the past, rather than the force of law and precedent. But this is generally true of questions of peace and war. And the president usually has the votes. Roosevelt in 1935 was an exception.

Presidential Leadership in Military Affairs

The constitutional and statutory apportionment of war powers between the president and Congress is one thing; the practice is another. In May 1975, Cambodian military forces captured an American merchant vessel, the *Mayaguez*, and its crew of thirty-nine, in international waters, apparently on the mistaken assumption that it was a spy ship. President Ford sent units of the air force, navy, and marines to retake the ship, an engagement that involved the sinking of Cambodian ships, a landing on Cambodian soil, and air strikes. Although the War Powers Resolution requires the president to consult in advance "in every possible instance," Ford did not. He made reports to Congress and its leaders after the fact, but gave them no opportunity to affect the course of the military engagement.[19]

Public support of the president's action was never in question. It was as if the government and a large majority of the people were anxious for an opportunity to make a successful display of American might and determination after the humiliation of withdrawal from Vietnam. Few were concerned about the letter of the law. One member of Congress did say that the president's action "appears to have been illegal and unconstitutional." She continued, "We have won no 'victory.' We have proved nothing to the world, except that this president is willing, as were his predecessors—to make hasty and ill-considered use of American military force against tiny countries regardless of the law." Some were disappointed that Ford had not tried a diplomatic solution before resorting to arms. There was more criticism when congressional hearings adduced evidence that the operation had been clumsy and costly. Minutes before the American attack, the Cambodians had announced on the radio that they were releasing the ship and crew. Excessive force had been used. Some of the bombing had been retaliatory, after the rescue had taken place. And more American lives had been lost than saved in the operation.[20] Still, the support for the president's strong and swift action, and the willingness of most people in Congress and in the country at least initially to accept his statement of the facts and his judgment that force was needed, suggest that in practice the War Powers Resolution, like the constitutional power of Congress to declare war, is optional.

Two years later as a private citizen, Gerald Ford reflected on his experience with the War Powers Resolution. He advised Congress to repeal it. For one thing, members of Congress are often out of town or otherwise inaccessible. "When a crisis breaks, it is impossible to draw the Congress into the decision-making process in an effective way," he said. "There is absolutely no way American foreign policy can be conducted or military operations commanded by 535 members of Congress even if they happen to be on Capitol Hill when they are needed." But if a president is confident that he can take action on his own during such a crisis because of his inherent "constitutional war powers to protect the lives and property of Americans," there is no impulse to consult anyway.[21] As Ford later summed it up,

> To have an affirmative action go right, gave me a great sense of confidence. It did not only ignite confidence in the White House, among the people here, it had an electrifying reaction as far as the American people were concerned. It was a spark that set off a whole new sense of confidence for them too. We had all gone through a very, very difficult eight months. This sort of turned the corner.[22]

The president's response to the capture of the *Mayaguez* was in the tradition of manly belligerence handed down to Gerald Ford from such rugged predecessors as Theodore Roosevelt, John Kennedy, and Lyndon Johnson (high-dominance types, in Lloyd Etheredge's classification, noted earlier).[23] The tradition proved more important than the provisions of the law.

"The victories of peace are great," said Theodore Roosevelt, "but the victories of war are greater. No merchant, no banker, no railroad magnate, no inventor . . . can do for any nation what can be done for it by its great fighting men." War meant honor and excitement. Peace was a condition of stagnation. He would "welcome almost any war," he once wrote privately, "for I think the country needs one."[24] This warlike man had been a weak, sickly boy, a pathetic and dependent child who turned himself into the model of physical and spiritual toughness for a generation of American youth. He was manly and courageous in everything to the end, even to the point of asking President Wilson for a combat command in World War I. And in all he exuded a boyish sense of adventure. Of his stint as assistant secretary of the navy, one member of Congress remarked, "Roosevelt came down here looking for war. He did not care whom he fought as long as there was a scrap." If there was no big war to fight, he would settle for a small one to keep the army and navy in practice.[25]

History seemed to repeat itself in John F. Kennedy. Also a pathetic child racked by a succession of illnesses, outdone in everything by an older brother, he grew into a bold and vigorous adult. He too was an outdoorsman, a physical fitness buff, a wartime hero of sorts, and a wealthy man who entreated the people to rise above materialism in pursuit of higher public goals. Like Roosevelt, he sought challenge. Kennedy went after the presidency despite unusual handicaps: He was young, inexperienced, and Catholic, and the odds were against him. But it was the kind of test to which he was drawn.

Kennedy's inaugural address could have been written by Theodore Roosevelt. It reflects the same motives.

> Let every nation know, whether it wishes us well or ill, that we shall pay any price, bear any burden, meet any hardship, support any friend, oppose any foe to assure the survival and the success of liberty. . . .
>
> To those peoples in the huts and villages of half the globe struggling to break the bonds of mass misery, we pledge our best efforts to help them help themselves, for whatever period is required. . . .
>
> Now the trumpet summons us again—not as a call to bear arms, though arms we need—not as a call to battle, though embattled we are— but a call to bear the burden of a long twilight struggle, year in and year out, "rejoicing in hope, patient in tribulation"—a struggle against the common enemies of man: tyranny, poverty, disease and war itself.
>
> Can we forge against these enemies a grand and global alliance, North and South, East and West, that can assure a more fruitful life for all mankind? Will you join in that historic effort?
>
> In the long history of the world, only a few generations have been granted the role of defending freedom in its hour of maximum danger. I do not shrink from this responsibility—I welcome it. I do not believe that any of us would exchange places with any other people or any other generation. The energy, the faith, the devotion which we bring to this endeavor will light our country and all who serve it—and the glow from that fire can truly light the world.[26]

The address illustrates a president's power to shape public and congressional opinion on questions of military policy. In domestic as well as foreign and military affairs, it was the peculiar contribution of John Kennedy to see the business of government as the detection and confrontation of crisis. "Kennedy cultivated . . . the use of crisis as an instrument of policy. From midday on January 20, 1961, until midday on November 22, 1963, the people of the United States lived in an atmosphere of perpetual crisis," wrote Henry Fairlie, "for what John Kennedy meant by action was a spectacular display of his power in a situation of maximum peril, as he defined it." The turbulence of the later 1960s had roots, he continued, "in the pitch of feverishness at which the American people had been kept for three years by the politics of crisis."[27] Even before January 20, in his campaign for the presidency, Kennedy had spoken alarmingly of a "missile gap" between the United States and the Soviet Union, which he was forced to admit was imaginary once he reached the White House.

Theodore Lowi argues that the dispersion of power in American politics frustrates policy leadership and tempts presidents to overstate both the seriousness of national problems and the efficacy of their solutions in order to bring pressure for action. Thus even in domestic affairs the language of war is employed—a program to help poor people becomes a "war on poverty" and a modest effort to hold down government expenditures a "war on waste."

But the rhetoric of the Kennedy inaugural was not contrived. Both its content and its passion were a straightforward expression of the president's feelings about the dangers of communism and the need for strong countermeasures. His closest adviser on military matters, General Maxwell D. Taylor, distilled this thinking in a report to the president later in the year, urging him "to express to his principal assistants and advisers his sense of the need of a changed attitude on the part of the government and of the people toward the emergency which confronts us." According to Taylor, the first requirement of such change was to recognize that "we are in a life and death struggle."[28] It was several years before Congress and the general public learned to be skeptical of the war rhetoric of the Kennedy and Johnson administrations.

Support for an expanding American role in the Vietnam War was sustained by an "incident" in the waters off North Vietnam in the summer of 1964. North Vietnamese torpedo boats allegedly fired on an American destroyer in the Gulf of Tonkin, and shortly after returned to attack it and another destroyer that had come to its aid. American forces badly damaged the North Vietnamese boats without incurring any significant damage themselves. Within a few days President Johnson had obtained the passage of the so-called Gulf of Tonkin Resolution by Congress, with only two senators and no representatives dissenting: "Resolved by the Senate and House of Representatives of the United States of America in Congress assembled, that the Congress approve and support the determination of the President, as Commander in Chief, to take all necessary measures to repel any armed attack against the forces of the United States and to prevent further aggression."[29] This defensively phrased resolution was received by the administration as the equivalent of a declaration of war and was routinely cited thereafter as justification for activities that were far more than defensive. What the public and Congress were not told, however, was that the resolution had been drafted in the Pentagon more than two months earlier as part of a plan for the widening of the war and that the navy was in the area in support of a broad covert campaign against the mainland of North Vietnam and its islands in the Gulf of Tonkin by South Vietnamese, American, and other forces under American command. At the time of the first torpedo boat attack, for example, South Vietnamese forces commanded and supplied by the Americans were engaged in amphibious attacks on two North Vietnamese islands. The shock and outrage expressed by the Johnson administration at what it characterized as an unprovoked attack were staged to trick the people and Congress into a righteous response that would become an excuse for waging war on North Vietnam. As the Pentagon Papers revealed later on, the president and his associates lied boldly and consistently about their policies and intentions throughout this period. Congress did not fully understand how it had been victimized until much later, and then in 1971 it futilely repealed the resolution.[30]

Similarly, Franklin Roosevelt seized upon a minor incident in September 1941 to crystallize public opinion and to some extent his own thinking on the menace of German submarine activity in the North Atlantic. Roosevelt was torn between Winston Churchill and others who wanted America to join Britain against Hitler and those who would limit the country's involvement to providing war materiel. Then came an encounter between a German submarine and the U.S. destroyer *Greer*. While on a routine trip to Iceland, the *Greer* was notified by a British plane that a submarine lay submerged several miles ahead. The *Greer* speeded up, found the submarine, followed it, and reported its exact position to the plane, which dropped depth charges without effect. After a time, the submarine fired two or three torpedoes at the *Greer*. The *Greer* responded with depth charges, lost the submarine's trail, picked it up again, and dropped more depth charges. Finally the *Greer* turned away and let British planes and ships continue the pursuit.

Roosevelt seized on the incident, such as it was, to depict the *Greer* and the United States as victims of German aggression. In a radio broadcast to the American people he said,

> The United States destroyer *Greer*, proceeding in full daylight toward Iceland, had reached a point southeast of Greenland. She was carrying American mail to Iceland. She was flying the American flag. Her identity as an American ship was unmistakable.
>
> She was then and there attacked by a submarine. Germany admits that it was a German submarine. The submarine deliberately fired a torpedo at the *Greer*, followed later by another torpedo attack.

No mention of the chase, the depth charges, the reporting of position to the British. Instead,

> I tell you the blunt fact that the German submarine fired first upon this American destroyer without warning, and with deliberate design to sink her. . . .
>
> It would be unworthy of a great nation to exaggerate an isolated incident, or to become inflamed by some act of violence. . . . We have

sought no shooting war with Hitler. We do not seek it now. But . . . when you see a rattlesnake poised to strike, you do not wait until he has struck before you crush him.

From now on, if German or Italian vessels of war enter the waters, the protection of which is necessary for American defense, they do so at their own peril.

Thenceforth, American warships could fire at will on any German warships in broad areas of the Atlantic designated as defense zones by the War Department. Congress would not declare war for another three months, after a genuine "incident" at Pearl Harbor, but meanwhile the president had managed to take a long step toward full involvement.[31]

None of this is new in American history. In 1846, President James K. Polk engineered an incident to induce Congress to declare war on Mexico. He wished to acquire the land between Texas and California. Mexico was unwilling to sell. So he provoked Mexico into giving him an excuse for war. The president sent American troops into disputed territory between the Rio Grande and the Nueces River. Mexico refused to react. Next he laid exaggerated claims against Mexico for the loss of American property in civil disturbances, and announced he would be satisfied with the cession of the land he desired. Mexico refused. Then some American soldiers were killed by Mexican troops near the Rio Grande, and Polk had his excuse. Mexico, he said, "had invaded our territory and shed American blood upon the American soil." Congress declared that Mexico had created a state of war. The way was open for the United States to acquire vast territories by force.[32] But the following year both houses began to look into the causes of the war, and early in 1848 the House of Representatives voted 85 to 81 to repudiate its part in the declaration of war. The war, it said, had been "unnecessarily and unconstitutionally begun by the President of the United States." One of those disavowing the declaration of war was Representative Abraham Lincoln, who explained himself in a letter to his friend W. H. Herndon:

Allow the President to invade a neighboring nation whenever he shall deem it necessary to repel an invasion, and you allow him to do so whenever he may choose to say he deems it necessary for such purpose, and you allow him to make war at pleasure. Study to see if you can fix any limit to his power in this respect, after having given him so much as you propose. If to-day he should choose to say he thinks it necessary to invade Canada to prevent the British from invading us, how could you stop him? You may say to him, "I see no probability of the British invading us;" but he will say to you, "Be silent: I see it, if you don't." . . .

This our convention understood to be the most oppressive of all kingly oppressions, and they resolved to so frame the Constitution that no one man should hold the power of bringing this oppression upon us. But your view destroys the whole matter, and places our President where kings have always stood.[33]

Clearly, the president is in a position to bring public and congressional opinion to his side. He may count on the rally-round-the-flag effect, as we have seen, and if he is unscrupulous—or believes sufficiently in what he is doing, which may amount to the same thing—he may release, withhold, and distort information to make the best case for his course of action. (And of course he may engage in undercover operations and even small wars entirely in secret.) The failure of the War Powers Resolution to control the actions of the president in the *Mayaguez* incident might have been expected. As Arthur S. Miller has put it, the president "can govern by *fait accompli*."[34]

The Legal Basis of Foreign Policy

In diplomacy, as in war, formal powers are divided between the executive and legislative branches. The president has the power, "by and with the advice and consent of the Senate, to make treaties, provided two thirds of the senators present concur." And he appoints ambassadors and other diplomatic officers with the advice and consent of a simple majority of the senators present and voting. He and Congress must cooperate in the usual way on legislation and appropriations related to foreign affairs, including such matters as the regulation of foreign commerce, the imposition of duties and excises, and consenting to agreements between states and foreign powers, which are separately mentioned in Article I. The president alone has the power to receive the ambassadors of other countries, which carries with it the greater power to recognize or deny recognition to those countries.

In diplomacy, as in war, the president enjoys more freedom of action than the words of the Constitution suggest. Congress, the courts, and the people tend to defer to assertion of authority by the president. But he cannot be as certain of the instant and fervent approval of the country in peaceful overtures and negotiations as he can in the deployment and support of troops.

The president's legal authority in foreign affairs is well stated in the Supreme Court's opinion in *United States* v. *Curtiss-Wright Export Corporation* in 1936.[35] The case tested the constitutionality of a joint resolution of Congress in 1934 allowing the president to prohibit the sale of arms by American manufacturers to Bolivia and Paraguay if in his judgment an embargo might "contribute to the re-establishment of peace between those countries." Fines and imprisonment were provided for those convicted of violating an embargo. Not long before it heard arguments in this case, the Supreme Court had twice ruled against what it regarded as excessive delegation of legislative authority to the executive. It felt one statute gave the president "an unlimited authority to determine the policy and to lay down the prohibition, or not to lay it down, as he may see fit. And disobedience to his order is made a crime punishable by fine or imprisonment." If the statute were held valid, said the Court, "it would be idle to pretend that anything would be left of limitations upon the power of the Congress to delegate its law-making function. . . . Instead . . . the Congress could at will and as to such subjects as it chose transfer that function to the President."[36] And, more generally, the Court had disappointed the president with a crabbed interpretation of the Constitution that denied him and the national government the power to regulate the economy. But that was in domestic affairs.

In the *Curtiss-Wright* case, the Court held that domestic and foreign affairs were profoundly different under the law.

> The two classes of powers are different, both in respect of their origin and their nature. The broad statement that the federal government can exercise no powers except those specifically enumerated in the Constitution, and such implied powers as are necessary and proper to carry into effect the enumerated powers, is categorically true only in respect of our internal affairs.[37]

The Court contended that the powers of the national government in foreign affairs were inherited whole from the British Crown via the government of the United States under the Continental Congress and the Articles of Confederation, according to the law of nations.

> It results that the investment of the federal government with the powers of external sovereignty did not depend upon the affirmative grants of the Constitution. The powers to declare and wage war, to conclude peace, to make treaties, to maintain diplomatic relations with other sovereignties, if they had never been mentioned in the Constitution, would have vested in the federal government as necessary concomitants of nationality.[38]

It is a strange argument, unconvincing to those legal scholars who have evidence that sovereignty was lodged in the several states during the revolutionary period and even more to those who prefer the Constitution to the law of nations as a source of internal law. But the Court went on to argue in less arcane terms that both the demands of the Constitution and the effective administration of government underlie executive discretion in foreign affairs.

Not only, as we have shown, is the federal power over external affairs in origin and essential character different from that over internal affairs, but participation in the exercise of the power is significantly limited. In this vast external realm, with its important, complicated, delicate and manifold problems, the President alone has the power to speak or listen as a representative of the nation. He *makes* treaties with the advice and consent of the Senate; but he alone negotiates. Into the field of negotiation the Senate cannot intrude; and Congress itself is powerless to invade it. As Marshall said in his great argument of March 7, 1800, in the House of Representatives, "The President is the sole organ of the nation in its foreign relations, and its sole representative with foreign nations."[39]

The Court concluded,

It is important to bear in mind that we are here dealing not alone with an authority vested in the President by an exertion of legislative power, but with such an authority plus the very delicate, plenary and exclusive power of the President as the sole organ of the federal government in the field of international relations—a power which does not require as a basis for its exercise an act of Congress, but which, of course, like every other governmental power, must be exercised in subordination to the applicable provisions of the Constitution.[40]

The joint resolution was not only constitutional, it was unnecessary. The Court went beyond the requirements of the case at hand and invested the president with inherent discretionary power in foreign affairs.

The doctrine of *Curtiss-Wright* has survived intact. The upshot has been that the president is presumed to be acting legally in conducting the foreign relations of the United States whatever he may do unless, as rarely occurs, he comes up against a specific legal prohibition in the Constitution or the statutes—and even then, as we shall see, he may yet have his way.

A year later Justice Sutherland wrote a similar opinion for the Court, this time expanding the power of the president to make agreements with other nations. In the case of *United States* v. *Belmont*, in language as sweeping and as tenuously related to existing law as that of *Curtiss-Wright*, the Court in effect allowed the president, in making agreements with other nations, to choose whether or not to follow Article II, Section 2, of the Constitution, which refers unequivocally to the need to seek Senate approval of treaties. The case upheld the president's power to make an agreement with the Soviet Union that tied U.S. recognition to various concessions, including the assignment to the United States of all money due the Soviet government from American nationals.[41]

In *Curtiss-Wright*, the Court had noted that the president *"makes treaties with the advice and consent of the Senate; but he alone negotiates,"* an interpretation consistent with practice since the first years of the republic. But another part of the Constitution, limiting the powers of the *states*, lists five kinds of international agreements: treaties, alliances, and confederations, which are denied to the States; and agreements and compacts, which are allowed only with the consent of Congress. By implication, then, treaties are not the only kind of agreements the *federal* government may make. The Constitution does not explain the differences among the several kind of agreements, and the Supreme Court in *United States* v. *Belmont* is silent on the point. But the Court permits presidential agreements or compacts, whatever they may be, without the advice and consent of the Senate.

> Governmental power over external affairs . . . is vested exclusively in the national government. And in respect of what was done here, the Executive had authority to speak as the sole organ of that government. . . .
>
> A treaty signifies "a compact made between two or more independent nations with a view to the public welfare." But an international compact, as this was, is not always a treaty which requires the participation of the Senate. There are many such compacts, of which a protocol, a modus vivendi, a postal convention, and agreements like that under consideration are illustrations.[42]

Aside from posing illustrations, the Court did not attempt to define the difference between a treaty and an executive agreement.

The Court might have dealt with the limited issue of a president's power to conclude agreements without Senate consent in the exercise of his explicit constitutional authority to recognize foreign governments, leaving the status of agreements in other contexts for later decision. Agreements made in pursuit of constitutional provisions, including the commander-in-chief role as well as the power of recognition, and of provisions of statutes and treaties might well have been viewed more favorably than other categories. Or the Court might have held that agreements were to be confined to lesser matters, such as the policing of boundaries and the private claims of citizens against other governments, or to policies taking complete and unambiguous effect at a given moment as opposed to those establishing rights and obligations to be administered over a period of time. Instead, Justice Sutherland was allowed to frame the issue in the most general terms.

The practical effect was to give presidents freedom to decide, on grounds of simple expediency if they wished, what to call a treaty and what to call an executive agreement. In September 1940, Franklin Roosevelt made an agreement with Great Britain to trade fifty old destroyers for the lease of sites for naval bases on British territory in the western Atlantic. Winston Churchill had been pleading for months for ships to make up for British losses in the naval war with Germany. Roosevelt vacillated. At first he argued that destroyers could not be turned over to Britain without legislation. But all signs were that neither house of Congress would approve. By midsummer the president was convinced that the survival of Great Britain and possibly therefore of the United States depended on ships and other support. His decision was to bypass the Senate and to make the gift of ships less objectionable at home by putting it in the form of an exchange. On his own, in this and related actions, as we have seen, Roosevelt maneuvered the nation from neutrality to limited belligerency.

Toward the end of World War II, Roosevelt made equally controversial agreements with the Soviet Union and Great Britain at Yalta, the most notable of a series of summit conferences among the superpowers in that period. The fate of vast territories and their populations was decided by the secret negotiations of a handful of men without recourse, in this country, to the Senate. In the early 1950s, conservatives in Congress under the leadership of Senator John Bricker of Ohio sought an amendment to the Constitution that in one version would have barred presidents from making executive agreements in lieu of treaties. By the time the complex amendment came up for a vote in the Senate, and failed, this provision had been dropped. Congress settled in 1972 for a statute requiring the president to inform Congress of the contents of all international agreements. Executive agreements now far outnumber treaties. In the first half-century under the Constitution, 60 of the 87 international agreements to which the United States was a party, and all of the important ones, were made in the form of treaties. In the next half-century, there were 215 treaties, again including the major agreements, and 238 executive agreements. In the third half-century, ending in 1939, there were 524 treaties and 917 executive agreements.[43] Since then executive agreements have greatly outnumbered treaties. And the trend has continued. The ordinary way of doing business now is without Senate participation.

Similarly, the president appears to have the authority to terminate a treaty without Senate consent, although there are no court decisions one way or the other and the Constitution is silent on the point. When he established full diplomatic relations with the People's Republic of China, President Carter announced his intention to terminate the American defense pact with Taiwan as of January 1, 1980. For his part, the president could cite a provision of the treaty allowing termination on one year's notice, a provision that, like the Constitution itself, made no mention of Senate participation, and could cite mixed but generally favorable precedent of presidential treaty termination in the nineteenth and twentieth centuries. Senator Barry Goldwater and others contended that Senate consent was implied in the Constitution and the treaty in question, and that in any event the Senate had passed a resolution in 1978 requiring the president to engage in "prior consultation" before making any changes in American policy toward Taiwan. The president seemed to have the weight of legal argument on his side, although it would no doubt have been politic to consult with the Senate before announcing his decision. [44]

A final kind of authority in foreign affairs is the power of the purse. It belongs to Congress, of course, subject to the veto of the president. Diplomacy itself is a minor item in the national budget and not readily regulated by Congress through appropriations, or through substantive legislation, for that matter. But the more a president's policy requires foreign aid and other large expenditures, the more it is open to congressional supervision.

In the decades after World War II, foreign aid programs were important in American foreign policy: the Marshall Plan for European reconstruction, technical assistance and food for underdeveloped countries, the Alliance for Progress in Latin America, and so forth. When it wished, Congress could assert its authority by holding down overall expenditures or, with equal effect, specifying in detail how the money it did allow would be spent.

In the exercise of this and other constitutional powers, the actual role of each branch has depended as much on political as on legal considerations.

The Conditions of Leadership

In foreign affairs, leadership tends to come from the president, and Congress merely facilitates or obstructs. Just which, depends in a general way on the opportunities for intervention available to Congress and its incentives for taking hold or backing off. In some situations, Congress is relatively passive, as when the executive withholds information on which it might act; in others there is some sharing of authority, as in the making of most treaties; and in still others Congress exercises its greatest authority, as in deciding upon economic assistance to other countries.

That there would be a large measure of secrecy in foreign affairs, as there is in matters of war and peace, must surely have been anticipated by the framers of the Constitution, although they did not touch the question directly. Hamilton, defending the Constitution in the *Federalist* No. 70, mentioned secrecy and decision, activity, and dispatch as favorable qualities of a single executive as opposed to a plural one.

Men often oppose a thing, merely because they have had no agency in planning it, or because it may have been planned by those whom they dislike. But if they have been consulted, and have happened to disapprove, opposition then becomes, in their estimation, an indispensable duty of self-love. They seem to think themselves bound in honor, and by all the motives of personal infallibility, to defeat the success of what has been resolved upon contrary to their sentiments. Men of upright, benevolent tempers have too many opportunities of remarking, with horror, to what desperate lengths this disposition is sometimes carried, and how often the great interests of society are sacrificed to the vanity, to the conceit, and to the obstinacy of individuals, who have credit enough to make their passions and their caprices interesting to mankind. Perhaps the question now before the public may, in its consequences, afford melancholy proofs of the effects of this despicable frailty, or rather detestable vice, in the human character.

Hamilton's argument for a single executive helps one understand why the constitutional convention itself met behind closed doors. It was not until fifty years had passed, when the likelihood of "the most bitter dissensions" had passed, that James Madison's invaluable notes of the proceedings were made public.

More to the point, John Jay argued for executive secrecy in foreign affairs in his discussion of the roles of president and Senate in the making of treaties in *Federalist* No. 64.

It seldom happens in the negotiation of treaties, of whatever nature, but that perfect *secrecy* and immediate *despatch* are sometimes requisite. There are cases where the most useful intelligence may be obtained, if the persons possessing it can be relieved from apprehensions of discovery. Those apprehensions will operate on those persons whether they are actuated by mercenary or friendly motives; and there doubtless are many of both descriptions, who would rely on the secrecy of the President, but who would not confide in that of the Senate, and still less in that of a large popular Assembly. The convention have done well, therefore, in so disposing of the power of making treaties, that although the President must, in forming them, act by the advice and consent of the Senate, yet he will be able to manage the business of intelligence in such a manner as prudence may suggest.

From the beginning, presidents have freely withheld information from Congress and the public. The reasons have varied. Protection of military secrets and foreign intelligence are generally acceptable unless, as in the later Nixon years, claims of "national security" are grossly overused.

Most would also agree to secrecy of high-level discussions between and within governments, in which options are explored frankly before the announcement of a decision. Without an assurance of secrecy, it is argued, international negotiations are likely to be disrupted by external pressures, and people within the government are afraid to give their best advice. The question is where to draw the line to allow the president a degree of confidentiality without depriving the public of information it deserves. Part of the answer has been to allow him to appoint members of his White House staff without Senate confirmation, symbolizing their responsibility to him alone, and not to call them to Capitol Hill for questioning. But, as Senator Fulbright once testified, problems arise when White House staff assume functions akin to those of cabinet members:

> No one questions the propriety or desirability of allowing the President to have confidential, personal advisers. President Wilson relied heavily on the advice and friendship of Colonel House, and President Roosevelt relied similarly on Harry Hopkins. President Nixon is certainly entitled to the private and personal counsel of Mr. Kissinger, but Mr. Kissinger in fact is a great deal more than a personal adviser to the President. Unlike Colonel House and Harry Hopkins, who had no staffs of their own, and even unlike Mr. Rostow, who at the end of 1968 had a substantive staff of no more than 12 persons, Mr. Kissinger presides over a staff of 54 "substantive officers" and a total staff of 140 employees.
>
> In addition, Mr. Kissinger serves as chairman of six interagency committees dealing with the entire range of foreign policy and national security issues and is also in charge of "working groups" which prepare the staff studies on which high level policy discussions are based. The National Security Council staff budget, which includes funds for outside consultants, stood at $2.2 million in fiscal year 1971, which is more than triple Mr. Rostow's budget in 1968. Mr. Kissinger's role is comparable to that of Colonel House in about the same way that a moon rocket is comparable to the Wright brothers' airplane; both could fly but there all meaningful comparison comes to an end.
>
> Mr. Kissinger's principal function—so we are told—is to define "options" for the President. On its face this might be taken for a disinterested, more or less clerical activity. But as people with experience in government know very well, the power to "define" options is the power to choose some and eliminate others, and that is a significant power indeed.
>
> One official has been quoted as saying that it gives Mr. Kissinger a "hammerlock" on foreign policy. Or, in the words of one reporter who has made a study of the Nixon administration's foreign policy methods, "Mr. Kissinger has become the instrument by which President Nixon has centralized the management of foreign policy in the White House as never before. . . . "
>
> I do not consider Mr. Kissinger's influence, or that of his new foreign policy bureau, as being in any way sinister, illegitimate, or even inappropriate—except in one respect: their immunity from accountability to Congress and the country behind a barricade of executive privilege.[45]

"Executive privilege" is a new term for an old practice. Although the Constitution requires the president to give Congress information on the state of the union and gives the Senate the power of advice and consent, from which one can reasonably infer a right to information relating to treaties and ambassadorial functions, presidents have not been uniformly generous with that information. George Washington, against the advice of his cabinet, gave the House of Representatives full and embarrassing information about what had gone wrong with General St. Clair's expedition against the Indians; four years later, he refused to give the House documents relating to a treaty with Britain, on the ground that treaties were the concern of the Senate, not the House. Strong presidents, especially, have resisted congressional inquiries. Theodore Roosevelt once prevented Congress from securing documents in a domestic matter by having them sent to the White House for safekeeping and informing Congress it would have to impeach him to get its hands on them.[46]

But it was Dwight Eisenhower, defending executive departments against Senator Joseph McCarthy's irresponsible investigations of subversive activities in the executive branch, who extended the notion of executive privilege from an occasional claim of confidentiality in and around the White House to a prohibition against the release of any internal executive-branch communication without White House approval. "This historic rule had been disclosure, with exceptions," remarked Arthur Schlesinger. "The new rule was denial, with exceptions." The ground had been laid for Richard Nixon's assertion of a constitutional right to keep Congress and the public in the dark about anything he wished.[47]

One of President Nixon's attorneys general, Richard Kleindienst, testifying before a Senate committee in opposition to legislation to curb executive privilege, asserted that the power to withhold any information in the possession of the executive branch derived from the separation of powers and could not be qualified by Congress or the courts. Were there, the senators asked, no constraints on executive discretion? "You could impeach the president of the United States and the vice president," snapped the attorney general. "You would have the speaker of the House of Representatives becoming the president. Then you could impeach the judiciary and appoint a new judiciary, and if you wanted to exercise your power you could have a whole new government." How could the president be impeached if Congress were denied all the evidence, inquired Senator Sam Ervin. The Senate needed no evidence to convict, said the attorney general, only votes. After a while, with elaborate sarcasm, Kleindienst thanked the senators for their "courteous hospitality" and walked out.[48]

Executive privilege in fact was subjected to limitation by the Supreme Court in the case of *United States* v. *Nixon*, as we shall see.[49] But whether that extraordinary case, arising from a criminal trial of Watergate conspirators, will have any effect on the ability of Congress to extract information on foreign affairs is unclear.

A more general remedy for the problem of inadequate information from the executive, on foreign and domestic affairs both, would be a question period, as in the British and Canadian parliaments, in which cabinet members would be held accountable to one or both houses for the running of their departments. Both Jimmy Carter and Walter Mondale endorsed the idea before their election in 1976. As a senator, Mondale argued in 1975, in his book *The Accountability of Power*, that weaknesses in policy might be corrected more quickly if cabinet members were subjected to no-holds-barred questioning by the Senate. "One Canadian official told me that it was his opinion that if we had had a question-and-report period in Congress, the war in Vietnam—because of its indefensibility—might have ended much earlier." (Mondale also contended that public questioning would strengthen the cabinet, because presidents would not want administration policies defended by men and women who were not capable, fully informed, and fully responsible for the affairs of their departments.)[50]

The executive has the upper hand in disputes about information under the present system, but in treaty making there is more equality between the branches. In 1978 Jimmy Carter had to work tooth and nail to win Senate support of the Panama Canal treaties. No president can take Senate support for granted. If he does, out of conviction that providence and public opinion are on his side and that the Senate will follow, he may be disappointed. The classic illustration is Woodrow Wilson's failure to court the Senate in his campaign to take the United States into the League of Nations. Although he was not obliged to bring the Senate into the negotiations leading to the making of the peace treaty and the League Covenant, it would have been politic to do so. Resistance to his leadership was all the greater when the Senate fell into Republican hands in the 1918 elections. Wilson would not work with the leaders of the Senate nor allow more than token Republican representation in the negotiations. When Senator Lodge suggested changes in the terms of American participation in the League, Wilson ruled out compromise and took his case to the people in order to force the issue. On a speaking tour for the League, he suffered an incapacitating stroke which ended whatever chance he might have had. The Senate voted against him. It is generally agreed that he could have had half a loaf or more if he had not been unyielding and self-righteous.

In laying the groundwork for the League's successor, the United

Nations, as World War II drew to a close, Franklin Roosevelt and Harry Truman took care that history did not repeat itself. Roosevelt cooperated with Republican leaders Thomas E. Dewey and John Foster Dulles during the election year of 1944, and he and Truman after him worked hand in hand with the Democratic and Republican leaders of the Foreign Relations Committee in the establishment of both the United Nations and the spirit of bipartisanship in foreign policy that prevailed to the end of the decade.[51]

In the areas of foreign policy requiring large sums of money, the power of Congress—of both houses rather than the Senate alone in this case—is at its greatest. The president must put himself at the mercy of the often unfriendly appropriations committees and their subcommittees. Once in a while, however, an inventive executive can avoid the judgment of Congress even on appropriations. Thomas Jefferson, suppressing doubts about the constitutionality of his course of action, vastly overspent the money available to him for the Louisiana Purchase in 1803 and was sustained by a grateful Congress. Theodore Roosevelt sent the fleet halfway around the world in a display of American military might and left it to Congress to supply the funds to bring the ships home. Richard Nixon, in an impulsive, imperial gesture, gave the president of Egypt a helicopter and later found funds for it in a discretionary account in the State Department intended for very different purposes. (Congress this time was sufficiently annoyed to reduce the fund in order to prevent a recurrence.) Somewhat differently, the Central Intelligence Agency was discovered making money in the 1960s and 1970s on its proprietary operations—an airline run under a cover name, for example—and plowing the profits back into expanded operations, a procedure that is legal enough in the case of government corporations such as the Tennessee Valley Authority but not for the CIA. But such exceptional cases aside, the president must go to Congress and ask for funding.

A good illustration of presidential skill in building support in Congress for foreign aid, against heavy odds, is Harry Truman's engineering of the passage of the European Recovery Program—the Marshall Plan—in 1948. To begin with, although the program made sense to him, Truman was under no Wilsonian illusion that it would therefore make sense to Congress. The election of 1946 had given control of both houses of Congress to the Republicans, many of whom were isolationist and economy-minded. Truman had fought hard with them on domestic legislation. His own popularity was low, and his party was scanning the field for a replacement to run for president in 1948.

The president took care not to mix his appeals for congressional action in domestic and foreign affairs. In the one, he was uniformly partisan (and unsuccessful); in the other, he was scrupulously bipartisan. Republican cooperation was bought with the assurance that credit would be shared. The president kept in close touch with key people in and out of government and backed up his private politicking with messages to Congress and the public to educate them on the importance of coming to the assistance of western Europe. His theme was anticommunism. There were costs: One of the first was McCarthyism. But whatever the ultimate wisdom of the president's cold war ideology, it provided consensus for his foreign policy and the large appropriations it required.[52]

Later presidents were less cooperative with Congress. Presidents Johnson and Nixon preferred to make their own foreign policy. They were defiant and devious. President Nixon made important overtures to the Soviet Union and China without involving congressional leaders of either party, as he might have to his advantage. With such treatment and the bitter experience of the war in Vietnam, Congress grew less compliant.

Conclusions

Late in 1966 Aaron Wildavsky wrote of the "two presidencies," one for domestic affairs, one for defense and foreign policy. The modern president had asserted far more effective control over defense and foreign policy, he argued, than over defense policy.[53] Although the president at the time, Lyndon Johnson, seemed to be an exception, since he was leading Congress and the country forcefully in both areas of policy, Wildavsky could cite the experience of several administrations in support of his distinction. Franklin Roosevelt from 1938 on did not get any important domestic measures through Congress. Harry Truman is credited with housing legislation at best. Eisenhower did not lead in domestic affairs. Kennedy had little success. Yet these presidents engineered American participation in the United Nations, the Marshall Plan, NATO, the test ban treaty, intervention in Vietnam—all for better or for worse, to be sure—and were responsible for many other foreign and military policies.

In foreign and military matters, these presidents enjoyed influence and freedom of action. There were rivals, said Wildavsky, but the president prevailed over them. The public, as he saw it, was slow to form strong opinions about foreign and military policy, but in the short run was supportive of the government. Interest groups were fewer and weaker in foreign than domestic affairs. Congress was passive, even deferential. The military, he believed, were disunited and as a result had less impact on policy than many supposed. The military-industrial complex was more influential in the allocation of funds than in determining the shape of the budget and its underlying policy. The State Department was weak and compliant.

Eight years later, Donald Peppers reexamined Wildavsky's argument in the light of new evidence.[54] From 1966 to the time of his study in 1974, there had been a dramatic loss of faith in presidents, and with it less public or congressional willingness to allow them free rein in any area of policy. The result was an erosion, though not an obliteration, of the distinction between the two presidencies. Vietnam offered lessons about the risks of presidential war; détente meant the president could no longer count on belligerent anticommunist consensus in support of foreign and military adventures; Watergate had made Congress, the bureaucracy, and the public more assertive. Point by point, Peppers found the rival centers of influence to have more direct or indirect impact on policy making than Wildavsky had found in 1966. He also saw a blurring of the distinction between foreign and domestic policy.

Peppers, too, may have been writing near the end of an era in the management of foreign affairs. By 1975, Secretary of State Kissinger was complaining that Congress had gone too far in controlling foreign policy, in particular for the Soviet Union, Latin America, and the Middle East, he said. "The attempt to prescribe every detail of policy by congressional action can, over a period of time, so stultify flexibility that you have no negotiating room left at all. We recognize that Congress must exercise ultimate policy control. But . . . I would hope that Congress would keep in mind that we need some flexibility."[55]

The legislation he had in mind included tariff legislation, aimed at the Middle East, that had unintentionally hurt South American oil-producing countries; a limit on Soviet credits from the Export-Import Bank for as long as the Soviet Union restricted the emigration of Jews and other Soviet citizens; the prohibition of military aid to Chile because of violations of human rights by the military junta; restriction of military aid to Turkey because of the Turkish invasion of Cyprus; reduced military and economic aid to Indochina; a rule that no more than 30 percent of American food aid could go to countries not in actual need, as determined by the United Nations; and more.[56]

Members of Congress continued to grumble about Kissinger's secretive and autocratic ways. But they did let up on the executive, and by the time Jimmy Carter took office they seemed less intent upon substituting their judgment for that of the White House and the State Department.[57]

The period that Peppers described began with the imperial presidencies of Lyndon Johnson and Richard Nixon and ended with the humdrum presidency of Gerald Ford, a natural time for Congress to reestablish its share of authority in foreign affairs. After that, Congress reverted to its more traditional role, falling back a step or two to let the president lead—but not by too much. It seemed enough to let the struggle with Kissinger stand as a warning to future administrations that Congress could be very unfriendly and obstructive if it were not consulted. And it continued to be heard on issues that mattered to the members and their constituents, including the Panama Canal, Taiwan and China, Strategic Arms Limitation Talks, military government in Argentina, trade with Cuba, and assistance to Indochina.

THE CABINET

The cabinet, consisting of the dozen or so heads of the major departments of the government (the number fluctuates) and others by invitation, is by tradition the president's principal advisory body, in theory. It enjoys the trappings of authority. It has its own room a few steps from the Oval Office, in a picturesque setting overlooking the Rose Garden. Americans regularly see pictures of the president seated with the vice president across the table and the secretaries arrayed on the right and left according to the seniority of their departments preparing to discuss matters of state. If there is a portrait of the executive branch, this is it. It is comparable to the formal portraits of the Supreme Court and the House and Senate, each too with its leader in the middle and seating arranged according to a plan that in one way or another puts the most honored members closest to the leader.

Cabinets, though, are invariably a disappointment to presidents and department secretaries alike. Still, each administration begins with ritual assurances that the cabinet is about to become active and important. "I plan a reorganized and strengthened cabinet," said Richard Nixon during his 1968 campaign for the Presidency.

> It's time we once again had an open administration—open to ideas *from* the people, and open in its communication *with* the people—an administration of open doors, open eyes, and open minds. . . .

We should bring dissenters into policy discussion, not freeze them out; we should invite constructive criticism, not only because the critics have a right to be heard, but also because they often have something worth hearing.

The president cannot isolate himself from the great intellectual ferments of his time. On the contrary, he must consciously and deliberately place himself at their center. . . .

This is one reason why I don't want a government of yes-men. . . .

As Theodore Roosevelt once put it, "the best executive is the one who has enough sense to pick good men to do what he wants done, and self-restraint enough to keep from meddling with them while they do it."

This requires . . . a cabinet made up of the ablest men in America, leaders in their own right and not merely by virtue of appointment—men who will command the public's respect and the president's attention by the power of their intellect and the force of their ideas.

Such men are not attracted to an Administration in which all credit is gathered to the White House and blame parceled out to scapegoats, or in which high officials are asked to dance like puppets on a presidential string. I believe in a system in which the appropriate cabinet officer gets credit for what goes right, and the president takes the blame for what goes wrong.

Officials of a new administration will not have to check their consciences at the door.[1]

These are not promises a president-elect fully intends to keep. They are more in the nature of a New Year's resolution to give up smoking once more or to love one's neighbors as oneself. Certainly Richard Nixon's plans for a strong cabinet and an open administration with the ablest men in America at his side were wishful thinking.

Aside from keeping a harmless myth alive, there are good reasons for these periodic statements of faith in the cabinet. First, all modern presidents but Eisenhower have been turned down by some of those they have invited to join the cabinet. Many qualified people find the work, the pay, or the life of politics unattractive. Presidents may be forgiven, perhaps, if they glamorize the cabinet at hiring time. Second, to praise the cabinet is to honor an old American distrust of monopoly of power in one leader. (The obligation to pay tribute to the principle that several heads are better than one is strongest when the vice president succeeds to the presidency—it is then also a promise of continuity.) Third, reliance on the cabinet is an attractive alternative to an ever-larger role for the White House staff. It is a simple and straightforward plan to hold the members responsible individually for the management of their departments and collectively for advising the president on programs and politics. But the cabinet has not proven very useful: in fact, the more one understands why not, the more one understands the presidency.

Cabinet Roles Compared

American cabinets resemble one another more than they resemble cabinets in other countries. Our experience with cabinets has fallen into a pattern set in George Washington's administration of rapport succeeded by a growing inability of the members to work with each other and, for that matter, with the president.

From one country to another, however, the dominant functions of cabinets vary greatly. B. W. Headey distinguishes six roles: departmental management, policy leadership, representative roles, cabinet roles, party and parliamentary roles, and public relations.[2] He finds departmental management more important in the American cabinet than in those of Canada, Britain, Australia, and the Netherlands, the other countries analyzed. A large proportion of American cabinet members have had previous experience running large organizations, sometimes governmental, more often private. Some of the most successful have had a dual background as executives in business and in the federal government. Departmental policy leadership is somewhat less important in the United States, in Headey's judgment (but of first importance in the Netherlands, where cabinet ministers are specialists, roughly a quarter of them promoted from civil service positions to head their departments). Representative roles are also of real, although secondary importance in the United States: Members act as representatives of regional, racial, occupational, and other segments of the society.

The other roles have less significance in the American system. Cabinet roles, which Headey defines as contributing to the collective decisions of the cabinet on issues not of direct concern to one's own department in addition to fighting for departmental programs, are emphasized in Great Britain, as are party and parliamentary roles. The American Constitution prohibits joint legislative-executive appointments, but it does not prohibit cabinet and party functions. They simply have not taken hold in the United States. Lastly, the public relations function of selling department and government programs to the legislature and the people is less significant in the United States than in the other countries studied.

The contrast between the British and the American systems is less stark than Headey's analysis suggests, however, if we consider that functions characteristic of the cabinet in one country can be found elsewhere in the other. As Richard Neustadt has noted, American counterparts of British cabinet ministers (in what Headey would call their cabinet, party, and parliamentary roles) can sometimes be discovered among the leaders of Congress, on the White House staff, and occasionally in the cabinet itself. (And the reverse—our departmental managers have counterparts in the top stratum of the British civil service.)[3]

The functions that predominate in the United States are performed by the members individually: Cabinet members are more useful to presidents for what they can accomplish in their respective departments and in private consultation in the White House than for what they have to say in the Cabinet Room. In Great Britain, cabinet roles are primarily collective and require as a bare minimum that the members meet regularly and work together. Proponents of cabinet reform in the United States believe the individual and collective functions are compatible. The evidence, as we shall see, is mixed.

Individual Roles

A typical role for an American secretary is departmental management (which in many parliamentary regimes is left largely to career civil servants). Although the Constitution allows the president to supervise the affairs of a department, he frequently delegates full responsibility to the secretary. Some energetic presidents have a highly selective interest in the affairs of the government: Woodrow Wilson, for example, paid little attention to domestic administrative matters. It was his preference to appoint secretaries he could trust and to leave departmental matters in their care. It was very different with the Department of State, however. His secretary of state, William Jennings Bryan, a political appointee, never had the president's confidence. Furthermore, Wilson was keenly interested in foreign affairs himself. The president and his adviser, Colonel House, therefore did much of the work of the State Department in the White House. With Wilson, as with other presidents, selectivity also resulted from the pressure of events: As war and the League of Nations took more of his time, he left more and more to the discretion of his cabinet secretaries. Similarly, the Vietnam and Watergate crises caused more delegation in the Johnson and Nixon administrations.

Calvin Coolidge, one of the weaker presidents, also delegated authority freely. It was not to save his energies for more important matters of state, however. Coolidge had a relaxed view of the office: He liked to sleep long hours, and had no interest in creating work for himself by stirring up the departments. He was canny enough to know that, at least in his day, the government would run itself if the president left it alone. His administrative strategy was "Sit down and keep still." He added, "If you see ten troubles coming down the road, you can be sure that nine will run into the ditch before they reach you and you have to battle with only one.''[4] And even that one could be turned over to a subordinate. In his autobiography, Coolidge wrote,

> The Presidency . . . is a place of last resort to which all questions are brought that others have not been able to answer. The ideal way for it to function is to assign to the various positions men of sufficient ability so that they can solve all the problems that arise under their jurisdiction. If there is a troublesome situation in Nicaragua, a General McCoy can manage it. If we have differences with Mexico, a Morrow can compose them. If there is unrest in the Philippines, a Stimson can quiet them.[5]

As this suggests, Coolidge, in contrast to Wilson, was most disposed to delegate in matters of foreign affairs.

Dwight Eisenhower delegated across the board. Even with respect to his greatest interests, national security affairs and balancing the budget, he insisted on being spared administrative detail. His administrative methods as president were influenced by his military experience, his age, his serious illnesses in office, and the fact that he was not much of a reader. He favored the appointment of businessmen to his cabinet because of their managerial ability. And he usually left them alone.

According to Harry Truman, who made good use of his cabinet members, the ideal relationship is reciprocal: The president stays out of the secretary's way in departmental matters, and the secretary defers to the president on questions of policy. President Truman came to this conclusion the hard way: His second secretary of state, James F. Byrnes, was in the president's opinion all too willing to make and proclaim foreign policy on his own. At the time of one of his greater indiscretions, when he was conducting negotiations without keeping the president informed of progress, Byrnes received a note from the president setting out his policy toward the Soviet Union and putting the secretary straight on the question of delegation: "I would like to pursue a policy of delegating authority to the members of the Cabinet in their various fields and then back them up in the results. But in doing that I do not intend to forgo the president's prerogative to make the final decision." Said Truman, "A Secretary of State should never have the illusion that he is President of the United States."[6]

Some years later, Truman developed a working relationship with Secretary of State Dean Acheson that came close to the ideal: There was candor, mutual respect, and a clear understanding where one's domain ended and the other's began.[7] Part of their understanding was that personnel decisions in the State Department would be the responsibility of the secretary, not the White House. If the president disagreed sufficiently with the secretary, he might replace him, but as long as Acheson was there he would control the department, and President Truman agreed.

Whether a president allows his cabinet members a free hand in making subcabinet appointments—or undercuts them by placing his own people in the departments, initially or afterwards—is the most important clue to the vitality of the role of the department manager. It is hard enough for a secretary to gain control of his department under the best of circumstances. Secretaries come and go (according to a count for the years 1960 through 1972, over four-tenths of them serve no more than two years) while civil servants stay on for decades, accumulating organizational skills.[8] But if key positions lying between the secretary and the civil service—under secretaries, assistant secretaries, deputy assistant secretaries, and the like—are filled by men and women who owe their jobs to the president, the secretary's job is more difficult still.

The alternatives can be seen in the staffing of the Departments of Defense and State in the Kennedy administration. In Robert McNamara, Kennedy found a secretary of defense who was by temperament and training, as president of the Ford Motor Company, a manager who required full control of his organization. It was he rather than Kennedy who chose all the key people in the Department of Defense. Some of his appointees were suggested by the president-elect or his recruiters, it is true, but they were named only if McNamara was entirely satisfied of their ability. In a number of cases he rejected the suggestions. For example, Kennedy proposed his friend Franklin D. Roosevelt, Jr., as assistant secretary of the navy, a post that had been held by three Roosevelts, including FDR. McNamara had someone else in mind. Some of his most important appointees were management specialists who could help him impose a new planning and budgeting system on the department. Dean Rusk, Kennedy's secretary of state, was a less forceful person and less interested in management. When he accepted the job of secretary of state, a number of important appointments in the department had already been decided, including Adlai Stevenson as ambassador to the United Nations and Chester Bowles as under secretary, both of whom had hoped to be secretary. But Rusk kept busy with policy and was content to leave much of the hiring that remained to Bowles.[9] His authority was further weakened by the appointment of McGeorge Bundy as assistant to the president for national security affairs. The relations of John Kennedy and Dean Rusk violated the Truman-Acheson rule in several respects.

President Nixon impulsively turned over responsibility for making subcabinet appointments to his cabinet members—and immediately after admitted to an aide that he had made a big mistake. Within a year the power was safely back in the White House, where it was used to displace liberals and others of questionable fidelity and to fill their positions with young loyalists from the president's staff. It was a clear sign of the president's growing distrust of his cabinet. [10]

After departmental management, the role an American cabinet member is most likely to play is the representation of a constituency. It too, of course, is an individual rather than a collective role. Representativeness has been important in the United States, though not as important as it has in Canada, we may note, where the representation of predominantly English-speaking, Protestant Ontario and French-speaking, Catholic Quebec—and to some extent the other regions of the country—has entailed a meticulous apportionment of places in the cabinet in order to keep the peace. (It is Headey's view that cabinet representativeness is a function of social cleavage.) [11] In the United States, less rigid recognition has been given regions, major religions, occupations, and, lately, blacks and women. Secretaries of "interest" departments, notably the Departments of Agriculture, Labor, Commerce, and Interior, are traditionally from the geographical and sometimes occupational constituencies served by their departments. In other cases, such as the appointment of a woman to head the Department of Health, Education, and Welfare (HEW) or a black to head the Department of Transportation, the constituency represented is not the specific clientele group of the department. And in still others there is a combination of the two: Arthur Goldberg, a Jewish labor lawyer, was appointed secretary of labor by President Kennedy. He had strong ties to organized labor and his appointment added religious diversity to the cabinet.

Jimmy Carter's secretary of housing and urban development, Patricia Harris, the daughter of a black Pullman-car waiter, considered it her job to speak "for people who are unable to provide for their own needs and who have been disadvantaged by this society." She criticized the president's 1980 budget for slighting HUD's programs. It "would risk the disaffection" of blacks and others politically important to the administration, she said. A White House aide countered, "The job of a secretary is to defend positions taken by a president, rather than publish something that will embarrass the president." But she vowed to speak her mind. [12] She survived the 1979 cabinet purge nonetheless.

Even when a secretary is not identified with the programs and clientele of his department at the time of appointment, he may soon be. There are good examples of the cooptation of a generalist secretary by the specialist bureaucracy in the Nixon administration. Robert Finch, an old friend and associate from California, was appointed to head the Department of Health, Education, and Welfare with a mandate from the president to be tough and cut costs. Within a few months he had come to believe in HEW and to support its programs, while the White House in the same period had become increasingly critical of the department. Caught between clashing forces, Finch left the department and soon after left the government. His successor, Elliot Richardson, was less torn emotionally than Finch, but he too showed sympathy for the people in HEW and defended them against their critics—by implication, against their critics in the White House. He was transferred to the Department of Defense. In 1972 John Ehrlichman summed up White House disappointment over the fate of presidential appointees: "We only see them at the annual White House Christmas party; they go off and marry the natives."[13]

The advantages of interest representation from the departmental point of view have been described by Hugh Heclo of the Brookings Institution:

> In every department in every recent administration, one of the chief ways political executives gained support in the bureaucracy was by being, or at least appearing to be, their agency's vigorous spokesman. "Fighting your counterparts in other departments creates confidence and support beneath you," one acknowledged. In reference to a strong advocate in his department, a civil servant said: "He was well regarded on the Hill and dealt from strength with [the interest group]. A lot of White House people were afraid of him. You could get more of what was wanted approved and through Congress." Less politically effective executives may be personally admired by civil servants but have little to offer in return for bureaucratic support. As one such cabinet secretary was described by a bureau chief: "He had charisma, a really fine and open man who had a lot of civil servants around here he liked. But he never got a grip on the department. He didn't really fight for what was needed and if he made a decision it was because he got maneuvered into it by the staff." Experienced bureaucrats recognize that such appointees leave their agencies and programs vulnerable to more politically aggressive competitors elsewhere. In this sense, career officials will typically prefer a strong if unpleasant advocate to an amiable weakling.[14]

Advocacy of departmental interests is not incompatible with support of the cabinet as a whole and the president if a secretary is willing to accept constraints—to speak up for the department, but to accept delays and compromises gracefully in the larger interests of the administration. Otherwise the members of the cabinet are a part of the problem, from the president's viewpoint, rather than of the solution. They may be, as critics of the American cabinet have contended, the president's natural enemies.

The picture of the cabinet as a conglomeration of special interests working in every direction but the president's is easily overdrawn, however. As Graham Wilson has shown, a department's clientele is likely in fact to consist of contending factions with very different policies.[15] The Department of Agriculture is commonly accepted as a nearly pure example of an agency in league with like-minded committees of the House and Senate and pressure groups outside the government. Since 1933, the department has administered farm price support programs that divert large sums of money from the treasury—and from consumers—to the farm community. It might be supposed that farmers would be fairly well agreed on the desirability of the subsidy, but in reality the major interest groups are bitterly divided, and the members of agriculture committees in Congress and the Secretaries of Agriculture have taken one side or the other depending largely on whether they were Democrats or Republicans. The Democrats and the National Farmers' Union have argued for subsidies in compensation for what they regard as the weak market position of the farmer, and the Republicans and the American Farm Bureau Federation have called for the gradual elimination of subsidies and the production controls that accompany them in order to return to a free, competitive market.

After the prosubsidy secretaries of agriculture of the New Deal and Fair Deal came a conservative Republican, Ezra Taft Benson, who agreed with his president, Dwight Eisenhower, that the best government was the least: "The blessings of abundance that we now possess have come down to us through an economic system that rests on three pillars—free enterprise, private property, and the market economy." Benson and Eisenhower faced a Democratic majority in Congress six of their eight years in office and were unable to scrap the farm program they inherited from Harry Truman, but with the free use of the veto on farm legislation they were able to induce Congress to chip away at it. When the Democrats won the presidency in 1960, a liberal Democrat, Orville Freeman, became secretary of agriculture. Once again the president and his secretary were in agreement on farm policy, but on one very different from the Republicans': They wanted stricter federal regulation of production, which they called "supply management," as the price farmers would have to pay for a guarantee.

With one exception, secretaries of agriculture since have fallen into this pattern, pushing for conservative or liberal policy according to party. The exception was President Nixon's first secretary, Clifford Hardin, a centrist who attempted to fashion compromises between the factions strongly committed to price supports or to their elimination. Hardin did not last long. Wilson concludes that the heads of other interest departments tend also to be more loyal to the White House than to organized interests. Presidents frequently reject names proffered by such interests for appointment to cabinet and subcabinet positions.

Wilson believes that students of the Department of Agriculture have missed the point by focusing on matters about which there is considerable consensus, such as the program to combat soil erosion, rather than the divisive and far more costly subsidy program. Another inference, which Wilson does not make but seems equally justified by his evidence, is that the committee-bureau-interest subgovernment continues to reign supreme in agriculture, maintaining the status quo in the face of opposition by the president *and* his secretary of agriculture. The point may be that the effective boundary between the adversaries is to be found between the secretary and his department rather than between the president and the secretary. If so, the secretaries of agriculture, labor, commerce, and interior may have a largely symbolic role and should not be expected to spur important policy changes.

Another cautionary statement about the importance of representativeness in the cabinet needs to be made, related to something noted in previous chapters. Presidential nominations and elections have become less dependent on the efforts of party organizations and their underlying coalitions and more dependent on candidates' personal organizations and treasuries and on direct appeals on television and radio unmediated by organized interests. As Nelson Polsby puts it, "The idea of a party as a coalition of interests bound together by the hope of electing a president is becoming an anachronism. Party is increasingly a label for names of individual voters who pick among alternatives marketed by the mass media."[16] One result, Polsby speculates, may be fewer client-oriented people in the cabinet. Another may be greater freedom for an unscrupulous president to issue unethical or unlawful orders to his subordinates.[17] An illegal order to the director of the Office of Economic Opportunity to shut the agency down, for example, might not have been issued had the director had even a mild concern about the people served by the agency. Stephen Hess views the matter more positively: Developments in the electoral process "have lessened traditional constraints on selecting the cabinet. Presidents will still incur obligations on the way to the White House, but more than ever before they will be free to choose their department heads on the basis of ability."[18] Perhaps.

Whatever lies in the future, it can be said that the practice so far has been for cabinet members to focus their attention on their respective departments—sometimes with presidential approval, sometimes not.

Collective Roles

Although collective functions are so important in Britain that one is able to speak of the cabinet as "the *assembly* of the principal ministers of the crown,"[19] in the United States the members normally do their most significant work outside one another's view. Still, the cabinet as a whole is more than a ceremonial institution, and the "inner cabinet" of secretaries of key departments is an influential group in most administrations.

The cabinet in the United States is at most an advisory rather than a decision-making body. Constitutional authority is vested in the president alone. There is no obligation to consult the cabinet, much less to be bound by its judgments. Lincoln's statement of the vote in his cabinet is good constitutional theory, whether he actually said it or not: "Seven noes, one aye—the ayes have it." It is true that George Washington allowed questions to be decided by a vote of his cabinet and that Thomas Jefferson revived the practice when he became president a few years later. But that was the end of it, except for two brief periods when the cabinet made decisions for weakened presidents: during the term of William Henry Harrison, who died of pneumonia on April 4, 1841, one month after his inauguration, and in the final chaotic days of the Buchanan administration two decades after.[20] Votes have sometimes been taken, but only to inform the president. Harry Truman did so; but he is also remembered as the president with the sign on his desk that said "The Buck Stops Here!"

> I never allowed myself to forget that the final responsibility was mine. I would ask the Cabinet to share their counsel with me, even encouraging disagreement and argument to sharpen up the different points of view. On major issues I would frequently ask them to vote, and I expected the cabinet officers to be frank and candid in expressing their opinions to me. At the same time, I insisted that they keep me informed of the major activities of their departments in order to make certain that they supported the policy once I had made a decision.[21]

The usual role of the cabinet as a group is simply to advise the president on issues he cares to bring before it. It is typically a diverse lot of people—generalists, specialists, politicians, businessmen, professionals—who can offer the president a good array of opinions on any subject. The drawback, often expressed in members' recollections of the tribulations of cabinet life, is that those who are uninformed on a subject may nevertheless hold forth, angering some of their colleagues and boring others. The following example from the Eisenhower administration was recorded by presidential assistant Emmet John Hughes:

> For world affairs, [Secretary of Defense Charles E.] Wilson reserved that curiously and coldly apolitical attitude so common among business leaders and so baffling even to conservative politicians. On all domestic matters, social or economic, the orthodoxy of his nineteenth-century views placed him well to the political right of Robert Taft and shoulder-to-

shoulder with William Knowland. But the senator from California would have been aghast to hear Wilson, addressing himself to problems of a Korean truce, blurt out to the cabinet one day: "Is there any possibility for a package deal? Maybe we could recognize Red China and get the Far East issues settled."[22]

This illustration cuts both ways, of course. Hughes meant it as an example of the foolishness of much that is said in cabinet meetings; but two decades later one cannot be so certain. It may have been one of the more sensible remarks made in an Eisenhower cabinet meeting—the sort of eccentricity that ought to be cultivated among advisers.

Eisenhower's cabinet, it should be noted, was atypical in a number of respects: It met regularly throughout his two terms, it had formal agenda and well-rehearsed briefings on departmental programs, and it was used by the president as a kind of pep rally with short talks on budget-balancing and other favorite themes. As a result, although there was not much debate, the members were reasonably well informed of one another's programs and of the president's views on a range of issues.

In any cabinet setting, full and candid discussion of departmental affairs for the benefit of the president is inhibited by the reluctance of members to air departmental problems before colleagues who are in competition for the president's favor. As one of Franklin Roosevelt's cabinet members said, it was better to be discreet in the formal session and to stay after for a private prayer meeting with the president on important items.[23]

Nothing has hurt the development of the cabinet as an advisory body more than leaks, however. Woodrow Wilson's experience and his disenchantment are typical. For most of his first year in office, he met with it twice a week, seeking what he called "common counsel"—debate and discussion, no voting, and at the end a sense of the meeting in the Quaker tradition. It worked well, until the president learned that his talkative secretary of the interior, Franklin K. Lane, was passing bits of the proceedings on to members of the press. The meetings were reduced to one a week, and from then on Wilson avoided the discussion of anything, particularly in foreign affairs, on which public disclosure could not be risked. However entertaining they were, the meetings were not a place for give-and-take on significant issues for the rest of his administration.[24]

Franklin Roosevelt's experience was very much the same. He too had leaks—for which, again, the secretary of the interior was thought to be responsible—and shortly eliminated the extra weekly session. The meetings were Wilsonian meanders through matters of minor importance or great generality. The only difference was that Roosevelt has more fun than Wilson. Truman remarked, "I believe Roosevelt took a great deal of pleasure in getting one member of the Cabinet to argue against another and in then hearing what they had to say. I watched him do it. He would beam when Ickes jumped on Hopkins, or Hopkins on Ickes. He sometimes seemed amused when Morgenthau raised mischief with the Secretary of State on how he was handling things. Roosevelt often made a game of it."[25]

In Britain, where the cabinet is directly and regularly involved in the making of government policy on all matters, it is a convention of the constitution that cabinet deliberations shall be kept secret, and that even the machinery of decision making itself shall be largely unknown to outsiders. Once a decision has been reached, it is supported by the members whether they favored or opposed it during cabinet debate: Anyone who cannot go along is expected to resign.[26] The public and the opposition party, as a result, cannot attack the final policy with information about the arguments pro and con or the compromises that went into it. It is a tidy system, much admired by Americans who have been troubled by leaks or open disputes in the cabinet. But it would be unlikely to work in the United States, where incentives are different. In Britain, party leaders control the government and the political careers of everyone in it: One who wants to stay in politics obeys the rules. In the United States, where there are many bases of political power and advancement—state and federal, and legislative and executive, to begin with—cabinet members who express independent views are not necessarily through in politics. And many others are not professional politicians, as they are in Britain, and may not be disturbed by the prospect of a quick return to their regular work.

The disabilities of the American cabinet are as much the result of a pluralistic political system as of specific errors of management by presidents. There is not much a president can do to turn the cabinet into a safe and effective advisory institution. That does not mean that the cabinet is useless, however. There are likely to be some members of any cabinet who can do for the president what the full cabinet cannot. Even in Britain, where the full cabinet has constitutional status, subgroups have been put into play for convenience and for confidentiality. The British cabinet has grown unwieldy in recent decades, fluctuating at times up to twice the size of the American. It is understandable, therefore, that subject matter committees should have been appointed to make recommendations to the cabinet as a whole. Further, an informal inner cabinet of key members has been convened to do preliminary work on items of great sensitivity and to report to the cabinet—some say to present it with *faits accomplis*. Two matters known to have been treated this way were the decisions to manufacture atomic bombs and to join Israel and France in an invasion of the Suez Canal area.[27]

There is an inner cabinet in the United States that is comparable except that it reports to the chief executive rather than to the full cabinet. It consists typically of the four original department heads: the secretaries of state, war (now defense), and the treasury, and the attorney general— whom George Washington brought together as the first cabinet. Thomas E. Cronin has described the role of these cabinet members as presidential counseling and strategic information gathering in addition to departmental management. The rest constitute the outer cabinet—although the wavering fortunes of HEW suggest the line between inner and outer is not fixed—and they, also in addition to departmental duties, or more in extension of those duties, perhaps, act mainly as advocates before the president. The outer cabinet member takes a departmental view of things; the inner member more easily adopts a presidential view. From his interviews with White House staff members, Cronin found a considerably higher level of trust of the inner cabinet than of the outer—the inner members were regarded as allies (though in the case of the State Department the trust did not extend beyond the Office of the Secretary), and, accordingly, the White House staff was more deferential to them than to the others.[28]

While inner cabinet secretaries, like others, normally enter public service from successful careers in business or the professions, they are much more likely to have had significant government experience in one or more of the inner cabinet departments and perhaps in the outer departments on the way up. And they, unlike outer cabinet members, may also have served in the White House at one time. They are often members of the group known as "in-and-outers," who can be called upon to take subcabinet and cabinet positions in one administration after another and perform departmental roles without adopting a narrow departmental perspective. They are also strong-minded people, on the whole, who can stand up to presidents when occasion requires. Elliot Richardson served at one time or another as law clerk to Associate Justice Felix Frankfurter, assistant to Senator Leverett Saltonstall, assistant secretary of HEW, special assistant to the attorney general of the United States, lieutenant governor and attorney general of Massachusetts, under secretary of state, secretary of HEW, secretary of defense, attorney general, and ambassador to Britain. James R. Schlesinger was director of strategic studies at the RAND Corporation, assistant director of the Bureau of the Budget and the Office of Management and Budget, chairman of the Atomic Energy Commission, director of central intelligence, secretary of defense, and then, with a change in administration from Republican to Democratic, assistant to the president and secretary of energy. Clark Clifford, who came to the White House in 1946 as a naval aide, proved so useful to President Truman that he was kept on as a presidential assistant and became an architect of cold war policy, then a prominent Washington attorney, served as adviser to Presidents Kennedy and Johnson, was appointed secretary of defense in 1968, and probably would have been secretary of state had Hubert Humphrey rather than Richard Nixon won the presidential election later that year.

The National Security Council (NSC), created in 1947, is meant to be an inner cabinet. Its statutory function is "to advise the President with respect to the integration of domestic, foreign, and military policies relating to the national security so as to enable the military services and other departments to cooperate more effectively in matters involving the national security."[29] Consisting of the president, the vice president, and the secretaries of state and defense, it has provided an official forum for consideration of military and foreign affairs and a formal reason, in addition to all the practical ones, for not bringing such matters before the full cabinet.

Early in his administration, President Nixon created a domestic counterpart of the NSC, the Domestic Council, which included all cabinet members except the secretaries of state and defense. But this experiment in dividing the cabinet in two, in effect, did not work to the president's satisfaction. In his State of the Union message of 1971, he proposed that Congress give him a reorganized cabinet, leaving only the inner cabinet intact:

> I propose . . . that we reduce the present twelve cabinet departments to eight.
>
> I propose that the Departments of State, Treasury, Defense and Justice remain, but that all the other departments be consolidated into four: Human Resources, Community Development, Natural Resources, and Economic Development.
>
> Let us look at what these would be:
>
> —First, a department dealing with the concerns of people—as individuals, as members of a family—a department focused on human needs.
>
> —Second, a department concerned with the community—rural communities and urban—and with all that it takes to make a community function as a community.
>
> —Third, a department concerned with our physical environment, and with the preservation and balanced use of those great natural resources on which our nation depends.
>
> —And fourth, a department concerned with our prosperity—with our jobs, our businesses, and those many activities that keep our economy running smoothly and well.

Under this plan, rather than dividing up our departments by narrow subjects, we would organize them around the great purposes of government. Rather than scattering responsibility by adding new levels of bureaucracy, we would focus and concentrate the responsibility for getting problems solved.[30]

Congress refused to enact the reorganization. In 1973, buoyed by a landslide reelection, President Nixon accomplished much the same thing in the form of a White House reorganization, over complaints that he lacked authority to do so without the consent of Congress.

The reorganization created a supercabinet by giving four cabinet secretaries dual appointments as counselors in the White House, each to oversee a number of departments and agencies in addition to their own. Secretary of the Treasury George P. Shultz was put in charge of economic affairs, Secretary of Agriculture Earl L. Butz of natural resources, HEW Secretary Caspar W. Weinberger of human resources, and Secretary of Housing and Urban Development James T. Lynn of community development. Together with Henry Kissinger, who was not yet secretary of state but was managing foreign affairs from the White House, they would be a small and loyal group through which the president hoped once for all to gain control of the executive branch. Winston Churchill had experimented briefly with supersecretaries whom he called "overlords." Richard Nixon's experiment was short-lived, too. Watergate began to unfold, and the president, realizing the imprudence of insisting upon a reorganization that was viewed as illegal, demeaning to the departments, and an insult to Congress, let the plan die. But this inner cabinet could at least in normal times have been largely instituted as others have in the past—which is to say informally, without congressional consent.

Leaving the Cabinet

On October 20, 1973, President Nixon ordered Attorney General Elliot Richardson to remove Special Prosecutor Archibald Cox, who had been appointed earlier in the year to investigate Watergate. Richardson refused, and resigned instead. The number-two man in the department, Deputy Attorney General William D. Ruckelshaus, was then ordered to perform the removal, and he too resigned rather than comply. Finally the solicitor general, the next in line of authority, carried out the president's order. Cox, Richardson, and Ruckelshaus made restrained but pointed public statements as they left office. It was the most spectacular confrontation of a president and a cabinet member in memory. What is more, the resignations had a powerful impact on public opinion, so that while the immediate effect was the removal of those who would not do the president's bidding, he was soon forced by public opinion to capitulate on the underlying issue of the release of evidence to the Watergate prosecutors.

The terms of Cox's appointment were clear: He was to have full authority to contest any assertions of executive privilege, and the attorney general was not to interfere with his decisions or actions and was not to remove him except for "extraordinary improprieties." Neither Cox nor Richardson, who appointed him, was willing to hold office without a strict guarantee of independence for the special prosecutor. With that guarantee, Cox went to work obtaining evidence that proved increasingly embarrassing to President Nixon. One batch of evidence the special prosecutor wanted was nine White House tapes (not the ones later to be the subject of a Supreme Court case and to reveal the details of criminal activity by the president himself) which the president refused to give up, even under the order of a federal appellate court. Not only that, the president ordered Cox to make "no further attempt . . . to subpoena still more tapes or other presidential papers of a similar nature." On Saturday, October 20, Cox held a press conference to say that he was "certainly not out to get the President of the United States," but that he felt obliged to go back to court to bring to its attention "what seems to me to be noncompliance."[31]

Then followed the resignations of Richardson and Ruckelshaus and the removal of Cox—the "Saturday Night Massacre." In a news conference after his resignation, Richardson said,

> The president . . . thought he had no choice but to direct the attorney general to discharge Mr. Cox. And I, given my role in guaranteeing the independence of the special prosecutor, as well as my belief in the public interests embodied in that role, felt equally clear that I could not discharge him. And so I resigned.
>
> At stake in the final analysis is the very integrity of the governmental processes I came to the Department of Justice to help restore. My own single most important commitment to this objective was . . . to the independence of the special prosecutor. I could not be faithful to this commitment and also acquiesce in the curtailment of his authority. . . .
>
> The rest is for the American people to judge. On the fairness with which you do so may well rest the future well-being and security of our beloved country.[32]

Said Cox, "Whether we shall continue to be a government of laws and not of men is now for Congress and ultimately the American people to decide."[33]

Public reaction was swift and deadly. Letters and telegrams poured in to Congress and the White House demanding the impeachment or the resignation of the president. The president and his staff had hoped the country would accept its claim that the removal of Cox was in the public interest. The "firestorm" of outrage and the president's falling popularity in public opinion polls made it clear that the people knew what was really going on. Cox had been fired because he was getting close to the truth. On October 23, the president's lawyer went to court and, referring to "the events of the weekend," announced that the president would comply with the order to deliver the tapes. The president had lost.

The resignations of Richardson and Ruckelshaus will be important in our history for exposing impropriety in the White House and rallying the public to veto a presidential decision. But they are very much the exception to the rule. Resignation from the cabinet and other responsible positions to protest and perhaps to reverse government policy happens too rarely to be considered one of the tools of American politics. The circumstances of the Cox firing were exceptional too, of course: a president hiding evidence of criminal activity.

In their book, *Resignation in Protest*, Edward Weisband and Thomas M. Franck demonstrate that in the United States public officials who have serious disagreements with their superiors on questions of policy tend not to resign and, if they do resign, do so politely and quietly, citing family reasons or ill health as the reason. Apart from the case of Richardson and Ruckelshaus, there has been only one rousing resignation in protest in this century that made a president reverse a decision. Secretary of the Interior Harold Ickes opposed Harry Truman's nomination of oilman Edwin W. Pauley to be under secretary of the navy, and likely secretary of the navy thereafter, on the ground that the national interest in the tidelands and other oil reserves would be jeopardized. The seventy-one-year-old Ickes resigned, held a press conference, and stirred up enough opposition to Pauley that the president was obliged to withdraw the nomination.[34]

Another public feud in the Nixon administration had more to do with the president's neglect of his cabinet than with policy. In 1970 Secretary of the Interior Walter J. Hickel, angry that he had seen the president alone only twice since his appointment sixteen months before and upset over the war in Vietnam, the recent invasion of Cambodia, and the president's loss of contact with advisers and with the public— particularly the young—wrote a long letter to the president which bluntly called for "enlightened" new approaches to solving problems, paying attention to young people ("We are in error if we set out consciously to alienate those who could be our friends"), calling off Agnew, who had been baiting them, and "Finally, Mr. President, permit me to suggest that you consider meeting, on an individual and conversational basis, with members of your Cabinet. Perhaps through such conversations, we can gain greater insight into the problems confronting us all, and most important, into solutions of these problems."[35] It was in effect a letter of resignation, and was made public. The president kept him on until after the November election, shunning him and his advice equally, and then fired him. (Whether a person resigns or is fired is sometimes a matter of timing. President Nixon tried to fire Acting Attorney General Ruckelshaus, too, and thought he had, but Ruckelshaus had beaten him to the draw with a letter of resignation. One is reminded of Harry Truman and Douglas MacArthur: "General Bradley came over to Blair House and . . . says if MacArthur hears he's going to be fired before he officially is fired, before he's notified, he'd probably up and resign on me. And I told Bradley, I says, 'The son of a bitch isn't going to resign on me. *I want him fired.*' "[36]

The more usual way of handling disagreement is exemplified by the behavior of Secretary of Defense Robert McNamara from 1966 to 1968. He was as responsible as anyone for the escalation of the war in Vietnam. But by 1966 he had second thoughts and in 1968 was in direct opposition to American policy. His objections to calls by the Joint Chiefs of Staff for more troops and more bombing in the north were overruled by the president. Still McNamara stayed on, managing the war and defending the president's war policy before Congress and the public. Ultimately he accepted the presidency of the World Bank and dropped from public notice, discreet to the end.[37]

Had he resigned in 1966 or 1967 and stated his concerns, he might have changed the course of the war. But he did not. "When I was at Ford," he once said, "if I didn't like a policy, I used to take it up with the chairman. If he ignored my criticism, I would take it to him again. Then, if that didn't help, and if it were something I felt strongly about, I might even go back a third time. But after that, I'd never raise that particular issue again. I'd just tend to my knitting." The reasons, according to Weisband and Franck, are a general aversion to tattling in our society and to breaches of confidence in the business and legal communities from which most high officials come. (Academics and professional politicians are considerably more willing to resign in protest.) Those who make their reasons known, with only one exception in the entire period studied, do not appear again in government positions at or above the level of the positions they have resigned.[38]

In Great Britain, resignation in protest is more common and more likely to be effective. More than half of those who resign speak out about their differences with the government. Foreign Secretary Anthony Eden and others resigned in 1938 in opposition to Prime Minister Neville

Chamberlain's policy of appeasement of the Axis powers, continued to speak out against the prime minister in Parliament, and in 1940, after helping to drive Chamberlain from office, joined Winston Churchill in forming a new government with a new war policy. The ritual to which most protesters adhere is to submit a letter of resignation with a statement of reasons to the prime minister, who makes it public along with his reply. A limited amount of confidential information may be revealed in support of one's resignation, with the prime minister's permission, which is readily obtained; and if he chooses to make a rebuttal, even more may then be revealed in response. Weisband and Franck's study shows that in Great Britain the political careers of those who resign in protest are no worse than the subsequent careers of those who resign quietly.[39]

Resignation in protest is a powerful form of dissent in any government. It is particularly so in Great Britain, where convention forbids open disagreement by those who remain in the cabinet but supports the right of dissent by one who resigns. In the United States, members of the cabinet are less careful to maintain a united front in public; but in the crucial cases in which disagreement has reached the breaking point there is almost always a conspiracy of silence that protects the careers of those involved and keeps the public in the dark.

Disagreement is institutionalized, even honored, in Congress and the judiciary. In the cabinet, however, it is viewed with disfavor, and when it occurs it is kept under wraps— except in the rare cases we have noted. No one argues that everything said in the cabinet and other presidential advisory bodies ought to become public information. Advisers should be able to offer the president a diversity of views without fear that their candor will be used against them or the administration. But that is not to say that all policy differences in cabinet meetings must be shrouded in secrecy either.[40]

THE WHITE HOUSE STAFF

Even if the cabinet were a sound and versatile instrument of government, presidents would need advice and assistance from other quarters. Views of all kinds—long-range, short-range, parochial, detached, inside, outside—are needed for informed decisions in the White House. But the recurrent inability of the cabinet to live up to expectations has given the search for people to help the president an urgency it would not otherwise have had. At one time or another, presidents have relied on cronies, members of the family, task forces of people from government and private life, friends in Congress, and others; but the main body of advisers and assistants in this century has been the White House staff.

These days if the cabinet lacks ability or discretion, the president can retreat immediately to a large, willing, and typically more loyal staff in the White House Office. There is no question of its usefulness. That is one side of the story. The other is that the White House staff has itself created new problems. It has contributed to the cabinet's low morale by sharing its power and prestige. It has sometimes insulated the president from the world and its problems with an artificially supportive and protective environment. And it has grown so large and assumed so many new tasks that more and more time and energy must now be spent on bureaucratic routines such as internal coordination and communication. Presidents experiment with improvements, it is true, but without learning a great deal from the errors of the past. And basic questions remain unanswered: Should its role be advisory only, or should it take on more and more operational responsibilities? Should the White House staff be structured, with vertical and horizontal divisions of labor, or be personal and informal?

Origin and Development

During his first term, Franklin Roosevelt prevailed on Congress to create a good number of agencies outside the major departments. Along with existing agencies, boards, and commissions, they created a monumental problem of coordination. By 1935, some of Roosevelt's advisers and the president himself recognized a need to simplify the organization of the executive branch and to strengthen the president's hand as manager. A Committee on Administrative Management was appointed, chaired by Louis Brownlow, which worked with the president and produced a set of recommendations in 1937. Roosevelt sent them to Congress with his support:

> The Committee has not spared me; they say, what has been common knowledge for 20 years, that the President cannot adequately handle his responsibilities; that he is overworked; that it is humanly impossible, under the system which we have, for him fully to carry out his constitutional duty as Chief Executive, because he is overwhelmed with minor details and needless contacts arising directly from the bad organization and equipment of the Government. I can testify to this. With my predecessors who have said the same thing over and over again, I plead guilty.[1]

The committee's report on the need for new assistants for the president reflected Roosevelt's preference for a personal staff outside the line of command—a narrow role rejected by some later presidents.

> The President needs help. His immediate staff assistance is entirely inadequate. He should be given a small number of executive assistants who would be his direct aides in dealing with the managerial agencies and administrative departments of the Government. These assistants, probably not exceeding six in number, would be in addition to his present secretaries, who deal with the public, with Congress, and with the press and the radio. These aides would have no power to make decisions or issue instructions in their own right. They would not be interposed between the President and the heads of his departments. They would not be assistant presidents in any sense. Their function would be, when any matter was presented to the President for action affecting any part of the administrative work of the Government, to assist him in obtaining quickly and

without delay all pertinent information possessed by any of the executive departments so as to guide him in making his responsible decisions; and then when decisions have been made, to assist him in seeing to it that every administrative department and agency affected is promptly informed. Their effectiveness in assisting the President will, we think, be directly proportional to their ability to discharge their functions with restraint. They would remain in the background, issue no orders, make no decisions, emit no public statements. Men for these positions should be carefully chosen by the President from within and without the Government. They should be men in whom the President has personal confidence and whose character and attitude is such that they would not attempt to exercise power in their own account. They should be possessed of high competence, great physical vigor, and a passion for anonymity.[2]

The committee recommended that they "be installed in the White House itself, directly accessible to the President."

Two years later Congress passed the Reorganization Act of 1939, which created six new presidential assistants. Instead of the consolidation of agencies requested, Congress gave the president limited authority, subject to legislative veto, to reorganize the executive branch. In his first reorganization shortly after, Roosevelt established the Executive Office of the President, which included the White House Office and the Bureau of the Budget. The latter had been in the Department of the Treasury and was to become a major instrument of presidential policy and administrative control, later under the name of the Office of Management and Budget.

The White House staff has since grown from a few dozen to several hundred. It has rivaled the cabinet in influence and under some presidents clearly surpassed the cabinet. It has not infrequently had young people in key positions and, except in the Eisenhower administration, a disproportionate number who have been with the new president on the way to the White House—thus the bands of New Yorkers, Missourians, Bostonians, Texans, Georgians, and others, one after another. It is a group that contrasts with the cabinet, whose members are older, established, and sometimes strangers to the president at the time of appointment. A president may hope for worldliness, managerial ability, and diversity among the members of his cabinet; at the top of his White House staff he is more likely to stress loyalty and trustworthiness.

Further generalization about the White House staff is difficult, however, except to say that it is an unusually compliant organization that reflects, even magnifies, the character and idiosyncracies of each new president. To understand the White House staff is to realize how differently it has served different presidents.

Franklin Roosevelt had a small staff in the White House, nine professionals and twenty-nine nonprofessionals by one count, in his first year in office. While the rest of the government grew under his leadership, the White House staff remained small, personal, and informal, at least until war came in 1941. Roosevelt's rule was that only important matters that could not better be handled in the departments should come before him and his staff. The members of the staff had easy access to the president; for example, during breakfast or the cocktail hour, when they might drift in to talk singly or in groups. It was Roosevelt's practice to give few fixed assignments, and even they, according to Richard Neustadt, "were sphere-of-action assignments, *not* programmatic ones."[3] This had three consequences:

1. The men on such assignments were compelled to be generalists, jacks-of-all-trades, with a perspective almost as unspecialized as the President's own, cutting across every program area, every government agency, and every facet of *his* work, personal, political, legislative, administrative, ceremonial.
2. Each assignment was distinct from others but bore a close relationship to others, since the assigned activities themselves were interlinked at many points. Naturally, the work of the Press Secretary and the Special Counsel overlapped, while both had reason for concern and for involvement, often enough, with the work of the Appointments Secretary—and so forth. These men knew what their jobs were but they could not do them without watching, checking, jostling one another. Roosevelt liked it so. (Indeed, he liked it almost too much; he positively encouraged them to jostle. He evidently got a kick out of bruised egos.)
3. Since each man was a "generalist" in program terms, he could be used for *ad hoc* special checks and inquiries depending on the President's needs of the moment. So far as their regular work allowed, the fixed assignment men were also general-utility trouble shooters. No one was supposed to be too specialized for that.[4]

In establishing the White House Office in 1939, the president noted that the staff would, as before, be "personal aides to the president and . . . have no authority over anyone in any department or agency." As the president's Committee on Administrative Management had specified, they "would not be assistant presidents in any sense," and would "issue no orders, make no decisions, emit no public statements."[5] What they did was political rather than administrative, and since for Roosevelt political influence rested on leadership of public opinion, much time was devoted to speechwriting and press relations.

Life in Roosevelt's White House Office was a volatile mixture of elation and frustration. His practice of assigning more than one person to a task was both useful and cruel. There was no doubt that the president enjoyed conflict among his advisers. There were a very few in his entourage who, serving a great and charming man, endured the moments of criticism and humiliation uncomplainingly and stayed with him to the end. Others who were less self-sacrificing or had ambitions of their own left sooner or later or were forced out. Roosevelt was not one for keeping a person on for sentimental reasons, one or two faithful retainers excepted. He ran through several sets of advisers in his dozen years in office. It was an exciting and disorderly environment for the president, shaped exactly to his needs.[6]

The White House staff was less important to Harry Truman than it had been to Roosevelt. Truman relied more on the cabinet. With some exceptions, such as Averell Harriman and Clark Clifford, the men Truman appointed to his staff were old friends, long on loyalty and short on ability and ethics. As I. F. Stone said, "The place was full of Wimpys who could be had for a hamburger." The peccadilloes of his staff tarnished Truman's image and in 1952 allowed the Republican party to characterize the Democrats as a party of corruption. In fact, unlike Roosevelt, Truman assigned responsibilities with some care in both the cabinet and the White House Office and kept the Missouri Gang out of important affairs. He would have been better off, however, to let an old friend go now and then, and like Roosevelt hire and fire primarily according to ability.[7]

Dwight Eisenhower's White House was formal and hierarchical, the very opposite of Franklin Roosevelt's. It was suited to a president with an orderly mind who wanted the staff to protect him from the hubbub of politics and the tiresome detail of administration. It had a division of labor rather than the roving and overlapping assignments characteristic of Roosevelt's staff, and one member of the staff managed the others. Eisenhower named Sherman Adams *the* assistant to the president, in the role of chief of staff to which the president had become accustomed in the military. (Harry Truman had originated the title, but had not meant it to signify preeminence over the rest of the staff.) Adams barred upstarts and senators, clerks and cabinet members from the Oval Office with equal rudeness and efficiency. No message of any kind went to the president without his approval. When he brought a problem to the president's attention, it was briefly stated and usually contained a recommended course of action. Adams did no more or less than what the president required: He ran a tight ship and screened out all but the few people and questions the president cared to face (and in so doing made it possible for the government to run without misstep each time the president was in the hospital with a serious illness).[8]

Franklin Roosevelt arranged his staff so that no one was in a position to obtain a monopoly of information on any subject and, therefore, to give advice without fear of contradiction. By gathering information from several sources, the president maintained his advantage over, and independence from, each member of his staff. It would have been unthinkable to put anyone in the position of dominating the entire staff. Eisenhower, who preferred peace and quiet to uproar, and solutions to problems, put Adams squarely in that position. Because of the force of his personality, however, Eisenhower was never in danger of being exploited by Adams. Quite the reverse: Adams drew much of the fire for what went wrong, and the president was happy to let him.

John Kennedy's White House resembled Franklin Roosevelt's—there were similarities in their personality and style and in addition a conscious effort by Kennedy and his advisers to do things Roosevelt's way. He did not rely much on the cabinet. ("Cabinet meetings are simply useless. Why should the Postmaster General sit there and listen to a discussion of the problems of Laos?") Increasingly he turned to members of the staff for action and advice; they were allowed to see the president when they wanted. Like Roosevelt, Kennedy was contemptuous of formal organization. He preferred rough-and-tumble. An important difference, however, was that he was a kinder, less manipulative man than Roosevelt. There was some of the mutual loyalty between president and staff that one found in Harry Truman's White House, and as a result less turnover than in Roosevelt's, even making allowance for the very different lengths of time Roosevelt and Kennedy served.[9] Theodore Sorenson, who came closer than anyone to being Kennedy's principal assistant, summed up the contrast between his White House and his predecessor's: "A reporter compared the Eisenhower-Kennedy methods of obtaining teamwork with the difference between football and basketball. The Eisenhower football method relied on regular huddles and rigid assignments. In the Kennedy administration all team members were constantly on the move."[10] Kennedy never had formal staff meetings. He dealt with staff members informally, separately or in clusters, according to need. He swept away the secretariats, coordinating committees, and formal agenda that had accumulated in the Eisenhower years.

Lyndon Johnson's White House was a less congenial place. It too was Rooseveltian in some respects: chaos, duplication, competitive administration, an absence of fixed assignments, no chief assistant. Eric Goldman, a Princeton professor of history who spent some time on Johnson's staff, witnessed "some of the most monumental confusion in all the not-too-tidy administrative history of the White House."

One sparkling winter morning I received three red-tagged "Rush" memos in my inter-office mail. The first two discussed a particular anti-poverty project and based their main points on two lengthy office conferences which had been held the day before, with no knowledge on the part of either group that the other one was meeting. The third concerned a different matter but, in a casual aside, mentioned that the anti-poverty project had been vetoed three days before.[11]

But Johnson's personality and psychic needs were different from Roosevelt's: He had an insatiable appetite for adulation and kept flatterers around to remind him of his greatness. One of the best, Jack Valenti, gave a memorable public speech about the president:

He is a sensitive man, a cultivated man, a warmhearted and extraordinary man. . . . The full spirit of the man never seems to be captured. . . . All around him everyone was in various states of shock, nearing collapse [after the assassination]. But the new President sat there, like a large gray stone mountain, untouched by fear or frenzy, from whom everyone began to draw strength. . . .

He began to give orders in clear, audible tones, yet the voice was soft, the words unhurried. And suddenly, as though the darkness of the cave confided its fears to the trail of light growing larger as it banished the night, the nation's breath, held tightly in its breast, began to ease and across the land the people began to move again. . . .

I sleep each night a little better, a little more confidently, because Lyndon Johnson is my President. For I know he lives and thinks and works to make sure that for all America and, indeed, the growing body of the free world, the morning shall always come.[12]

Johnson also had strong-willed and able people on his staff, such as Joseph Califano, later a member of the Carter cabinet, and Bill Moyers, who went on to be a newspaperman and broadcaster. But the effective people had to be unassuming or they aroused the president's jealousy and, like Moyers, were forced out. Life in the Johnson White House was best put in words by Eric Goldman:

President Johnson's attitude toward his staff was essentially feudal. He was the head of the duchy with all rights thereto appertaining. When he did not like the length of a Special Assistant's hair, he told him to go to a barbershop; he ordered a secretary to enroll in a charm school. He expected aides to be available at any time for any function. They were as likely to be asked to phone the tailor ("These damn pants hitch up too much") as to confer with an ambassador. . . .

The President could berate his aides in lashing language. Sometimes he did this collectively, as when he exploded at three of them in his office,

"How can you be so goddamn stupid! Why can't I get men with the brains of the Kennedy bunch?" More often, he would turn on a single staff member. On a number of occasions I saw an aide emerge from a presidential session white-faced and shaking, swearing that he could not stand it another day.

All effective Presidents have used a carrot-and-stick technique with their staff in order to keep the men on their toes and in their place. President Johnson carried the tactic to his own extreme. He would heap praise on a particular aide for a period, much to the discomfiture of the others, then suddenly shift his attitude, giving the man no assignments, rejecting his suggestions *in toto*, scarcely speaking to him. Just as suddenly, the assistant would be lifted from hell and transformed into an angel once again.[13]

Both to satisfy his own intense curiosity about everything that was going on in the White House and the bureaucracy and to keep after his burgeoning Great Society programs, Johnson and his staff gave more and more attention to management and implementation. He was forever looking over subordinates' shoulders, figuratively and literally. Later he did the same to the military fighting his war in Vietnam.

After some experimentation, the Nixon White House came to resemble that of Eisenhower more than any other, at least in one important respect: hierarchy. As Richard Nathan has shown, President Nixon tried a number of ways of controlling the executive branch. At first, he stressed the importance of strong and independent cabinet members. A year later, unlike Eisenhower less than pleased with the results of this experiment, he began to build the White House staff into what Nathan calls a "counterbureaucracy," recovering some of the authority that had been delegated to the cabinet, isolating the president from its members, requiring them to clear statements with the White House, and bypassing them in dealing with the departments.[14]

The next phase, in 1973, however, was to farm out young Nixon loyalists from the White House to subcabinet positions in the departments and to rely more on them than on either the cabinet or the White House Office. This move was abruptly overcome by Watergate and the resignations of H. R. Haldeman and John Ehrlichman.

The White House counterbureaucracy, while it lasted, was the most determined attempt ever made to control the executive branch from the center. Agencies were subordinated to layers of authority in the White House, and at the top of the now vast hierarchy, guarding the president, was H. R. Haldeman, less canny than Sherman Adams but every bit as rude and imposing. The demeanor of the staff and the preponderance of Germanic names (Haldeman, Ehrlichman, Ziegler, Klein, Kissinger, Schultz, etc.) suggested such unflattering imagery as the "Berlin Wall" and the "Fourth Reich." But for all its toughness, the counterbureaucracy was not effective. It brought to mind the truism that one cannot cure the ills of bureaucracy with more bureaucracy. The counterbureaucracy is better understood as an extension of Nixon's traits of loneliness and suspicion and his need for perfect control, of himself and others, than as a valid attempt to manage the executive branch.

Since then there have been no new experiments. Gerald Ford, an open and gregarious man, eliminated much of the Nixon superstructure and returned the White House Office to the ease and informality of the Kennedy era. One long-time White House staff member thought it was "a little like the slaves after the Civil War. They don't know yet what to do with their freedom and they're going this way and that."[15] (Russell Baker of the *New York Times* noted that Ford had cats, unlike most modern presidents, who have had dogs. Cats are self-possessed, contemptuous of humans, studiously ungrateful, and—speculated Baker—more likely than a dog to give a president a realistic and balanced view of life. Dogs are invariably grateful and agreeable: They sit and smile and praise their masters for everything they do, right or wrong. They are, on the whole, a bad influence. If Baker is correct, and there is no reason to believe he is, cat people should be expected to have advisers who are capable of independent thinking, and dog owners to have advisers who smile and wag their tails.[16]

Jimmy Carter tried to take hold of the executive branch and bring it under control in the spring of 1978 when his standing in the polls was at its lowest and his ability as a leader was in doubt. After a year of reliance on the cabinet, he had come to the conclusion Richard Nixon had reached eight years before, that stronger control of the bureaucracy by the White House staff was required. Department heads were told that henceforth the president's policies would take precedence over theirs, that speeches and congressional testimony were to be cleared with the White House, and that lesser political appointments in their departments would be under White House control. Cabinet members' aides were required to meet regularly with White House personnel to report and to be briefed—a replay of Nixon's counterbureaucracy.[17] Then in 1979 he fired nearly half the cabinet at one blow and elevated presidential assistant Hamilton Jordan to the Haldeman-like position of chief of staff.

Problems

One of the sourest and most influential books on presidents and the people around them is *The Twilight of the Presidency* by George Reedy, who served for a time as press secretary to Lyndon Johnson. Its argument is that the White House has become an institution that corrupts presidents and their assistants and cuts them off from the world. People who become president, prudent as they may have been in the past, come to share the awe that the public has for those who follow in the footsteps of Jefferson, Jackson, and Lincoln, says Reedy, and in the process lose their grasp on reality. Presidential assistants, for their part, often fawn and flatter their way into favor and reinforce presidential misperceptions. No one on the inside, alas, ever tells a president to go climb a tree. (There was one trusted aide in Franklin Roosevelt's White House, Louis H. Howe, who was reputed to have the spirit and the leave to tell the president to go to hell. But he died in 1936, and then there was no one.) Even senators, who assert their independence on the Hill, are reverent and deferential when they meet a president on his home ground. [18]

For White House staff—the king's courtiers—"there is only one fixed goal in life," according to Reedy:

> It is somehow to gain and maintain access to the president. This is a process which resembles nothing else known in the world except possibly the Japanese game of *go*, a contest in which there are very few fixed rules and the playing consists of laying down alternating counters in patterns that permit flexibility but seek to deny that flexibility to the opponent. The success of the player depends upon the whim of the president. Consequently, the president's psychology is studied minutely, and a working day in the White House is marked by innumerable probes to determine which routes to the Oval Room are open and which end in a blind alley.
>
> The techniques are astonishingly simple and require not subtlety but a willingness to test human credulity to its outermost limits. Basically, the methodology is to be present either personally or by a proxy piece of paper when "good news" arrives and to be certain that someone else is present when the news is bad. The battle-wise assistant develops to its highest degree the faculty of maintaining physical proximity coupled with the ability to disappear (by ducking down a hallway or stepping behind a post) at the right moments. The White House is architecturally well adapted to such tactics, since there are plenty of hallways and a plethora of concealing pillars. [19]

Doris Kearns, another who witnessed White House catering to presidential whims, has described the eagerness of Lyndon Johnson's staff to bring him reports on questions of state and, at his slightest wish, quantities of peanut brittle, shirts, felt-tipped pens, cottage cheese, even an automatic soft-drink dispenser—an endless variety of offerings for the purpose of staying in his good graces. [20]

The chief executive of any large organization has problems getting objective information from his subordinates, with a realistic balance of good news and bad. But in the White House straight talk is a rarity. Gerald Ford read *The Twilight of the Presidency* and recommended it to his staff.[21]

It may have been unfair for Reedy to have attempted generalizations from experience in Johnson's White House, for surely there has been less self-deception and deception by staff in some other administrations—Franklin Roosevelt's and Gerald Ford's, to mention two. And even in the Johnson White House there was some relief from consensus now and then. But although the problems Reedy describes may be less acute in some presidencies than in others, they seem nonetheless to be there.

Richard Nixon's White House presents many illustrations of the scramble for preferment described by Reedy, and of honest advice freely given, as well. The staff was a mixture of the civilized and the uncivilized. Each appealed to one side of the president's divided nature. There was one capable group of assistants, holding various staff and cabinet posts over the years, largely specialists, outspoken and loyal—Henry Kissinger in foreign affairs, the flamboyant Daniel Patrick Moynihan in urban affairs and the problems of welfare, George Schultz in economics, and others—who were intellectuals, well known before joining Nixon, and familiar with the workings of government. They had the self-possession to act simultaneously as professionals and as the president's loyal subordinates, two roles that often clash. They suppressed their distaste of the president's dark side and those who served it. They showed the president full deference—along with big doses of blarney in Moynihan's case ("I would like to speak first of the theme, 'Forward Together.' This appeal was very much in evidence in your very fine acceptance speech in Miami, and during the campaign the logic of events, and your own sure sense of them, brought it forward even more insistently.")[22] Of the three, Kissinger had the greatest administrative ability, and Moynihan the least. Kissinger was far more useful to the president, therefore. He drove his staff, presented well-researched policy options to the president, made his recommendations, and carried them out. He mastered theory and practice alike. Moynihan's role was more academic.[23]

Many of the rest of Nixon's advisers were involved in Watergate and went to prison for it. It is useful on several grounds to distinguish between H. R. Haldeman and John Ehrlichman, the principal members of the White House staff, and the others. Haldeman and Ehrlichman were old associates, intensely loyal to the president. Haldeman was a California advertising man who took up with Nixon in the campaign of 1956. Ehrlichman, a college friend of Haldeman who became a lawyer, specialized in zoning, and opened a practice in Seattle, joined Haldeman during the 1960 campaign. They had been close to Nixon since. And, as the tapes made clear, they were blunt and unaffected in their private exchanges with the president and, on Watergate matters at least, curiously egalitarian—Haldeman seemed to overrule the president as much as the president overruled Haldeman. These men were not the flatterers Reedy described. They gave their advice straight and hard.

Yet Haldeman and Ehrlichman failed the president (and he them). Perhaps it was because they had so little of substance to offer. They had no governmental experience before coming to the White House, no interest in policy except in the pursuit of power and prestige, and were fairly well limited to wondering about the public relations value of anything that came before the president—"Will it play in Peoria?" was Ehrlichman's recurrent question. "They were efficient only at the things that didn't *matter*, like motorcade organizing and memo routing. But their memos, like most of their minds, had no *content*. Essentially, they were a bunch of advance men, and when the confetti had been thrown and the parade was over, they really didn't seriously know what to do," said one newsman of Haldeman, Ehrlichman, and the others. There was no problem of communication. There just was nothing of consequence to say.[24]

The remainder were courtiers in Reedy's sense, the lesser figures on the staff, good-looking, cheerful young men—none of the severity of Haldeman and Ehrlichman—bowing, scraping, and happily doing whatever they were told. There was John Dean, the lawyer with the fine memory who helped cover up Watergate and later recounted it in detail to a Senate investigating committee; Dwight Chapin, a puppy of the sort Russell Baker must have had in mind, responding to a colleague who mentioned consumerism as a profitable issue: "By God, that's absolutely right. . . . I've been saying that for over a year now. People don't know where we stand on the Nader business. We need a stronger posture—be for it or against it, I don't care which, but one or the other!"[25] There was Egil Krogh, director of the Plumbers, a counterespionage unit in the White House, contrite after pleading guilty to burglarizing the office of Daniel Ellsberg's psychiatrist for information on the Pentagon Papers leak and on Ellsberg himself:

> While I early concluded that the operation had been a mistake, it is only recently that I have come to regard it as unlawful. I see now that the key is the effect that the term "national security" had on my judgment. The very words served to block critical analysis. It seemed at least presumptuous if not unpatriotic to inquire into what the significance of national security was.[26]

There was Charles Colson the dirty tricks man, always in perfect submission to authority, first military, then presidential, and then religious. And others. They were willing to do what most bureaucrats were not, and, as he became more and more desperate, Nixon relied increasingly on them.

Lyndon Johnson and Richard Nixon were opposites in one respect: Johnson needed people around him—even when he went to the bathroom, it is said—while Nixon avoided the company of others, shut in the Oval Office or hidden away in his retreat in the Executive Office Building. Johnson often used his staff as a cheering squad; Nixon more typically used his to take care of things out of his sight and to protect him from contact with outsiders. Despite the differences, the two presidents ended in the same predicament, insulated from reality, suspicious of all who disagreed with them, clinging to unworkable strategies to the bitter end. James David Barber may well be correct that the main reason in each case was a compulsive, active-negative personality. But it is interesting that, instead of serving as counterweights, their staffs only reinforced the presidents' personal limitations and made it possible for them to maintain unrealistic views of Vietnam, Watergate, dissent, civil disturbance, and more broadly, the ways of democracy.

There is another deficiency in the White House advisory system—of the staff and members of the cabinet and subcabinet in varying combinations—that has nothing to do with whether the president is an active-negative or not. It is a phenomenon much better understood now than a few years ago. It is simply that in time of crisis, the president's advisers, like any other group of people, may rush impulsively and self-righteously toward an inhumane decision. George Homans put the underlying problem in the form of a hypothesis in 1950: "A decrease in the frequency of interaction between the members of a group and outsiders, accompanied by an increase in the strength of their negative sentiments toward outsiders, will increase the frequency of interaction and the strength of positive sentiments among the members of the group, and vice versa."[27]

Some evidence of the importance of the small group theory of Homans and others to an understanding of the relation of a president and his advisers was presented in *The Korean Decision* by Glenn Paige in 1968. It was not a study of the White House staff, because in crisis President Truman preferred to rely on cabinet and subcabinet officers, though not the full cabinet; nor, as Paige is careful to note, does one case study prove a theory. But it was important in developing hypotheses applicable to other crisis decisions which have often involved interactions of presidents and their staffs. Paige traced the daily decisions made by the president in company with various groups of advisers; the pressures from outside, which reinforced each enlargement of American commitments; and the information available and the use that was made of it.

He found among other things that in the week in mid-1950 in which the decision was made to intervene fully in Korea with ground troops ad hoc groups were convened, rather than the cabinet as such; the decision makers developed warm feelings toward each other and wanted to be with one another; both the president and his advisers felt it appropriate that the president play the part of a strong leader; there was a tendency toward selective recall of old intelligence themes (such as the adequacy of South Korean forces) even in the face of new information to the contrary; as the crisis wore on, more and more was felt to be at stake (from protection of Americans in Korea to protection of American interests in the Far East to containment of the Soviet Union and so on); as values proliferated, the decision makers became more and more willing to take risks; and the decision makers increasingly avoided contact with those who might disagree with them (Congress, for example).[28]

Later, with the help of the literature on small group dynamics and other studies of presidents and their advisers during the Pearl Harbor and Korean crises, the Bay of Pigs invasion, and the escalation of the war in Vietnam, Irving Janis described a more general set of characteristics, all dysfunctional, to which he gave the Orwellian name "groupthink." According to Janis, groupthink is a pernicious kind of conformity in decision-making groups, occurring most frequently in those that are cohesive, insulated from others who might contribute to its decision, and under the sway of a leader who promotes his own solution "even when the leader does not want the members to be yes-men and the individual members try to resist conforming"—all common enough in the White House.[29] It stems from esprit de corps, and is different from conformity induced by coercive leadership. Thus, groupthink is more likely to occur in the camaraderie of a Kennedy White House than under the whip of a Lyndon Johnson.

All of this is obvious enough. There must be few people indeed who have not been caught up in the warmth and elation of group decision making—the sense of shared purpose in politics, bureaucracy, business, sports, and other social settings. What Homans described as "negative sentiments toward outsiders" is less obvious. In the White House, the amiability of the group and its "exhilarating sense of omnipotence" is likely to lead to "irrational and dehumanizing actions directed against outgroups"—"solidarity against an evil enemy and complete unanimity about everything that needs to be done." Although the members of the group may be entirely humane as individuals, together they may arrive at unnecessarily inhumane judgments.[30] Janis describes the symptoms of groupthink:

1. An illusion of invulnerability, shared by most or all the members, which creates excessive optimism and encourages taking extreme risks.
2. Collective efforts to rationalize in order to discount warnings which might lead the members to reconsider their assumptions before they recommit themselves to their past policy decisions.

3. An unquestioned belief in the group's inherent morality, inclining the members to ignore the ethical or moral consequences of their decisions.
4. Stereotyped views of enemy leaders as too evil to warrant genuine attempts to negotiate, or as too weak and stupid to counter whatever risky attempts are made to defeat their purposes.
5. Direct pressure on any member who expresses strong arguments against any of the group's stereotypes, illusions, or commitments, making clear that this type of dissent is contrary to what is expected of all loyal members.
6. Self-censorship of deviations from the apparent group consensus, reflecting each member's inclination to minimize to himself the importance of his doubts and counterarguments.
7. A shared illusion of unanimity concerning judgments conforming to the majority view (partly resulting from self-censorship of deviations, augmented by the false assumption that silence means consent).
8. The emergence of self-appointed mindguards—members who protect the group from adverse information that might shatter their shared complacency about the effectiveness and morality of their decisions.[31]

His conclusion is that the more a group displays the symptoms of groupthink, the poorer its decisions will be.

Reedy and Janis are both concerned about irrationality in the presidential advisory system, but their focus is somewhat different. Reedy emphasizes the difficulty a president faces obtaining good information and advice from aides caught up in the petty business of competing for presidential favor. Janis is more concerned about periods of cooperativeness and high common purpose in the White House. Reedy describes daily routine, Janis the occasional historic decision. The two are in agreement that the White House, with and without presidential complicity, has ways of cutting itself off from valuable information on the outside.

Remedies

The White House Office has been useful to presidents, who have relied on it increasingly for both advice and management and, not surprisingly, promoted its growth from a personal staff into an impersonal bureaucracy. Criticisms of the staff have come largely from those who feel it has contributed to executive autocracy: members of Congress, the public, students of foreign and military policy-making procedures, and other outsiders. The White House Office has made it possible for presidents to control their immediate environment and sometimes overcontrol it by shutting out all discomforting points of view. If a president wants to surround himself with yes-men or hawks or old friends without experience in government, to take some modern examples, he is free to do so. He may in the process isolate himself from those who could help him be a good president.

A number of remedies have been suggested either to control the growth of the White House staff and its authority or to control the effects of its growth. Four deserve mention: limiting the size of the staff, requiring Senate confirmation of top White House Office appointments, institutionalizing dissent in the advisory system, and reallocating personnel and responsibilities between the White House Office and the cabinet.

Presidents usually promise to reduce the size and authority of the White House staff as they come into office. It goes along with the promise to improve the position of the cabinet. The longer they are in office, however, the more difficulty they have keeping either promise. The Ford and Carter administrations provide two good illustrations of the promise and the performance. Gerald Ford had good reason to cut the staff down to size. Richard Nixon's White House staff had been arrogant, power hungry, and to a considerable extent corrupt, and there was agreement that the time had come for pruning. Furthermore, Ford was a simpler and more direct person than most of his predecessors and seemed suited to a return to simpler, more direct forms of administration. In his confirmation hearings for vice president, he had favored a middle position between cabinet government and White House government, adding, "I do not think that the cabinet officers should be beholden to some person in the White House who is appointed by the president." In the first week of his administration, an aide announced, "We think the White House staff is too big, a ridiculous kind of structure with the Domestic Council and the OMB involved in policy and cabinet members being figureheads."[32]

But within a year Ford asked Congress for almost twice as many top-level staff positions as he had first had, increasing those in the $36,000 range or above from 54 to 95. The bill died in the Senate.[33]

President Carter called for a sharp reduction for roughly the same reasons. He was even more interested than Ford in symbols of the restoration of a simpler White House, and cutting the staff was in harmony with reducing limousine privileges and wearing jeans to the Oval Office. There was some chagrin, therefore, at the discovery that the White House staff had grown by 145 to a new high of 655 during the first month of his administration. Most of the increase could be explained by the need to answer the high volume of mail and telephone calls that greeted the new administration. Later in that year, however, the president announced that the number had been cut to 578, of which 461 were full time (although 485 were authorized), 17 part time, and 100 detailed;

and he proposed but never accomplished a reduction of full time staff to 340.[34]

Another remedy, sometimes suggested in the same breath, is to require Senate confirmation of key White House staff members. Because, in the words of the President's Committee on Administrative Management, they were to be people "in whom the president has personal confidence and whose character and attitude is such that they would not attempt to exercise power in their own account," accountability to the Senate had seemed inappropriate when the White House Office was created. They were "the president's men," as the director of the Bureau of the Budget was, even though from its creation until the creation of the Executive Office of the President in 1939 the bureau was in the Treasury Department. The principle of exempting the president's immediate assistants was reaffirmed by the first Hoover Commission in 1949.[35]

But during the Nixon administration, Congress began to have doubts. There were two reasons: the growth and abuse of power in the White House and the repeated refusal of members of the White House staff to answer congressional requests for information or to appear as witnesses before committees. Henry Kissinger was the worst offender, in congressional eyes. Long before his appointment as secretary of state late in 1973, he had become secretary of state de facto. William P. Rogers had the title, but Kissinger had the power. As a presidential assistant, Kissinger felt no obligation to respond to congressional queries. He was the president's man, and his information and advice did not need to be shared with Congress. But to members of Congress this meant they were denied access to the real secretary of state. Said Senator Fulbright, chairman of the Foreign Relations Committee,

> It is ironic that the president's top foreign policy adviser will answer questions from a Tass or AP correspondent but not those which trouble members of the Foreign Relations Committee. . . .
> Make no mistake about it, the handles of power are being centralized in the White House at a rapid pace. Our system of checks and balances is being fast eroded in the process and both Congress and the American people are the losers. . . .
> This is a subversion of our constitutional processes. . . . We must find—if we intend to keep some of the influence which the Constitution gives to this body—ways to bring Mr. Kissinger before the Senate.[36]

In making public statements, said Fulbright, "he is no longer an actual personal adviser of the president. He is, for all practical purposes, the Secretary of State." When he became secretary of state, he was willing to testify, although not about his discussions with the president, invoking a traditional distinction governing the testimony of cabinet officers.

In 1973, bills were introduced in Congress to require Senate confirmation of appointments to the positions of director and deputy director of the Office of Management and Budget (which had been taking on more and more operating responsibilities over the years, particularly in the reorganization in which it changed from BOB to OMB) and the three White House Office positions of executive director of the Domestic Council, executive director of the International Economic Policy Council, and executive secretary of the National Security Council. Speaking of the White House Office positions, which his bill covered, Senator Percy assured his colleagues that he did not propose disturbing the old Rooseveltian relationship of president and adviser:

> It is not intended to intervene between the president and his assistants. . . . Each of the three posts affected by the bill has an operating function created by law or reorganization plan. Each of these officials has an enormous impact on the lives of American citizens, on formation of policy, and the administration of the laws.
>
> I trust that all congressional committees would . . . recognize that the executive privilege to have a confidential relationship [between president and adviser] cannot and must not be invaded by Congress. But when the same person is in a dual capacity or responsibility, we cannot evade our responsibility by saying that such person's activities are totally exempt from congressional confirmation or oversight.[37]

Confirmation and oversight went together, in the senators' minds. Said Senator Roth, "Requiring senatorial confirmation of the nominations of these three important executive office officials would also help to guarantee their availability as witnesses before the committees of Congress."[38]

Senator Percy's bill passed the Senate, but not the House. The measure requiring confirmation of the two top officials of the Office of Management and Budget passed both houses but was vetoed by President Nixon. A similar act, which exempted incumbent OMB officials from the requirement of confirmation, was signed by the president in 1974. Other attempts have been made since to require confirmation of members of the White House Office, without success. They remain "the president's men."[39]

A third remedy, for the prevention of premature consensus either in time of crisis or in more routine affairs, is the institutionalization of dissent. Knowing the tendency of the White House advisory system to overwhelm those who disagree with a decision toward which the group appears to be converging, a president may take steps to protect dissenters and keep debate alive until the decision is made. Early in the Vietnam War, Under Secretary of State George W. Ball, an independent-minded liberal, foresaw with great clarity the futility of American involvement—

the escalation, the difficulty of withdrawal, and the cost. He stayed on, and year after year pressed his arguments before the president and the cabinet, who respected him as a person, tolerated his dissent, and were unmoved.[40] Alternatively, a member of the staff may assume the role of devil's advocate, representing but not necessarily believing in a major policy position that seems in danger of neglect in a policy debate. McGeorge Bundy was once described as the "guardian of options and protector of the president" in the Johnson White House for jumping in on the losing side of policy debates and marshalling facts that others had failed to put before the president.[41]

But there can be no assurance that a dissenter will be taken seriously, whether his dissent is voluntary or role playing. If he is known to be arguing for the sake of argument, he is particularly vulnerable; but even a sincere dissenter such as Ball may have little impact. In fact, any form of institutionalized dissent may only give a group a false sense of its fairmindedness and make it even more pig-headed than it would have been without dissent.

Alexander George has argued, further, that devil's advocacy is of uncertain utility because

> "Competence, information, and analytical resources bearing on the policy issue may be unequally distributed. . . . As a result, one policy option may be argued much more persuasively than another. And there is no assurance, of course, that the policy option which is *objectively* the best will be presented persuasively, for this requires that its advocate possess adequate competence, information, and analytical resources. Deprived of a persuasive presentation, that policy option may lose out to an inferior one that happens to have more effective sponsorship.

His remedy, "multiple advocacy," would require the president to see that "a range of interesting policy options on any given issue" was represented by advocates from the staff or other parts of the government who did have such resources, including "power, weight, and influence," and that enough time was set aside for a thorough debate. The system would not be ad hoc. There would be "presidential-level participation in organizational policy making in order to monitor and regulate the workings of multiple advocacy."[42]

Of all the modern presidents, only Franklin Roosevelt was at ease with dissenters. He did in his disordered way build dissent into the system with his penchant for competitive administration. It is harder to imagine other presidents putting up with multiple advocacy for long, particularly if it worked.

A final remedy must be mentioned, not because it is likely to be adopted but because it offers insight into the strengths and weaknesses of both the White House staff and the cabinet. Stephen Hess of the Brookings Institution suggests that White House and cabinet would both be better off if the people typically appointed to White House posts were in the cabinet and cabinet people in the White House.

> There is much to recommend having potential presidential aides step down, rather than up, to White House service. For example, Clarence Randall under Eisenhower and Peter Peterson under Nixon, both former chief executives of major corporations, had little incentive to limit their advice to what might comfort the president and were not overawed in his presence. Ironically, however, persons of substantial achievement, unless they are too old, are often made department secretaries rather than presidential assistants. The irony is twofold. The successful executive's experience may have limited applicability or may even prove counterproductive in running a department. (To paraphrase Charles Wilson: what works for General Motors will not necessarily work at the Department of Defense.) On the other hand, the energy-laden young White House aides may sometimes be exactly what is needed in the departments to make the lions of bureaucracy do the President's bidding. Stamina gives department executives an important advantage that presidential counselors do not need in the same abundance. Loyalty is necessary in political executives who head departments, where centrifugal forces work to pull an appointee away from the President; wisdom is the necessary quality at the White House, where counselors will be the last barrier between a President and a possibly ill-advised decision. Thus under the present system the President may have the wrong people in the wrong jobs at both ends, White House and departments.[43]

George Reedy said, "There should be a flat rule that no one be permitted to enter the gates of the White House until he is at least forty and has suffered major disappointments in life."[44]

In the 1930s, the White House staff was small, it reported directly to the president, and its members confined themselves largely to advising, speechwriting, and other services that, in the words of the President's Committee on Administrative Management, did not interpose them between the president and his department heads. In the decades since, the staff has become large and impersonal, and its members have often found themselves in the chain of command. Because of its size, the staff has left the intimacy of its early days far behind, to be sure, but in form and function it is still adaptable to each president's requirements. Under a Kennedy, it is fluid and informal. Under an Eisenhower, it is structured, with access to the president restricted to a favored few.

The reason it is large and powerful is, simply, that presidents one after another have been disappointed with the cabinet and the bureaucracy and have turned—not always wisely—to the White House staff for help. The staff has been loyal and responsive, on the whole—excessively so, at times. Whether Congress will respond with controls to inhibit the accumulation of power in the White House Office is hard to say. Even in the wake of Watergate, when the incentive to impose controls was greatest, Congress was reluctant to do so. The consensus seems to have been that presidents should have virtually a free hand in arranging their staff, despite the possibility of abuses.

THE CIVILIAN
BUREAUCRACY

It is understandable that presidents should want to control the federal bureaucracy, in order that their policies might be carried out in more or less the form intended. No president should be expected to allow bureaucrats, with their legendary powers of delay, obstruction, and obfuscation, to have the upper hand. Mastery of the bureaucracy is a challenge policy-minded presidents are unlikely to ignore.

But try as they may, presidents have only limited success as administrators. Normally they can overcome overt disloyalty, but to bring the bureaucracy into ready compliance with the president's views of the Constitution, the laws, and the public interest either by persuasion or by coercion is more difficult than it seems. There are ways of manipulating bureaucrats from above, as we shall see, but none of them works very well. Most presidents try gamely, then in time retreat to concentrate on other responsibilities.

The problems of control are similar with respect to civilian and military agencies, but the stakes are different. Responsiveness and co-ordination are more important in military than in domestic affairs. Less dissent and openness are expected than in civilian agencies. It is best, therefore, to examine the military separately.

In this chapter, we shall consider the questions why, how, and how well presidents have played the role of manager of the civilian agencies in the executive branch.

Why Presidents Want to
Manage the Bureaucracy

Traditionally, the two main reasons for asserting control of the bureaucracy have been to carry out policies and to hold down costs. One is positive, of special concern to activists; the other negative, more of interest to dedicated budget balancers. Most presidents maintain both interests to some degree.

Consider the case of President Nixon and public school desegregation. A year after taking office, Nixon announced a policy that reaffirmed the rightness of the original desegregation decision but that carefully limited the further movement of the government toward racial balance in the schools. He promised compliance with Supreme Court decisions but not with what he deemed excessively liberal lower court decisions. He was especially critical of busing.

> I am dedicated to continued progress toward a truly desegregated public school system. But, considering the always heavy demands for more school operating funds, I believe it is preferable, when we have to make the choice, to use limited financial resources for the improvement of education— for better teaching facilities, better methods, and advanced educational materials—and for upgrading of the disadvantaged areas in the community rather than buying buses, tires, and gasoline to transport young children miles away from their neighborhood schools. . . .
>
> In some communities, racially mixed schools have brought the community greater interracial harmony, in others they have heightened racial tension and exacerbated racial friction. Integration is no longer seen automatically and necessarily as an unmixed blessing for the Negro, Puerto Rican, or Mexican-American child. . . .
>
> The school . . . is a place not only of learning, but of living—where a child's friendships center, where he learns to measure himself against others, to share, to compete, to cooperate—and it is the one institution above all others with which the parent shares the child. . . .
>
> Whatever makes the schools more distant from the family undermines one of the important supports of learning. . . .
>
> The notion that an all-black or predominantly black school is automatically inferior to one which is all or predominantly white . . . inescapably carries racist overtones.

The president then went on to prescribe standards of enforcement for the Justice Department and HEW that amounted to a general slowdown of the federal desegregation effort. For example,

> In devising local complicance plans, primary weight should be given to the considered judgment of local school boards—provided they act in good faith and within constitutional limits.

The neighborhood school will be deemed the most appropriate base for such a system.

Transportation of pupils beyond normal geographic zones for the purpose of achieving racial balance will not be required. . . .

De facto racial separation, resulting genuinely from housing patterns, exists in the South as well as the North; in neither area should this condition by itself be cause for federal enforcement actions.[1]

Shortly afterward, the Nixon administration was rebuffed by the Supreme Court on the questions of the speed of desegregation and the appropriateness of busing as a means of integration, but in the long run the clear command of the executive branch had its way. President Nixon backed up his policies with the removal of recalcitrant officials, including the head of the Office of Civil Rights in HEW.

The reason the president went to such lengths to state his policy in detail and to direct compliance by the agencies concerned was that the issue was one in which he had a keen interest. Polls showed widespread opposition to federal desegregation policies. To strengthen his support in the country and to maintain a base in the South, he repudiated the outright integrationist policies of the liberal Democratic administrations of Kennedy and Johnson. There were few black votes to lose, since blacks had never supported him in any number. His explicit public command to his subordinates was designed to minimize resistance to a change in policy among federal bureaucrats in the Justice Department and HEW who were dedicated to the spirit of *Brown* v. *Board of Education* and would not easily be persuaded to alter course.

As for holding down costs, no president in our history had a greater interest in economy in government, and to that end no man looked more closely into departmental operations, than William Howard Taft. His department heads were instructed to send up budget requests "as low as possible consistent with imperative governmental necessity." President and cabinet went over the budget in fine detail to make cuts where they could. Proudly he told Congress of the money saved, of budgets "cut to the quick." He required the people in every agency to clear requests for money or legislation through the heads of their departments, in effect giving the latter an absolute veto over unnecessary items.[2]

In 1910, Taft appointed a Commission on Economy and Efficiency to explore these concerns further. Over the next two years, the commission made many recommendations for the improvement of departmental management. Its proposals for an executive budget were not approved by Congress at first, because the House of Representatives was not in the hands of the president's party. Indeed, Congress prohibited even the informal implementation of such a budget. But many of

Taft's ideas were embodied in the Budget and Accounting Act of 1921, after the Republicans had taken control, and became standard practice in government.[3]

But making sure that the laws are executed faithfully and economically is not the only reason presidents delve into agency affairs. There are others, some a reflection of the narrower interests of party or clique or of the president himself.

There is, for example, a limited amount of patronage to be dispensed in filling jobs at the subcabinet level—under secretaries and assistant secretaries of departments, their assistants, members of independent boards and commissions, and the like. About 2,000 positions in the executive branch may be filled by the president by political appointment, about half with Senate confirmation; another several thousand appointments, including many reserved for lawyers, are subject to presidential influence, although the number that may fairly be called patronage is a matter of debate.[4] The president appoints people to whom he has become indebted on the way to the White House and others who are party loyalists and come with good recommendations from party leaders whose favor he values. Similarly, a president will wish to reward and court racial, ethnic, occupational, and other segments of the population, and women, of late, with these appointments. President Ford hired more members of minorities than his predecessor, and President Carter far more than Ford. Until the proportions in high federal position mirror those of the general population, the pressures are likely to remain.[5]

Patronage is a fact of life in national politics, to which serious objection is raised only if it becomes too blatant. It includes more than jobs. Early in 1974 a congressional investigation uncovered the "responsiveness" program, a massive effort in the first term of the Nixon administration to rechannel federal grants, contracts, loans, and subsidies to people who would support the president's reelection and to solicit illegal campaign contributions from beneficiaries of federal programs and from federal employees. The program was conceived and managed by the White House under the supervision of H. R. Haldeman. It extended to the manipulation of criminal investigations and civil actions brought by the Justice Department and the Equal Employment Opportunity Commission. Presidents long have been willing to bend federal programs for partisan purposes. But in this, as in other aspects of the conduct of the Nixon administration, it was the single-mindedness with which the interests of the White House were pursued, to the exclusion of concern about faithful execution of the laws, that provided a break with the past.[6]

The Nixon administration also provides an unparalleled chronicle of abuses of federal agencies by a president, sometimes for personal gain, summarized in the first two articles of impeachment prepared by the Judiciary Committee of the House of Representatives in 1974. The Internal Revenue Service, for example, was called upon to provide adverse information about the president's political opponents and also to approve a faked tax return for the president himself. The Secret Service provided illicit forms of crowd control for the president, spied on Senator McGovern for the White House, and improperly approved the addition of valuable improvements to the president's estates in California and Florida in the name of national security. The FBI illegally tapped the phones of newsmen at White House request. (When he was asked about the use of agencies for warrantless surveillance and other activities contrary to federal law, the unrepentent former president argued, "Well, when the president does it, that means that it is not illegal." "By definition," added the interviewer. "Exactly, exactly," responded Nixon.)[7]

Still another reason why presidents wish to manage the bureaucracy is the sheer love of power. Presidents tend to be manipulative. Unmanipulative people usually do not reach the office unless, as in the case of Gerald Ford, it is by accident. Lyndon Johnson's power drive often took the form of overcontrol of subordinates, as much for his own gratification as to see that policy was carried out.

In sum, from the point of view of the public, not all presidential assertion of control is to be applauded. Some is useful, to be sure, in getting the work done. Some amounts to an obstruction of the legitimate business of government. And some is simply extraneous.

Whatever their intentions, to serve broad or parochial interests, presidents sooner or later are frustrated in their efforts to manage the bureaucracy. Franklin Roosevelt, a man who did not give up easily, once said,

> The Treasury is so large and far-flung and ingrained in its practices that I find it almost impossible to get the action and results I want—even with Henry [Morgenthau] there. But the Treasury is not to be compared with the State Department. You should go through the experience of trying to get any changes in the thinking, policy, and action of the career diplomats and then you'd know what a real problem was. But the Treasury and the State Department put together are nothing compared with the Na-a-vy. The admirals are really something to cope with—and I should know. To change anything in the Na-a-vy is like pounding a feather bed. You punch it with your right and you punch it with your left until you are finally exhausted, and then you find the damn bed just as it was before you started punching.[8]

It was the same a generation later. A White House aide complained,

> President Nixon doesn't run the bureaucracy; the civil service and the unions do. It took him 3 years to find out what was going on in the bureaucracy. And God forbid if any president is defeated after the first term, because the bureaucracy has another 3 years to play games with the next president.[9]

Thomas E. Cronin, interviewing a sample of people who had been on the White House staff between 1961 and 1970, found that conflict with the departments was the norm. Nearly two-thirds said they had experienced considerable difficulty in working with federal executive departments, and another 25 percent moderate difficulty. Among the reasons given, nearly half cited bureaucratic parochialism, weak and unimaginative agency leadership, and the capture of agency leaders by narrow special interests. Somewhat fewer mentioned red tape and inept staff work. Interestingly, these White House staffers were also willing to find fault with themselves. Some 51 percent cited White House staff insensitivity toward agency officials as a source of conflict and strain, 44 percent mentioned presidential and staff communication failures, and 37 percent usurpation of agency roles and excessive interference in agency affairs.[10] There is every reason to suppose that the criticisms of agency behavior would have been as severe had members of subsequent administrations been interviewed.

Are presidents wrong to expect to be managers? No, if their goal is to assert working control over a limited number of programs in which they have a strong interest. Yes, if it is to command the willing obedience of the bureaucracy at large. As Harry Truman said of his successor, Dwight Eisenhower, "He'll sit here and he'll say 'Do this! Do that!' *And nothing will happen.* Poor Ike—it won't be a bit like the Army. He'll find it very frustrating."[11]

But few presidents have the managerial experience to make realistic assessments of what can and cannot be done in the Oval Office. Effective administration is as complex, subtle, and taxing a trade as, say, legislative leadership. One would not expect a freshman legislator to be an effective majority leader; one should not expect a president to be a born manager. Many presidents have had no real managerial background. Franklin Roosevelt came fully prepared to office: assistant secretary of the navy, to acquaint him with high-level federal administration, and governor of New York, to train him in the role of chief executive in the largest public bureaucracy short of the federal government. But compare his successors: Jimmy Carter had experience as a chief executive, though, to be sure, of a much smaller state than New York and unsupplemented by any federal experience (aside from being a relatively junior naval officer, which hardly counts). Harry Truman, Lyndon Johnson, and Richard Nixon served in the executive branch only as vice presidents, which is not as helpful as the title implies. Franklin Roosevelt neglected Harry Truman's training in the months of their service together. Richard Nixon and Lyndon Johnson on the contrary, were involved in a variety of White House affairs as vice president, although neither was anywhere near being the number-two man in the Eisenhower and Kennedy administrations, respectively. Eisenhower had been a general and, briefly, a university president. John Kennedy and Gerald Ford were legislators without significant executive experience.

Donald Matthews made a study some years ago of the incompatibility of legislative and executive roles from the perspective of the Senate. Former governors, especially of larger states, had trouble adjusting to legislative ways—the seniority system, the hazing of junior members, and so forth—and other senators had difficulty accepting them. Egos clashed. Instead of learning the system, former governors (perhaps to their credit) became increasingly frustrated with the Senate's norms and grew more and more unconforming. Former state legislators and members of the U.S. House of Representatives, by contrast, adjusted easily and effectively to Senate behavior patterns. [12] The Senate was a different place then, more respectful of seniority than it is now, but Matthews' study remains suggestive of the difficulties of moving from one branch to another.

A degree of naiveté seems to be built into the American system, which, unlike the British, does not guarantee a balanced legislative, executive, and political background for chief executives. A president may know that bureaucracies are not easily manipulated from above without fully understanding how independent and even disloyal subordinates can be in the normal operation of a large organization. Franklin Roosevelt's experience served him well. He knew what to expect. His response as president was, first, not to devote a great deal of his time to administration. He was content to make his mark as a political leader. Second, as we shall see, in programs that were important to him he was a tough and largely successful administrator. He was in the Madisonian tradition, accepting the selfishness and intractability of human nature and arranging institutions to make the most of it.

Controlling the Bureaucracy Through Policy

There are three common ways to try to control the bureaucracy. One is to prod and constrain by policy directives (in the broad sense, including budgetary controls). Another is to control through hiring, firing, and other personnel actions. A third is the power of reorganization. Separately or together, they work indifferently at best.

The Constitution requires the president to "take care that the laws be faithfully executed."[13] The laws sometimes designate the president as the responsible officer, more often the heads of departments and other subordinates. But the words of the statutes are not controlling. As a practical matter, even when the law assigns personal responsibility, presidents must almost always act through others. There is too much to be done.

A more interesting question is whether the president may intervene in the administration of programs that have been assigned by Congress to his subordinates. It was James Madison's view when this was discussed in Congress in 1789 that the president had the authority to "inspect and control" the activities of his subordinates. Subsequently, in 1823, a much narrower view was expressed by the attorney general: A president, he said, could do barely more than put a stop to criminal dereliction of duty by his subordinates. President Andrew Jackson a few years later reasserted and enlarged Madison's interpretation. An act of Congress granting powers to a department secretary, he said, "did not, as it could not change the relation between the president and secretary—did not release the former from his obligation to see the law faithfully executed nor the latter from the president's supervision and control."

Custom and judicial decision wavered between these positions afterward. In an 1838 case involving the president's powers over the postmaster general, the attorney general argued that it was the president's duty to decide how and when the laws were to be executed:

> The head of a department is subject to the power of the president "to call upon him for his opinion in writing, upon any matter appertaining to the duties of his office." This implies, plainly, that he is, as to these duties of his office, subject to the president's control. For why should he give any account of his opinions upon matters appertaining to those duties if he is independent of the president?[14]

The Supreme Court disagreed:

> The executive power is vested in a president; and so far as his powers are derived from the Constitution, he is beyond the reach of any other department, except in the mode prescribed by the Constitution through the impeaching power. But it by no means follows, that every officer in every branch of that department is under the exclusive direction of the president. Such a principle, we apprehend, is not, and certainly cannot be claimed by the president.
>
> There are certain political duties imposed upon many officers in the executive department, the discharge of which is under the direction of the

president. But it would be an alarming doctrine, that Congress cannot impose upon any executive office any duty which they may think proper, which is not repugnant to any rights secured and protected by the Constitution; and in such cases, the duty and responsibility grow out of and are subject to the control of the law, and not to the direction of the president. And this is emphatically the case, where the duty enjoined is of a mere ministerial as opposed to discretionary character. . . .

It was urged at the bar, that the postmaster-general was alone subject to the direction and control of the president, with respect to the execution of the duty imposed upon him by this law; and this right of the president is claimed, as growing out of the obligation imposed upon him by the Constitution, to take care that the laws be faithfully executed. This is a doctrine that cannot receive the sanction of this court. It would be vesting in the president a dispensing power, which has no countenance for its support, in any part of the Constitution; and is asserting a principle, which, if carried out in its results, to all cases falling within it, would be clothing the president with a power entirely to control the legislation of Congress, and paralyze the administration of justice.[15]

Later on, however, the Supreme Court adopted a more sympathetic view of presidential authority. In 1926, for example, it said that

The discretion to be exercised is that of the president in determining the national public interest and in directing the action to be taken by his executive subordinates to protect it. In this field his cabinet officers must do his will. . . .

The ordinary duties of officers prescribed by statute come under the general administrative control of the president by virtue of the general grant to him of executive power, and he may properly supervise and guide their construction of statutes under which they act in order to secure that unitary and uniform execution of the laws which Article II of the Constitution evidently contemplated in vesting general executive power in the President alone. Laws are often passed with specific provision for the adoption of regulations by a department or bureau head to make the law workable and effective. The ability and judgment manifested by the official thus empowered, as well as his energy and stimulation of his subordinates, are subjects which the president must consider and supervise.[16]

The Court indicated that there were certain decisions of a quasi-judicial character in which presidential intervention might be inappropriate, but they were exceptional.

Although extensive, the president's supervisory authority to "take care that the laws be faithfully executed" is still, as the words imply, far short of unfettered discretion. In denying the president the power to substitute his solution to the problem of a national emergency created by a wartime steel strike for that designed by Congress, the Supreme Court in 1952 said,

> In the framework of our Constitution, the president's power to see that the laws are faithfully executed refutes the idea that he is to be a lawmaker. The Constitution limits his function in the lawmaking process to the recommending of laws he thinks wise and the vetoing of the laws he thinks bad. The president's order does not direct that a congressional policy be executed in a manner prescribed by Congress—it directs that a presidential policy be executed in a manner prescribed by the president. . . . The power of Congress to adopt such public policies as those proclaimed by the order is beyond question. . . . The Constitution does not subject this lawmaking power of Congress to presidential . . . supervision or control.[17]

Similarly, in the impoundment cases the federal courts denied Richard Nixon authority to order the withholding of vast sums of appropriated money, holding that presidential discretion in interpreting the law must be devoted to carrying out, not thwarting, the intentions of Congress. The president's power to decide which laws he will enforce vigorously, or less than vigorously, and when and how he will enforce them does give him limited legislative authority under the "take care" clause. But when he goes so far as to ignore the will of Congress or actively to subvert its purposes, he may be called to account by the other branches.

It is a different matter when Congress has been silent and the president issues executive orders with the combined effect of legislation and execution. Soon after he became president, for example, John Kennedy issued an executive order to deal with the problem of discrimination in government employment and in private employment conducted under government contract. A Committee on Equal Employment Opportunity was established and given powers to enforce policies of nondiscrimination and affirmative action. The president delayed sending civil rights proposals to Congress another two years, however, because there seemed to be little chance of passage.[18] Had he submitted civil rights legislation and been rebuffed by Congress, such an executive order would have been on even shakier legal ground.

In addition to general supervision—or, in practice, selective supervision—of the bureaucracy under the "take care" clause, the president has the powers of legislative and budgetary clearance to influence the work of the executive branch. The president and his aides in the Office of Management and Budget approve requests for authority and money going from the agencies of government to Congress. The clearance procedure is designed to keep agencies from making any demands on Congress that are inconsistent with the president's policies. It serves two purposes simultaneously: It is a part of the legislative process, allowing the president to fashion a coherent program for the consideration of Congress; but it also gives him a carrot and a stick as manager of the bureaucracy. He can allow expansion of programs and appropriations in favored agencies by sending the requests along to Congress with his approval, or he can deny requests for new authority and deny or trim requests for money as a sign of his displeasure.

The Budget and Accounting Act of 1921 formalized the practice of gathering agency budgets for submission to Congress as a single executive budget with the imprint and approval of the president. It created the Bureau of the Budget or BOB (now the OMB) to help him. Since then, clearance has been used variously to hold down spending, to shape new White House programs, and as a fiscal control of the economy. Stronger presidents have used clearance the most; weaker ones have let it languish. The legislative clearance function, instituted soon after, became an instrument of control during the presidency of Franklin Roosevelt, once his first flurry of legislation had been enacted. The BOB or OMB has since reviewed each policy proposal and made a positive, neutral, or negative judgment: It can find a proposal "in accord with the program of the president," less enthusiastically tag it "consistent with the objectives of the administration," unenthusiastically let it go to Congress with "no objection from the standpoint of the administration's program," or prohibit its transmittal by finding it not to be in accord with the president's programs—a prohibition that wily bureaucrats can circumvent if they care to make the effort. Legislative clearance reached its high point under Harry Truman. After Truman, important legislative matters tended to be handled by the White House staff instead, either directly or on appeal.[19]

Just how powerful these clearance procedures are has been the subject of debate. Budget decisions tend to be incremental at the stages of executive clearance and legislative appropriation. Whatever the powers of the president and Congress to intervene in agency operations by raising or cutting funds, the practice is to give agencies more or less what they have enjoyed in the past—plus a proportionate part of any government-wide increase each year. Incrementalism is the natural result of competition among the agencies and their friends in Congress and the country. A president who tries to break out of this pluralistic political marketplace by recommending that a program be curtailed or abolished may stir up more opposition than he can handle.[20]

In his first year in office, Jimmy Carter directed the executive branch to use zero-base budgeting, which had been tried by some private firms and had been introduced in Georgia by Carter as governor. Zero-base budgeting is designed to break the hold of incrementalism by forcing units to analyze the consequences of various funding levels (including no funding at all, in theory), justify their programs from the ground up, assign priorities to their programs, and send details to the chief executive for decision. Along with sunset laws, which provide for the expiration of an agency's authorization after a stated period unless Congress sees reason to provide a new lease on its life, zero-base budgeting is meant to allow president and Congress to rid the government of functions that are no longer needed. It remains to be seen whether president and Congress will make much use of these devices. Similar efforts have failed in the past. The only tangible effect has been an increase in paperwork. What matters is power, not formal authority and budgetary devices.

The most talented presidents have known better than to try to control too much. Coolidge was not alone in believing that some problems would take care of themselves if they were left alone. A. Lee Fritschler, in his book *Smoking and Politics*, describes the years of warfare among government agencies, Congress, and interest groups, once the link between smoking and disease had been demonstrated, over what if anything was to be done to curb smoking in the United States, or, if not to curb, then to warn the public of the health hazard. Lyndon Johnson, president during much of this period, refused to intervene. He might have taken the side of the tobacco industry or of those concerned about the public health. But since it was a matter he cared little about and one with the potential of creating more enemies than friends, whichever way he intervened, he let it alone.[21]

The initiatives of the Federal Trade Commission in bringing about cigarette hazard labeling were unusually visible and controversial, but otherwise not uncharacteristic of federal agencies. Agencies often propose new policies and compete for the president's attention and Congress's largesse. Some agency initiatives may be unwelcome, some must be vetoed because of limited resources, but the agencies often are a source of ideas that help the president shape his legislative programs from year to year. This is one of the benefits of bureaucracy, from the president's point of view. He can learn from it as well as try to keep it under control.

Max Weber said long ago that bureaucracy has two sides. Bureaucracy, which he defined as an organization with, among other things, hierarchy, a division of labor, specialists, and written rules, was in his view the most predictably efficient way of organizing work for any master, public or private, because it mobilized expertise impersonally, and excluded friendship, nepotism, and political patronage. The difficulty was, however, that the experts were in a position to use their knowledge to take control of the organization.

The question is always who controls the existing bureaucratic machinery. And such control is possible only in a very limited degree to persons who are not technical specialists. Generally speaking, the trained permanent official is more likely to get his way in the long run than his nominal superior, the Cabinet minister, who is not a specialist.[22]

It is interesting to see who predominates in practice, the bureaucrat whose authority is based on knowledge, or the department head, the president, and Congress, whose authority is hierarchical. A generation ago two political scientists framed the problem in a public debate. Herman Finer of the University of Chicago took the view that bureaucrats should be strictly controlled from above—ultimately by the people, to whom the executive and legislature are responsible—to curb their natural tendency to do things wrong, inadequately, or too zealously (malfeasance, nonfeasance, and what he termed "overfeasance"). "We in public administration must be aware of the too good man as well as the too bad; each in his own way may give the public what it doesn't want." Carl Friedrich of Harvard contended that policy was inevitably made by bureaucrats and political leaders both. "Public policy, to put it flatly, is a continuous process, the formation of which is inseparable from its execution." The highly trained people characteristic of modern bureaucracy could be counted on to use their sense of professionalism, their "inner check," to fill in the gaps in the statutes and executive orders. Unlike Finer, Friedrich saw the bureaucracy as having a positive contribution to make to the policy process.[23]

Some presidents have seen the bureaucracy exclusively from Finer's perspective, as something to be kept on a short leash. More often, however, they have had a mixed view that bureaucrats need to be led, pushed, curbed, lobbied, and often bypassed, but also consulted on a wide range of issues on which they have superior knowledge.

Controlling the Bureaucracy Through Personnel

By hiring people who are loyal and firing those who are disloyal (and setting an example for those who might be tempted), a manager can elicit a degree of compliance with his policies among subordinates. No president could function without these controls. Each appoints a sizable team of assistants, cabinet and subcabinet officers, and others, and in time must make replacements as some work out and some do not. But his power to hire and fire is circumscribed by law and attenuated by the sheer number of people he must supervise. He is in a very different position from, say, that of the autocratic manager of a small, nonunionized manufacturing plant (or peanut business).

In the early years of the republic, presidents had no trouble controlling the executive branch. Congress usually gave the chief executive administration authority directly, from prescribing the duties of department heads to approving lighthouse construction contracts, and did not tie him down with personnel regulations. He could appoint and remove subordinates at will, although in practice civil servants, who tended to be from the upper classes, probusiness, and bound by a gentlemanly standard of ethics, enjoyed permanent tenure. More to the point, the bureaucracy was small enough to be managed directly. The State Department headquarters consisted of a secretary and two clerks in 1789, and by 1800 still had only eight clerks plus a messenger. In that year, the Treasury Department, the largest, had only seventy-eight people in its central office. George Washington supervised more people on his plantation in Virginia than in any of the executive departments' central offices. Management of the government was a matter of dealing at first hand with a few officials and trusting a somewhat larger body of subordinates to do their duty.[24]

Then in 1828, for political rather than managerial purposes, President Andrew Jackson announced that from then on federal employees would be subject to replacement by each incoming president. He defended his system of rotation in office (or spoils system, as it came to be known by its opponents) on every ground except the most important one, which was the political advantage to his party of being able to reward the faithful with office. In his inaugural address he said,

> There are, perhaps, few men who can for any great length of time enjoy office and power without being more or less under the influence of feelings unfavorable to the faithful discharge of their public duties. Their integrity may be proof against improper considerations immediately addressed to themselves, but they are apt to acquire a habit of looking with indifference upon the public interests and of tolerating conduct from which an unpracticed man would revolt. Office is considered as a species of property, and government rather as a means of promoting individual interests than as an instrument created solely for the service of the people. Corruption in some and in others a perversion of correct feelings and principles divert government from its legitimate ends and make it an engine for the support of the few at the expense of the many. The duties of all public officers are, or at least admit of being made, so plain and simple that men of intelligence may readily qualify themselves for their performance; and I can not but believe that more is lost by the long continuance of men in office than is generally to be gained by their experience. I submit, therefore, to your consideration whether the efficiency of the Government would not be promoted and official industry and integrity better secured by a general extension of the law which limits appointments to four years.
>
> In a country where offices are created solely for the benefit of the

people no one man has any more intrinsic right to official station than another. Offices were not established to give support to particular men at the public expense. No individual wrong is, therefore, done by removal, since neither appointment to nor continuance in office is matter of right. The incumbent became an officer with a view to public benefits, and when these require his removal they are not to be sacrificed to private interests. It is the people, and they alone, who have a right to complain when a bad officer is substituted for a good one. He who is removed has the same means of obtaining a living that are enjoyed by the millions who never held office. The proposed limitation would destroy the idea of property now so generally connected with official station, and although individual distress may be sometimes produced, it would, by promoting that rotation which constitutes a leading principle in the republican creed, give healthful action to the system.[25]

No one could suggest that the duties of government are "plain and simple" today, and even in Jackson's day some positions were professional: auditors, chief clerks, scientific positions in the Coast Survey, the Naval Observatory, and the Smithsonian Institution, and the entire regular army and navy, for example. These and many more were customarily exempt from rotation, particularly at the higher levels.[26]

From the outset there was controversy about rotation in office. One celebrated observer of Jacksonian democracy, Alexis de Tocqueville, was particularly sour:

I shall not remark that the universal and inordinate desire for place is a great social evil; that it destroys the spirit of independence in the citizen, and diffuses a venal and servile humor throughout the frame of society; that it stifles the manlier virtues: nor shall I be at pains to demonstrate that this kind of traffic only creates an unproductive activity, which agitates the country without adding to its resources: all these things are obvious. But I would observe, that a government which encourages this tendency risks its own tranquility, and places its very existence in great jeopardy. . . .

Amongst democratic nations, as well as elsewhere, the number of official appointments has, in the end, some limits; but amongst those nations, the number of aspirants is unlimited; it perpetually increases, with a gradual and irresistible rise, in proportion as social conditions become more equal, and is only checked by the limits of the population.

Thus, when public employments afford the only outlet for ambition, the government necessarily meets with a permanent opposition at last; for it is tasked to satisfy with limited means unlimited desires. It is very certain that, of all people in the world, the most difficult to restrain and to manage are a people of office-hunters. Whatever endeavors are made by rulers, such a people can never be contented; and it is always to be apprehended that they will ultimately overturn the constitution of the country, and change the aspect of the state, for the sole purpose of making a clearance of places.[27]

As it became clear that rotation in office was lowering the efficiency and prestige of the public service, reformers pressed for a system of tests, at first "pass" examinations to assure a minimum level of competence and later, under the Civil Service Act of 1883, competitive examinations to admit the most qualified people to public employment and a Civil Service Commission to provide enforcement. In the years after, the rules and coverage of the merit system were both extended to the point where the president was effectively barred from using the civil service for patronage. The loss to the chief executive was not serious, however: Federal patronage was largely under the control of members of Congress and their states' party organizations and hardly, therefore, a cohesive influence in support of executive authority. As Herbert Kaufman put it, in 1883 public administration was passing from reliance on representativeness to a new faith in neutral objectivity, which was also reflected in the creation of independent regulatory commissions from 1887 onward. The goal was to separate administration from politics.[28]

The quest for Jacksonian representativeness has resumed from time to time, as in the community action programs of the 1960s, which involved the poor and minorities in the administration of welfare and rehabilitation programs. But under the merit civil service, and in the absence of an affirmative action quota system, a degree of unrepresentativeness by race, ethnicity, class, and sex is inevitable in any bureaucracy, particularly at the higher levels, because who is both trained and willing to compete successfully for better-paying jobs in government and elsewhere is heavily determined by the social system. The tension between representativeness and the examination system remains.

While the unrepresentativeness of bureaucracy, in the sense of failure to match the demographic qualities of a larger population, may make a very great difference to groups that are un- or underrepresented, it may not make much difference in the way programs are administered. A recent study, for example, confirms that, by measures of class, education, religion, and region, the United State foreign service is highly unrepresentative, but goes on to demonstrate that foreign service officers who differ in such background characteristics do not in any systematic way differ in attitudes related to their work.[29] Not all such studies come to the same conclusion, but at least they suggest collectively that unrepresentativeness does not necessarily affect output.

Unrepresentativeness by party, however, may matter to a president. When Dwight Eisenhower and Richard Nixon came to office in 1953 and 1969, respectively, they faced predominantly Democratic bureaucracies. Eisenhower removed a modest number of positions from the merit system so that Republicans could be appointed without delay, but he was a passive president and largely unconcerned about implementation of new programs and therefore about making the bureaucracy responsive. But President Nixon was an activist who launched new programs and scuttled old ones. No president ever tried harder, against greater odds, to make the bureaucracy responsive to the White House.

In a study of the attitudes of political executives and top career bureaucrats during the early Nixon years, Joel Aberbach and Bert Rockman documented the gap in values and beliefs between the new Republican administration and the largely Democratic civil service. The differences were compounded by the tendency of civil servants in social service agencies (Health, Education, and Welfare, Housing and Urban Development, and the Office of Economic Opportunity) to have particularly liberal views favoring a more active social service role for the federal government.[30]

The response of the Nixon administration was to experiment with ways, some legal and some illegal, to overcome the bureaucracy in the offending agencies (an endeavor that should be distinguished from concurrent efforts to use the Internal Revenue Service, the intelligence agencies, and other organizations for unlawful purposes associated with Watergate). With the acquiescence of the Civil Service Commission, the supposed watchdog of the merit system, the White House introduced a patronage plan for higher-level civil service that required systematic bending and breaking of the rules. Pressures from the White House time and again resulted in the use of civil service regulations regarding the creation and description of positions to hire loyal Republicans rather than, as originally intended, to prevent hiring on political grounds. For instance, additional qualifications not by chance matching those of someone the White House wanted to place might be added to a job description so that the favored person became the only one on a list of hopefuls who qualified for a position.[31]

Civil Service Commission members complained that it was hard to stand up to White House pressures because of their dual (and inconsistent) roles of protecting the merit system and serving as personnel managers for the government. President Carter's solution to this old problem was to split the functions into two agencies, one clearly political and one clearly nonpolitical. In 1978 a reorganization plan and supporting legislation were approved, replacing the commission with an Office of Personnel Management and a Merit System Protection Board, effective in 1979.

There is one more question concerning a president's powers of personnel management: whether he may freely remove his appointees (as distinguished from those hired under merit civil service rules) if he is unhappy with their performance. Most high positions in the government are filled by the president with the advice and consent of the Senate, although some, such as members of the White House Office, are by law the president's alone to fill. What role the Senate should have in the *removal* of people it has confirmed was not settled until the Supreme Court's decision in *Myers* v. *United States* in 1926. Except for impeachment, the Constitution is silent on removal. From the beginning, some interpreted the silence to mean that department heads and other high officials were removable only by impeachment, a view supported by Chief Justice John Marshall in the case of *Marbury* v. *Madison* in 1803: "As the law creating the office gave the officer a right to hold it for five years, independent of the executive, the appointment was not revocable, but vested in the officer legal rights which are protected by the laws of his country."[32]

Another view was that the president could remove his appointees at will, by himself. In the debate on the establishment of a Department of Foreign Affairs (later to be called the Department of State), Congress adopted this option for the secretary of state, in a form that implied that the removal power stemmed from the Constitution, and in the opinion of some thereby made this the official option for all removals. Another interpretation was that where Senate approval was needed for appointment it was needed for removal. Alexander Hamilton said in the *Federalist* No. 77,

> It has been mentioned as one of the advantages to be expected from the coöperation of the Senate, in the business of appointments, that it would contribute to the stability of the administration. The consent of that body would be necessary to displace as well as to appoint. A change of the Chief Magistrate, therefore, would not occasion so violent or so general a revolution in the officers of the government as might be expected, if he were the sole disposer of offices.

Still another was that Congress, exercising its "necessary and proper" powers, might by statute decide how executive officials should be removed.

President Andrew Johnson was impeached and nearly convicted in 1868 for alleged violation of the Tenure of Office Act of 1867, which required Senate consent for removal of presidential appointees who had been confirmed by the Senate. The act, passed over Johnson's veto, had been intended to saddle him with subordinates sympathetic to the reconstruction policies of Congress. The acquittal of Johnson lent some support to the view that presidents were meant to have full discretion in removals. The Tenure of Office Act was repealed in 1887.

A similar act of Congress passed in 1876, requiring that certain classes of postmaster "shall be appointed and may be removed by the president by and with advice and consent of the Senate," was tested before the Supreme Court in the *Myers* case. Woodrow Wilson had fired one Frank Myers, postmaster of Portland, Oregon, without Senate approval. Myers, and after his death his heirs, sued the government for the salary he would have received had he been allowed to serve his full term. In a learned opinion written by former President William Howard Taft, by then chief justice, the Court held that the Tenure of Office Act of 1867 had been unconstitutional and that the 1876 act was equally so.

> When a nomination is made, it may be presumed that the Senate is, or may become, as well advised as to the fitness of the nominee as the president, but in the nature of things the defects in ability or intelligence or loyalty in the administration of the laws of one who has served as an officer under the president, are facts as to which the president or his trusted subordinates, must be better informed than the Senate, and the power to remove him may, therefore, be regarded as confined, for very sound and practical reasons, to the governmental authority which has administrative control. The power of removal is incident to the power of appointment, not to the power of advising and consenting to appointment, and when the grant of the executive power is enforced by the express mandate to take care that the laws be faithfully executed, it emphasizes the necessity for including within the executive power as conferred the exclusive power of removal. . . .
>
> Our conclusion on the merits . . . is that Article II grants to the president the executive power of the government, i.e., the general administrative control of those executing the laws, including the power of appointment and removal of executive officers. . . .

Taft stressed the need for closeness between a president and his immediate subordinates:

> Each head of a department is and must be the president's alter ego in matters of that department where the president is required to exercise authority. . . .
>
> He must place in each member of his official family, and his chief executive subordinates, implicit faith. The moment that he loses confidence in the intelligence, ability, judgment or loyalty of any one of them, he must have the power to remove him without delay. To require him to file charges and submit them to the consideration of the Senate might make impossible the unity and coordination in executive administration essential to effective action.[33]

One may wonder what all this has to do with a postmaster in Portland. Clearly Taft, with the feeling of a man who has faced the challenges of the presidency, was using a minor issue as an excuse to make broad rules that would have their greatest impact on policy-making positions. His motives were revealed in private correspondence published long after:

> I am strongly convinced that the danger to this country is in the enlargement of the powers of Congress, rather than in the maintenance in full of the executive power. Congress is getting into the habit of forming boards who really exercise executive power, and attempting to make them independent of the president after they have been appointed and confirmed. This merely makes a hydra-headed executive, and if the terms are lengthened so as to exceed the duration of a particular executive, a new executive will find himself stripped of control of important functions, for which as head of the government he becomes responsible, but whose action he cannot influence in any way.[34]

The *Myers* case once and for all settled the question whether the Senate could share the removal power, but it did not assure presidents control of the growing number of independent regulatory commissions, governed by boards whose members have fixed staggered terms and protection from presidential removal except for "cause"—malfeasance and the like. Franklin Roosevelt removed a member of the Federal Trade Commission over a policy disagreement in 1933, confident that *Myers* provided a legal rationale. But in *Humphrey's Executor v. United States*, the Supreme Court sustained an award of back salary and affirmed the power of Congress to create agencies with mixed executive, legislative, and judicial functions and to shield them from presidential interference. Of the Federal Trade Commission, the Court said:

> Its duties are performed without executive leave and, in the contemplation of the statute, must be free from executive control. In administrating the provisions of the statute in respect of "unfair methods of competition"— that is to say in filling in and administering the details embodied by the general standard—the commission acts in part quasi-legislatively and in part quasi-judicially. . . . To the extent that it exercises any executive function—as distinguished from executive power in the constitutional sense—it does so in the discharge and effectuation of its quasi-legislative or quasi-judicial powers, or as an agency of the legislative or judicial departments of the government.[35]

One way a president asserts control over regulatory commissions is year by year to appoint members who share his political values. It takes time—three to four years to appoint a majority of the members of a seven-person commission, and, as in the case of members of the Supreme Court, displays of independence from the president who makes the appointment are common. A president may have some success in leading, even without formal controls, but not as much as he would like.

And so it is that the White House periodically proposes gathering the functions of the regulatory commissions into cabinet departments. Congress, for its part, guards the independence of these agencies from the president (though not from the legislature). In 1977, for example, a Senate committee proposed that the two kinds of controls now exercised by the president and his people over agencies generally no longer apply to regulatory commissions. These controls are budgetary and legislative clearance by the OMB and the litigation of the agencies' civil cases by the Department of Justice. The committee felt that it sapped the independence of the regulatory agencies for officials responsible to the president to be in a position to veto requests for money and authority to Congress and to decide which cases initiated by a commission would be taken to court or appealed.[36]

This is a power struggle between branches of the sort the framers of the Constitution anticipated and approved. It is also a disagreement about the nature of government decisions and the kinds of institutions best suited to make them. Few quarrel with the principle that ordinary judicial decisions, in the sense of applying general rules to specific disputes, are appropriately made by people insulated by law and custom from political pressures. Today many judicial decisions are made within the bureaucracy, ultimately subject to appeal to the regular courts. A new class of civil servant, the administrative law judge, whose tenure is protected by special civil service regulations, has been created to make many of these decisions. Administrative law judges often try cases within the independent regulatory commissions.

There is less agreement, however, about the quasi-legislative functions of the commissions such as rule making. Some people agree with the Supreme Court in the *Humphrey* case that sublegislation can be drawn objectively and nonpolitically under a general congressional standard. If they are right, independence is not illogical. Others contend that filling in the gaps in statutes inevitably involves policy making, and that the only question is whether the policy making will be most heavily influenced by the president or by the separate interests that cluster about the regulatory agencies.

Controlling the Bureaucracy Through Reorganization

Typically both kinds of controls considered so far, policy and personnel, are at stake when a president undertakes a reorganization of part of the executive branch. Reorganization is the most radical strategy for improving the president's management of the functions of government. Both its uses and its limitations can be seen in the creation of the

Department of Energy by the president and Congress in 1977. Jimmy Carter made an issue of energy in his first year in office. He proposed new regulations and backed them up with a plan to collect energy programs then scattered throughout the federal government into one department directly responsible to the White House. Congress responded quickly. The new Department of Energy was given all the powers of the Federal Energy Administration, the Energy Research and Development Administration, and the Federal Power Commission and was given additional authority from the Departments of the Interior, Housing and Urban Development, Commerce, and Defense and from the Interstate Commerce Commission.

Clearly the potential for coordination of energy policy was enhanced by reorganization. But, not unexpectedly, President Carter lost to Congress on a crucial point. The secretary of energy was denied the ultimate power to determine energy prices. Instead, a bipartisan Federal Energy Regulatory Commission composed of five members with four-year staggered terms was created within the new department, with authority to set the price of electricity, gas, and oil—in effect reconstituting the Federal Power Commission, augmented by powers from the Interstate Commerce Commission. Except for a provision that on the declaration of a national emergency by the president the secretary might fix oil prices subject to the veto of either house of Congress, the new commission was only nominally within the Department of Energy. Congress refused the president his most important request.[37]

Reorganizations below the level of cabinet departments may be accomplished by means of executive orders, pursuant to general legislation, as well as by separate acts of Congress. But the pattern is much the same: Congress is careful not to give the president too much control over key functions. For example, President Carter was given limited reorganization authority for a period of three years. Either house could veto a reorganization plan within sixty days of its submission by the president; no more than three plans could be pending before Congress at any time; and no reorganization could abolish any function mandated by statute or extend or expand any agency functions. Clearly, any major surgery would have to be performed by separate legislation.[38]

Similar reorganization authority has been granted presidents from Woodrow Wilson's time onward. The largest batch of reorganizations was prompted by the two Hoover Commissions, chaired by the former president, which issued recommendations in 1949 and 1955. The first commission was interested in strengthening the cabinet-level departments by grouping the many existing agencies, including regulatory commissions, into departments and by centralizing authority in department secretaries. It made some 273 recommendations in all, many accomplished sooner or later, including the creation of a welfare department. The second commission, with a more conservative interest in cutting government functions, was less successful.[39]

Congress has allowed the creation of new departments from time to time, sometimes after lengthy debate. In addition to the Department of Energy, there have been HEW, HUD, and the Department of Transportation since World War II, and the transformation of the Post Office from a department into a government corporation in the false hope that it would work more efficiently. But other departmental reorganizations have been rejected by Congress. Lyndon Johnson failed to secure the consolidation of the Department of Commerce and Labor in 1967, and Richard Nixon was denied his 1971 plan for consolidating the Departments of Agriculture, the Interior, HEW, Labor, Commerce, Transportation, and HUD into the Departments of Natural Resources, Human Resources, Economic Development, and Community Development.

In January 1973 President Nixon announced another major reorganization, but this time, emboldened by a decisive victory over George McGovern in the November election, he did not seek congressional approval. Four assistants to the president were to act for him "to integrate and unify policies and operations" in domestic affairs, foreign affairs, economic affairs, and executive management. Below them there would be three supersecretaries, in the fields of natural resources, human resources, and economic development. Below the supersecretaries would be the cabinet. But the pressures of the Watergate investigation intervened, and the plan died. In May, press secretary Ron Ziegler revealed in characteristically misleading language that the plan, "as originally announced and conceived, would be moved aside at this time."[40]

Most presidents, including Nixon, have believed in what Harold Seidman describes as the orthodox theory of reorganization, exemplified by this statement of purposes in the Reorganization Act of 1949:

1. To promote the better execution of the laws, the more effective management of the executive branch of the Government and of its agencies and functions, and the expeditious administration of the public business.
2. To reduce expenditures and promote economy, to the fullest extent consistent with the efficient operation of the Government.
3. To increase the efficiency of the operations of the Government to the fullest extent practicable.
4. To group, coordinate, and consolidate agencies and functions of the Government, as nearly as may be, according to major purposes.
5. To reduce the number of agencies by consolidating those having similar functions under a single head, and to abolish such agencies or functions thereof as may not be necessary for the efficient conduct of the Government.
6. To eliminate overlapping and duplication of effort.[41]

Reshuffling alone does not produce more coordination and efficiency, however. There is rarely one logical departmental home for a complex governmental function—wherever it ends up, a typical bureau will still need to coordinate its work with bureaus in a number of other agencies. Where should bureaucrats who arrange grain shipments to foreign countries be placed—in the Department of State or of Agriculture? Among foreign or domestic affairs? Which of the several agencies now concerned with the improvement of waterways has the most logical claim? Should conservation functions be grouped in one agency or be seen as natural concomitants of programs in agriculture, parks and recreation, energy, transportation, urban development, etc.?

It *can* make a difference if a seriously divided function is given its own high-level organization. Thus conservationists long pressed for a Department of Conservation not because it was "logical" or because it made sense from the president's perspective, but because it stood to make conservation a more visible and powerful function of government with a high-level official to speak for it before the president and Congress. In 1978, in the debate on the creation of a Department of Education, interest groups favoring increased federal support of education were divided as to whether promotion of the function from the Office of Education in HEW to departmental status would help or hurt their cause. The National Education Association felt it would enhance the status of educational programs. The American Federation of Teachers argued that educational interests were better off inside a large, multiconstituency department than isolated and vulnerable by themselves.[42] As this example suggests, the president's desire for improving the management of a governmental function is not the only reason for reorganization.

Franklin Roosevelt was less persuaded than any other modern president of the benefits of rationalization and consolidation of the executive branch. First of all, he rejected the orthodox argument that reorganization saves money. "We have to get over the notion that the purpose of reorganization is economy. . . . The reason for reorganization is good management."[43] But in the pursuit of good management, President Roosevelt frequently put new functions in new agencies rather than trust them to existing agencies, which he tended to regard as too set in their ways. Further, he believed in duplicating and overlapping functions. By giving two agencies with mutually suspicious administrators similar responsibilities, Roosevelt was assured a good flow of information (including everything derogatory each could say about the other), competitiveness, and a capacity for experimentation and continued organizational flexibility that other presidents lacked.

Roosevelt gave a large amount of responsibility for relief for the unemployed to Harry Hopkins, a general-purpose aide, and to Harold

Ickes, the combative secretary of the interior. They were very different men, each effective in his own way. One was more concerned with getting things done, the other with doing things correctly; and so their approaches to solving the problems of hunger and poverty were different. They fought for funds and authority, played bureaucratic tricks on each other, Ickes in particular complaining bitterly about Hopkins and threatening more than once to resign (although in fact he outlasted Roosevelt in office), and together did exactly what the president wanted of them.[44]

Roosevelt understood that bureaucrats are to some extent in business for themselves and must be offered treats for good behavior, have their ears pulled, or be left to fight things out on their own. Anthony Downs has described five kinds of bureaucrats: self-interested "climbers" and "conservers" and mixed-motive "zealots," "advocates," and "statesmen." Climbers want ever more power, income, and prestige; conservers want security and to retain what power, income, and prestige they have. Zealots are loyal to fairly narrow policies above everything else; advocates to a broader range of policies—both are interested in power as a means to their ends. Statesmen are loyal to the general welfare and may feel out of place in the typical bureau. All but the statesmen are primarily promoters of their personal interests or of parochial organizational interests.[45] Roosevelt made particularly good use of advocates such as Ickes and of liberal zealots, and avoided conservers, who according to Downs tend to dominate (and stagnate) older agencies, by creating new agencies with advocates and zealots attracted from other agencies or private life.

Just how serious Roosevelt was about reorganization is indicated by this memorandum to his budget director:

> I agree with the Secretary of the Interior. Please have it carried out so that fur-bearing animals remain in the Department of the Interior. You might find out if any Alaska bears are still supervised by (a) War Department (b) Department of Agriculture (c) Department of Commerce. They have all had jurisdiction over Alaska bears in the past and many embarrassing situations have been created by the mating of a bear belonging to one Department with a bear belonging to another Department.
>
> F.D.R.
>
> P.S. I don't think the Navy is involved but it may be. Check the Coast Guard. You never can tell![46]

Even the strongest of chief executives can be blocked by alliances of bureaus, congressional committees, and constituents. There may be pork-barrel benefits at stake, as in the periodic consideration of moving Army Corps of Engineers civilian functions to a more appropriate department. Or Congress may balk at reorganization plans that cannot be fitted to the existing committees of the House and Senate. President Nixon's plan for taking functions from the Departments of Agriculture, Commerce, Labor, and Transportation, which have fairly well-defined clienteles, and rearranging them into functional departments of community development, economic affairs, human resources, and natural resources meant a serious dislocation in the relations of the executive and other key parts of the political system. It was received in Congress with the same lack of enthusiasm that would attend a proposal, say, to elect U.S. senators from census districts without regard to state boundaries. Although in the abstract it might make sense for a senator to represent the St. Louis metropolitan area, covering parts of Missouri and Illinois, it probably would not make sense to the senators now elected in Missouri and Illinois, their party organizations, their state governments, and state-based interest groups.

Even more generally, Congress usually is reluctant to add to presidential authority in the aggregate. The members' Madisonian sense of balance—professional jealousy, perhaps—leads them to look suspiciously on any proposal that will tip the balance further in the direction of the White House. It is no accident that the executive branch, after years of reorganization, still does not resemble the ideal of the Hoover Commission as expressed in the 1949 act. Hundreds of functions are carefully tucked away in the care of regulatory commissions, independent agencies, government corporations, institutes, boards, councils, and committees.[47]

As "representativeness" in politics and administration was found by Kaufman to be largely displaced by "neutral competence" with the advent of the merit system and independent commissions, so was neutral competence in time challenged by the third principle, "executive leadership." The reorganization movements in the states and the national government in this century and the growth of the Executive Office of the President, and the renewed interest in the strong-mayor plan locally, have aimed at centralizing and politicizing previously dispersed and insulated function under the aegis of a chief executive.[48] But executive leadership has never taken complete hold, at least in the minds of bureaucrats and members of Congress. The principle of neutral competence remains a powerful counterbalance to assertions of presidential authority.

THE MILITARY
BUREAUCRACY

In the United States, the formal military chain of command goes from the president as commander in chief at the top through the National Security Council and the secretary of defense to the Joint Chiefs of Staff and the commanders of unified and specified commands. The services maintain their separate identity, but the secretaries of the army, navy, and air force are outside the chain of command for combat purposes. (In more detail: within the White House Office, the president has an assistant for national security affairs, a key post that has been occupied by such influential people as McGeorge Bundy and Henry Kissinger, and the assistant's professional staff. The National Security Council, established by Congress in 1947, is chaired by the president. Its members are the vice president and the secretaries of defense and state. By statute, the chairman of the Joint Chiefs of Staff is the military adviser to the council, and the director of central intelligence is its intelligence adviser. The Central Intelligence Agency is under the direction of the council and the president. The Joint Chiefs of Staff consists of a chairman, who is the chief military officer of the armed services, appointed by the president, and the chief officers of the army, navy, and air force.)[1]

There is constant competition for power among the components of this system, horizontally among the separate services and vertically within and between the military and their civilian superiors, and there are shifting patterns of influence as a result. Furthermore, the values of the competitors tend to differ from each other and also from one period to another—sometimes the military are more warlike and the civilian leaders more restrained, but as often it is the reverse, as we shall see. Military policy depends on the values of whoever predominates at any given time. It may or may not be the president. (In 1945, critical questions such as whether or not to push on to Berlin or leave it to the Russians were made by the military, because the president was dying.)[2]

There are differences between policy making in military and civilian programs. Now and then at least, strategic military decisions are more crucial—to invade, to bomb, to retreat, to disarm—and it is therefore important to take pains to make the right decision; whereas trial and error is ancient and honorable conduct in civilian programs. Also, strategic military decisions and decision processes are far more likely to be secret than their civilian counterparts, which means that the participants are harder to identify, their values may not be a matter of public record, and their mistakes may be swept under the rug. (Other kinds of decisions, such as the general level of military appropriations or the building or closing of bases, are handled more openly.)

Another difference is that strategic military decisions, particularly in time of crisis, are more likely than domestic decisions to be made by a few people at the top of the formal hierarchy. Democratic theory would tend to regard them as no better than a necessary evil. Theodore Lowi argues, however, that crisis decisions are the best our pluralistic political system produces:

> They combine intensity of conflict with shortage of time. Politically this means a very narrow scope of participation and extremely limited range for bargaining. The public and public-serving institutions are far removed. Decisions are made by an elite and are usually highly legitimate— if we may measure by the largely ceremonial and affirmative responses crisis decisions tend to receive.[3]

In crises such as the Berlin blockade, the Korean invasion, and the Cuban missile crisis of 1962, there is little time to involve more than a few high officials and perhaps a small number of trusted advisers not currently in office. The result, Lowi contends, is clear-headedness and good decision making.

When there is time for bargaining among the many centers of power in the political system, however, decisions tend to be inferior, Lowi argues. He cites the creation of the Defense Department in 1947 and 1949 as an example of the muddled policy that is likely when all of the vested interests affected have an opportunity to make their claims. A widely discussed proposal to unify the armed forces was set aside in favor of a compromise that retained the separate services, linked at the top by the joint chiefs, the secretary of defense and two years later a Department of Defense, the National Security Council, and the president. Lowi considers it a confederation: a decentralized form of organization closer to the pre-1947 arrangement than to unification. (In his opinion, the additional coordination that occurred in the 1960s under Secretary of Defense Robert McNamara was largely the work of a single forceful personality and did not do away with the independent political power of the army, navy, and air force.)[4]

But in military as in domestic affairs, Lowi reminds us, whether policy making is centralized or decentralized depends on the issue.

Civilian Control: Great Cases

In the United States, the question typically asked first concerns the adequacy of civilian control of the military. Samuel P. Huntington makes a useful distinction between what he calls *subjective* and *objective civilian control*—and finds neither quite characteristic of the United States today. Subjective control occurs when the military leadership has the same interests and values as the political leadership of society. If a nation's officer corps and political leaders are both drawn from the aristocracy, as in late-eighteenth-century Europe, or if there is a militia drawn from the citizenry in time of trouble—a democratic institution in a democratic society—as in the American Revolution, then there is subjective control. The framers of the Constitution were agreed on a citizen militia for the new republic. Although they prohibited members of Congress from resigning to take civil office, they did not bar them from resigning to take military office. Legislators were expected to take up arms with men from other walks of life. The military would consist of amateurs, and civilian-mindedness would be assured.[5]

Objective civilian control is the subordination of the military to the rule of a single legitimate civilian authority. The military in this case does not mirror the state, but is instead constrained by it. Once a professional standing army evolved in the United States, objective control became the only possible form of civilian supremacy. But it has remained imperfect, Huntington contends, because the framers divided control over the military between president and Congress and between the states and the nation rather than provide a single powerful supervising authority.

> The Framers' concept of civilian control was to control the uses to which military authority might be put rather than to control the military per se. They were more afraid of military power in the hands of political officials than of political power in the hands of military officers. Unable to

visualize a distinct military class, the Framers could not fear such a class. But there was need to fear the concentration of authority over the military in any single governmental institution. As conservatives the Framers wanted to divide power, including power over the armed forces.[6]

So it is that the National Guard and the Reserves are strong political forces at the state and national levels, and compete with the regular services for the attention of the president and Congress.

> Objective civilian control is maximized if the military are limited in scope to professional matters and relegated to a subordinate position in a pyramid of authority culminating in a single civilian head. The military clauses of the Constitution, however, provide for almost exactly the opposite. They divide civilian responsibility for military affairs and thereby foster the direct access of the professional military authorities to the highest levels of government.[7]

The wartime presidency of Abraham Lincoln illustrates the competition for power characteristic of the system. Early in the fighting, Congress established the Committee on the Conduct of the War, which kept close watch on the military, frequently called generals to testify about operations, and acted as chief critic of the president's war policies. The militia was (and remained until 1903) under dual state and national control during hostilities. More than any other wartime president, Lincoln made use of his constitutionally ambiguous power as commander in chief to make his own military decisions instead of leaving them to the generals. One result was a spectacular competition between Lincoln and his commander of the Army of the Potomac and later chief general, George B. McClellan, which is noteworthy because it directly raised the question of civilian control.

George McClellan was a proud and popular general who was quick to give Lincoln detailed advice on running the country but slow to follow his orders. McClellan was so certain of the rightness of his own views that he habitually blamed those around him for what went wrong rather than accept responsibility or change his ways. As criticism of his inactivity mounted, Lincoln's orders to get on with the fighting became more and more explicit: In one series, he set a date "for a general movement of the land and naval forces of the United States against the insurgent forces," commanded the Army of the Potomac to seize and occupy Manassas Junction, and added a memorandum to McClellan explaining why that course of action should be taken rather than an attack on Richmond. McClellan disobeyed. He stayed put for months. "He has got the slows," admitted Lincoln. Again and again Lincoln turned aside advice that he be fired: "I would remove him tomorrow if convinced it were for the good of the service." Instead, the president grew openly critical and sarcastic: When McClellan wrote asking for more horses and mules, he replied, "I have just read your despatch about sore-tongued and fatigued horses. Will you pardon me for asking what the horses of your army have done since the battle of Antietam that fatigues anything?" He referred to the Army of the Potomac as "General McClellan's bodyguard."[8]

But after more than a year of McClellan's "slows," Lincoln removed him. "Alas for my poor country!" said the general. Two years later, McClellan ran for president against Lincoln and lost, though not by much. His wartime sluggishness was interpreted by many as sheer cowardice, but it stemmed at least in part from divided sympathies. He was not as committed to the Union cause as Lincoln.

Whatever his motives, however, he was so disobedient as to force the president to get rid of him and assert the principle of civilian supremacy.

In 1951, President Harry Truman removed General of the Army Douglas MacArthur in an equally painful affirmation of civilian control after a somewhat shorter period of vacillation and negotiation. MacArthur, hero of the battle of the Pacific in World War II, was supreme commander of the United Nations forces in Korea and commander of United States forces in the Far East. He was a political general in several senses of the term: He was a man who had spent much of his life and virtually all his later life in the Far East and felt he understood the people and cultures of the region better than most; he had been supreme allied commander in Japan after the war and had supervised the swift transition of its political system from autocracy to democracy; and he was a hero among conservative Republicans, particularly, who thought of him as a possible candidate for the presidency and who had tempted him with candidacy in 1948. He was a big, handsome man, proud and egotistical, and something of a dandy. "Mac," as he was known, was in all of these respects but stature very much like "Little Mac" McClellan. General MacArthur designed his own gaudy uniforms, spoke and wrote poetically, played the role of hero outrageously, and had ill-concealed disdain for the political and military opinions of his commander in chief.

But General MacArthur's disobedience was the reverse of McClellan's: He wanted an all-out war in Korea, while the president wanted a limited one. In June 1950, North Korean forces invaded South Korea. Harry Truman responded immediately with the promise of American support under the aegis of the United Nations. MacArthur was put in charge. With a well-executed amphibious landing at Inchon, he began a rapid removal of North Koreans from the south, and also began to show a penchant for disagreeing publicly with the president on strategic military policy. Truman had announced a policy of "neutralizing" the

Nationalist Chinese stronghold of Formosa by employing American forces to defend the island from attack from the mainland and equally to prevent the Nationalists from attacking the mainland. MacArthur was openly supportive of the Nationalists and their designs on the mainland, and made his disagreement with Truman known in a message to be read to the annual convention of the Veterans of Foreign Wars in Chicago. This led to a meeting with the president on Wake Island in October to settle their differences. It was stiff and tense, but the two seemed to reach an understanding. The war continued to go well. MacArthur was confident it would be short: He promised victory by Thanksgiving. Shortly, however, reports arrived from the battlefield that soldiers of the People's Republic of China were fighting side by side with the North Koreans. MacArthur thought little of it—he had assured the president all along that neither the Russians nor the Chinese were likely to become involved in the war. The push northward went on, farther and farther into North Korean territory. Then the Chinese launched a massive counteroffensive, beating back MacArthur's forces and inflicting heavy losses. He had walked into a trap. He was in trouble and would continue to be.[9]

The general resumed public statements on the need for measures directed at the Chinese mainland, to which the president responded with a general gag order through the joint chiefs: "Until further written notice from me . . . no speech, press release, or other public statement concerning foreign policy should be released until it has received clearance from the Department of State." Another order followed, clearly meant for MacArthur, but still not addressed to him in person: "Officials overseas, including military commanders and diplomatic representatives, should be ordered to exercise extreme caution in public statements, to clear all but routine statements with their departments, and to refrain from direct communication on military or foreign policy with newspapers, magazines, or other publicity media in the United States." Two days later, however, the general went public again with a message of "profound thanks" to the American Legion for their demand that the White House authorize the bombing of China. He advised the joint chiefs of the need, in addition, to allow the Nationalists both to attack the mainland and to contribute troops to the war in Korea. And he backed up his internal advice with a statement to the press that "expansion of our military operations to the coastal areas and interior bases would doom Red China to the risk of imminent military collapse." This ran directly counter to the president's policy of limiting the conflict to the Korean peninsula.[10]

Then, in March 1951, the general arranged with the Republican minority leader of the House of Representatives, Joseph W. Martin, Jr., to have his war policy read into the record:

My views and recommendations with respect to the situation created by Red China's entry into the war against us in Korea have been submitted to Washington in most complete detail. Generally these views are well known and clearly understood, as they follow the conventional pattern of meeting force with maximum counterforce as we have never failed to do in the past. Your view with respect to the utilization of the Chinese forces on Formosa is in conflict with neither logic nor this tradition.

It seems strangely difficult for some to realize that here in Asia is where the Communist conspirators have elected to make their play for global conquest, and that we have joined the issue thus raised on the battlefield; that here we fight Europe's war with arms while the diplomats there still fight it with words; that if we lose the war to communism in Asia the fall of Europe is inevitable. Win it and Europe most probably would avoid war and yet preserve freedom. As you point out, we must win. There is no substitute for victory.[11]

President Truman had no choice but to relieve MacArthur of his command, adding, "Full and vigorous debate on matters of national policy is a vital element in the constitutional system for free democracy. It is fundamental, however, that military commanders must be governed by the policies and directives issued to them in the manner provided by our laws and Constitution. In time of crisis, this consideration is compelling."[12] He went on to praise the general's "distinguished and exceptional service" to his country. Years later, with less charity, Truman said, "I fired him because he wouldn't respect the authority of the President. . . . I didn't fire him because he was a dumb son of a bitch, although he was, but that's not against the law for generals. If it was, half to three-quarters of them would be in jail."[13]

Harry Truman's popularity, low at the time, fell further. Public opinion polls showed support for MacArthur two to one over the president. Washington was inundated with angry letters and telegrams. MacArthur was summoned by his friends in the Senate to tell his side of the story in closed-door hearings and to address Congress and the nation on the radio and television. He reiterated his view that the war should be carried to the mainland and concluded movingly,

The world has turned over many times since I took the oath on the plain at West Point, and the hopes and dreams have long since vanished, but I still remember the refrain of one of the most popular barracks ballads of that day which proclaimed most proudly that old soldiers never die; they just fade away.

And like the old soldier of that ballad, I now close my military career and just fade away, an old soldier who tried to do his duty as God gave him the light to see that duty. Good bye.[14]

The president never regained his popularity. The general did fade away, despite some thought that he might run for president. And when the dust had settled, there was fair agreement that President Truman, right or wrong on policy, had done what a president must do to an insubordinate officer.

No other case of insubordination by a commanding officer has ever been as spectacular. But the problem crops up now and then in less serious cases, and the McClellan and MacArthur precedents are dusted off to put the offending officer in his place. In 1977 Major General John K. Singlaub, chief of staff of American forces in South Korea, was recalled to the United States, reprimanded by President Carter, and reassigned for having publicly criticized the president's plan for the gradual removal of American troops from South Korea ("If we withdraw our ground troops on the schedule suggested, it will lead to war.") The withdrawal plan was known to be unpopular in the Pentagon, not to mention South Korea and Japan, but General Singlaub was the only military officer to air his complaints in the press. The next year, from his new post in Georgia, General Singlaub again spoke out against White House policy—this time a decision to delay production of neutron weapons pending negotiations on arms control with the Soviet Union. He also remarked that the newly ratified Panama Canal treaties were unnecessary. The general was allowed to retire. Then, freed from constraints, he enjoyed brief notoriety as a conservative spokesman and and general-purpose critic of practically every important military decision the president had made since his inauguration.[15]

Secretary of Defense Harold Brown noted in the Singlaub case that the military "are not only allowed but they are encouraged to express their views during the determination of policy through the chain of command." An officer may make "public statements before policy is arrived at." After the policy is determined, however, "it . . . becomes his responsibility to support that policy publicly if he plans to stay in the military." General Singlaub seems to have believed in civilian control also, in his fashion, but not as that principle is understood by presidents. "Blind, unquestioning obedience to decisions on military matters which were made without reference to the nation's military advisers may not be in the best long-term interests of the United States," he said.[16]

Civilian Control: Routine Matters

Not all problems of civilian control involve open refusal to obey a command or to hold one's tongue, followed by removal (and some dabbling by the offender in civilian politics thereafter). In fact, the president is far more likely to face threats to civilian control in more subtle and routine forms—many of them amounting to no more than standard maddening bureaucratic behavior.

A fully effective commander in chief needs good information from his military, paramilitary, and intelligence services in order to make good decisions, and he needs obedience down the line once the decisions are made. This is far more difficult to secure than one might suppose. A sampling of cases from the administrations of John F. Kennedy and his successors illustrates the problem.

When he took office in 1961, Kennedy inherited the Central Intelligence Agency's plan to return Cuban exiles to their homeland to overthrow Fidel Castro. Kennedy approved of the idea and stipulated that American involvement remain secret and that his option of calling off the operation be kept open until the last minute. Within a few weeks, the plan was perfected with the assistance of the Joint Chiefs of Staff, and an invasion was launched at the Bay of Pigs that failed instantly. Kennedy accepted the blame, and properly so, but it was also clear that he had been let down by the CIA. The agency was incorrect in its estimates of the relative strength of its forces and Castro's: It had predicted that the Cuban air force would pose no problem to the invaders (it was small, "entirely disorganized," "for the most part obsolete and inoperative," and its fighting ability "almost nonexistent") and that the establishment of a beachhead would set off anti-Castro uprisings all over the island. It had further predicted, mistakenly, that if something did go wrong the invading forces could escape to the hills and continue their struggle for the liberation of Cuba as guerillas, as Castro had some years before. The self-assurance and enthusiasm of Kennedy's CIA advisers obscured the weakness of their plan. (There is, however, a theory that the CIA and the military knew the invasion of exiles would not work and hoped to trap the president into overt military support.)

The president was ill served by the CIA on the operational side, too. Increasingly he had been led to believe that the plan could not be aborted once under way, because too many exiles had been mobilized, trained, and fired up for the invasion and could not be let go without political repercussions. And the sponsorship of the United States was not kept secret. It was symbolic of the entire misbegotten operation that the first people ashore were American frogmen, contrary to the president's orders, and that they were immediately picked up by Cuban patrols.[17]

Looking back on the Bay of Pigs invasion, Kennedy saw that he had been sold a bad plan by zealous bureaucrats and had not been obeyed in the implementation of the plan. Civilian control had been tenuous at best. He vowed to be less trusting next time.

The following year, during the Cuban missile crisis, President Kennedy took pains to weigh intelligence and advice more carefully and not to be swept along by consensus. When it was all over, he had reason to be content with both the procedure and the outcome. Intelligence reports were better than in the Bay of Pigs episode. They were slow in coming, it is true: Graham Allison has shown that the strategic decisions of the United States would have been different if information about Soviet missiles had come earlier or later, but also that the intelligence function, like others, rests on standard operating procedures that are characteristic of all large organizations.

Less than a month before the discovery of the missiles, the U.S. Intelligence Board had concluded that the Soviet Union was very unlikely to place offensive missiles in Cuba. It may be hard to believe that the United States should have been so slow to discover the truth, particularly with information on suspicious activity from CIA informants—a five-inch stack of reports on missiles alone, including data on the arrival of large-hatch Soviet ships riding high in the water, a sketch of a missile being transported by truck to the western part of the island, and the report of a boast by Castro's private pilot that "we have everything, including atomic weapons." But even information that proves true may not be credible by itself. The CIA had received many reports of missiles in Cuba in the past, all false, some planted by Cuban refugees. Clearly, it could not abruptly accept the latest as true. Other bits and pieces of the missile story were "in the system," but took time to reach the analysts and to work their way to the top. The best information came from photographs taken by high-flying U-2 spy planes, which made regular trips over Cuba. But after a U-2 was shot down over mainland China, the scope of flights over Cuba had been temporarily restricted by the government, to reduce the risk of a similar incident in Cuba and a buildup of international pressure to end all U-2 flights over unfriendly territory. The taking of the pictures that clearly showed missiles was thus delayed about a month. Allison argues that what critics regarded as the failure of American intelligence—its delay in coming to the right conclusion—can be understood as the product of organizational routines designed to balance risks: Speeding up the transmission of information from agents would have posed additional personal dangers; jumping to conclusions from isolated reports would have triggered a damaging international response; and so forth.[18]

Similarly, when President Kennedy ordered a naval blockade to prevent further shipments of military equipment to Cuba, there were problems of implementation, also resulting from organizational routines—in this case the desire of the navy to run the blockade its way rather than bow to the special demands of the White House. The president wished to afford the Soviet Union every opportunity to give in gracefully, in effect using the blockade as a political tactic rather than—as the navy seemed to prefer—as a purely military maneuver. When President Kennedy moved the blockade line closer to Cuba from its original 500 miles in order to allow the Soviet Union more time for compliance, the navy ignored his order and enforced the original line. Later, when some ships stopped in the water, the civilians guessed correctly that the blockade was working, while the navy ominously and incorrectly assumed the ships were waiting for submarine escorts. Lest the navy blunder, Secretary of Defense McNamara asked the chief of naval operations exactly what he planned to do. The admiral was upset that a civilian should question him on naval procedures; the secretary was upset that the admiral was unwilling to provide details. How would submarines be handled? Would there be Russian-speaking officers available? What would happen, McNamara asked, if a Soviet captain would not say what he was carrying?

The chief of naval operations waved the *Manual of Naval Regulations* in the secretary's face: "It's all in there."

Replied the secretary, "I don't give a damn what John Paul Jones would have done. I want to know what you are going to do, now."

"Now Mr. Secretary," retorted the admiral, "if you and your deputy will go back to your offices, the navy will run the blockade."[19] The admiral was made an ambassador soon after and sent to Portugal, and McNamara stepped up his efforts to make the navy play his game rather than theirs. ("The admirals are really something to cope with—and I should know. To change anything in the Na-a-vy is like punching a feather bed," as FDR said.) It was the kind of firsthand control that Lincoln occasionally enjoyed by visiting the battlefield.

It was Lyndon Johnson, however, more than any president since Lincoln, who monitored military engagements and intervened in day-to-day decision making. He approved specific targets in Vietnam, after long study and discussion of maps and air reconnaissance photographs to assess the benefits and costs of destroying each bridge, barracks, oil depot, airfield, or factory—the costs always including the possibility of extending the war beyond Vietnam.

> I never knew as I sat there in the afternoon, approving targets one, two, and three, whether one of those three might just be the one to set off the provisions of those secret treaties. In the dark at night, I would lay awake picturing my boys flying around North Vietnam, asking myself an endless series of questions. What if one of those targets you picked today triggers off Russia or China?

Night and day he would go to the Situation Room in the basement of the White House and absorb reports from the battlefield. He seemed to have nearly perfect control of the military.[20]

But, as Doris Kearns and others have demonstrated, the president had a feebler hold on the conduct of the war in Vietnam than his hours in the Situation Room indicated. He was confused about what he saw and heard, we now know, miscalculating the physical and psychic impact of the bombing on the Vietnamese people and miscalculating the ability of the adversary to fight an effective war on the ground. His boundless faith in American know-how can be seen in his plans for the economic improvement of Southeast Asia—at the same time as he was widening the war against the people and the land.

> These countries of Southeast Asia are homes for millions of impoverished people. Each day these people rise at dawn and struggle through until the night to wrest existence from the soil. They are often wracked by disease, plagued by hunger and death comes at the early age of 40.
>
> The American people have helped generously in times past. . . . Now there must be a much more massive effort to improve the life of man in that conflict-torn corner of our world. . . .
>
> There is much to be done. The wonders of modern medicine can be spread through villages where thousands die every year from lack of care. Schools can be established to train people in the skills that are needed to manage the process of development.

If it could be done in America, it could be done in Vietnam.

> I want to leave the footprints of America in Vietnam. I want them to say when the Americans come, this is what they leave—schools, not long cigars. We're going to turn the Mekong into a Tennessee Valley.[21]

The president was also regularly misinformed about the very events he monitored in the White House basement. Targets were identified and hit, and damage assessed, with far less accuracy than the president was led to believe. Because of the difficulty of pinpoint bombing, the tendency of the air force was to saturate whole areas, with only a modest effort to distinguish military and civilian targets, and to report more damage to the one and less to the other than the facts warranted. Some of the most devasting criticism of the remote-control war in Vietnam came from a disaffected ex-commandant of the marines, General David M. Shoup, who in 1969 wrote, "The U.S. bombing effort in both North and South Vietnam has been one of the most wasteful and expensive hoaxes ever to be put over on the American people." The reason, in his judgment, was that the air force, navy, and marines were "target-grabbing," vying for good records in bombing contests over Vietnam and lying about the success of their missions in order to compete for the favor of the president and Congress. The president and the American people alike were victims of falsified reports from the field, to which was added Lyndon Johnson's tendency to hear what he wanted to hear.[22]

A memorable case of false reporting from Vietnam came to light in 1972, during the Nixon administration, as the result of a letter to a senator from an air force sergeant in Thailand. "I and other members of wing intelligence," the letter began, "have been falsifying classified reports for missions into Vietnam. That is, we have been reporting that our planes have received hostile reactions such as [antiaircraft and missile] firings whether they have or not." An investigation showed that General John D. Lavelle, commander of the Seventh Air Force, had ordered at least twenty-eight unauthorized raids into North Vietnam over a period of four months in 1971 and 1972. In 1969 the secretary of defense had authorized bombers escorting unarmed reconnaissance planes over North Vietnam to attack antiaircraft and surface to air missile sites if and only if the enemy made offensive moves. The Pentagon allowed "protective reaction" strikes. General Lavelle ordered what he called "planned protective reaction" strikes instead.[23]

The general had two sets of records kept: One was factual and remained in his headquarters; the other falsely described one of several possible kinds of hostile enemy action to justify each American attack. Neither the Pentagon nor the president knew that the air war in the North had been expanded in violation of orders until the whistle was blown. General Lavelle contended that his breach of instructions and false reporting had the tacit approval of his superiors, which was denied by the Pentagon. Lavelle was recalled, demoted, and allowed to retire. It is not known how widespread such disobedience was during the war. It was not unique, certainly. There had previously been unauthorized bombings of Hanoi and of Soviet ships in Haiphong harbor. And there was a massacre of civilians in My Lai—unauthorized, to be sure, and unknown in Washington until eighteen months after the fact when a letter arrived from an enlisted man, as in the Lavelle incident.

A different problem of civilian-military relations, outside the usual pattern of faulty information up the line and disobedience to orders coming down, was revealed in the final year of the Nixon administration. The Pentagon was discovered spying on the White House. A Navy clerk assigned to the National Security Council diverted the most secret "eyes only" documents to his superiors in the navy. Just how many original documents and copies were transmitted is uncertain—many, according to the clerk; not so many, according to the admiral most directly involved. But it is agreed that the clerk had the confidence of the

White House, including then presidential assistant Henry Kissinger and his deputy, General Alexander M. Haig; that he accompanied them on six trips overseas; and that he gave the Pentagon information on secret peace negotiations with Le Duc Tho of North Vietnam in Paris, on secret talks on disarmament with the Soviet Union, and on Kissinger's secret trip to China in 1971. Some of the information came from private reports from Kissinger to the president. The intelligence went to the chairman of the Joint Chiefs of Staff, Admiral Thomas H. Moorer, and was passed on to the ranking members of the staff of the joint chiefs under a security system to guard against secondary leaks.[24]

As interesting as the spying operation itself is the question why the Pentagon should have wanted the information. Because of the risks, it had to be more than normal curiosity. One possibility among many is that the joint chiefs were worried about White House negotiations with long-time adversaries such as China and the Soviet Union. By not taking the military chiefs into his confidence on important policy shifts, President Nixon may have created suspicions in the Pentagon that led to the spying. What the military planned to do with the information is also unknown, but had they concluded that the nation was in jeopardy they might have sabotaged any of the negotiations by leaking secret documents.

The immediate outcome of the discovery of the spying operation was the removal of the clerk and the military liaison staff from the White House. But no steps were taken against the Pentagon. Admiral Moorer was reappointed chairman of the Joint Chiefs of Staff. And the White House, for reasons of its own, resisted further inquiry into the matter.

In all of the struggles for control of strategic military policy, to repeat Theodore Lowi's point, there is a relatively small cast of characters: a president contending with generals and admirals, or sometimes with obstreperous functionaries in the Central Intelligence Agency. By contrast, there are many decisions on other matters that are made in a larger arena. Those associated with the so-called military industrial complex are an example.

As Dwight Eisenhower left office, he cautioned the American people:

> Until the latest of our world conflicts, the United States had no armaments industry. American makers of plowshares could, with time and as required, make swords as well. But now we can no longer risk emergency improvisation of national defense; we have been compelled to create a permanent armaments industry of vast proportions. Added to this, three and a half million men and women are directly engaged in the defense establishment. . . .

This conjunction of an immense military establishment and a large arms industry is new in the American experience. The total influence—economic, political, even spiritual—is felt in every city, every State house, every office of Federal government. We recognize the imperative need for this development. Yet we must not fail to comprehend its grave implications. Our toil, resources and livelihood are all involved; so is the very structure of our society.

In the councils of government, we must guard against the acquisition of unwarranted influence, whether sought or unsought, by the military-industrial complex. The potential for the disastrous rise of misplaced power exists and will persist.

We must never let the weight of this combination endanger our liberties or democratic processes. We should take nothing for granted. Only an alert and knowledgeable citizenry can compel the proper meshing of the huge industrial and military machinery of defense with our peaceful methods and goals, so that security and liberty may prosper together.[25]

For the military-industrial complex to function, there need not be a conspiracy among the military defense industries, legislators from districts with defense plants and military bases, and others; it is enough that they have common interests and a supporting belief in the over-riding importance of a strong and well-equipped military establishment. Middle-level Pentagon officers can be counted on these days to favor military buildup and military solutions to foreign policy problems: A study by Lloyd Etheredge reveals, among other things, that 83 percent think the use of American force in Vietnam was justified, compared with 65 percent in the State Department and 36 percent in a control group from the Office of Management and Budget.[26]

To a president, the military-industrial complex can be a formidable adversary. In halting production of the B-1 bomber, for example, Jimmy Carter had to overcome the effects of a massive public relations campaign by Rockwell International, the prime contractor, and by a host of allied interests. A lobby called the American Security Council suggested that opposition to the B-1 bomber was a communist plot. ("Foremost among the groups opposing the B-1 bomber is the Communist Party of the Soviet Union and other Communist parties.") A special episode of the television serial, "The Six Million Dollar Man," was produced, with the assistance of the Department of Defense, showing the redoubtable Steve Austin beating off the attempts of the East Germans to sabotage the B-1 sufficiently to affect its performance in a test flight. There were lavish hunting trips for Pentagon officials paid by Rockwell, letter-writing campaigns, and so on.[27]

President Eisenhower himself contended successfully with the military-industrial complex. Budget reduction had been one of his promises in the campaign of 1952, and he meant to apply it to defense as well as domestic programs. Also, however, he was bent on keeping the country's defenses strong. He hoped to do both at once by placing more reliance on nuclear deterrence and less on conventional forces and trusting allies on the periphery of the Soviet Union to provide ground troups for conventional warfare. In Eisenhower's view, the savings would mean a sounder economy and in the long run, therefore, a greater readiness to compete with the Soviet Union. Overspending on defense would ultimately weaken the economy and the ability of the United States to respond to Soviet threats. He had his way. Defense spending *was* held down during his administration, particularly for conventional forces in the army and navy. It made a difference that Eisenhower was the nation's most admired general. With the help of Republican publicity in which his policy of "massive retaliation" was touted as a "new look," offering "more bang for the buck," he was able to gain broad public support and put down most of the opposition in Congress and the Pentagon. Any other president would have been more vulnerable to conservative criticism.[28]

In the end, the policy of keeping costs down and protecting the country with threats of nuclear attack in support of local defense efforts gave way to John Kennedy's policy of graduated deterrence, based on the ability to strike back with strategic nuclear weapons, conventional forces, or unconventional counterinsurgency forces as needed. Whether he was right or wrong, Eisenhower was unusually successful in overcoming pressures to escalate armaments and to expand the nation's military commitments. It was Eisenhower who rejected the advice of the secretary of state and the chairman of the Joint Chiefs of Staff in 1954 that the United States go to the aid of the French on the brink of defeat in Indochina.

Militaristic Civilians

One need only compare Dwight Eisenhower and John Kennedy to put to rest any simple theory that generals seek war and civilians seek peace. In much of our history, the military have been anything but adventurous—the United States has, in fact, never been led into war by the military.[29] Nor does civilian control assure caution in the deployment of armed forces. This is not to say that the principle of civilian control of the military has no value, but only that it is by itself no guarantee of prudence in military policy making. It is equally important that the people of the country be wise and responsible and elect presidents and members of Congress in their image.

The war in Vietnam illustrates the problem. There was a good measure of civilian control: Presidents Kennedy and Johnson went to war with their eyes wide open, with the benefit of reasonably good intelligence. It is impossible to read the Pentagon Papers and other documents of the period and entertain any thought that the civilians were systematically victimized by the military, as one can argue with respect to Kennedy and the CIA in the Bay of Pigs operation.

Before he became president, Kennedy had read and liked retired General Maxwell Taylor's pungent criticisms of the strategy of massive retaliation. Taylor, a former army chief of staff, became, progressively, adviser, special military representative, and chairman of the Joint Chiefs of Staff under Kennedy. He was a maverick nurtured by the president. Together the two men perfected the strategy of graduated deterrence and "flexible response." There were to be no more failures like the Bay of Pigs. In a 1961 report to the president made public in 1977, Taylor wrote,

> Paramilitary operations such as Zapata [the Bay of Pigs landing] are a form of Cold War action in which the country must prepare to engage. If it does so, it must engage in it with a maximum chance of success. Such operations should be planned and executed by a governmental mechanism capable of bringing into play, in addition to military and covert techniques, all other forces, political, economic, ideological, and intelligence, which can contribute to its success.

The report was consistent with the belligerent, interventionist tone of the inaugural address. Said Taylor,

> We are in a life and death struggle which we may be losing, and will lose unless we change our ways and marshal our resources with an intensity associated in the past only with times of war.

He advocated immediate consideration of several measures, including

- The announcement of a limited national emergency.
- A re-examination of emergency powers of the President as to their adequacy to meet the developing situation.
- The review of any treaties . . . which restrain the full use of our resources in the Cold War.
- The determination to seek the respect of our neighbors without the criterion being international popularity.

And concluded with the proposal of an "affirmative program" in Indochina. Escalation of American armed force in Vietnam began immediately.[30]

In both the Kennedy and Johnson administrations, the inner circle of the White House consisted of civilians, Taylor excepted, who were capable, successful (the best and the brightest, David Halberstam called them), and adventurous. One of the most important figures was Robert McNamara, secretary of defense from 1961 to 1968, whose strengths and weaknesses exemplify both the boldness and the wrongheadedness of the Vietnam period.

McNamara came to the Department of Defense from the presidency of the Ford Motor Company, where he was known as a tough and successful manager. He had taught at Harvard Business School and during World War II had been assigned by the army air forces to help organize and systematize its long-range bomber program. At Ford his forte was systems analysis, with which he modernized an organization grown stodgy and uncompetitive. With computerized statistical techniques, he cut costs, coordinated operations, and produced a car that would compete with the Chevrolet.

McNamara was a far more active and informed secretary of defense than his predecessors, in the style of his presidency of Ford. His was the most forceful assertion of civilian control the Pentagon had ever experienced. He enlarged the Office of the Secretary with systems analysts brought in from the outside and instituted a new management technique known as the Planning, Programming, Budgeting System, or PPBS. It was more than a new way of making annual requests for appropriations. It was a decision-making system with which McNamara meant to transform a pluralistic bureaucracy into a monolithic one.

One way to understand PPBS is to compare it with the decision-making system it replaced. Traditionally the separate services had enjoyed a good deal of autonomy in deciding how their annual appropriations would be spent, an arrangement not greatly affected by the legislation of 1947 and 1949. Civilians, including presidents other than Eisenhower, had typically deferred to the expertise of the military on the allocation of appropriations for specific programs and weapons systems. Furthermore, technical information on the performance of the separate services was insufficient for the secretary, the president, and Congress to make informed judgments, particularly comparative judgments. Decision making in the defense department, in sum, was decentralized and beyond the grasp of most civilians.

PPBS was designed to change this. It required each unit precisely and quantitatively to report its contributions to the major programs of the department, such as "strategic retaliatory forces" and "continental air and missile defense forces," and to spell out the unit costs of each of the contributions. The same kind of analysis was required in looking from one to five years into the future: Once a projected level of output in each program for the department as a whole was set, the optimum contributions of each unit could be determined by comparing unit costs and finding the combination of army, navy, air force, and marine corps contributions that produced the most for a given amount of money or, alternatively, cost the least for a given level of output. This was cost-benefit analysis, the core of PPBS. As McNamara described it,

> Let me give you one hypothetical example to illustrate the point. Suppose we have two tactical fighter aircraft which are identical in every important measure of performance, except one—Aircraft A can fly ten miles per hour faster than Aircraft B. However, Aircraft A costs $10,000 more per unit than Aircraft B. Thus, if we need about 1,000 aircraft, the total additional cost would be $10 million.
> If we approach this problem from the viewpoint of a given amount of resources, the additional combat effectiveness represented by the greater speed of Aircraft A would have to be weighed against the additional combat effectiveness which the same $10 million could produce if applied to other defense purposes—more Aircraft B, more or better aircraft munitions, or more ships, or even more military family housing. And if we approach the problem from the point of view of a given amount of combat capability, we would have to determine whether that given amount could be achieved at less cost by buying, for example, more of Aircraft B or more aircraft munitions or better munitions, or perhaps surface-to-surface missiles. Thus, the fact that Aircraft A flies ten miles per hour faster than Aircraft B is not conclusive. We still have to determine whether the greater speed is worth the greater cost. This kind of determination is the heart of the planning-programming-budgeting or resources allocation problem within the Defense Department.[31]

The most dramatic effect of PPBS was to bring to the Office of the Secretary decisions that previously had been made at a lower level. On policy questions, the role of the separate services was reduced to supplying information that the secretary could use to approve or disapprove the continuance of present efforts and the initiation of others.

The energy and personality of Robert McNamara were a powerful reinforcement of PPBS. He was a professional: He did his homework and was ready, even anxious, to overwhelm generals, admirals, and members of Congress with his superior grasp of the facts—something they had not encountered in the amateurs who had occupied the office before him.

> He was marvelous with charts and statistics. Once, sitting at CINC-PAC for eight hours watching hundreds and hundreds of slides flashed across the screen showing what was in the pipe line to Vietnam and what was already there, he finally said, after seven hours, "Stop the projector.

This slide, number 869, contradicts slide 11." Slide 11 was flashed back and he was right, they did contradict each other. Everyone was impressed, and many a little frightened.[32]

At its worst, McNamara's self-assurance led to the dogmatic defense of his own kind of evidence and his own solutions.

PPBS must inevitably be judged by the policy it helped produce—above all the disaster of American involvement in Vietnam. It is not difficult, with the luxury of hindsight, to discover why McNamara's decision-making system failed. PPBS was a fad, like zero-base budgeting years later, according to its proponents a universal cure for the ills of bureaucracy. It promised to reduce human error and bias in decision making with hard data and computers. Those who believed in PPBS considered their logic invincible, which is one reason it took so long to realize that the Vietnam War was a mistake.

PPBS failed because it dealt best with quantifiable variables such as the number and power of missiles and bombs, and worst with intangibles such as the ingenuity and determination of the enemy. What worked in Detroit as a method of designing cost-effective cars was largely irrelevant to the problem of fighting a guerilla war in the jungles of Vietnam.[33] Worse, it helped to insulate McNamara from reality, even when military intelligence was realistically pessimistic about the war, and it kept alive the myth that the war could be won from the air. Another reason for the failure of PPBS was that it set much store in planning, with insufficient respect for the dimness of the future. In 1964 McNamara confidently predicted that the American troops would be home by Christmas 1965. Throughout the war, which lasted ten years longer than McNamara promised, the Pentagon kept saying it could see the light at the end of the tunnel.

McNamara and his decision-making system were better at making innumerable small decisions on the elimination of waste and duplications of effort among the services than at figuring out what the Americans were up against in Indochina. But while they predominated they lent such an air of precision and authenticity to strategic military decisions that dissent was all but impossible.

McNamara had taken hold of the Department of Defense, shaken it, and managed it with zest and determination for seven years. He established civilian control, with the help of PPBS. But it was not a fair test of willpower, as Eisenhower's "new look" had been, because the civilians were at least as hungry for war as the military. PPBS lingers on as a supplementary management and budgeting tool in several parts of the federal government, but after McNamara it had no real importance in the Pentagon. Decision making reverted to its traditional decentralized state, which meant that, along with a degree of sloppiness characteristic of pluralism, there was an opportunity for more people to complain when policy seemed to be going wrong. In 1977 Secretary of Defense Harold Brown, a disciple of McNamara, reinstituted some central budgetary controls; but he was less anxious than McNamara to march to war with their help.[34]

There is another side of the question of civilian-military relations: To most people, civilian control requires the exclusion of the professional military from a role at home, in domestic politics. In the 1960s and 1970s this principle was threatened by a series of incidents that, like the war in Vietnam, resulted from a lack of restraint among the civilians in charge rather than from military adventurism. Increasingly, the White House turned to the armed services for domestic purposes not authorized by law and in some instances expressly forbidden by statute or by the Constitution.

There seem to be two kinds of reasons why presidents make use of the military for domestic functions. Sooner or later every president is frustrated by the separation of powers, checks and balances, and intractable bureaucrats. It is tempting then to turn to the military, with its promise of obedience. (When President Nixon ordered the chairman of the joint chiefs to have an officer who had been convicted for his part in the My Lai massacre returned from jail to his quarters, the chairman said "Yes, sir." Remarked Nixon, "Anyone else would have answered 'Yes, but. . . .' ")[35] As commander in chief, the president can impose his will without the statutory restrictions he encounters in dealing with the civilian bureaucracy (to which one may add that every modern president except Dwight Eisenhower and perhaps Jimmy Carter has also enjoyed the glamor and excitement of association with the military). Military officers tend to be efficient—they usually are retired early if they are not, whereas civil servants stay on until a mandatory retirement age. And they are likely to be discreet.

The mixture of the military and the political in the career of General Alexander M. Haig is a case in point. In 1969, a colonel at West Point, he was brought to the White House as a member of presidential assistant Henry Kissinger's National Security Council staff. His experience was largely in staff rather than command positions. Haig did well, was given great responsibility, and by 1972 had been promoted to four-star general. At his request, he was returned to a military job, as vice chief of staff of the army. When H. R. Haldeman was forced out of office by Watergate revelations in 1973, however, President Nixon turned to Haig. As the president's principal assistant, Haig assumed more responsibility for policy than Haldeman had enjoyed, defended the president against his critics, deliberately misled Watergate investigators, kept the

White House going as the president's position deteriorated, and in the end discussed a pardon with Vice President Ford and helped urge the president to resign when the damning contents of the June 23rd tape became known. He had enormous power, acting as president at times when Richard Nixon was taken up with his defense against impeachment. President Ford appointed him supreme allied commander in Europe, over criticism that he was a "political" general, raised to power by the White House rather than by success as a soldier.

Haig served his presidents well. His only public misstep seems to have been to admonish Deputy Attorney General William Ruckelshaus, who had refused to fire Special Prosecutor Archibald Cox, "You have received an order from your commander in chief!"—which of course he had not, since the president is not commander in chief of civilian agencies. It suggested that Haig was unclear about the distinction between war powers and domestic powers.

Another side of White House use of the military (and the paramilitary) in domestic affairs is illustrated by the political intelligence activities of the army and the CIA in the late 1960s and early 1970s. The army collected, computerized, and disseminated information from 1967 to 1969 on some 18,000 civilians who either were involved in urban rioting and other civil disturbances or seemed likely to be, indiscriminately spying on groups that advocated violence and a good many that did not, including the National Association for the Advancement of Colored People and the Daughters of the American Revolution. This "Continental United States Intelligence" operation, or "Conus Intel," was part of a vast domestic surveillance and intelligence network that worked with the knowledge and approval of Presidents Kennedy, Johnson, and Nixon. The CIA conducted "Operation CHAOS" from 1967 to 1974 to discover contacts between foreign governments and dissident groups in the United States. Like Conus Intel, it netted dissidents of all kinds. The 1947 statutory charter of the CIA explicitly prohibiting domestic intelligence operations was ignored. Operation CHAOS accumulated information on more than 300,000 people and organizations from surveillance of antiwar and other demonstrations, from infiltration of political organizations, and from informants.[36]

Presidents Johnson and Nixon were both pathologically suspicious of dissenters; Nixon, in addition, needed the CIA to cover up Watergate.

A final form of abuse, the involvement of the military in a coup d'etat by a president seeking unlimited power or perpetuation in office, has never happened. But it was enough of a possibility a few years ago for responsible officials to take steps to prevent it. In the final days of the Nixon administration, Secretary of Defense James R. Schlesinger, in consultation with the chairman of the Joint Chiefs of Staff, asserted close control over the military services in order to thwart any attempt by the president or his aides to interfere with the impeachment process by force of arms. Secretary Schlesinger was convinced the president would be forced from office shortly and was concerned that the legitimacy of the government might be threatened by an illicit involvement of the military. He therefore exercised his statutory responsibility of transmitting orders from the president to the services, stayed close to the Pentagon, and would have nullified an improper command. Several years before, General Earle G. Wheeler, chairman of the Joint Chiefs of Staff, had listed the prevention of a seizure of power by a military clique first among the functions of the JCS. Perhaps he and Schlesinger were playing hypothetical war games; perhaps, though, they understood the fragility of constitutional constraints on the military.[37]

Opinion polls show a high level of popular confidence in the military. It is not considered infallible, but neither is it seen as a threat. As one student of the military puts it, "People are not afraid of the military."[38] And the military, for its part, schools itself in the doctrine of civilian control. There is no doubt of the consensus on this point, inside and outside the military. Disobedience is almost unthinkable. Still, in a number of ways short of disobedience, there are ever-present problems of abuse in the system, from an excess of military or civilian zeal.

THE SUPREME COURT

John Marshall, chief justice of the United States from 1801 to 1835, deserves much of the credit for making the Supreme Court an independent political force great enough to compete with presidents. He made an ordinary court extraordinary by asserting its authority to find acts of the other branches of government unconstitutional—a point on which the Constitution is silent—and by leading it into the middle of one debate after another decade after decade on great questions of national power.

Marbury v. *Madison*, in which Marshall established the power of judicial review by denying the Court a lesser power granted by Congress some years earlier, is a complex case. In finding Section 13 of the Judiciary Act of 1789 unconstitutional on the questionable ground that it amounted to an unwarranted extension of the Court's original jurisdiction, the Court assumed the authority to have the final say on the obedience of the rest of the government to the dictates of the Constitution. Marshall's language is strong and uncompromising:

> If an act of the legislature, repugnant to the Constitution, is void, does it, notwithstanding its invalidity, bind the courts, and oblige them to give it effect? Or, in other words, though it be not law, does it constitute a rule as operative as if it was a law? This would be to overthrow in fact what was established in theory; and would seem, at first view, an absurdity

too gross to be insisted on. It shall, however, receive a more attentive consideration.

It is emphatically the province and duty of the judicial department to say what the law is. Those who apply the rule to particular cases, must of necessity expound and interpret that rule. If two laws conflict with each other, the courts must decide on the operation of each.

So if a law be in opposition to the Constitution; if both the law and the Constitution apply to a particular case, so that the court must either decide that case conformably to the law, disregarding the Constitution; or conformably to the Constitution, disregarding the law, the court must determine which of these conflicting rules governs the case. This is of the very essence of judicial duty.[1]

Hardly anyone in our judicial tradition would argue with Marshall's conclusion that the courts must favor the Constitution when it conflicts with a statute (and, by extension, with the actions of the executive). The problem is that diagnosing conflict between the Constitution and a statute is a matter of judgment and therefore of disagreement. Section 13 is a good example, since most legal scholars feel it was not inconsistent with the Constitution.

Supreme Court majorities since have wavered between similarly uninhibited application of the Constitution—although rarely with Marshall's force of argument—and the restraint that comes of being less certain that there is one clear or prudent answer to each case. Presidents prefer restraint. Roger Taney, chief justice from 1836 to 1864, provides illustrations of both restraint and activism vis-à-vis the president. In the well-known case of *Luther* v. *Borden*, Taney, writing for the Court, deferred to the decision of President John Tyler, acting with congressional authorization, to support one of two competing Rhode Island governments and to mobilize troops against the other in pursuit of the constitutional mandate to guarantee a republican form of government to every state in the union. Which government to support, said Taney, was a "political question" and therefore inappropriate for the Court to judge.

The high power has been conferred on this court of passing upon the acts of the State sovereignties, and of the legislative and executive branches of the federal government, and of determining whether they are beyond the limits of the power marked out for them respectively by the Constitution of the United States. This tribunal, therefore, should be the last to overstep the boundaries which limited its own jurisdiction. And while it should always be ready to meet any question confided to it by the Constitution, it is equally its duty not to pass beyond its appropriate sphere of action, and to take care not to involve itself in discussions which properly belong to other forums. No one, we believe, has ever doubted the proposition, that, according to the institutions of this country, the sovereignty in every State resides in the people of the State, and that they may alter and change their form of government at their own pleasure. But whether they have changed it or not by abolishing an old government, and establishing a new one in its place, is a question to be settled by the political power. And when that power has decided, the courts are bound to take notice of its decision, and to follow it.[2]

But it was Taney in a more activist mode who opposed Abraham Lincoln's seemingly unconstitutional suspension of habeas corpus in 1861. Taney ordered the release of a southern agitator, John Merryman, from the military prison in which he was being held without trial. The general in charge turned away the messenger carrying Taney's order to produce the prisoner. Taney responded with a contempt order against the general. To no avail: Lincoln and his general ignored the order. Said Taney,

> I had supposed it to be one of those points of constitutional law upon which there was no difference of opinion, and that it was admitted on all hands, that the privilege of the writ could not be suspended except by Act of Congress. . . .
>
> The Constitution provides . . . that "no person shall be deprived of life, liberty or property, without due process of law." It declares that "the right of the people to be secure in their persons, houses, papers and effects, against unreasonable searches and seizures, shall not be violated; and no warrant shall issue, but upon probable cause, supported by oath or affirmation, and particularly describing the place to be searched, and the persons or things to be seized." It provides that the party accused shall be entitled to a speedy trial in a court of justice.
>
> These great and fundamental laws, which Congress itself could not suspend, have been disregarded and suspended, like the writ of habeas corpus, by a military order, supported by force of arms. . . . I can only say that if the authority which the Constitution has confided in the judiciary department and judicial officers, may thus, upon any pretext or under any circumstances, be usurped by the military power, at its discretion, the people of the United States are no longer living under a government of laws, but every citizen holds life, liberty and property at the will and pleasure of the army officer in whose military district he may happen to be found.[3]

It has been back and forth ever since. The justices have proved equally adept at deciding grand issues of public policy when it suited them and fending those issues off when it seemed inappropriate or untimely to take them on. By 1936, Justice Brandeis could offer a whole catalogue of by then traditional reasons why the Court need not accept disputes brought to its door or decide them on broad grounds once presented. In addition to political questions, the Court might avoid cases brought by people insufficiently affected by the governmental action questioned, by those who had failed to take their complaints to every other possible legal forum before coming to the Supreme Court, and by those for whom a decision could no longer make a difference (if a party to the suit had died, for example), and cases of such technical complexity that the Court could better defer to specialists in the bureaucracy. And if it accepted a case, the Court might reach a decision narrowly—by statutory rather than consitutional construction, for instance.[4] It was not at all in the spirit of John Marshall. But his tradition of judicial activism has remained very much alive, alongside that of Brandeis and the other apostles of restraint. The result has been dual precedents from which the justices might choose whenever they were presented with a ticklish question of presidential power.

Confrontation

No group of cases has caused the Court to ponder activism versus restraint more than those involving presidents. One reason is that presidents can threaten everything from simply ignoring decisions that go against them to launching attacks on the Court. The possibility of open conflict sets an outer limit to judicial activism, therefore, beyond which the Court would seriously risk its authority. The members of the Court do not provoke the wrath of a president lightly. They wish to be right, but they also wish to remain effective.

The deadliest disputes between the president and the Supreme Court, in addition to Lincoln versus Taney, occurred in the administrations of Thomas Jefferson, Franklin Roosevelt, and Richard Nixon. Each of these presidents felt gravely threatened by the federal judiciary and moved to put it down. None was able to carry out his plan of attack, but in each instance the attempt was enough to cause the Court concern and to remind it of the risks of overextending its authority.

Before the adoption of the Lame Duck Amendment in 1933, a president and Congress could work well into the postelection year, passing laws, making appointments, and otherwise upsetting a new administration waiting in the wings. The Judiciary Act of 1801 was a mischievous piece of legislation passed by the Federalists under John Adams after they had lost the election of 1800 to Jefferson. It created new federal judgeships, relieved the justices of the Supreme Court of their onerous circuit duty, and reduced the membership of the Court from six to five when the next death or resignation occurred in order to delay the appointment of a Jeffersonian. The Federalists hoped to have a judiciary, and a Supreme Court, that with the benefit of life tenure would be a counterforce to Jeffersonians in the White House and Congress for years to come. Adams appointed Federalists to the new judicial posts and filled a vacancy in the chief justiceship with Secretary of State John Marshall.[5]

Jefferson had cause to be unhappy with the judiciary. He had planned to fill the chief justiceship with his own man, but the vacancy had come too soon; his fellow Republicans had suffered from energetic enforcement of the Sedition Act of 1798; he was dismayed at the open partisanship of some of the federalist judges; and capping it off was the act of 1801. It was in this setting that William Marbury came, after the new president had taken office, to ask that the Supreme Court order the new secretary of state, James Madison, to deliver his (Marbury's) commission as a justice of the peace, a petty position to which he had been appointed and confirmed but for which, in the turmoil of the transition, he had failed to receive a commission. In a preliminary round, Marshall ordered Madison to show cause why the commission should not be delivered, and Madison ignored him.

Then, while the case of *Marbury* v. *Madison* was pending, the Jeffersonians attacked. In 1802, they passed new legislation that repealed the 1801 measure, took the recently appointed judges' jobs from them, and postponed the next session of the Supreme Court until the following year in order to make it impracticable for the Court to find the 1802 legislation unconstitutional. When the Court at last resumed its work in 1803, it decided Marbury's suit and did so masterfully. Rather than order the delivery of the commission, which Marbury did not really want by then and which Madison surely would not deliver, Marshall persuaded the Court to avoid the issue by finding the statute on which Marbury's suit was based unconstitutional.

The decision led the Republicans to think about impeachment. They warmed up on a drunken and insane federal district judge, John Pickering (rejecting the claim of his family that, *because* he was insane, he could not be impeached and tried, and in the process setting a precedent for impeachment for offenses other than indictable crimes). Samuel Chase, a Supreme Court justice who had made brazen anti-Republican remarks from the bench, was impeached and brought to trial in the Senate. It was supposed that Marshall would follow, and one by one the Federalists would be removed and replaced. "Removal by impeachment," said one senator, is nothing more than a declaration by Congress that "you hold dangerous opinions, and if you are suffered to carry them into effect you will work the destruction of the nation." Chase, however, was acquitted on all counts with the help of defections among the Republicans. The plans to do in the rest of the Federalists were abandoned. The judiciary was safe for the moment.

But in 1807 came another bitter encounter. Aaron Burr, almost chosen president when the 1800 election had been thrown into the House of Representatives, and named vice president instead, was accused by Jefferson of treason for trying to break away some of the western territory from the United States. The case came before John Marshall, sitting as a circuit judge, who angered Jefferson by accepting bail for Burr, issuing subpoenas to the president to produce papers requested by the defendant, and sticking to tight constitutional standards ("Treason against the United States, shall consist only in levying war against them, or in adhering to their enemies, giving them aid and comfort. No person shall be convicted of treason unless on the testimony of two witnesses to the same overt act, or on confession in open court.")[6] Again there were rumors of impeachment if Marshall failed to convict Burr. But Burr was acquitted. When the administration brought lesser charges against him, he was acquitted again, in Marshall's court. The long struggle was over. It had demonstrated the vulnerability of the Supreme Court and the other federal courts to political attack and, equally, the powers of resistance of a well-led Court.

Mortal combat occurred again in the 1930s, between the Court and Franklin Roosevelt. By 1935, the legislation that Congress had passed for the president during and after the emergency session of 1933 had begun to reach the Supreme Court for review. One after another, major programs were struck down. On "Black Monday"—May 27, 1935—the Court voided the National Industrial Recovery Act and the Frazier-Lemke Act for the relief of farm mortgagors, and added for good measure that the president had acted unconstitutionally in removing a federal trade commissioner for political reasons. All three cases were unanimous.[7]

President Roosevelt had been thinking about what to do about the Supreme Court for some time. In 1935 he put some options before the cabinet: constitutional amendments to reverse Court decisions, in the manner of the Income Tax Amendment of 1913; an amendment to allow Congress to reenact any measure voided by the Court; and packing. In early 1937, his spirit renewed by a landslide reelection, Roosevelt sent Congress a court-packing bill to give the president the power to appoint an additional justice for any member who passed the age of 70, increasing the size of the Court from nine to a maximum of fifteen. Since most members of the Court were already over 70, the bill would allow the president to appoint enough liberals to make the Court change course at once.

The fine irony was that the plan had been devised by Associate Justice McReynolds, one of Roosevelt's most dedicated antagonists, when he was attorney general many years earlier. McReynolds' plan had been directed at all federal courts *except* the Supreme Court; Roosevelt proposed that it apply *only* to the Supreme Court. The president was less than honest about his motives when he sent the plan to Congress: He put the enlargement of the Supreme Court in with a bill to increase the number of judges at all levels, reduce caseloads, and provide speedier justice; and he justified it all together in the name of efficiency. Certainly no one inside or outside of Congress was misled. Everyone knew it was a bill designed to turn the Supreme Court sharply left. Vice President Garner, presiding over the Senate when the president's message was read, gave a broad hint of trouble ahead, ostentatiously holding his nose with one hand and signaling thumbs down with the other. To help it along, the president went on radio with a fireside chat, this time with more candor. He said,

> The American form of government [is] a three horse team provided by the Constitution to the American people so that their field might be plowed. . . .
>
> The three horses are, of course, the three branches of government— the Congress, the executive, and the courts. Two of the horses are pulling in unison today; the third is not. . . .
>
> It is the American people themselves who are in the driver's seat.
> It is the American people themselves who want the furrow plowed.
> It is the American people themselves who expect the third horse to pull in unison with the other two. . . .
>
> We have . . . reached the point as a nation where we must take action to save the Constitution from the Court and the Court from itself.[8]

But the bill foundered.

And then, abruptly, the Court began to decide cases in the president's favor—the "switch in time that saved nine." Associate Justice Owen Roberts and Chief Justice Charles Evans Hughes tipped the balance in a series of cases in March and April, and the resignations of older justices followed. From 1937 on, the Court exercised judicial restraint on domestic regulatory and welfare legislation, and reserved its activism for the defense of individual liberties under the Bill of Rights and the equal protection clause.

The president had had his way with the Court, but not with Congress. Court packing died in the Senate. The causal relation between Roosevelt's attack and the collapse of the anti-New Deal forces on the Court is unclear still. It was not, as some supposed at the time, a simple matter of giving in to the president's threat. The crucial switch of Justice Roberts in the case of *West Coast Hotel Company* v. *Parrish* appeared after the introduction of the court-packing bill, but his vote in the case occurred well before, and could not have been prompted by the plan. Much later, however, Roberts admitted that the Court had been under strain from criticism of its New Deal decisions and an expectation that the president would try some remedy.[9] One of the lessons of the confrontation may have been that presidents cannot easily tamper with the Court; but another, surely, was that it is risky for the Supreme Court to stay out of step with Congress, the president, and the public too long.

Still another great confrontation came during the Nixon presidency. As a conservative, Richard Nixon had every reason to be displeased with the performance of the Court from the time of the public school desegregation in 1954 to his inauguration in 1969. The Warren Court had curbed the anticommunist efforts of the federal and state governments, given new meaning to the First Amendment, and broadened the constitutional rights of minorities and criminal defendants. In the first weeks of his administration, Nixon was to be further disappointed by a new flurry of liberal decisions, beginning with the assertion that high school students had the right to wear black armbands as a war protest in school and going on to reverse a number of criminal convictions—of civil rights activists for demonstrating in Chicago and marching in Birmingham in the face of opposition by local authorities, of a man who disparaged and burned an American flag as a civil rights protest, of former Harvard professor Timothy Leary for the possession of marijuana, of a Ku Klux Klan leader (on the grounds that the First Amendment protected advocacy of the use of force and of the violation of law unless such advocacy was directed to inciting or producing imminent lawless action), and of a man convicted of possessing obscene material in the privacy of his home—finishing with a decision voiding state laws that denied welfare benefits to residents of less than a year.[10]

It was no surprise, therefore, that President Nixon made the most of Earl Warren's resignation by naming a conservative federal judge, Warren Burger, to the chief justiceship. Burger was sworn in (on June 23, 1969, the day the Court handed down an important pair of search-and-seizure cases limiting the power of the police to search a suspect's house without a warrant)[11] with a mandate to turn the Court around. At most, however, the Court became more moderate. It did grow less liberal during the Nixon years, but it never quite stopped handing the White House rude disappointments.

When another vacancy occurred that year, upon the resignation of Associate Justice Abe Fortas, President Nixon proposed the name of Clement Haynsworth of South Carolina. Like Burger, Haynsworth was a conservative senior federal appellate judge who might be expected to help undo some of the work of the Warren Court. Opposition to the appointment developed in the Senate, however, as the unfolding of his record revealed the extent of his conservatism, particularly in civil rights cases. While the confirmation was pending, the Supreme Court handed down still another decision certain to displease the president: In *Alexander* v. *Holmes*, decided in October 1969, a unanimous Court, including Chief Justice Burger, chided the administration for attempting to slow public school desegregation in Mississippi.[12] Previous administrations had gone to court many times to ask for desegregation orders, but never to ask for a slowdown. In a *per curiam* opinion that by its very terseness suggested that the point was beyond argument, the Court said that "Continued operation of segregated schools under a standard allowing 'all deliberate speed' for desegregation is no longer permissible." Further delay was out of the question. It was against this background that debate proceeded on the Haynsworth nomination. Then new information came to light that portrayed Haynsworth as ethically insensitive. He had, among other things, decided a case involving a company in which he owned stock. His nomination was rejected. Angrily, President Nixon said, "Especially I deplore the nature of the attacks that have been made upon this distinguished man. His integrity is unimpeachable, his ability unquestioned. The Supreme Court needs men of his legal philosophy to restore the proper balance to that institution."

Then, out of bitterness, Nixon made a nomination that one careful scholar of the Court has characterized as very likely the worst in our entire history: G. Harrold Carswell, another federal judge from the South, had a record of opposition to civil rights and an unusual number of reversals of his decisions by higher courts. Whereas Haynsworth enjoyed the support of the bench and bar in the South, Carswell did not. Some eminent southerners, not to mention northerners, recommended that he be voted down by the Senate. Senator Russell Long of Louisiana responded gamely, "Does it not seem . . . that we have had enough of those upside down, corkscrew thinkers? Would it not appear that it might be well to take a B student or a C student who was able to think straight, compared to one of those A students who are capable of getting us a 100 percent increase in crime in this country?" And Senator Roman Hruska of Nebraska added that even if Carswell was mediocre, "There are a lot of mediocre judges and people and lawyers. They are entitled to a little representation, aren't they, and a little chance? We can't have all Brandeises and Cardozos and Frankfurters and stuff like that there."[13] As the debate grew warmer, President Nixon intervened with a constitutional argument that seemed to suggest that the Senate's power of confirmation might be used to support but not to oppose a presidential nomination:

> What is centrally at issue in this nomination is the constitutional responsibility of the President to appoint members of the Court—and

whether this responsibility can be frustrated by those who wish to substitute their own philosophy or their own subjective judgment for that of the one person entrusted by the Constitution with the power of appointment. . . . If the Senate attempts to substitute its judgment as to who shall be appointed, the traditional constitutional balance is in jeopardy.

Then a reporter dug up a speech Carswell had delivered over two decades earlier, a fervent defense of white supremacy. His nomination, too, was rejected.

President Nixon, willfully misconstruing the Senate vote, retorted, "I have reluctantly concluded . . . I cannot successfully nominate to the Supreme Court any federal appellate judge from the South who believes as I do in the strict construction of the Constitution." He deplored the criticism of Haynsworth and Carswell as "vicious assaults on their intelligence, their honesty, and their character." He concluded, "As long as the Senate is constituted the way it is today, I will not nominate another southerner and let him be subjected to the kind of malicious character assassination accorded both Judges Haynsworth and Carswell." His next nominee, Judge Harry Blackmun of Minnesota, was confirmed without difficulty.

In 1971, Justices Hugo Black and John Marshall Harlan resigned within days of one another and gave the president his third and fourth appointments to the Court. By that time, the Court had further angered the president with such decisions as *New York Times* v. *United States*, which denied the administration's request for a court order prohibiting publication of the Pentagon Papers, and *Swann* v. *Charlotte-Mecklenburg*, which declared busing a legitimate means of overcoming *de jure* segregation in the public schools. President Nixon had made his opposition to busing clear. In this, its first pronouncement on busing, the Court was unanimous. The opinion of the Court was written by Chief Justice Burger.[14]

President Nixon considered a number of people for the new posts, foremost among them an Arkansas bond lawyer and a woman judge in California, both so demonstrably unqualified that the American Bar Association's screening committee, which had found no fault with Haynsworth or Carswell, refused to endorse them. It split on the bond lawyer, six voting "not qualified" and six "not opposed," and unanimously declared the woman judge "not qualified."[15] The legal community and the public were outraged to learn of the president's intentions. Another round of defeats in the Senate was inevitable. The president substituted the names of Lewis Powell and William Rehnquist, however, just before going on television to announce his appointments. Although Powell was a southern conservative and Rehnquist an ideologist of the far right, they were regarded as honest and capable. The

Senate voted to confirm, giving the lie to the president's complaint that the Senate had set its mind against southerners and conservatives.

It is interesting to speculate why the president had tried to name a succession of people of inferior qualifications to the Court. It cannot have been out of ignorance, since the identity of highly qualified men and women of all persuasions and regions was no secret in the legal community and became a matter of public knowledge whenever the search began for a new member of the Court. Lewis Powell, for example, had been on most lists from the beginning. The appointments must be assumed to have been calculated. Angered and frustrated by the liberalism of the Court, even into his administration, the president was increasingly attracted to pure and simple conservatives—good soldiers rather than independent thinkers. Rebuffed again and again, he grew vindictive and in the end must have meant to humiliate the Court and the Senate both. It would have been difficult to find people of the stature of Black and Harlan, and in fact he never did, but the bond lawyer and the judge from California would have mocked their memory.

Jefferson's weapon was impeachment, Franklin Roosevelt's was court packing, and Nixon's was mediocrity. These differences aside, the lesson of the grand confrontations of presidents and the Supreme Court is that the political branches will move against the Court when they feel they have been pushed too far by its decisions. In each of these instances, the independence and authority of the Court were at stake.

There is another kind of attack that worked once and might work again, and that is alteration of the Court's appellate jurisdiction. So far it has not been used by presidents, but only by Congress acting on its own initiative. It is a powerful threat, and might at any time be passed at the suggestion of a president.

Article III of the Constitution gives the Court narrowly defined original jurisdiction, and appellate jurisdiction over a range of subjects and persons "with such exceptions, and under such regulations as the Congress shall make." Under this authority, Congress makes periodic changes in the flow of litigation to the Court and in the mechanisms by which the Court can accept or reject the cases presented to it. The usual purpose is to improve the Court's supervision of the federal and state judicial systems. But it can also be used to curb the Court if it is on the verge of handing down an unpopular decision. The leading case is *Ex parte McCardle* (1869). William McCardle, a newspaper editor in Mississippi during Reconstruction, was arrested on charges of publishing libelous and incendiary articles and was held for trial before a military tribunal. He appealed to the Supreme Court under a provision of the Habeas Corpus Act of 1867. The case was argued, and then, within days, Congress repealed the provision of the law that had allowed McCardle to bring his case. When the repealer was vetoed by Andrew Johnson, Congress overrode the veto. Its concern was that the Court, which earlier had found the wartime trial of a resident civilian by a military tribunal unconstitutional when and where civil courts were open for business, might go on to find Reconstruction unconstitutional.[16]

The justices might have decided that the power of Congress to alter the jurisdiction of the Court did not include the right to intervene in a case already before the Court. Instead, they ordered reargument to consider the question the following term, over Justice Grier's dissent: "By the postponement of this case, we shall subject ourselves, whether justly or unjustly, to the imputation that we have evaded the performance of a duty imposed on us by the Constitution, and waited for Legislative interposition to supersede our action, and relieve us from responsibility."[17] When they came to a final decision months later, they agreed unanimously that Congress had made it impossible for them to proceed with the case. *Ex parte McCardle* was dismissed. Congress had found a way to exercise surer and more selective control over the Court than the all-out war Jefferson had attempted.

In the 1950s the Supreme Court's controversial decisions on civil rights, defendants' rights, and the anticommunist programs of the federal and state governments gave rise to many proposals for reforming the Court. The one that came closest to passing was an offspring of *McCardle*. Senator William Jenner of Indiana introduced a bill that would have withdrawn the Court's appellate jurisdiction in several specific areas in which, in the opinion of many on the right, it had given communists an unfair advantage. Unlike the legislation aimed at the Court in the McCardle incident, Jenner's bill would not have undone pending litigation, but it would have allowed Congress and the executive to ignore the offending cases as precedent. After acrimonious debate, the bill came to a vote in August 1958 and lost forty-one to forty-nine.[18]

A few years later, in the mid-1960s, Congress considered still another way of curbing the Court: constitutional amendments to modify or reverse the Court's decisions on reapportionment, school prayer, and the rights of criminal suspects. The closest any of the proposals came to passage were the majority votes in the Senate in 1965 and 1966 for an amendment to allow the states to apportion one legislative chamber on a basis other than population and in 1966 for an amendment to permit voluntary prayer in the public schools—but each time the vote fell short of the two-thirds required to propose constitutional amendments to the states.

Still another form of confrontation is the president's refusal to obey the Court's orders. The list is familiar and brief. John Marshall expected

Thomas Jefferson and his secretary of state, James Madison, not to deliver Marbury's commission if asked—which is one reason why, in 1803, he chose not to ask. In 1832, President Andrew Jackson is reputed to have responded to a Supreme Court decision about a missionary to the Cherokee Indians, "John Marshall has made his decision; now let him enforce it." But the decision was directed to a Georgia court, not to the president, and the response therefore was more in the nature of an observation than a confrontation. Abraham Lincoln, in his inaugural address of 1861, with the hurtful *Dred Scott* decision of 1857 in mind, gave the Supreme Court a polite but firm warning not to overstep its authority again.

> I do not forget the position assumed by some that constitutional questions are to be decided by the Supreme Court, nor do I deny that such decisions must be binding in any case upon the parties to a suit as to the object of that suit, while they are also entitled to very high respect and consideration in all parallel cases by all other departments of the government. And while it is obviously possible that such decision may be erroneous in any given case, still the evil effect following it, being limited to that particular case, with the chance that it may be overruled and never become a precedent for other cases, can better be borne than could the evils of a different practice. At the same time, the candid citizen must confess that if the policy of the government upon vital questions affecting the whole people is to be irrevocably fixed by decisions of the Supreme Court, the instant they are made in ordinary litigation between parties in personal actions the people will have ceased to be their own rulers, having to that extent practically resigned their government into the hands of that eminent tribunal. Nor is there in this view any assault upon the court or the judges. It is a duty from which they may not shrink to decide cases properly brought before them, and it is no fault of theirs if others seek to turn their decisions to political purposes.[19]

It was in this spirit that Lincoln ignored the order of Chief Justice Taney to release John Merryman from Fort McHenry in 1861.

More recently, Franklin Roosevelt appeared ready to defy the Supreme Court in 1935 if it should rule that holders of government bonds might receive payment in gold. If the Court went the wrong way, he planned to nullify the decision. "To stand idly by and to permit the decision of the Supreme Court to be carried through to its logical, inescapable conclusion would imperil the economic and political security of this nation."[20] And in 1974 Richard Nixon announced that he would accept a "definitive" judicial decision on the disposition of the White House tapes sought by the special prosecutor. Without saying what he meant by "definitive," the president left open the possibility that he would defy a decision that did not meet his standards, a point to which we shall return in the next chapter.

Judicial Deference

In the long run, the confrontations of the Supreme Court and the political branches—the attempts to impeach, pack, ignore, and humiliate the Court and to overcome its decisions by constitutional amendment or the withdrawal of appellate jurisdiction—have not weakened the Court. If anything, the struggle for survival has given the Court strength. But the threat is always there. The president and Congress have so many ways of retaliating when the Court displeases them that the justices, aware of the history of confrontation, are inclined not to be too bold. The Court is likely to challenge a president head on only when he is too weak to fight back.

Wartime cases raise these strategic questions most clearly. There is, for example, *Ex parte Quirin*, the case of the German saboteurs, which came before the Court in 1942. Eight Germans trained in a sabotage school near Berlin, who had lived in the United States and could pass as Americans, were sent by submarine to New York and Florida with explosives for use against war industries. They buried their uniforms on the beaches, proceeded to major cities, and were promptly picked up by the FBI. President Roosevelt issued two executive orders, one declaring that enemies entering the United States for purposes of sabotage and espionage were "subject to the law of war and to the jurisdiction of military tribunals," the other establishing a military commission to try the saboteurs. According to the first order, there was to be no recourse to the civil courts.

The Supreme Court was in a difficult situation. It suspected, as John Marshall had in the *Marbury* case, that a wrong decision would be ignored by the executive. In fact, the Court was never certain while the case was pending whether the men were still alive or had been put to death under the terms of the presidential orders. It also knew, as Marshall did, that if it backed down meekly in the face of stern reality, it would be open to criticism for cowardice. The solution, which lacked the force and bite of *Marbury*, was to accept the case for review and then to uphold the president's authority. To take the case at all required some nerve, in view of the public clamor for swift justice. The Court could take some satisfaction in demonstrating that it and the Constitution had the final say, even in the heat of war. But the Court probably could not have saved the accused men if it had thought the military trial unconstitutional, and that may have influenced the direction of its decision.[21]

During the late 1960s and early 1970s, the Supreme Court regularly turned away challenges to the constitutionality of the war in Vietnam. Usually the cases were brought by young men about to be drafted into the army or shipped to Vietnam. In one interesting case, *Massachusetts* v. *Laird*, the point was raised by a state on behalf of its citizens, under the terms of a 1970 state law forbidding the use of Massachusetts residents in the war in the absence of a congressional declaration. The Court refused the case, and Justice Douglas equally predictably filed a dissent, spelling out the many reasons why the Court should face up to the issue.

> We have never ruled, I believe, that when the federal government takes a person by the neck and submits him to punishment, imprisonment, taxation, or to some ordeal, the complaining person may not be heard in court. The rationale in such cases is that the government cannot take life, liberty, or property of the individual and escape adjudication by the courts of the legality of its action.
>
> This is the heart of this case. It does not concern the wisdom of fighting in Southeast Asia. Likewise no question of whether the conflict is either just or necessary is present. We are asked instead whether the executive has power, absent a congressional declaration of war, to commit Massachusetts citizens to armed hostilities on foreign soil. Another way of putting the question is whether under our Constitution presidential wars are permissible.[22]

Why should the majority of the Court refuse to consider the question of the lawfulness of a war? It was an important question, and it raised a plausible objection to American involvement based on a straightforward reading of Article I, which grants Congress, not the president, the power to declare war. The formal answer, had the court chosen to give reasons, might have been that it was a political question of the kind raised in *Luther* v. *Borden*, appropriately decided by the political branches.[23] A more practical answer was that the Court would have invited trouble in taking such a case and especially deciding it against the president. For all of its seeming unpopularity, the war in Vietnam had the support of a majority of the people, Congress, and the president until the very end.

The cases of *Ex parte Quirin* and *Massachusetts* v. *Laird* are part of a pattern of decision established in the last century: When war powers are tested in wartime, the Court usually supports the president. By contrast, when war powers are tested after the war is over, which happens because it sometimes takes years to bring an appeal before the Court, the Court is notably less permissive. A few leading cases make the point.

In the Civil War, President Lincoln had his way with the Court— though he and the Chief Justice disagreed about Merryman, as we have seen. In the *Prize Cases*, the Court upheld Lincoln's blockade of southern ports in sweeping language.

> If a war be made by invasion of a foreign nation, the president is not only authorized but bound to resist force by force. He does not initiate the war, but is bound to accept the challenge without waiting for any special legislative authority. And whether the hostile party be a foreign invader, or States organized in rebellion, it is nonetheless a war. . . .
>
> Whether the president is fulfilling his duties, as commander in chief, in suppressing an insurrection, has met with such armed hostile resistance, and a civil war of such alarming proportions as will compel him to accord to them the character of belligerents, is a question to be decided *by him*, and this Court must be governed by the decisions and acts of the political department of the government to which this power was entrusted. "He must determine what degree of force the crisis demands." The proclamation of blockade is itself official and conclusive evidence to the Court that a state of war existed which demanded and authorized a recourse to such a measure, under the circumstances peculiar to the case.[24]

A while later, in 1864, the Court entirely avoided the sensitive issue of the trial of civilians by military commissions by refusing to take the case of Clement Vallandigham, a southern sympathizer who was tried and convicted in Ohio for publicly expressing sympathy for the Confederate cause and harboring disloyal sentiments. He had said to a large meeting in Ohio in 1863 that the war was wicked, cruel, and unnecessary, "not waged for the preservation of the union, but for the purpose of crushing out liberty." He was, he said, "at all times and upon all occasions resolved to do what he could to defeat the attempts now being made to build up a monarchy upon the ruins of free government." The military commission sentenced him to prison for the duration of the war. The Supreme Court refused to review, arguing that it had no original jurisdiction to take a case from a military commission and appellate jurisdiction only with respect to courts, of which the commission was not one. Had it wished to regard the commission as a court, it might simply have done so.[25]

A similar case reaching the Court in 1866, after the war was over, was decided differently, though the Court was except for one member the same as in *Vallandigham*. In 1864, Lamdin Milligan, a citizen of Indiana, was tried by a military commission in Indianapolis for involvement with the Sons of Liberty, an organization aimed at overthrowing the government of the United States, for conspiring to seize munitions stored in military arsenals; for liberating prisoners of war, for resisting the draft, and for other acts of disloyalty. He was sentenced to death.

Milligan initiated appeals through the civil courts. When the Supreme Court reviewed the case, it made a bold declaration of individual rights:

> Had this tribunal the legal power and authority to try and punish this man?
>
> No graver question was ever considered by this court, nor one which more nearly concerns the rights of the whole people; for it is the birthright of every American citizen when charged with crime, to be tried and punished according to law. The power of punishment is alone through the means which the laws have provided for the purpose, and if they are ineffectual, there is an immunity from punishment, no matter how great an offender the individual may be, or how much his crimes may have shocked the sense of justice of the country, or endangered its safety. By the protection of the law human rights are secured; withdraw that protection, and they are at the mercy of wicked rulers, or the clamor of an excited people. If there was law to justify this military trial, it is not our province to interfere; if there was not, it is our duty to declare the nullity of the whole proceedings.[26]

Then noting that there was no fighting going on in the area in which Milligan had been arrested and that the civil courts were open and operating, the Court ordered Milligan's release (assuming he had not already been hanged, a point on which they were uncertain). "The Constitution of the United States," it said, "is a law for rulers and people, equally in war and in peace, and covers all classes of men, at all times, and under all circumstances."[27] The president had no authority to establish military commissions outside the theater of war. Several members of the Court would have denied the power to Congress as well, but that was not at issue.

We may be allowed some cynicism about *Ex parte Milligan*. The Constitution has never applied equally in war and peace. There has been a strong consensus of president, Congress, and courts throughout our history that it should not. As Lincoln put it,

> Was it possible to lose the nation, and yet preserve the Constitution? By general law life *and* limb must be protected; yet often a limb must be amputated to save a life; but a life is never wisely given to save a limb. I felt that measures, otherwise unconstitutional, might become lawful, by becoming indispensable to the preservation of the Constitution, through the preservation of the nation.

The pattern can be seen in the cases testing the power of the president and Congress to establish martial rule within the United States in World War II. During the war, all of the important decisions, including *Ex parte Quirin*, went in favor of the president. The exclusion and relocation of people of Japanese ancestry from the western part of the country, citizens and aliens alike, violated many of the guarantees of the Constitution, and is now agreed to have been a grievous mistake. All persons of Japanese ancestry, including 70,000 American citizens, were cleared from the three West Coast states and parts of Arizona and sent to detention camps in the interior. The Supreme Court reviewed the program for the first time in *Hirabayashi v. United States* in 1943. Hirabayashi had been convicted on two counts, violation of a curfew requiring people of Japanese ancestry to remain in their homes at night and refusal to appear at a relocation center, and given three months in jail on each count, the sentences to run concurrently. The Supreme Court upheld the conviction for violation of the curfew, a relatively minor invasion of rights in wartime, and thus was able to avoid the more serious question of the lawfulness of the relocation program on the ground of mootness— Hirabayashi would have to serve his sentence in any event. As in *Ex parte Vallandigham*, the Court had made the most of a technicality in order to avoid the embarrassment of a decision.[28]

When the Court faced the issue of exclusion in *Korematsu v. United States*, it decided in favor of the president, and of Congress, which had subsequently ratified the president's order:

> Korematsu was not excluded from the Military Area because of hostility to him or his race. He *was* excluded because we are at war with the Japanese Empire, because the properly constituted military authorities feared an invasion of our West Coast and felt constrained to take proper security measures. . . . We cannot—by availing ourselves of the calm perspective of hindsight—now say that at the time these actions were unjustified.[29]

Justice Roberts dissented:

> This is not a case of keeping people off the streets at night as was *Hirabayashi v. United States*, nor a case of temporary exclusion of a citizen from an area for his own safety or that of the community. . . . On the contrary, it is the case of convicting a citizen as punishment for not submitting to imprisonment in a concentration camp, based on his ancestry, and solely because of his ancestry, without evidence or inquiry concerning his loyalty and good disposition towards the United States.[30]

After the war was over, the Court was less deferential. In *Duncan v. Kahanamoku*, a case much like *Milligan* but without its rhetorical flourishes, the Court reversed the wartime conviction of a civilian tried by a military tribunal in Hawaii for assaulting two marine sentries at a navy yard. Under the Hawaiian Organic Act passed by Congress in 1900 the governor, with the approval of the president, was authorized to declare martial law in the islands. But the Court, in an opinion by Hugo Black, who had written the opinion of the court in *Korematsu*, held that the governor and the president had exceeded the intent of Congress in allowing military trials of civilians at a time more than two years after the attack on Pearl Harbor when the civil courts were operating and military danger had subsided.[31]

The pattern, then, is judicial restraint during wars and reassertion of the wartime rights of individuals afterwards. Along the way, there have been some thoughtful alternatives offered in separate opinions. In *Duncan* v. *Kahanamoku*, for example, Justice Burton argued against hindsight: The courts must "put themselves as nearly as possible in the place of those who had the constitutional responsibility for immediate executive actions," he said. "For this Court to intrude its judgment into spheres of constitutional discretion that are reserved either to the Congress or to the chief executive, is to invite disregard of that judgment by the Congress of by executive agencies under a claim of constitutional right to do so."[32] Reserving the right of the Court to set the outer limits of executive discretion in war as in peace, Burton was content to concede the benefit of any doubt in wartime and to stick with that principle in deciding wartime cases after the war was over. The Constitution works differently in times of war and peace and, he thought, the Court should be candid about it.

In *Korematsu*, Justice Jackson took a different position: The Constitution should not be stretched for the sake of expediency in time of war, but neither should the military be required to conform to conventional tests of constitutionality. His solution to the dilemma was for the courts simply to look the other way and not review military decisions.

> Much is said of the danger to liberty from the Army program for deporting and detaining these citizens of Japanese extraction. But a judicial construction of the due process clause that will sustain this order is a far more subtle blow to liberty than the promulgations of the order itself. A military order, however unconstitutional, is not apt to last longer than the military emergency. . . . But once a judicial opinion rationalizes such an order to show that it conforms to the Constitution, or rather rationalizes the Constitution to show that the Constitution sanctions such an order, the Court for all time has validated the principle of racial discrimination in criminal procedure and of transplanting American citizens. The principle then lies about like a loaded weapon ready for the hand of any authority that can bring forward a claim of an urgent need.[33]

Virtually everyone agrees that the president must have vast discretion in wartime but, as we have seen, there is less agreement on how to reconcile military expediency and constitutional principle.

The Supreme Court's treatment of presidential authority in *domestic* affairs is much simpler. More often than not, the president acts in the domestic arena in conformity with acts of Congress. Since 1937 the Court has with few exceptions approved domestic legislation fashioned by the president and Congress; and since 1935 it has approved all delegations of authority to the president contained in that legislation. Only when the president acts without statutory authorization does he run the risk of a judicial rebuff.

Before 1937 the Supreme Court was more interested in protecting property rights than nonproperty rights. It favored business and tended to be unsympathetic toward the claims of dissidents, criminal defendants, the poor, and minorities. After 1937 its interests reversed. Increasingly it used the Bill of Rights and the Fourteenth Amendment to defend the beleaguered and the underprivileged (with some notable exceptions, such as *Korematsu*), and just about gave up pleasing businessmen by finding regulatory and welfare legislation unconstitutional, as it had in the early years of the New Deal. The Constitution had not changed, but the values of the Court's members had.

A secondary dispute between Franklin Roosevelt and the Court arose over the constitutionality of delegating large amounts of policy-making authority to the president, as noted in an earlier chapter. In 1935 the Supreme Court struck down the National Industrial Recovery Act for, among other reasons, unlawfully delegating authority to the president. Under the act, codes of fair competition for each industry were to be approved and enforced by the president. But what constituted fair or unfair competition was undefined. It was left to the discretion of the president, without standards or guidelines, and that, said the Court, was unconstitutional.[34] But the Court never again objected to delegation of authority to the president. When President Nixon declared a wage-price freeze under the Economic Stabilization Act of 1970, which gave him vast discretionary authority "to issue such orders and regulations as he may deem appropriate to stabilize prices, rents, wages, and salaries at levels not less than those prevailing on May 25, 1970," the courts raised no objection. A lower federal court reviewed the act and obligingly concluded that there was a general understanding about what might be done to stabilize prices, in contrast with the National Industrial Recovery Act, which was a shot in the dark—a brand new economic experiment that indeed left the president on his own to set the direction of policy.[35]

Thus the president has free rein in matters of war and peace, almost without exception, and we shall consider the exception next. (That the Court tends to recant ex post facto, as in *Ex parte Milligan* and *Duncan* v. *Kahanamoku*, is of no real importance.) In domestic matters, he has been similarly favored by the permissiveness of the post-1937 Court with respect to presidentially inspired legislative programs and to the delegation of legislative authority to the executive.

The Steel Seizure Case

There is one case that deals more directly with presidential prerogative than any other in our history, a wartime case that went against the president, with an overly simplistic opinion of the Court and a concurring opinion that states the limits on presidential authority with rare cogency. In *Youngstown Sheet & Tube Co.* v. *Sawyer*, the Steel Seizure case, the Court denied President Truman the authority to take over the steel mills for the purpose of preventing a strike.[36] The facts are simple. From December 1951 to April 1952 the United Steelworkers of America threatened to strike, and the intervention of the Federal Wage Stabilization Board proved to be of no avail. At the last minute, the president, believing a strike would jeopardize the war effort in Korea, ordered his secretary of commerce to seize and operate the steel mills until the danger of a strike had passed. The steel industry brought suit to prevent the seizure, and within days the issue was before the Supreme Court. Hugo Black's opinion of the Court was short and to the point.

> The president's power, if any, to issue the order must stem from an act of Congress or from the Constitution itself. There is no statute that expressly authorizes the president to take possession of property as he did here. Nor is there any act of Congress . . . from which such a power can fairly be implied.
>
> It is clear, that if the president had authority to issue the order he did, it must be found in some provision of the Constitution. . . .
>
> The order cannot properly be sustained as an exercise of the president's military power as commander in chief. . . . Nor can the seizure order be sustained because of the several constitutional provisions that grant executive power to the president. In the framework of our Constitution, the president's power to see that the laws are faithfully executed refutes the idea that he is to be a lawmaker. . . .
>
> The Founders of this Nation entrusted the lawmaking power to the Congress alone in both good and bad times.[37]

The trouble with this is that while Black recognizes no inherent authority at all in the executive, the history of the presidency suggests that presidents do act on their own with the blessing of the Court. The *Korematsu* case may not be an admirable example, but it remains good law, and the opinion of the Court, we may recall, was written by Black. Yet he cited no precedent in the Steel Seizure case. The weakness of Black's opinion is underscored by the fact that a majority of the Court (counting the separate opinions of six concurring and dissenting members) agreed that under some circumstances a president *might* exercise inherent or emergency powers.

Robert Jackson, in his concurring opinion, made a more realistic assessment of presidential power:

> 1. When the president acts pursuant to an express or implied authorization of Congress, his authority is at its maximum, for it includes all that he possesses in his own right plus all that Congress can delegate. In these circumstances, and in these only, may he be said (for what it may be worth) to personify the federal sovereignty. If his act is held unconstitutional under these circumstances, it usually means that the federal government as an undivided whole lacks power. A seizure executed by the president pursuant to an act of Congress would be supported by the strongest of presumptions and the widest latitude of judicial interpretation, and the burden of persuasion would rest heavily upon any who might attack it.
>
> 2. When the president acts in absence of either a congressional grant or denial of authority, he can only rely upon his own independent powers, but there is a zone of twilight in which he and Congress may have concurrent authority, or in which its distribution is uncertain. Therefore, congressional inertia, indifference or acquiescence may sometimes, at least as a practical matter, enable, if not invite, measures on independent presidential responsibility. In this area, any actual test of power is likely to depend on the imperatives of events and contemporary imponderables rather than on abstract theories of law.
>
> 3. When the president takes measures incompatible with the expressed or implied will of Congress, his power is at its lowest ebb, for then he can rely only upon his own constitutional powers minus any constitutional powers of Congress on the subject. Courts can sustain exclusive presidential control in such a case only by disabling the Congress from acting upon the subject. Presidential claim to a power at once so conclusive and preclusive must be scrutinized with caution; for what is at stake is the equilibrium established by our constitutional system.[38]

Jackson put Harry Truman's seizure order in the third category because Congress had rejected seizure in such situations—though over the years providing for it in various other circumstances—and had instead passed the Taft-Hartley Act providing for the use of a temporary injunction and, if necessary, an appeal to Congress for new legislation. (In 1979 a federal court, later overruled, cited Jackson's concurrence in striking down key provisions of President Carter's 1978 executive order on wage and price guidelines. The court found the president's assumption of authority to withhold government contracts from noncomplying companies unjustified either by acts of Congress or by the Constitution.)[39]

But as Jackson knew, better than Black, there are ambiguities in even the best classification systems. It is not always clear whether a president is acting in concert with Congress. Sometimes the statutes are unclear. When its use of warrantless wiretaps was challenged, for example, in a case involving an investigation of the dynamiting of a CIA field office in Michigan, the Nixon administration argued that the president had been given the authority by Congress, a category-one contention that the Court rejected—the act in question was neutral, it said. The government then fell back on the argument that the president's independent power to protect the national security sufficed, a category-two rationale also rejected by the Court, which concluded that the president was not exempt from the requirements of the Fourth Amendment in domestic national security investigations.[40]

Sometimes even the silence of Congress is ambiguous. If Congress has not acted on a given matter and the president has, is congressional silence to be taken as acquiescence? There is precedent for this view. But what then is to be made of President Kennedy's executive order establishing a Committee on Equal Employment Opportunity to enforce a policy of nondiscrimination in government employment and in private employment under government contract. In court, the government got away with a far-fetched argument that nondiscrimination in government contracts could be justified by a 1949 act concerned with "efficiency and economy" in procurement. On the contrary, everyone knew in 1949 and in 1961 that congressional silence represented an unwillingness to legislate civil rights. The executive order might better have been regarded as defiance of the will of Congress. But the courts upheld the order.[41]

There is another point in the Steel Seizure case that never quite breaks the surface: the importance of the political context. It is subsumed by Justice Jackson's principle that "any actual test of power is likely to depend on the imperatives of events and contemporary imponderables rather than on abstract theories of law." By mid-1952 President Truman's popularity was at a low point; his party was looking for a new candidate for November; the war in Korea was stalemated and unpopular; and a steel strike did not appear as calamitous as it might have in World War II. Furthermore, President Truman was all too clearly playing politics by refusing to use the temporary injunction provided by the Taft-Hartley Act, probably because he had condemned the act in 1947 as a slave labor law, vetoed it, and watched Congress override his veto. Five years later, he knew that if he invoked the act and it worked he would look silly and the Republicans would say so. He was on weak footing, therefore, when he approached the Supreme Court. It is quite possible the Court would have decided differently had the president been less vulnerable.

The same forces can be seen at work in the case of *United States v. Nixon*, in which a unanimous Court ordered the president to release tapes of conversations with his advisers for use in a criminal trial.[42] A long time from now, the case may best be remembered for having allowed a limited claim of executive privilege, but its immediate impact was to help drive Richard Nixon from office. He was at the time widely regarded as having engaged in criminal conduct, and his arguments that his actions were governed by considerations of national security and the protection of the presidency had become a bad joke. The opinion of the Court does not go into such "imperatives of events and contemporary imponderables," but it may be supposed that the justices were fully aware of the political and legal importance of their decisions. It is believed, in fact, that they drew together in unanimity out of concern that the president would refuse to obey a split decision. Afterward it was revealed that the president had been undecided about compliance until the last minute.

Perhaps the central lesson of the Steel Seizure case and *United States* v. *Nixon* is that the Supreme Court, though normally restrained, does have power to rise up and smite a president. Another is that it is most likely to do so when the president has already been forced to his knees in the political wars (or, as in *Milligan* and *Kahanamoku*, after the death of the president in question). Still another lesson, some would argue, is the view of Oliver Wendell Holmes, Jr., that

> Great cases like hard cases make bad law. For great cases are great not by reason of their real importance in shaping the law of the future but because of some accident of immediate overwhelming interest which appeals to the feelings and distorts the judgment. These immediate interests exercise a kind of hydraulic pressure which makes what was previously clear seem doubtful, and before which even well-settled principles of law may bend.[43]

Controlling the Court

Presidents expect Supreme Court majorities to go against them from time to time, but they are likely to be sharply disappointed when their own appointees join those majorities. In the Steel Seizure case, two of President Truman's four appointees voted for the steel companies, and that was enough to swing the decision against the president. In *United States* v. *Nixon*, all four of the president's appointees voted for the release of the tapes, and his chief justice wrote the opinion of the Court. It bears repeating that the Court is generally deferential to presidents—Franklin Roosevelt's first term aside—and members are not on the whole unkind to those who appointed them. But decisions that do go the wrong way rankle, all the more if one's own appointees have been disloyal.

There are many examples. Theodore Roosevelt was furious with Justice Holmes for his vote against the government in an important antitrust case two years after his appointment to the Court. Roosevelt had had good sense to appoint the independent-minded Holmes, already a towering figure in American jurisprudence. Still, he wanted Holmes to vote right on antitrust. Before making the appointment, he had questioned Senator Henry Cabot Lodge, of Holmes's home state of Massachusetts, and found Holmes sound—he thought—on antitrust, labor, race, and other key issues. As it happened, the president won his case five to four, with Holmes dissenting. But he was no less incensed. "I could carve out of a banana a judge with more backbone than that," he growled. Holmes was amused to learn of the remark. He would, he said, "call the shots as I see them in terms of the legal and constitutional setting." A while later, Holmes said to a labor leader, "What you want is favor, not justice. But when I am on my job, I don't give a damn what you or Mr. Roosevelt want." Normally he would enforce a law even, as he once said, if it made him vomit. As for antitrust legislation, he said, "Of course I know, and every other sensible man knows, that the Sherman law is damned nonsense, but if my country wants to go to hell, I am here to help it."[44]

Theodore Roosevelt was less concerned about the party affiliation of a prospective appointee than what he called a man's "real politics." Discussing Horace Lurton, a Democrat, Roosevelt said,

> The nominal politics of the man has nothing to do with his actions on the bench. His real politics are all important. . . . He is right on the Negro question; he is right on the power of the federal government; he is right on the Insular business; he is right about corporations; and he is right about labor. On every question that would come before the bench, he has so far shown himself to be in much closer touch with the policies in which you and I believe.[45]

But, as Harry Truman noted, "Packing the Supreme Court simply can't be done. . . . I've tried it and it won't work. . . . Whenever you put a man on the Supreme Court he ceases to be your friend. I'm sure of that." Perhaps President Truman suffered more than most because he did appoint an undistinguished lot of good friends to the Court and expected them to act like good friends on the bench.[46]

Dwight Eisenhower was furious about the performance of two of his appointees, Earl Warren and William J. Brennan. His nomination of Earl Warren to the chief justiceship was frankly political, to reward a presidential contender and the contender's state of California, but Eisenhower and his advisers had every reason to believe from Warren's record as state attorney general and governor that he would be a proper conservative—he had among other things favored the relocation of Japanese-Americans and opposed President Truman's steel seizure. Soon after his confirmation, however, Warren led the Court to a unanimous decision declaring the unconstitutionality of racial segregation in the public schools, a principle that was soon extended to other forms of segregation.[47]

Eisenhower said nothing publicly against the school desegregation decision while in office, but neither did he lend it any moral support. The impression grew that he found desegregation distasteful. When the governor of Arkansas used the national guard to prevent court-ordered school integration in Little Rock in 1957, Eisenhower had no choice but to require obedience to the federal government. He put the Arkansas national guard under Pentagon command, sent in federal paratroops, and assured integration by keeping Little Rock High School under military guard for the remainder of the school year. Still, he could not help regarding the chief justice at least as much to blame as the governor of Arkansas for the trouble in Little Rock.

In the years following, Warren led the Court to a succession of liberal decisions. William Brennan was a willing collaborator. When someone later asked Eisenhower if he had made any mistakes in office, he replied, "Yes, two, and they are both sitting on the Supreme Court."[48]

President Nixon had fewer decisions to complain about, but as a more active president than Eisenhower he was more likely to be directly affected when the Court spoke, as we have seen in the cases on busing, surveillance, and the White House tapes. On most issues, the four Nixon appointees were in agreement, and with the help of one or two swing men were able to turn the Court away from the liberalism of the Warren period. It was only after Nixon had left office that they began to lose their cohesiveness.[49]

A footnote to the tale of Richard Nixon and the Court: It was reported in 1977 that three of his appointees had voted to hear the appeals of John Mitchell, H. R. Haldeman, and John Ehrlichman from their convictions in the Watergate cover-up case. It takes four votes to bring a case before the Court. Since one of Nixon's appointees, William Rehnquist, excused himself because he had been assistant attorney general under Mitchell, the vote went five to three against the convicted men. According to reports based on a leak from the Supreme Court, Chief Justice Burger delayed final consideration of the appeal in the hope of changing one vote among the five in order to take the case for argument. He failed, and the three conspirators were forced to serve out their sentences.[50]

To sum up: The Supreme Court has the power to strike down the legislative programs of presidents and executive actions taken on their own authority. One reason the Court has kept its great power, however, is that it avoids serious clashes with the president. History suggests that presidents will retaliate if they are not treated with deference by the Court. Only when the president is out of office or merely hanging on is the Court likely to attack his programs and decisions.

SUCCESSION

The United States has enjoyed peaceful and orderly transitions from one president to the next without exception from the beginning of the republic. It honors its revolutionary heritage in principle, and in practice is as unrevolutionary as a nation can be. Every four years, even in war, presidential elections are held as the Constitution requires, and the losers accept the outcome. They may grumble, and certainly set about laying plans for the next election, but they do not seriously consider an assassination or a coup d'etat. It is a remarkable record.

Because of the oddities of the electoral system and the chance that someone who has lost the popular vote may be elected president, the willingness of the majority, not just the minority, to be good losers may be tested at any time. It is one thing to accept the results of an electoral system when it works, quite another when it breaks down. But each time the winner of the popular vote has lost the presidency, in the elections of 1824, 1876, and 1888, the outcome was in fact broadly accepted. And when the transition has come between elections, upon the death or resignation of a president, though the person promoted from the vice presidency may have been a disappointment, the people have accepted the lawful transfer of authority. A succession has never provoked a constitutional crisis in the United States.

In this chapter we shall consider transitions occurring between elections, caused by the death or resignation of a president, by his disability, or by impeachment and conviction.

Death or Resignation

Legally, the death or resignation of a president presents relatively few problems; it is disability that raises the most difficult questions of interpretation, even with the clarifications of the Twenty-Fifth Amendment. Death or resignation leads to a transition that is uncomplicated legally, however aggravating politically.

The original Constitution provided that

> In the case of the removal of the President from office, or of his death, resignation, or inability to discharge the powers and duties of the said office, the same shall devolve upon the Vice President, and the Congress may by law provide for the case of removal, death, resignation, or inability, both of the President and Vice President, declaring what officer shall then act as President, and such officer shall act accordingly until the disability be removed or a President shall be elected.[1]

The vice president, in succeeding to the powers and duties of the office on the death or resignation of the president (leaving "inability" aside for the moment), probably was meant to become acting president only, not president, but when John Tyler took the title along with the office in 1841 he set a lasting precedent. The Twenty-Fifth Amendment, adopted in 1967, affirmed the tradition: "In case of the removal of the President from office or of his death or resignation, the Vice President shall become President."[2]

Under the terms of the Constitution, it is up to Congress to decide what is to be done if both the presidency and the vice presidency become vacant. A law enacted in 1792 put the president pro tempore of the Senate next in line, followed by the speaker of the House.[3] In the unlikely event that all four offices were vacant at once, the law provided for the selection of a new president and vice president by electors chosen by the several states. In 1866, Congress passed a new law of succession designating the secretary of state in the event of a double vacancy, if he met the constitutional qualifications for the presidency, and after him the secretary of the treasury, and so on through the cabinet. Then, in 1947, feeling it was undemocratic for the next person in the line of succession to be an unelected official, President Truman asked Congress to put the speaker and the president pro tempore at the head of the line, followed by the cabinet, and that is the way it has been since.[4]

With the passage of the Twenty-Fifth Amendment, resort to a line of succession is less likely than it seemed to Harry Truman, who served without a vice president for nearly four years. The amendment says, "Whenever there is a vacancy in the office of the Vice President, the President shall nominate a Vice President who shall take office upon confirmation by a majority vote of both Houses of Congress."[5] It was not long before the provision had its debut: Spiro Agnew resigned the vice presidency in 1973, having bargained with the Department of Justice for light treatment in criminal court in return for leaving office immediately; Gerald Ford was named vice president and confirmed by Congress; then in 1974 Richard Nixon resigned; Ford became president; and the next vice president, Nelson Rockefeller, was named by Ford and confirmed by Congress. A new president had been named by a man in the process of being driven from office and had in turn named his successor—all far removed from the will of the people. There was talk of trying a new amendment.

The main criticism of the vice presidency, however, is not that it may at times be filled in an undemocratic way, but that vice presidents are by tradition chosen with at least as much concern for their ticket-balancing value as for their likely ability to do well as president. And there is a good chance that a vice president will become president either by the death or resignation of the incumbent (as did John Tyler, Millard Fillmore, Andrew Johnson, Chester A. Arthur, Theodore Roosevelt, Calvin Coolidge, Harry Truman, Lyndon Johnson and Gerald Ford) or by election (John Adams, Thomas Jefferson, Martin Van Buren, and Richard Nixon), which is about the only reason anyone takes the job. As Mr. Dooley said in 1906,

> Ivry mornin' it is his business to call at th' White House an' inquire afther th' prisidint's health. Whin told that th' prisidint was niver betther he gives three cheers, an' departs with a heavy heart. . . .
>
> Aside fr'm th' arjoos duties iv lookin' afther th' prisidint's health, it is th' business iv th' vice-prisidint to preside over th' deliberations iv th' Sinit. Ivry mornin' between ten an' twelve, he swings his hammock in th' palachial Sinit chamber an' sinks into dhreamless sleep. At times th' vice-prisidint rises fro'm his hammock an' says: 'Th' Sinitor will come to ordher.' 'He won't,' says th' Sinitor. 'Oh, very well,' says th' presidin' officer; 'he won't,' an' dhrops off again. It is his jooty to rigorously enforce th' rules iv th' Sinit. There ar-re none.[6]

As a candidate and during the first months of his term of office, the vice president usually is depicted as a full working partner of the president: one who gets along with the president, agrees on major issues, and is privy to the information he may need to act as president. The reality is different. The two are likely to represent different factions of the party, may even have been rivals for the presidency, and invariably are rivals in the sense that the vice president wants to be president sooner or later. When he became vice president, John Adams said, "I am nothing, but I may be everything."

As vice president, Harry Truman was so left out that he had to be informed of the existence of the atom bomb program by the secretary of war when he succeeded to the presidency. Dwight Eisenhower made some pretense of keeping Richard Nixon at hand as an apprentice, but in fact the two men were not close politically or socially. Asked by a reporter what decisions vice president Nixon had been responsible for in his administration, Eisenhower replied, "If you give me a week, I might think of one." When it came his turn, President Nixon, according to one aide, "froze out" Vice President Spiro Agnew. A reporter once asked Nixon if he had told Agnew about his plans for a diplomatic opening to China. He responded incredulously, "Agnew? Agnew? Of course not."[7]

Most presidents and vice presidents have an understanding that the latter will keep up appearances, whatever the reality. When he was vice president, Lyndon Johnson played the role of loyal subordinate despite the antagonism he and Kennedy had for one another. As president, Johnson demanded no less of Hubert Humphrey. Throughout the tragic escalation of the war in Vietnam, Vice President Humphrey publicly supported the policy of the administration and helped to rally the liberal wing of the party behind the president despite deepening private misgivings. Even when he had become the Democratic candidate for president in 1968, he remained a spokesman for Johnson's war policy, bowing to his will until late in the campaign. The pact between the two men was strong enough to overcome what Humphrey perceived as his own interest and the interest of his party and the country. Humphrey and Johnson were unusually well qualified for the vice presidency. They had been leading presidential contenders in their own right and powerful Senate leaders—only a few vice presidents in our history have been as well prepared to help a president run the country. But they, like the rest, were reduced to abject subordination. Afterwards Humphrey admitted, "The only time I saw Johnson was when he ran out of people to chew on and raised hell with me."[8]

One of the roles commonly taken by vice presidents is that of hatchetman for the president, who is thus able to appear statesmanlike above the political fray. President Eisenhower sent Richard Nixon to conduct a tough and dirty campaign in the mid-term elections of 1954, and President Nixon sent Spiro Agnew out to do the same in 1970—with equally bad results. Later, President Nixon used his new vice president, Gerald Ford, to lead a campaign against the critics of Watergate, while the president laid low and sent out word from the White House that he was too busy with foreign affairs to pay heed to domestic squabbles. Ford lashed out at the "few extreme partisans" who were "bent on stretching out the ordeal of Watergate for their own purposes." Those who were pursuing the investigation of Watergate were acting from narrow partisan motives, he said. "Their aim is total victory for themselves and the total defeat not only of President Nixon but of the policies for which he stands. If they can crush the President and his philosophy, they are convinced that they can dominate the Congress and, through it, the nation," said Ford. "A relatively strong group of political activists" were trying, he continued, "to cripple the President by dragging out the preliminaries to impeachment as long as they can, and to use the whole affair for maximum political advantage." If they succeeded, he said, "with the super-welfare staters in control of the Congress, and the White House neutralized as a balancing force, we can expect an avalanche of fresh government intervention in our economy, massive new government spending, higher taxes, and a more rampant inflation." Incredibly, even in the final hours of the Nixon administration, after he had been privately informed of the existence of a tape that would drive the president from office, Gerald Ford kept up his attack on the motives of those who favored impeachment. True to the pattern, when he had become president and was seeking reelection, Ford assumed the role of president of all the people, removed from battle, and deployed vice-presidential candidate Robert Dole as *his* hatchetman, also without success.[9]

Because of all the difficulty recruiting capable vice presidents and finding a proper role for them in office—it has more than once been suggested that the office be abolished. Arthur Schlesinger has proposed a constitutional amendment to that effect, leaving the line of succession under the control of Congress and providing for the prompt election of a new president. The merit of this plan is that the country would soon have someone in office who enjoyed the confidence of a majority of the people. Former senator and presidential candidate Eugene McCarthy has proposed as an alternative that, along with abolition of the vice presidency, we empower the electoral college to reconvene and fill vacancies in the presidency (requiring electors to exercise independent judgment, whereas traditionally most people have been praying they would not).[10]

Presidential Disability

When a president is disabled, the procedures for succession are less certain. Under the original Constitution, quoted earlier, the vice president was to take over the powers and duties of the office if the incumbent were disabled. The framers of the Constitution probably meant the vice president to step aside if the president recovered. But that was not the only possible interpretation of the text. And when presidents were disabled, the ambiguity of the Constitution was one reason nothing at all was done.

The first case was the eighty days between the shooting of President James A. Garfield and his death in September 1881. There were a number of urgent questions of foreign and domestic policy that needed attention and could not be delegated to department heads, but the president was too ill to do more than sign a single extradition paper. For a time there was hope he would recover from the wound. The cabinet met to consider whether Vice President Arthur might take over the duties temporarily. It decided four to three, however, that once he had done so he could not constitutionally hand the office back to Garfield, a view held by only a small minority of legal scholars at the time. Neither Vice President Arthur nor the cabinet wanted to do anything to distress the president and further endanger his life, so they did nothing.

The next serious presidential disability was Woodrow Wilson's— the result of a stroke—lasting from September 1919 through the end of his term in March 1921. He was at times capable of doing a modest amount of work, but for long periods could do nothing. He went eight months without seeing his cabinet, and read and signed only those papers his wife and doctor felt he could manage without worsening his condition. The Versailles Treaty and U.S. participation in the League of Nations were under consideration in the Senate but had only intermittent attention in the White House. Bills became law without his signature.

During this long period, the few faint suggestions that Vice President Marshall might act as president were slapped down by the president and those around him. Wilson seemed not fully aware of the seriousness of his disability, for one thing: He even thought he might run for reelection in 1920. His family and doctor were under no such illusion, but they wished to protect him, as a patient, from the loss of his office. They discouraged cabinet discussion of succession. Secretary of State Lansing was fired for having suggested it. ("When Lansing sought to oust me, I was on my back. I am on my feet now and I will not have disloyalty about me.") Wilson hung on for nearly a year and a half.

In the case of both Garfield and Wilson, there was concern that, once given up, the presidency could not be taken back by the president. That apparent misconstruction of the Constitution was one reason why those around the president shied away from succession. In both circumstances, the vice president was reluctant to lay claim to the office, perhaps for fear of appearing to be self-serving, though in both the public interest clearly called for it. And in both cases the cabinet chose not to force the issue. For all these reasons, the disability provision of Article II was a failure.

The Twenty-Fifth Amendment was designed to correct the deficiencies. The president may now give up the powers and duties of his office if he is disabled and get them back when he is fit. And if disabled but unable or unwilling to make the decision to step aside, he is to be displaced—there is now a clear mandate and, further, a sharing of the responsibility for this difficult decision by the vice president and the cabinet, which may make it easier on them all.

> *Section 3.* Whenever the President transmits to the President pro tempore of the Senate and the Speaker of the House of Representatives his written declaration that he is unable to discharge the powers and duties of his office, and until he transmits to them a written declaration to the contrary, such powers and duties shall be discharged by the Vice President as Acting President.
>
> *Section 4.* Whenever the Vice President and a majority of either the principal officers of the executive departments, or of such other body as Congress may by law provide, transmit to the President pro tempore of the Senate and the Speaker of the House of Representatives their written declaration that the President is unable to discharge the powers and duties of his office, the Vice President shall immediately assume the powers and duties of the office as Acting President.
>
> Thereafter, when the President transmits to the President pro tempore of the Senate and the Speaker of the House of Representatives his written declaration that no inability exists, he shall resume the powers and duties of his office unless the Vice President and a majority of either the principal officers of the executive department, or of such other body as Congress may by law provide, transmit within four days to the President pro tempore of the Senate and the Speaker of the House of Representatives their written declaration that the President is unable to discharge the powers and duties of his office. Thereupon Congress shall decide the issue, assembling within 48 hours for that purpose if not in session. If the Congress, within 21 days after receipt of the latter written declaration, or, if Congress is not in session, within 21 days after Congress is required to assemble, determines by two-thirds vote of both houses that the President is unable to discharge the powers and duties of his office, the Vice President shall continue to discharge the same as Acting President; otherwise, the President shall resume the powers and duties of his office.

Still, there is no assurance that disability will be handled better in the future than in the past. Even the provisions of the Twenty-Fifth Amendment are not self-executing. Even they will require some courage and intelligence in their administration, particularly if the disability should be mental rather than physical.

Impeachment

The remaining way for the presidency to become vacant is by the impeachment and removal of the incumbent. The relevant portions of the Constitution are

Article II, Section 4

> The President, Vice President and all civil officers of the United States shall be removed from office on impeachment for, and conviction of, treason, bribery, or other high crimes and misdemeanors.

Article I, Section 2.

> The House of Representatives . . . shall have the sole power of impeachment.

Article I, Section 3.

> The Senate shall have the sole power to try all impeachments. When sitting for that purpose, they shall be on oath or affirmation. When the President of the United States is tried, the Chief Justice shall preside: And no person shall be convicted without the concurrence of two thirds of the members present.
>
> Judgment in cases of impeachment shall not extend further than to removal from office, and disqualification to hold and enjoy any office of honor, trust, or profit under the United States: but the party convicted shall nevertheless be liable and subject to indictment, trial, judgment, and punishment according to law.

Article II, Section 2.

> The President . . . shall have power to grant reprieves and pardons for offenses against the United States, except in cases of impeachment.

And Article III, Section 2.

> The trial of all crimes, except in cases of impeachment, shall be by jury.

Under these provisions, one president, Andrew Johnson, was impeached but not convicted, and another, Richard Nixon, resigned in order to avoid impeachment.

Impeachment has two sides. It is a legal process resembling indictment and trial. It is also a political contest when a president is involved, with the partisan emotions and calculations of an election and even a few of the anxieties that attend a presidential assassination. Those who would impeach a president must prevail legally *and* politically.

The basic legal question is whether a person may be impeached for an offense that is not an indictable crime. The words of Article II, "treason, bribery, or other high crimes and misdemeanors," are open to very different interpretations: both the disinterested ones of legal scholars and the less trustworthy ones of lawyers hired to make the best possible case for the prosecution or the defense. The broadest possible view of the impeachment power was expressed by Gerald Ford—not in 1974 when he was defending Richard Nixon, to be sure, but four years earlier in arguing for the impeachment of liberal Supreme Court Justice William O. Douglas.

> [Impeachment, he said,] relates solely to the accused's right to hold civil office; not to the many other rights which are his as a citizen and which protect him in a court of law. . . . What then, is an impeachable offense? The only honest answer is that an impeachable offense is whatever a majority of the House of Representatives considers it to be at a given moment in history.
>
> Something less than a criminal act or criminal dereliction may nevertheless be grounds for impeachment.[11]

In one sense, it is correct that the House—or the Senate, ultimately—decides what an impeachable offense is because it has the last say: Few legal scholars believe there could be a judicial appeal of an impeachment or a conviction. Therefore whatever Congress in its wisdom decides impeachment is, it is. It is another thing to imply that Congress might reach its judgment without the guidance of Article II, however, or of the provision of Article III that judges shall hold office "during good behavior." By any reasonable interpretation of the Constitution, Douglas was not impeachable. The House so voted. Much later, Ford publicly apologized for his part in this misuse of the impeachment power.

At the other extreme is the contention that impeachment is limited to the more serious offenses for which one may be indicted and tried in a regular criminal court. For example, Representative Edward Hutchinson, ranking Republican member of the Judiciary Committee during its consideration of the impeachment of Richard Nixon, contended that

> The meaning of the words treason and bribery are self-evident. They are crimes, high crimes directed against the State. To me the meaning of the words high crimes and misdemeanors is equally obvious. It means what it says that a President can be impeached for the commission of crimes and misdemeanors which like other crimes to which they are linked

in the Constitution, treason and bribery, are high in the sense that they are crimes directed against or having great impact upon the system of government itself.

Thus, as I see it, the Constitution imposes two separate conditions for removal of a President. One, criminality, and two, serious impact of that criminality upon the government.[12]

The White House argued similarly that

The words "treason, bribery, or other high crimes and misdemeanors," construed either in light of present-day usage or as understood by the framers in the late 18th century, mean what they clearly connote— criminal offenses. Not only do the words inherently require a criminal offense, but one of a very serious nature committed in one's governmental capacity.

And it added supporting evidence:

This criminality requirement is reinforced by judicial construction and statutory penalty provisions. It is further evidenced by the criminal context of the language used in the other constitutional provisions concerning impeachment, such as Art. III, Sec. 2, Clause 3, which provides in part, "the trial of all crimes, except in cases of impeachment, shall be by jury."[13]

The majority of the Judiciary Committee took a middle position in 1974. Early in the year, the staff reported to the committee, "To confine impeachable conduct to indictable offenses may well be to set a standard so restrictive as not to reach conduct that might adversely affect the system of government. Some of the most grievous offenses against our constitutional form of government may not entail violations of the criminal law." The intent of the framers of the Constitution and practice since its adoption, the staff suggested, emphasize "the significant effects of the conduct—undermining the integrity of the office, disregard of constitutional duties and oath of office, abrogation of power, abuse of the governmental process, adverse impact on the system of government. Clearly, these effects can be brought about in ways not anticipated by the criminal law."[14]

The three articles of impeachment voted by the Judiciary Committee, which would have become the basis for debate in the full House on the impeachment of President Nixon had he not resigned, listed both criminal and noncriminal offenses, in keeping with the staff interpretation of the Constitution. Article I charged the president with obstructing and impeding the administration of justice by covering up the Watergate break-in. "This concealment," said the committee, "required perjury, destruction of evidence, obstruction of justice—all of which are crimes." And it involved "false and misleading public statements as part of a deliberate, contrived, continued deception of the American people"—which is a violation of the oath of office but not activity for which one might be sent to jail. Article II also charged a combination of indictable offenses and violations of the oath of office through the abuse of powers that only a president possesses: ordering wiretaps on political "enemies," using tax returns to gather intelligence, and so on. In the words of the committee, by his misuse of the Internal Revenue Service, the Federal Bureau of Investigation, and other units of the government, the president "engaged in conduct that violated the rights of citizens, that interfered with investigations by federal authorities and congressional committees, and that contravened the laws governing agencies of the executive branch of the federal government. This conduct, undertaken for his own personal political advantage and not in furtherance of any valid national policy objective, is seriously incompatible with our system of constitutional government." Article III charged the president with refusal to supply information needed by the Judiciary Committee to complete its investigations. The Republican minority did not support the second and third charges, but agreed that President Nixon had in the end incriminated himself on the first, obstruction of justice.[15]

The records of the Constitutional Convention do not say that the framers intended impeachment for conduct that was not criminal in the ordinary sense, but it is a fair inference. Impeachment was considered at first for "malpractice or neglect of duty." This was changed in the Committee on Detail to "treason, bribery or corruption," then simplified to "treason or bribery." When the question came before the full convention, George Mason proposed that "maladministration" be added, to which James Madison objected that "so vague a term will be equivalent to a tenure during the pleasure of the Senate." Mason then suggested the addition of "high crimes and misdemeanors" instead, and that became the final language without dissent. Madison's objection to the word "maladministration" did not mean he wished to allow impeachment for indictable offenses only, but simply that he wanted some limitation to the impeachment power. In the convention he said, "Some provision should be made for defending the community against the incapacity, negligence or perfidy of the chief magistrate. . . . He might pervert his administration into a scheme of peculation or oppression. He might betray his trust to a foreign power." In the Virginia ratification convention Madison said, "If the President be connected, in any suspicious manner with any person, and there be grounds to believe that he will shelter him," he would be subject to impeachment.[16] And as a member of the first Congress two years later, he said,

It may, perhaps, on some occasion, be found necessary to impeach the President himself; surely, therefore, it may happen to a subordinate officer, whose bad actions may be connived at or overlooked by the President. . . .

I think it absolutely necessary that the President should have the power of removing from office; it will make him, in a peculiar manner, responsible for their conduct and subject him to impeachment himself, if he suffers them to perpetrate with impunity high crimes or misdemeanors against the United States, or neglects to superintend their conduct, so as to check their excesses.[17]

Clearly Madison took a broad view of impeachment, even to the point of suggesting that a president might be impeached for tolerating misbehavior in his subordinates. Alexander Hamilton, a coauthor with Madison of the *Federalist*, wrote in No. 65 that impeachable offenses are those "which proceed from the misconduct of public men, or, in other words, from the abuse or violation of some public trust."

Further, the phrase "high crimes and misdemeanors" had been well known in English law where it had been used since the fourteenth century, in impeachments, not in the criminal law. It meant political offenses—crimes against the state. Blackstone's *Commentaries on the Laws of England*, familiar to all the framers, defined high misdemeanors as "the mal-administration of such high officers as are in public trust and employment."[18]

There is also a record of impeachments in the United States to consult. Twelve people have been impeached: nine judges, one senator, one cabinet member, and one president. Four were convicted, all judges. The charges have included many of a noncriminal nature. The most recent conviction, of District Judge Halsted Ritter in 1936, is a good example. He was charged with both kinds of offenses, including income tax evasion, a statutory crime; but he was acquitted of all but one charge, that his conduct had brought his court "into scandal and disrepute, to the prejudice of said court and public confidence in the administration of justice." President Nixon's lawyers argued, with some plausibility, that precedents involving judges were not relevant to his case, on the theory that the constitutional standards for the impeachment of judges and presidents differ, a point on which scholars disagree.[19]

The one precedent clearly relevant to the Nixon case, however, the impeachment and near conviction of President Andrew Johnson in 1868, was used to advantage by both sides. Ten of the eleven articles of impeachment voted by the House of Representatives were related to President Johnson's supposed violation of the Tenure of Office Act of 1867, which forbade the removal without Senate consent of certain officials during the term of the president by whom they were appointed.

Whether there was a violation depends on one's reading of the ambiguous words of the statute. The charges included indictable offenses. The other article, which did not, accused the president of ridiculing Congress.

The Judiciary Committee staff included the Johnson case among the ten in which there were allegations of offenses other than violations of the criminal law. President Nixon's lawyers, on the other hand, characterized it as a vindication of the narrow view of the impeachment power: "His acquittal strongly indicates that the Senate has refused to adopt a broad view of 'other high crimes and misdemeanors' as a basis for impeaching a president." One cited the action of the House, the other of the Senate. Which aspect of the Johnson impeachment is most important as a matter of law is endlessly debatable; but which is most important practically is clearer. It takes more than evidence of unindictable political offenses and more than evidence of lesser indictable political offenses to remove a president. Roughly the same lesson can be drawn from the Nixon case.[20]

Andrew Johnson's real offense, which did not appear in the articles of impeachment, was that he and the Radical Republicans who dominated Congress disagreed on policy for the defeated South. Once Congress had enacted a Reconstruction program over his veto, President Johnson did what he could to sabotage its implementation. He issued orders contradicting the requirements of acts of Congress, obstructing the efforts of federal commanders to challenge the voting registration of suspected Confederate sympathizers, denying the power of military commanders to issue decrees with the force of law or remove civilian officials and appoint new ones, and more.[21]

It was a bitter but honest disagreement. Johnson wished to be conciliatory toward the white South, to allow life—except for slavery—to go on very much as it had before the war. Congress wanted to protect blacks, to abolish discrimination along with slavery and to impose harsh military rule on the South until new ways of self-governance were learned. Regardless of whose policy was wiser, when the president interfered with the administration of lawful acts of Congress he might straightforwardly have been charged with the political offense of failure to execute the Reconstruction program faithfully. Instead, in an attempt to find a more specific legal excuse for removing him, the House of Representatives charged violations of the Tenure of Office Act and related acts of criminal conspiracy. The act was of doubtful constitutionality, and, although passed to limit Andrew Johnson's power over military and civilian appointees, its application to his removal of Secretary of War Stanton was also doubtful. The impeachment as it was framed by the House was devious and clumsy, and it failed.

In the case of Richard Nixon, although the House seemed likely to vote for impeachment on the basis of evidence available to it before the revelation of the "smoking gun" on August 5, 1974, and although the special prosecutor's office felt it already had a good criminal case against the president (which it chose not to prosecute), there was real question whether the required two-thirds could be mustered for conviction in the Senate. Before August 5, Congress had masses of convincing evidence against the president, including tapes of the president's involvement in the cover-up. For example, the president congratulated John Dean on September 15, 1972:

> Well, the whole thing is a can of worms. As you know, a lot of this stuff went on. And the people who worked [unintelligible] are awfully embarrassed. But the way you've handled it, it seems to me, has been very skillful, because you—putting your fingers in the leaks that have sprung there.[22]

Later, on March 22, 1973, President Nixon told John Mitchell and John Dean,

> I don't give a s___ what happens. I want you all to stonewall it, let them plead the Fifth Amendment, cover up or anything else.[23]

Then came the smoking gun, a full and detailed confession of a felony by the president, proof beyond the shadow of a doubt (conviction in a criminal court requires proof only beyond reasonable doubt), which generated pressures that most of the president's defenders in Congress found irresistible. Four days later there was a new president.

On June 23, 1972, six days after the second Watergate break-in, the president told H. R. Haldeman to order the CIA to stop the FBI from proceeding with its investigation of the source of the money found on the burglars, which was leading back to the Committee for the Re-Election of the President. The special prosecutor had known of White House efforts to use the CIA in the cover-up, but it had no hard evidence that the president was involved. The tape made it clear.

> *Haldeman:* Now, on the investigation, you know the Democratic break-in thing, we're back in the problem area because the FBI is not under control, because Gray doesn't exactly know how to control it and they have—their investigation is now leading into some productive areas—because they've been able to trace the money—not through the money itself—but through the bank sources—the banker. And, and it goes in some directions we don't want it to go. Ah, also there have been some things—like an informant came in off the street to the FBI in Miami who

was a photographer or has a friend who is a photographer who developed some films through this guy Barker and the films had pictures of Democratic National Committee letterhead documents and things. So it's things like that that are filtering in. Mitchell came up with yesterday, and John Dean analyzed very carefully last night and concludes, concurs now with Mitchell's recommendation that the only way to solve this, and we're set up beautifully to do it, ah, in that and that—the only network that paid any attention to it last night was NBC—they did a massive story on the Cuban thing.

President: That's right.

Haldeman: That the way to handle this now is for us to have Walters [of the CIA] call Pat Gray and just say, "Stay to hell out of this—this is ah, business here we don't want you to go any further on it." That's not an unusual development, and ah, that would take care of it.

President: What about Pat Gray—you mean Pat Gray doesn't want to?

Haldeman: Pat does want to. He doesn't know how to, and he doesn't have . . . any basis for doing it. Given this, he will then have the basis. He'll call Mark Felt in. . . .

President: Yeah.

Haldeman: He'll call him and say, "We've got the signal from across the river to put the hold on this." And that will fit rather well because the FBI agents who are working the case, at this point, feel that's what it is. . . .

Haldeman: And you seem to think the thing to do is get them to stop?

President: Right, fine.[24]

The tape made the difference. The Constitution seems to say one thing about the meaning of impeachment and Congress another. Polls of the Senate showed a readiness to convict after the release of the tape, not before. The effective meaning of impeachable offense seems to be felonious behavior at which one is caught red-handed. But without tapes, any future president who engages in criminal activity may be able to let his subordinates take the blame, as Richard Nixon was able to do until near the end. And clearly a president who merely tolerates corruption will be untouchable.

The unwillingness of Congress to use its impeachment power except in the presence of demonstrated criminality matches the public opinion poll results during the last year of the Nixon administration, which showed a larger and larger majority who felt the president had participated in the cover-up, but a far smaller portion who wanted him to be impeached. When the June 23rd tape came to light, even those who interpreted the impeachment power broadly were grateful for the evidence of criminal behavior and a quick resolution of the sorry affair.

Acceptance of the White House definition of impeachable offenses was the price paid for forcing Nixon out.

A No-Confidence Vote?

The constitutional devices for removing a president temporarily or permanently do not work easily, we know from long experience. Whether they work at all is an open question. The original disability provision certainly was no help when Presidents Garfield and Wilson were unable to function for long periods, nor during Franklin Roosevelt's fourth term, when he was dying; but one might say it supported the informal agreement of President Eisenhower and his vice president, Richard Nixon, for the transfer of authority during brief periods of incapacity. The disability clauses of the Twenty-Fifth Amendment have not been tested, nor has there been any obvious presidential disability since the adoption of the amendment. But it is not at all clear that the problem of belling the cat, as Arthur S. Miller put it,[25] has been solved by the amendment. The vice president and the cabinet together may or may not be more able and willing to displace the president than vice presidents alone have been in the past; and the amendment's explicit reassurance to presidents that they may have their powers back may or may not be enough to induce a president to step aside voluntarily. The impeachment power is at hand to remove a president who has confessed to the commission of a serious indictable crime in office, but it is doubtful that Congress and the public will invoke it for political offenses and dereliction of duty, as the framers of the Constitution seem to have intended.

The provisions relating to presidential removal, particularly to disability under the Twenty-Fifth Amendment and to impeachment, were carefully designed to be neither too hard nor too easy to use—to stand ready for real emergencies but not to destabilize the political system by regular use for partisan advantage. It should be no wonder, though, that these provisions of the Constitution, like others, should have been molded by political and social forces and notably in this case by the reluctance of people inside and outside the government to threaten a president's tenure.

During the painfully long time it took to force President Nixon out of office, from the spring of 1973 as Watergate began to unravel and Haldeman and Ehrlichman resigned to the release of the tape and the presidential resignation in August 1974, people began to think about ways of removing presidents without having to accuse them of anything. In February 1974, Representative Henry S. Reuss introduced H. J. Res. 903, a proposed amendment to the Constitution for the removal of the president upon the adoption of a resolution of no confidence by three-fifths of those present and voting in each house. With the president removed, the vice president (or next in line if that office were vacant) would act as president until a new election for president and vice president was called, within 90 to 110 days, or to coincide with congressional elections if they were approaching. The new president and vice president would serve out the regular term if most of it were left; otherwise, the date of the next scheduled presidential election would be postponed two years.

According to its proponents, a vote of no confidence would do two useful things. It would allow the removal of those who in theory should be declared disabled or guilty of high crimes and misdemeanors, but without need for Congress to make a specific finding of physical or mental impairment or of guilt. It would also make possible the removal of someone who had simply lost the confidence of the people. From the firing of Special Prosecutor Cox in October 1973 (if not before) until the disclosure of the tape the following August, Richard Nixon was a man on the run. In his last months in office, polls showed that a majority of the people wanted him out of office—putting together those who felt he was guilty of impeachable or indictable offenses and those who simply felt he had lost his usefulness as president. With the option of a no-confidence vote, Congress might have removed the president early on and spared the country the trauma of impeachment proceedings.

Lyndon Johnson would have been a likely subject of a no-confidence vote in the latter half of his 1965–1969 term, after he had lost his popularity in the polls for leading the nation deeper and deeper into war and for unrest at home. Harry Truman was in comparable trouble during the last years of his administration, and like Lyndon Johnson was pressured into a decision not to run for reelection. Herbert Hoover, burdened with the Great Depression his first year in office, never gained the confidence of the people—when his world of free enterprise and limited government fell apart in 1929, it might have been good for the country to bring in a new person with new values. Perhaps Franklin Roosevelt would have become president in 1930, Dwight Eisenhower in 1950, Robert Kennedy or Richard Nixon in 1967, and Gerald Ford in 1973. None of these cases is cited to say with any certainty that Congress should or would have exercised its no-confidence power if the Reuss amendment or its equivalent had been in effect at the time, but to point to circumstances in which it would at least have been a live question.

The prime objection to the no-confidence vote is that it might weaken the presidency. If Congress wished, it could limit the country to active presidents who lasted just long enough to offend three-fifths of Congress and passive presidents who held onto office by leaving policy to Congress. Since the voters have increased split-ticket voting in the last generation to the point that the chances of electing a Congress of one party and a president of another are about even, the normal conflict of Democrats and Republicans might be enough to produce regular no-confidence votes. If it took only three-fifths of those present and voting to oust a president, compared with two-thirds to override a veto, the temptation in Congress to remove a president who exercised the veto might be irresistible. We would then have, to use Woodrow Wilson's term for the imbalance of the late nineteenth century, congressional government.[26]

To meet this objection, Representative Reuss issued a new proposal several months later, in August 1977. H. R. Res 1111 contained two important changes: A president who suffered a no-confidence vote in Congress would not be displaced immediately, but would serve until the inauguration of his successor, and the vote would lead to a new congressional election at the same time as the presidential election. Clearly Congress would think twice about removing a president if it were removing itself at the same time. Further, H. J. Res. 1111 required the entire Senate to stand for reelection (each new senator to be elected for the term his or her predecessor had been serving). The new proposal was an effort to balance incentives in a way that would allow Congress to act when need arose but that would keep it from removing presidents frivolously. It is possible, though, that the price for Congress to pay would be too great and the amendment would not be used at all. Or it might conceivably be used by a president to have his way with Congress by threatening an impasse that would bring public pressure for dissolution.[27]

A no-confidence plan would end any incentive to make a general-purpose instrument of impeachment: No-confidence votes would cover borderline cases—thus most cases—of misbehavior as well as inability.

The simplest solution to all problems of succession would be to apply existing provisions of the Constitution firmly and fearlessly to presidents who ought to be removed for one of the reasons stated. But if they have not been applied in that manner so far, perhaps one should not be optimistic that new provisions would fare better.

Some of the difficulty of predicting whether reforms would make things better or worse can be seen in the old debate about what should be borrowed from Britain and to what effect. (There is rarely any call for borrowing from other countries.) The idea of the executive as a creature of the legislature was given a full hearing in the Philadelphia Convention and rejected. A century later, as we have seen, Woodrow Wilson pointed to the British system as a source of ideas for strengthening our presidency, and many people since have proposed British solutions for American political stagnation—a fusion of powers to overcome the ills of separation, responsible parties to replace the weak and heterogeneous Democratic and Republican organizations, and most recently a no-confidence vote to give Congress and the people added control of the executive. Some of the proposals have been meant to strengthen presidential power over Congress, some the reverse.

The amended Reuss proposal would have imported one of the links between the British executive and legislature: It would have given the legislature the power to remove the executive without giving the executive the power to dissolve the legislature, as in Britain, and without requiring the executive to have the confidence of the legislature for its very existence or to appear before the legislature from time to time to answer its questions.[28]

There are two ways of thinking about the problem of borrowing institutions piece by piece, which might be called *contextual* and *noncontextual*. According to the contextual school, one must understand an institution in its structural and functional setting and not expect it to work its old way in a new environment. By this logic, for example, the United States should not experiment with parliamentary government unless it is willing to reform its parties, which in turn would require new nominating procedures, and so on. Further, borrowers should be well aware of the way an institution works on home ground before thinking of importation. The no-confidence vote has not worked in Britain as some Americans think, Arthur Schlesinger argued recently—the last time it was used to remove a government that had enjoyed majority support in the legislature was in 1885, he noted (soon after, the *coalition* government of James Callaghan was ousted by a 310 to 311 vote of no confidence). Nor has its indirect effect, as a threat, been to enhance the legislature's control of the executive. On the contrary, he says,

> Suppose a constitutional amendment gave Congress or the president the power to dissolve the government—both the presidency and the Congress—and call for new elections. The question is: would this strengthen the executive or the legislative? The British example leaves no doubt about the answer. The power of dissolution would play into the hands of the executive. For once legislators have to face the electorate themselves, they will not be likely to force no-confidence votes. Presidents would be able to use the threat of new elections to keep rebellious legislators in line.[29]

William Livingston of the University of Texas is even less optimistic about borrowing. He posits a basic incompatibility between the two systems:

> The American constitution concentrates on the curbing of governmental power—on dividing it among a variety of governmental agencies and making sure that the total power of the state cannot be concentrated in

one set of hands. The British system, on the other hand, is designed to concentrate power in a single set of hands—legally the Parliament, politically the Cabinet—and then provide adequate means by which the users of power are held accountable for the way it is used. The American constitution seeks to preserve liberty by preventing the too effective use of governmental power. The British constitution protects it by providing means by which the users of power are rendered accountable to the people whom they are intended to serve.[30]

Since accountability in Britain stems from the threat of the next election rather than the threat of dissolution, in his view, it would be wrong to expect the no-confidence vote to make presidents accountable to Congress in the United States.[31]

James Sundquist of the Brooking's Institution belongs to the other school. He argues for a no-confidence vote without any supposition that it would work or need to work in the British manner. It would have the salutary effect of reaching presidents (1) against whom only a circumstantial case of criminal behavior has been made; (2) who have abused their authority, (3) who have suffered mental or emotional breakdown, which he feels the Twenty-Fifth Amendment will be unable to handle; and (4) those in whom the public has lost confidence. Its function would be to remedy specific deficiencies of the American system rather than to establish closer links between the government and the people in the fashion of the British. Sundquist believes that if Congress were given the no-confidence power and the executive were not given the power of dissolving the legislature, which the cabinet has in Britain, the effect, far from being disruptive, would be to exert a restraining influence on the presidency and restore a proper balance of power between the branches.[32]

Whether the no-confidence vote would work to the advantage of Congress, the president, or at all is uncertain—the speculations on its effects are a good reminder of the difficulties of political engineering. What is more certain is that until there is another succession crisis as serious as Watergate, interest in reform will be insignificant.

PRESIDENTS AND POLICY

It seems right that the last word in this study should be an assessment of presidents' influence on policy—of the difference they make, in other words. We have seen the challenge of finding the causes of presidential behavior, observed that behavior in various contexts, and now, finally, focus on impact. (We have in fact considered effects all along in a succession of institutional settings, but there is some advantage in a separate second look, with illustrations.)

If policy is understood as the sum of the visible, formal decisions of the three branches of government, a president's influence on policy is the effective part he plays in this process. The president, Congress, the Supreme Court, and other parts of the government influence and are influenced by one another in a continuing pattern of circular causation, as the framers of the Constitution intended. The output is public policy. But there is increasing awareness that such formal decisions do not always produce their intended results. Policy, therefore, may also be understood to include the impact, empirically determined, of formal decisions on society and the world. In that case, the difference a president makes is a product of his relative influence among government policy makers and the influence of the government on its environment. Lyndon Johnson had more hand in formulating the Economic Opportunity Act of 1964 than the Voting Rights Act of 1965, but the Voting

Rights Act worked better than the Poverty Program, and one could conclude that the president's support of the Voting Rights Act had a greater ultimate impact.

The President's Effect on Policy

Graham Allison's study of decision making in the Cuban missile crisis in 1962, noted earlier, exemplifies the intragovernmental conception of effect, primarily. His concern is to show three distinct but complementary ways to explain the making of the decision to confront the Soviet Union with a naval blockade of Cuba and force the removal of Soviet missiles. The rational actor frame of reference takes foreign affairs "as the more or less purposive acts of unified governments," the organizational process framework regards governmental actions "as *outputs* of large organizations functioning according to regular patterns of behavior," and the bureaucratic politics framework "as a *resultant* of various bargaining games among players in the national government."[1] The first puts emphasis on the president and the secretary of state; the second on entire organizations and their standard operating procedures; and the third on individual participants—high-ranking officials, their subordinates, and ad hoc advisers from Congress and outside government. In the synthesis of these approaches, which Allison prefers to any one alone, the president's role, however substantial, is seen as molded by the pressures and the clashes of the organizations and individuals around him. President Kennedy faced down a dangerous antagonist with finesse and firmness; however, he had to act through organizations such as the navy and the CIA, each with its parochial perceptions and limited repertoires; and his choice of strategies was influenced by the debates of advisers like the hawkish Dean Acheson and the more moderate Robert Kennedy.

In the absence of careful assessments such as Allison's, the conventional wisdom is that when there is leadership in Washington it is likely to be the president's, since the rest of the political system is largely incapable of it. Presidents get much of the credit for what Congress and the bureaucracy do and much of the blame for their inactivity or mistakes, even when there is not much the White House might have done for better or worse. The model of the strong president dominates our casual assessments of power relations within the government.

There are cases in which the presidential role is unambiguous, to be sure: When Franklin Roosevelt asserted emergency authority to close the banks in 1933, received immediate support from Congress, and calmed public fears with a fatherly fireside chat on the radio as he set about reopening the banks under proper regulation, there was no doubt who was in charge. But such instances aside, the temptation is to fall back on subjective judgment.

The problem of subjectivity can be seen in the writings of presidential historian Arthur M. Schlesinger, Jr. In his three-volume *The Age of Roosevelt*, he favors the heroic view of his subject as master of his age, as the title suggests, acting on his environment rather than acted on.[2] Compare, however, the treatment of Richard Nixon in *The Imperial Presidency* some years later.[3] Schlesinger, who disliked Nixon from the outset and worked against him in one election after another, might have been disposed to blame him for the excesses of his administration in the way he commended Roosevelt for the New Deal. Instead, he crosses the line into historical determinism. "Nixon's Presidency," he writes, "was not an aberration but a culmination. It carried to reckless extremes a compulsion toward presidential power rising out of deep-running changes in the foundations of society." In his view, the imperial presidency is an accumulation of war-making authority in the executive, a "war-magnified Presidency," with powers that spill over into domestic affairs.[4]

The theme of *The Imperial Presidency* is the force of institutional history. Presidents are carriers of tradition: "The developing presidential claim to control the flow of information received a comprehensive statement from President Tyler in 1843." The office has a life and importance transcending individual presidencies: "In the course of the early nineteenth century, the Presidency thus strengthened its control of information, secured its monopoly of diplomacy and enlarged its theory of defensive war."[5] The Locke-Jefferson-Lincoln tradition of executive prerogative of which he writes assumes a reality of its own.

Presidents are not bound by tradition, Schlesinger explains. They have the option "to ride the new tendencies of power or to resist them." He also describes the presidency as "a peculiarly personal institution." Yet the pressure to build on the past rather than spurn it is hard to resist. John Kennedy "gratefully accepted the royal prerogative." And in this century, strong political and economic forces have reinforced the tradition. "As the parties wasted away, the Presidency stood out in solitary majesty as the central focus of political emotion, the ever more potent symbol of national community." Moreover, "At the same time, the economic changes of the twentieth century"—depressions and war—"had conferred vast new powers not just on the national government but more particularly on the Presidency."[6]

And so the executive branch "continued, it seemed inexorably, to accumulate power at the expense of Congress." (In Schlesinger's account of the New Deal, by contrast, there is nothing inexorable at all about

Franklin Roosevelt's leadership of Congress. He receives credit for wringing everything humanly possible out of Congress from the first 100 days onward.) Even Dwight Eisenhower, the most passive of modern presidents, was swept along. "The casual adoption by Eisenhower of the doctrine of absolute executive privilege showed how the combination of congressional delinquency with the executive perspective could lead even a Whig administration to aggrandize the Presidency."[7] Schlesinger's early view was that a president such as Andrew Jackson or Franklin Roosevelt made all the difference. In *The Imperial Presidency*, the differences from one president to the next are marginal.

One may argue, of course, that Franklin Roosevelt *was* dramatically different from his immediate predecessors, or that Richard Nixon did build on the excesses of his predecessors. But these two works, and most others on the presidency, differ markedly, without proof, on whether what happens in the presidency is in general attributable to the man or to the office and the times.

Theodore Lowi's special contribution to the debate has been to demonstrate that the involvement of the president in policy making depends on the nature of the policy. Redistributive policy, the reallocation of wealth, rights, or other important values from one part of the society to another, tends to involve the president heavily; distributive policy, which is government subsidy and other tangible benefits for specific individuals, groups, and corporations, tends *not* to involve the president materially—it is handled by bureaus, congressional committees, and well-defined outside interests; and regulatory policy, which is government control over businesses and private individuals, is characterized by a moderate amount of presidential involvement.[8] One would expect the role of the president to differ, then, from the formulation of policy for universal government health insurance, say, to cotton subsidies, and to occupational safety regulation.

In foreign affairs, similar distinctions apply. In general, the president has considerably more discretion in foreign than in domestic matters, although there are some questions, particularly those with domestic pork-barrel implications, that provoke the full interplay of economic interests and congressional parochialism. The summit meeting of President Carter, Prime Minister Menachem Begin of Israel, and President Anwar Sadat of Egypt at Camp David in 1978 is a nearly pure example of policy making by a president and key advisers without the involvement of Congress, the lesser bureaucracy, and outside interests (although the participants were free to take the positions of those institutions and interests into account, and did). The deliberations were kept entirely secret to assure that others would not interfere, and try as it might the press could spring no leaks. Since no treaties, appropriations, or other legal obligations for the United States were to result from the meeting, the president was at liberty not to invite congressional leaders.

A classic study of the relative influence of the president and Congress in the policy-making process is Lawrence H. Chamberlain's *President, Congress and Legislation*.[9] He examined the legislative history of ninety of the most important measures passed by Congress between 1880 and 1940 to assess the contributions of the president, Congress, and pressure groups from the formative to the final stages. Unless the president was clearly more influential than Congress (as in the Agricultural Adjustment Act of 1933, for example) or Congress than the president (e.g., the Sherman Antitrust Act of 1890), Chamberlain classified an act as the joint product of presidential and congressional influence (e.g., the Federal Reserve Act of 1913). Of the ninety, he judged only nineteen to be presidential—and thirty-five congressional, twenty-nine joint presidential-congressional, and seven in which pressure group influence predominated. Even during the administrations of Woodrow Wilson and Franklin Roosevelt, the influence of Congress in getting legislation written and passed was considerable.

Years later, to discover whether there had been any change in the relative influence of the two branches since, William M. Goldsmith of Brandeis University extended the analysis to the most important legislation passed between mid-1945 and 1964, omitting the war years 1941 to mid-1945 as an exceptional period in which presidential leadership was greatly favored. For the sake of comparability, Goldsmith took care to follow Chamberlain's criteria of selection and evaluation. He found a substantially greater involvement of the president in legislation. Of sixty-three acts, twenty-six were classed as presidential (e.g., the National Security Act of 1947), seven as congressional (e.g., the Taft-Hartley Labor-Management Relations Act of 1947), twenty-eight as joint presidential-congressional (e.g., the Civil Rights Act of 1964), and only two attributable primarily to pressure groups (e.g., fair trade amendments to the Federal Trade Commission Act in 1952).[10] Presidential influence now underlies most major legislation, but Congress often shapes or—if one considers the many White House requests that are lost in Congress each session—obstructs measures that come before it.

Enlightening as they are, studies such as Lowi's, Chamberlain's, and Goldsmith's have a quality that invites criticism: They are to a large extent subjective. Others have found it difficult to apply their concepts (redistributive, distributive, regulatory, presidential influence preponderant, congressional influence preponderant, etc.) with any precision to the complex facts of politics or to build theories on the original framework. It is one thing to understand the difference between redistributive and regulatory policy in the abstract, for example, and another to classify a given statute as one, the other, or a combination of both. Thus George D. Greenberg and others contend, in a recent critique of public policy studies, that "Lowi never specifically addresses the problem of how to classify a policy correctly when it has attributes of more than one of his policy types, but one can infer from the general tone of his articles that he does not expect classification to present a major problem." They go on to say,

> The problems in operationalizing Lowi's hypotheses illustrate the special difficulties of theory construction and testing in the field of public policy studies. His provocative ideas cannot be meaningfully operationalized without considerable effort by the researcher to add greater specificity and precision, a process in which the researcher must often, without adequate guidance, make important assumptions about what the theory is trying to say.[11]

The same might be said of Goldsmith's application of Chamberlain's classification to recent legislation and of any subsequent efforts to apply their concepts to legislation from the mid-1960s on.

Richard I. Hofferbert adds, in criticism of Lowi, that "The bait has not been taken by other researchers. Lowi's insightful review is often noted in critical essays, but there is no instance in the literature I have read where his classification scheme has been examined with specific data and tested propositions."[12] (It is ironic that Lowi introduced his classification with similar criticisms of the pluralist and elitist case studies of an earlier generation of political science: "The main trouble with all these approaches is that they do not generate related propositions that can be tested by research and experience. Moreover, the findings of studies based upon any one of them are not cumulative.")[13] Progress has been made, however, since Hofferbert wrote his critique. A study by Lance T. LeLoup illustrates the possibility of measuring intragovernmental influence in policy making with some precision.

LeLoup raised the question of the importance of presidential attention and support in the life and well-being of federal agencies. He took changes in the appropriations for eight agencies over a period of twelve years, from 1960 through 1971, as the dependent variable to be explained. He tested the following as independent variables: previous percentage changes in an agency's budget requests, previous changes in appropriations, agency size, degree of agency hierarchy, congressional conflict, congressional partisanship, and, of particular interest here, presidential attention and support. Each variable was expressed as a quantitative index. Presidential attention and support were measured by the number of times the president mentioned an agency in his public statements in a given year (presidential attention) and the tone in each instance—positive, neutral, or negative (presidential support).[14]

The correlations of the several independent variables with the dependent variable, percentage change in appropriations, were expressed in the form of a path model—causal chains leading directly or indirectly to the dependent variable. These indicated a surprisingly large impact of the president on agency appropriations. Contrary to the theory of Aaron Wildavsky and others that congressional and constituent support are crucial to an agency at budget time, LeLoup's study suggests that presidential favor is paramount. (A possible weakness of the analysis is that the eight agencies were chosen in part because of the evident interest of the White House in their affairs. The several with a reputation for close relations with constituent groups, too, may provide a reasonably good test of the president's influence, however.)

LeLoup's study is exploratory. It would be interesting to have similar data for all agencies (or at least a representative sample) for a longer period, perhaps broken down by policy area, as a test of Lowi's principle that policy determines politics. Other studies reported in the same volume point in that direction. Some day, skeptics notwithstanding, we may have studies that refine and synthesize the work of Lowi, Chamberlain, Goldsmith, LeLoup, and others in a comprehensive analysis of the president's role in different areas of domestic policy making. For the time being, we must get along with partial theories and partial data.

The Impact of Government Policy on Society

In assessing the broader influence of the president we encounter a comparable mixture of subjective and objective studies, the former setting out bold conclusions and the latter clarifying and sometimes debunking old truths.

One of the more influential impressionistic studies of this generation was Daniel Patrick Moynihan's *Maximum Feasible Misunderstanding*, a devastating critique of the community actions programs of the War on Poverty by a social scientist, administrator, and later senator, who had helped write the legislation. It was his stern conclusion that "the program was carried out in such a way as to produce a minimum of the social change its sponsors desired, and bring about a maximum increase in the opposition to such change, of the kind they feared."[15] Lyndon Johnson's War on Poverty went wrong, as did his war in Vietnam. In the late 1970s, the country settled into a period of conservatism based in part on second thoughts, such as Daniel Patrick Moynihan's, on the ability of the government to effect social change.

An equally valuable and far more precise study of the impact of presidential decision making on the society at large is Edward R. Tufte's

Political Control of the Economy. Tufte gathered the published findings on the manipulation of the economy by presidents seeking reelection, added even more of his own, and put them all together in a comprehensive empirical study that is also a fine detective story with a real villain.[16]

Tufte was interested in testing the popular theory that incumbent administrations "turn on the spigot surely and swiftly and fill the trough so that it counts with the electorate," pays old political debts, and improves the party's chances in forthcoming elections. He might have selected any of a number of economic variables for study, including the most widely followed, inflation and unemployment. A relationship *can* be found between each of them and the electoral cycle in the United States in the period examined, from 1946 to the late 1970s: The unemployment rate does indeed tend to be relatively low at election time, and four of the six years in which both unemployment and inflation declined were presidential election years. But real disposable income, which is directly and immediately affected by changes in taxes and in transfer payments such as social security and veterans' benefits, is the most manipulable in the short run and proves to be the most interesting.[17]

To begin with, an exploratory examination of twenty-seven countries[18] indicated that nineteen, including the United States, had political business cycles by this measure: Short-term growth in real disposable income per capita was found more often in election years than in non-election years. In the United States, the relationship between the electoral calendar and changes in annual disposable incomes is striking. Not only are there differences between presidential election years and others, but when years are distinguished according to degrees of electoral importance to the president, corresponding degrees of economic improvement are found. In presidential election years when the incumbent is seeking reelection—when the stakes are highest, that is—the economic change is greatest. In mid-term election years, when the stakes are next greatest, the change is somewhat less. In presidential election years when the president is not seeking reelection, the economic change is still less. And in years without elections it is least.[19]

It may be assumed that elections trigger economic conditions rather than vice versa in the United States, since the electoral timetable is fixed by the Constitution. In a parliamentary system, the relationship is ambiguous, because governments frequently schedule elections when they have the best chance of winning—they may exploit economic conditions as they occur, conditions for which they may or may not be responsible. Such ambiguity as there is in the United States concerns not whether there has been political manipulation of the economy but the extent to which responsibility belongs to the president, to Congress, or to others. (Tufte supposes that some manipulation may result from agencies simply trying to protect themselves from White House criticism if an election goes wrong.)[20]

In any event, the record shows that government payments go up before elections. Social security payments tend to go up in election years; social security *contributions* tend to go up in off years. And payroll deductions are set so that many people complete their social security payments (and thus have more to spend) before November. Veterans' benefits also rise in election years. Federal payments to state and local governments to be passed on directly to the people go up too.[21]

The one administration in the post-World War II era in which real income did *not* tend to rise in election years was that of Dwight Eisenhower. In all four national elections held during his two terms in office it fell, instead, and in three of the four odd years it rose. Eisenhower was elected on a platform calling for budget reduction, he believed in it, and he held to it. He rejected the advice of Vice President Nixon and others that government spending be stepped up before the 1960 election. Unlike other presidents, Eisenhower also did nothing to manipulate unemployment rates in election years. He won reelection because of his great personal popularity, but his economic policies hurt his party. In the elections of 1954 through 1960, the 1956 presidential vote excepted, Republicans did badly.[22]

Richard Nixon believed he had lost the election of 1960 to John Kennedy because of Eisenhower's economic policy. His book, *Six Crises*, written in 1962, shows his commitment to economic manipulation for political ends. In 1972, seeking reelection, he did everything he could to increase real per capita disposable income, including an unusual amount of manipulation of transfer payments.[23]

As an aide described it, the policy was to "open the sluices" in 1971 and 1972, and then to use the short-term remedy of wage and price controls, a discretionary presidential action, to delay the inflation that would inevitably follow. Tufte estimates that some 75 million people benefited from this increased flow of money from the government in 1972. To be certain of public gratitude, the White House launched an expensive public relations campaign to credit the president with all that was being done for pensioners, veterans, and other beneficiaries of government programs. A statement was sent to each of 25 million social security beneficiaries in October 1972, shortly before the election, that said,

> Your social security payment has been increased by 20 per cent, starting with this month's check, by a new statute enacted by the Congress and signed into law by President Nixon on July 1, 1972.
> The President also signed into law a provision which will allow your social security benefits to increase automatically if [sic] the cost of living goes up.[24]

Another effort, documented by the Senate Watergate Committee, was the production and distribution of illustrated brochures by many federal agencies in 1972, at White House direction, describing President Nixon's concern and accomplishments for the elderly—a massive mailing of campaign literature at government expense, sprinkled with phrases such as

> The U.S. Department of Agriculture is striving to make President Nixon's goal for "a new national attitude on aging" a reality. . . .
> The President's commitment to seeing that special housing requirements of older Americans are met has resulted in channeling a significant part of the Nation's housing production to meet elderly needs at all income levels. . . .
> As President Nixon has pointed out, "Old age . . . should be a time of pride and fulfillment." . . .
> One of the President's primary objectives in the health-care area is to make it easier for older Americans to stay at home and remain independent.[25]

How much all of the manipulation of pocketbooks and public opinion contributed to the landslide reelection of Richard Nixon is a matter of speculation. Incumbent presidents (and members of Congress) have a natural advantage in elections, to be sure. Few, however, according to evidence such as Tufte's, are content to leave the election to nature.

One effect of political control of the economy is clear: The tendency of president and Congress to use short-term stimulants and depressants in order to win elections virtually precludes the development of long-range economic policy.[26] In areas of policy where immediate payoff is less likely, president and Congress are more inclined to make decisions for their long-range implications. Civil rights policy is a case in point.

Tufte's analysis, which happens to be of the seamy side of American politics, is a model of the work that might be done in every area of public policy to clarify the impact of government on society. Together with studies of the intragovernmental influence of presidents, such as those noted earlier in the chapter, they would take some of the guesswork out of our assessment of the importance of the presidency.

Speculations

Let us conclude with some points of perspective.

Although our everyday interest in the presidency may center on power relations within the government and the impact of government programs on society, there is some reason to suspect the presence of larger historical, economic, and psychological forces at work that affect the specific causal relationships and policy processes we have examined so far. Two studies of national moods, one by an historian, another by a psychologist, illustrate the value of a broader focus—the two have been chosen in part for the striking use they make of empirical evidence.

Many years ago, historian Arthur M. Schlesinger, the father of the Arthur Schlesinger whose works we have examined, described mood shifts from left to right and back in American politics—periods averaging 16.6 years of alternating action and inaction (which he also called *liberalism* and *conservatism*): 1765−1787, left; 1787−1801, right; 1801−1816, left; 1816−1829, right; 1829−1841, left; 1841−1861, right; 1861−1869, left; 1869−1901, right; 1901−1918, left; 1918−1931, right; and 1931 through the year he was writing, 1939, left. He explained, "Apparently the electorate embarks on conservative policies until it is disillusioned or wearied or bored, and then attaches itself to liberal policies until a similar course is run."[27]

(According to his son, in 1967, Schlesinger first played with the idea of a regular fourteen-year cycle—at least in this century—in the 1920s. He wondered if Wilson's loss of Congress to the conservative Republicans in 1918 might not have begun a period of quiescence destined to last until 1932, and so on, alternating with periods of activism. That would foretell quiescence in 1946—the year Truman lost Congress to the Republicans; activism in 1960—the year Kennedy won the presidential election; quiescence in 1974—when Gerald Ford replaced Richard Nixon; and activism again in 1988; all as if one could imagine some great cosmic clock ticking slowly just out of earshot. It is a game one should not take too seriously in this form, but it tempts speculation.)

Then came Harvard psychologist David C. McClelland, with a causal theory that went well beyond Schlesinger's "disillusioned or wearied or bored" explanation. It is McClelland's view, expressed in *Power: The Inner Experience* and other works, that the times (or public moods, more precisely) determine the selection and conduct of presidents.[28] Years ago, as we have noted, McClelland developed projective measures of a number of motives, notably the need for power, affiliation, and achievement. The people he studied were given tasks such as telling stories about ambiguous pictures—one might describe a picture of two people together as friends enjoying one another's company, another see it as a critical superior and a compliant subordinate, a third as competitors, and so forth. The three motives of interest to McClelland appeared in many guises in these stories, but their central meanings were simple: The need for power was the desire to have influence or impact on another; the need for affiliation was the desire to love and be loved; and the need for achievement was the desire to do something better than it had been done before.[29] Putting many themes and nuances together, McClelland could depict the motivational pattern and the maturity of each person he studied.

Next he found a way to chart the motives of whole societies over a period of several centuries by content analysis of their popular literature—children's textbooks, bestselling novels, and hymns—measuring the rise and fall of each motive from a mean. The result was a picture of a society in which the need for power might be high and the need for affiliation low in one period and the reverse some years later. Then he related popular moods and political and social events. In a number of countries and historical periods, a high level of achievement orientation was found to be followed by increased economic growth. "If the popular literature of the country was particularly achievement-oriented, there would be a larger than usual number of individuals with high achievement motivation who would behave in an active entrepreneurial fashion, ultimately kicking off rapid economic growth for the country as a whole." Lately he has found a similar relation between the power and affiliation motives and periods of social reform and war. In both studies, McClelland feels justified in interpreting the regular succession of motivational pattern and societal activity as cause and effect. "We have some basis for arguing for a motivational determination of history," he argues, if the increases in need for power regularly precede wars. "If they accompany or follow wars, we might prefer a Social Darwinian interpretation of history in which we conceive of an event as calling forth the kind of motivation needed to cope with it."[30]

The specific finding of interest here is that a relatively high societal need for power accompanied by a relatively low need for affiliation is followed by a period of political or social reform that in time is followed by war, with great though not perfect regularity—at least in the United States and Great Britain—and when this pattern is absent, reform and war do not ensue. McClelland describes this motivational configuration as "imperial," on the supposition that it underlay the building of the great empires of the past. It is also the pattern he has found associated with successful leadership of large organizations, when accompanied by "activity inhibition," which is a measure of self-control derived from the frequency of the use of the word *not* in imaginative stories.[31]

"Whether a country goes to war depends on its state of mind: an imperial motivational pattern sets in motion forces likely to lead to war whenever serious provocations occur," says McClelland. Periods of high power motivation and low affiliation motivation have been followed in this country by the reform eras of Jeffersonian democracy, Jacksonian populism, abolitionism, progressivism, the New Deal, and the struggle for civil rights—and these were followed, respectively, by the War of 1812, the Mexican War, the Civil War, World War I, World War II, and the Vietnam War. (The Spanish-American and Korean Wars are not predicted by the psychological data, and the timing of mood and war are irregular in the Vietnam period.) "The paradox of reform movements is that they have an unintended consequence: They seem to create an action orientation that makes war possible."[32]

McClelland notes that his and others' organizational studies have shown that an effective, expanding organization, under a manager with the imperial pattern of motives, is likely to have high morale and, unfortunately, feelings of hostility and punitiveness toward outsiders.[33] Belligerency may be the price to be paid for effective collective action in the organization and in the nation—although McClelland holds out the hope that people may learn, as he believes the Quakers have, to be both reformist and pacifist.

McClelland's associates who studied the motivations of American presidents found the high-power, low-affiliation pattern in Franklin Roosevelt and Lyndon Johnson and the low-power, high-affiliation pattern in Dwight Eisenhower and Gerald Ford, to cite examples.[34] It is McClelland's view, putting national and individual studies together, that presidents and their policies are products of their times. Presidents are brought to office, he says, and conditioned there, by the force of the national mood—by a yearning either for brotherhood or for power.

This is a humbling thought for president and electorate alike.

NOTES

CHAPTER 1

1. Theodore J. Lowi, "American Business, Public Policy, Case-Studies, and Political Theory," *World Politics*, 16, no. 4 (July 1964), 677–715; *The End of Liberalism* (New York: Norton, 1969); "Decision Making vs. Policy Making," *Public Administration Review*, 30, no. 3 (May–June 1970), 314–325; "Four Systems of Policy, Politics, and Choice," *Public Administration Review*, 32, no. 4 (July–August 1972), 298–310.

CHAPTER 2

1. Theodore Roosevelt, *An Autobiography* (New York: Macmillan, 1913), pp. 372, 378.

2. William Howard Taft, *Our Chief Magistrate and His Powers* (New York: Columbia University Press, 1916), pp. 139–140, 143–144.

3. Malcolm Moos, *The Republicans* (New York: Random House, 1956), pp. 268–270.

4. Arthur M. Schlesinger, "Tides of American Politics," *Yale Review*, 29, no. 2 (December 1939), 22.

5. David C. McClelland, *Power: The Inner Experience* (New York: Irvington, 1975), pp. 7–8, 252–253, 255, 274.

6. Richard E. Donley and David G. Winter, "Measuring the Motives of Public

Officials at a Distance: An Exploratory Study of American Presidents," *Behavioral Science*, 15, no. 3 (May 1970), 227–236.

7. David G. Winter, "What Makes the Candidates Run," *Psychology Today*, July 1976, pp. 45–49, 92.

8. See McClelland, *Power*, generally.

9. Lloyd S. Etheredge, "Personality Effects on American Foreign Policy, 1898–1968," *American Political Science Review*, 72, no. 2 (June 1978), 444.

10. Ibid., p. 439.

11. Doris Faber, *The Mothers of American Presidents* (New York: New American Library, 1968), pp. xii–xiii.

12. Lucille Iremonger, *The Fiery Chariot* (London: Secker & Warburg, 1970).

13. Harold D. Lasswell, *Psychopathology and Politics* (Chicago: University of Chicago Press, 1930), pp. 75, 184; also "Democratic Character," in his *Political Writings* (New York: Free Press, 1951), pp. 463–525.

14. E.g., Alexander L. and Juliette L. George, *Woodrow Wilson and Colonel House* (New York: Day, 1956), whose account is followed here.

15. Sigmund Freud and William C. Bullitt, *Thomas Woodrow Wilson: A Psychological Study* (Boston: Houghton Mifflin, 1967).

16. George and George, *Woodrow Wilson*, pp. 114–116.

17. Robert C. Tucker, "The Georges' Wilson Reexamined: An Essay on Psychobiography," *American Political Science Review*, 71, no. 2 (June 1977), 606–618.

18. Edwin A. Weinstein, James W. Anderson, and Arthur S. Link, "Woodrow Wilson's Personality: A Reappraisal," *Political Science Quarterly*, 93, no. 4 (Winter 1978), 585–598.

19. James David Barber, *The Presidential Character: Predicting Performance in the White House*, 2nd ed. (Englewood Cliffs, N.J.: Prentice-Hall, 1977), pp. 12–13.

20. Ibid., p. 18.

21. Ibid., pp. 7–10.

22. Ibid., pp. 6, 12–13.

23. Erwin C. Hargrove, "What Manner of Man: The Crisis of the Modern Presidency," in *Choosing the President*, ed. James David Barber (Englewood Cliffs, N.J.: Prentice-Hall, 1974), pp. 17–21.

24. Barber, *Presidential Character*, p. 12.

25. Alexander L. George, "Assessing Presidential Character," *World Politics*, 26, no. 2 (January 1974), 255–259.

26. Barber, *Presidential Character*, p. 418.

27. Ibid., p. 442.

28. Ibid., p. xi.

29. Ibid., pp. 5−6.

CHAPTER 3

1. Richard M. Nixon, "My Side of the Story," *Vital Speeches*, October 15, 1952, pp. 11−15.

2. Richard M. Nixon, *Six Crises* (New York: Doubleday, 1962), pp. 119, 124.

3. Richard M. Nixon, "The Watergate Affair," *Vital Speeches*, May 16, 1973, pp. 450−452.

4. Jules Witcover, *Marathon: The Pursuit of the Presidency, 1972-1976* (New York: Viking Press, 1977), pp. 198, 232; Joseph Lelyveld, "The Selling of a Candidate,"*New York Times Magazine*, March 28, 1976, p. 66.

5. *New York Times*, January 26, 1978, p. A15.

6. Ibid., March 16, 1975, sec. 2, p. l.

7. Ibid., January 26, 1978, p. A15; *Washington Post*, January 30, 1978, p. A2.

8. John Herbers, *No Thank You, Mr. President* (New York: Norton, 1976), p. 44.

9. Ibid., p. 24.

10. Dwight D. Eisenhower, *Public Papers: 1958* (Washington, D.C.: U.S. Government Printing Office, 1959), pp. 610−614.

11. David Halberstam, "Press and Prejudice," *Esquire*, April 1974, p. 110.

12. Quoted in Julius Duscha, "The White House Watch over TV and the Press," *New York Times Magazine*, August 20, 1972, p. 9. © 1972 by The New York Times Company. Reprinted by permission.

13. *New York Times*, November 2, 1973, p. 24; December 17, 1973, p. 75.

14. Ibid., May 6, 1973, p. 55.

15. *New York Times* v. *Sullivan*, 376 U.S. 254 (1964).

16. Anthony Lewis, "Nixon and a Right of Reply," *New York Times*, March 24, 1974, sec. 4, p. 2.

17. *Miami Herald* v. *Tornillo*, 418 U.S. 241 (1974).

18. Carl Bernstein and Bob Woodward, *All the President's Men* (New York: Simon & Schuster, 1974), pp. 171, 247.

19. Duscha, "White House Watch," p. 95.

20. *Red Lion Broadcasting Co.* v. *Federal Communications Commission*, 395 U.S. 367 at 388 (1969).

21. Quoted in Leonard W. Levy, *Jefferson & Civil Liberties* (Cambridge, Mass.: Belknap Press of Harvard University Press, 1963), pp. 60, 69.

22. Theodore C. Sorenson, *Kennedy* (New York: Harper & Row, 1965), chap. 12; Henry Fairlie, *The Kennedy Promise* (New York: Doubleday, 1973) p. 215.

23. *Near v. Minnesota*, 283 U.S. 697 at 716 (1931).

24. *New York Times*, June 14, 1978, p. A14.

25. John E. Mueller, "Presidential Popularity from Truman to Johnson, *"American Political Science Review*, 64, no. 1 (March 1970), pp. 136–148; Richard A. Brody and Benjamin I. Page, "The Impact of Events on Presidential Popularity: The Johnson and Nixon Administrations," in *Perspectives on the Presidency*, ed. Aaron Wildavsky (Boston: Little, Brown, 1975), pp. 136–148; James A. Stimson, "Public Support for American Presidents: A Cyclical Model," *Public Opinion Quarterly*, 40, no. 1 (Spring 1976), 1–21; Henry C. Kenski, "The Impact of Economic Conditions on Presidential Popularity," *Journal of Politics*, 39, no. 3 (August 1977), 764–773.

26. Mueller, "Presidential Popularity," pp. 20, 31–32.

27. Stimson, "Public Support," p. 10.

28. Mueller, "Presidential Popularity," pp. 21–22; *New York Times*, January 31, 1979, p. A10.

29. Nixon, *Six Crises*, pp. 231, 303.

30. Kenski, "Impact of Economic Conditions," pp. 764–773.

31. Brody and Page, "Impact of Events," pp. 140–141.

32. Samuel Kernell, Peter W. Sperlich, and Aaron Wildavsky, "Public Support for Presidents," in *Perspectives*, ed. Wildavsky, pp. 148–181.

33. Fred I. Greenstein, *Children and Politics* (New Haven, Conn.: Yale University Press, 1965); Robert D. Hess and Judith V. Torney, *The Development of Political Attitudes in Children* (New York: Doubleday, Anchor Books, 1968); David Easton and Jack Dennis, *Children in the Political System* (New York: McGraw-Hill, 1969).

34. Greenstein, *Children and Politics*, pp. 41, 55.

35. Hess and Torney, *Development*, p. 45.

36. Ibid., pp. 43, 55.

37. Ibid., pp. 48, 205; Greenstein, *Children and Politics*, p. 115.

38. Easton and Dennis, *Children*, pp. 89, 138, 177, 199, 201, 365–366, 372.

39. Ibid., pp. 203–204.

40. Stanley A. Renshon, "Assumptive Frameworks in Political Socialization Theory," in *Handbook of Political Socialization*, ed. Stanley A. Renshon (New York: Free Press, 1977), p. 10.

41. Martha Wolfenstein and Gilbert Kliman, eds., *Children and the Death of a President* (New York: Doubleday, Anchor Books, 1965), pp. xvi–xviii, 220.

42. Dean Jaros, Herbert Hirsch, and Frederic J. Fleron, Jr., "The Malevolent Leader: Political Socialization in an American Sub-Culture," *American Political Science Review*, 62, no. 2 (June 1968), 564–575.

43. Jack Dennis and Carol Webster, "Children's Images of the President and of Government in 1962 and 1974," *American Politics Quarterly*, 3, no. 4 (October 1975), 394, 397.

44. Dean Jaros and John Shoemaker, "The Malevolent Unindicted Co-Conspirator: Watergate and Appalachian Youth," *American Politics Quarterly*, 4, no. 4 (October 1976), 483–506.

45. F. Christopher Arterton, "The Impact of Watergate on Children's Attitudes Toward Political Authority," *Political Science Quarterly*, 89, no. 2 (June 1974), 269–288; "Watergate and Children's Attitudes Toward Authority Revisited," *Political Science Quarterly*, 90, no. 3 (Fall 1975), 477–496.

46. Arterton, "Impact of Watergate," pp. 276, 287.

47. Arterton, "Watergate and Children's Attitudes," pp. 494–495.

48. Fillmore Sanford, "Public Orientation to Roosevelt," *Public Opinion Quarterly*, 15, no. 2 (Summer 1951).

49. Samuel Kernell, Peter W. Sperlich, and Aaron Wildavsky, "Public Support for Presidents," in *Perspectives on the Presidency*, ed. Aaron Wildavsky (Boston: Little, Brown, 1975), pp. 148–181.

CHAPTER 4

1. Art. II, Sec. 1.

2. Abridged from *The American Presidency*, Revised Edition, © 1960 by Clinton Rossiter. Reprinted by permission of Harcourt Brace Jovanovich, Inc.

3. James Bryce, *The American Commonwealth*, 2nd ed. rev. (London: Macmillan, 1891), Vol. 1, pp. 73–75.

4. Harold J. Laski, *The American Presidency: An Interpretation* (New York: Harper & Row, 1940), pp. 51–53.

5. Hugh Heclo, "Presidential and Prime Ministerial Selection," in *Perspectives on Presidential Selection*, ed. Donald R. Matthews (Washington, D.C.: Brookings Institution, 1973), pp. 21–24.

6. Austin Ranney, *Participation in American Presidential Nominations, 1976* (Washington, D.C.: American Enterprise Institute for Public Policy Research, 1977), p. 1.

7. H. L. Mencken, *A Carnival of Buncombe*, ed. Malcolm Moos (Baltimore, Md.: Johns Hopkins Press, 1956), p. 1.

8. Commission on Party Structure and Delegate Selection, *Mandate for Reform* (Washington, D.C.: Democratic National Committee, 1970), pp. 10–11.

9. Ibid., pp. 34–35.

10. *Congressional Quarterly*, July 10, 1976, p. 1803.

11. John W. Soule and Wilma E. McGrath, "A Comparative Study of Presidential Nominating Conventions," *American Journal of Political Science*, 19, no. 3 (August 1975), p. 510.

12. Denis G. Sullivan and others, "Candidates, Causes, and Issues: The Democratic Convention, 1976," in *The Impact of the Electoral Process*, ed. Louis Maisel and Joseph Cooper (Beverly Hills, Calif.: Sage, 1977), p. 117.

13. Judith H. Parris, *The Convention Problem* (Washington, D.C.: Brookings Institution, 1972), pp. 62–68; William R. Keech and Donald R. Matthews, *The Party's Choice* (Washington, D.C.: Brookings Institution, 1976), pp. 182–183, 211.

14. Parris, *Convention Problem*, pp. 104–105.

15. Richard Reeves, *Convention* (New York: Harcourt Brace Jovanovich, 1977), pp. 238–239.

16. Parris, *Convention Problem*, pp. 118–119.

17. Theodore H. White, *The Making of the President—1964* (New York: Atheneum, 1965), p. 200.

18. Norman Mailer, *St. George and the Godfather* (New York: New American Library, 1972), pp. 180–182.

19. Keech and Matthews, *Party's Choice*, pp. 157–213.

20. Ibid., pp. 160–161.

21. Ibid., p. 160; Leon D. Epstein, "Political Science and Presidential Nomination," *Political Science Quarterly*, 93, no. 2 (Summer 1978), 181.

22. Ibid., pp. 166–167.

23. Herbert B. Asher, "The Media and the Presidential Selection Process," in *Impact*, ed. Maisel and Cooper, p. 219.

24. Donald R. Matthews, "Presidential Nominations: Process and Outcomes," in *Choosing the President*, ed. James David Barber (Englewood Cliffs, N.J.: Prentice-Hall, 1974), pp. 58–59.

25. Asher, "Media," pp. 214–215.

26. Keech and Matthews, *Party's Choice*, p. 121.

27. Philip E. Converse and others, "Continuity and Change in American Politics: Parties and Issues in the 1968 Elections," *American Political Science Review*, 63, no. 4 (December 1969), 1083–1105.

28. Keech and Matthews, *Party's Choice*, pp. 243–245.

29. Nelson W. Polsby and Aaron Wildavsky, *Presidential Elections*, 4th ed. (New

York: Scribner's, 1976), p. 111; *Congressional Quarterly*, July 10, 1976, pp. 1806–1808; *New York Times*, September 1, 1976, p. 10.

30. Jules Witcover, *Marathon: The Pursuit of the Presidency 1972-1976* (New York: Viking Press, 1977), pp. 199–214; Reeves, *Convention*, pp. 9–10.

31. *New York Times*, January 21, 1975, p. 17.

32. *Cousins* v. *Wigoda*, 419 U.S. 477 (1975).

33. Witcover, *Marathon*, pp. 209–210.

34. Matthews, "Presidential Nominations," pp. 53, 61.

35. Keech and Matthews, *Party's Choice*, p. 33.

36. Ibid., p. 21.

37. Donald R. Matthews, "Winnowing," in *Race for the Presidency*, ed. James David Barber (Englewood Cliffs, N.J.: Prentice-Hall, 1978), p. 57; F. Christopher Arterton, "The Media Politics of Presidential Campaigns," in *Race for the Presidency*, ed. Barber, p. 39.

38. Gerald M. Pomper, "The Decline of the Party in American Elections," *Political Science Quarterly*, 92, no. 1 (Spring 1977), 21–41.

39. Ibid., p. 26.

40. Ibid., p. 31; *Buckley* v. *Valeo*, 424 U.S. 1 (1976).

41. Heclo, "Presidential and Prime Ministerial Selection," p. 28.

42. Ibid., p. 46.

43. John C. Calhoun, *Works*, ed. Richard K. Crallé (New York: Appleton Century Crofts, 1858), Vol. 6, pp. 240–241.

44. Austin Ranney, "Changing the Rules of the Nominating Game," in *Choosing*, ed. Barber, pp. 72–73.

45. James I. Lengle and Byron Shafer, "Primary Rules, Political Power, and Social Change," *American Political Science Review*, 70, no. 1 (March 1976), 29.

46. *New York Times*, June 10, 1978, p. 7.

CHAPTER 5

1. V. O. Key, Jr., "A Theory of Critical Elections," *Journal of Politics*, 17, no. 1 (February 1955), 3–18; Angus Campbell and others, *The American Voter* (New York: Wiley, 1960), pp. 531–538; James L. Sundquist, *Dynamics of the Party System* (Washington, D.C.: Brookings Institution, 1973), chap. 1; Walter Dean Burnham, *Critical Elections and the Mainsprings of American Politics* (New York: Norton, 1972), chaps. 1–2.

2. Norman H. Nie, Sidney Verba, and John R. Petrocik, *The Changing American Voter* (Cambridge, Mass.: Harvard University Press, 1976), pp. 175–189.

3. Ibid., p. 167.

4. Kristi Anderson, "Generation, Partisan Shift, and Realignment: A Glance Back at the New Deal," in *The Changing American Voter*, ed. Nie, Verba, and Petrocik, chap. 5.

5. Campbell, *American Voter*, p. 537.

6. Ibid., pp. 55–58.

7. Ibid., p. 124.

8. Kevin Phillips, *The Emerging Republican Majority* (New Rochelle, N.Y.: Arlington House, 1969).

9. John H. Kessel, "Strategy for November," in *Choosing the President*, ed. James David Barber (Englewood Cliffs, N.J.: Prentice-Hall, 1974), pp. 95–119.

10. John Bartlow Martin, *Adlai Stevenson of Illinois: The Life of Adlai E. Stevenson* (New York: Doubleday, 1976), pp. 606–607.

11. Kessel, "Strategy for November," pp. 98–101.

12. Martin, *Stevenson*, pp. 639–640.

13. Quoted in Theodore C. Sorenson, *Kennedy* (New York: Harper & Row, 1965), pp. 190–191.

14. For another interpretation, see Benjamin I. Page, "A Theory of Political Ambiguity," *American Political Science Review*, 70, no. 3 (September 1976), 742–752.

15. Harold Hotelling, "Stability in Competition," *Economic Journal*, 39, no. 1 (March 1929), 41–57.

16. Arthur Smithies, "Optimum Location in Spatial Competition," *Journal of Political Economy*, 49, no. 3 (June 1941), 423–439.

17. Anthony Downs, *An Economic Theory of Democracy* (New York: Harper & Row, 1957), pp. 117–122.

18. Herbert McCloskey, Paul J. Hoffmann, and Rosemary O'Hara, "Issue Conflict and Consensus Among Party Leaders and Followers," *American Political Science Review*, 54, no. 2 (June 1960), 406–427.

19. Campbell, *American Voter*, p. 231.

20. Ibid., pp. 248–249.

21. Ibid., p. 250.

22. Philip E. Converse, "The Nature of Belief Systems in Mass Publics," in *Ideology and Dissent*, ed. David Apter (New York: Free Press, 1964), pp. 206–261.

23. Benjamin I. Page and Richard A. Brody, "Policy Voting and the Electoral Process: The Vietnam War Issue," *American Political Science Review*, 66, no. 3 (September 1972), 979–995.

24. Ibid., p. 987.

25. Ibid., p. 983.

26. Ibid., p. 982.

27. Ibid., p. 987

28. Benjamin I. Page, *Choices and Echoes in Presidential Elections* (Chicago: University of Chicago Press, 1978), pp. 76–90.

29. Quoted in Joe McGinnis, *The Selling of the President 1968* (New York: Trident Press, 1969), pp. 154, 240–241.

30. *New York Times*, May 4, 1977, p. 1; Henry Fairlie, "Sweet Nothings," *New Republic*, June 11, 1977, pp. 17–19.

31. Committee on Political Parties, American Political Science Association, "Toward a More Responsible Two-Party System," *American Political Science Review*, 44, no. 3 (September 1950), pt. 2, 1–2.

32. Ibid., p. 13.

33. Evron M. Kirkpatrick, "Toward a More Responsible Two-Party System: Political Science, Policy Science, or Pseudo-Science?" *American Political Science Review*, 65, no. 4 (December 1971), 968.

34. Austin Ranney, *Curing the Mischiefs of Faction* (Berkeley: University of California Press, 1975), pp. 44–45.

35. James McGregor Burns, "The Democrats' Opportunity," *New Republic*, July 21, 1973, pp. 18–21.

36. Theodore H. White, *The Making of the President—1964* (New York: Atheneum, 1965), p. 217.

37. Ibid., pp. 331–397.

38. Page, *Choices*, p. 95.

39. Nie, Verba, and Petrocik, *Changing American Voter*, p. 143.

40. Ibid., p. 199.

41 Ibid., pp. 202, 204.

42. Richard G. Niemi and Herbert F. Weisberg, "Do Voters Think Ideologically?" in *Controversies in American Voting Behavior*, ed. Richard G. Niemi and Herbert F. Weisberg (San Francisco: W. H. Freeman, 1976), pp. 76–79.

43. Nie, Verba, and Petrocik, *Changing American Voter*, pp. 123–135.

44. George F. Bishop and others, "The Changing Structure of Mass Belief Systems," *Journal of Politics*, 40, no. 3 (August 1978), 781–787.

45. Arthur H. Miller and others, "A Majority Party in Disarray: Policy Polarization in the 1972 Election," *American Political Science Review*, 70, no. 3 (September 1976), 757.

46. Nie, Verba, and Petrocik, *Changing American Voter*, pp. 156–183.

47. Ibid., p. 48.

48. Ibid., pp. 49–54.

49. Leon D. Epstein, "Political Science and Presidential Nomination," *Political Science Quarterly*, 93, no. 2 (Summer 1978), 191; Steven J. Brams, *The Presidential Election Game* (New Haven, Conn.: Yale University Press, 1978), pp. 25–29.

50. Arthur H. Miller, "Partisanship Reinstated? A Comparison of the 1972 and 1976 U.S. Presidential Elections," *British Journal of Political Science*, 8, no. 2 (April 1978), 133, 140.

51. Ibid., p. 150.

52. Ibid., pp. 130–132, 152.

53. Nie, Verba, and Petrocik, *Changing American Voter*, pp. 1–2.

54. Robert Axelrod, "Communication," *American Political Science Review*, 72, no. 2 (June 1978), 622.

55. Everett Carll Ladd, Jr., with Charles D. Hadley, *The Transformation of the American Party System* (New York: Norton, 1975), p. 231.

56. Epstein, "Political Science," p. 147.

57. Walter Dean Burnham, "Jimmy Carter and the Democratic Crisis," *New Republic*, July 3 and 10, 1976, pp. 17–19.

58. Wallace S. Sayre and Judith H. Parris, *Voting for President* (Washington, D.C.: Brookings Institution, 1970), p. 23.

59. *U.S. Constitution*, Art. II, Sec. 1.

60. Herbert Agar, *The Price of Union* (Boston: Houghton Mifflin, 1950), p. 40.

61. *Federalist* No. 68.

62. Sayre and Parris, *Voting*, p. 26.

63. Ibid., pp. 26–27.

64. Ibid., p. 28.

65. Ibid., pp. 37–38.

66. Ibid., p. 32.

67. Ibid., pp. 10–11.

68. *Wesberry* v. *Sanders*, 376 U.S. 1 (1964).

69. Quoted in Nelson W. Polsby and Aaron Wildavsky, *Presidential Elections*, 4th ed. (New York: Scribner's, 1976), p. 267.

70. *Congressional Quarterly*, March 10, 1979, p. 408.

71. Sayre and Parris, *Voting*, p. 129.

72. John H. Yunker and Lawrence D. Longley, "The Biases of the Electoral College," in *Perspectives on Presidential Selection*, ed. Donald R. Matthews (Washington, D.C.: Brookings Institution, 1973), pp. 172–203.

CHAPTER 6

1. Dumas Malone, *Jefferson the President: First Term, 1801–1805* (Boston: Little, Brown, 1970), pp. 89, 142.

2. Ibid., pp. 90–109, 141–143.

3. Woodrow Wilson, *Congressional Government* (New York: Meridian Books, 1956), pp. 47–49.

4. Woodrow Wilson, *Cabinet Government in the United States* (Stamford, Conn.: Overbrook Press, 1947), pp. 7–11, reprinted from the *International Review*, August 1879.

5. Woodrow Wilson, *Constitutional Government in the United States* (New York: Columbia University Press, 1908), pp. 68–71.

6. Arthur S. Link, *Wilson: The New Freedom* (Princeton: Princeton University Press, 1956), pp. 149–155, 187.

7. Ibid., p. 187.

8. Rexford G. Tugwell, *The Democratic Roosevelt* (Baltimore, Md.: Penguin Books, 1969), p. 234.

9. Quoted in Barry D. Karl, "Executive Reorganization and Presidential Power," 1977 *Supreme Court Review* (1978), p. 23.

10. Lawrence H. Chamberlain, *The President, Congress, and Legislation* (New York: Columbia University Press, 1946), pp. 450–452.

11. 48 Stat. 22 (1933). Emphasis added.

12. E.O. 6101, April 5, 1933.

13. *Panama Refining Co. v. Ryan*, 293 U.S. 388 (1935); *Schechter Poultry Corp. v. United States*, 295 U.S. 495 (1935).

14. E.g., *Yakus v. United States*, 321 U.S. 414 (1944); *Fahey v. Mallonee*, 322 U.S. 245 (1947).

15. James McGregor Burns, *Roosevelt: The Soldier of Freedom* (New York: Harcourt Brace Jovanovich, 1970), pp. 433–437.

16. Jong R. Lee, "Presidential Vetoes from Washington to Nixon," *Journal of Politics*, 37, no. 2 (May 1975), 522–546.

17. Ibid., pp. 530–546.

18. *Congressional Quarterly*, January 1, 1978, pp. 3–5.

19. *New York Times*, January 2, 1978, p. 11.

20. *Congressional Quarterly*, December 24, 1977, pp. 2631–2635.

21. Ibid., October 14, 1978, p. 2925.

22. *New York Times*, April 17, 1977, sec. 1, p. 1.

23. Ibid., May 24, 1977, p. 1; July 21, 1977, p. A11.

24. John F. Manley, "Presidential Power and White House Lobbying," *Political Science Quarterly*, 93, no. 2 (Summer 1978), 275.

25. *Congressional Quarterly*, October 14, 1978, p. 2924.

26. John R. Bolton, *The Legislative Veto* (Washington, D.C.: American Enterprise Institute for Public Policy Research, 1977).

27. Ibid., p. 2.

28. Ibid., p. 10.

29. Ibid., p. 11.

30. Bruff and Gellhorn, 90 *Harv. L. Rev.* 1369 at 1420 (1977).

31. Ibid., p. 1425.

32. Quoted in Bruce Miroff, *Pragmatic Illusions* (New York: McKay, 1976), p. 277.

33. Harry S. Truman, *Memoirs*, vol. 2: *Years of Trial and Hope* (New York: Doubleday, 1956), p. 208.

34. Wilson, *Constitutional Government*, p. 71.

35. Theodore Roosevelt, *An Autobiography* (New York: Macmillan, 1913), pp. 371–372.

36. Robert E. Sherwood, *Roosevelt and Hopkins: An Intimate History* (New York: Harper & Row, 1948), pp. 631–632; Message to Congress, September 7, 1942, quoted in Robert Hirschfield, *The Power of the Presidency*, 2nd ed. (Chicago: Aldine, 1973), pp. 109–111.

37. E.O. 8802, June 25, 1941; E.O. 9981, July 26, 1948; E.O. 10925, March 6, 1961; E.O. 11063, November 20, 1962; Ruth P. Morgan, *The President and Civil Rights* (New York: St. Martin's Press, 1970), pp. 69–72.

38. Ibid., pp. 87–88.

39. Louis Fisher, *Presidential Spending Power* (Princeton, N.J.: Princeton University Press, 1975), pp. 148, 162–163.

40. Ibid., pp. 158, 169–170, 177, 184, 192–194.

41. Ibid., pp. 190–192; *Train* v. *City of New York*, 420 U.S. 35 (1975).

42. 88 Stat. 297 (1974).

43. *U.S. Constitution*, Art. II, Sec. 2.

44. *Congressional Quarterly*, February 4, 1978, p. 299.

45. *New York Times*, February 2, 1977, p. 1.

46. Ibid., August 28, 1977, sec. 4, p. 3; September 14, 1977, p. 31.

47. Ibid., May 23, 1976, sec. 4, p. 16.

48. Ibid., February 6, 1978, p. A1.

49. *Williams* v. *Phillips*, 360 F. Supp. 1363 (D.D.C. 1973).

50. *Buckley* v. *Valeo*, 424 U.S. 1 at 109–137 (1975).

CHAPTER 7

1. *Federalist*, no. 69.

2. Art. I, Sec. 8; Art. II, Sec. 2.

3. James Madison, *Notes of Debates in the Federal Convention of 1787* (Athens: Ohio University Press, 1966), p. 476.

4. Message to Congress, July 4, 1861, quoted in Robert Hirschfield, *The Power of the Presidency*, 2nd ed. (Chicago: Aldine, 1973), pp. 76–77.

5. Arthur M. Schlesinger, Jr., *The Imperial Presidency* (Boston: Houghton Mifflin; London: Andre Deutsch Limited, 1973), p. 184.

6. Ibid., p. 133; *New Republic*, January 29, 1972, p. 19.

7. Quoted in Schlesinger, *Imperial Presidency*, pp. 187–188.

8. *Mottola* v. *Nixon*, 318 F. Supp. 538 at 541–543 (N.D.Cal. 1970).

9. *Congress and the Nation*, Vol. 3: *1969–1972* (Washington, D.C.: Congressional Quarterly Service, 1973), pp. 911–921.

10. *New Republic*, February 10, 1973, p. 28; *New York Times*, July 1, 1973.

11. 87 Stat. 555 (1973).

12. 119 *Congressional Record* S34990–991, October 25, 1973.

13. Alexander Bickel, "The Need for a War-Powers Bill," *New Republic*, January 22, 1972, p. 17.

14. *New Republic*, January 5, 1972, p. 14.

15. James Thomas Flexner, *Washington: The Indispensable Man* (Boston: Little, Brown, 1974), p. 284.

16. Quoted in Hirschfield, *Power*, pp. 50–54.

17. Ibid., pp. 56–57.

18. Sidney Warren, *The President as World Leader* (New York: McGraw-Hill, 1964), pp. 189–190.

19. 1975 *Congressional Quarterly Almanac* 310–311.

20. Ibid.

21. *New York Times*, April 12, 1977, p. 14; May 23, 1975, p. 35.

22. Quoted in Roy Rowan, *The Four Days of Mayaguez* (New York: Norton, 1975), p. 223.

23. Lloyd S. Etheredge, "Personality Effects on American Foreign Policy," *American Political Science Review*, 72, no. 2 (June 1978), 434–451.

24. Quoted in Warren, *President as World Leader*, p. 18.

25. Henry F. Pringle, *Theodore Roosevelt* (New York: Harcourt, Brace, 1931), pp. 171, 176.

26. John F. Kennedy, *Public Papers: 1961* (Washington, D.C.: U.S. Government Printing Office, 1962), pp. 1–3.

27. Henry Fairlie, "Camelot Revisited," *Harper's Magazine*, January 1973, pp. 74–76.

28. Tad Szulc, "Kennedy's Cold War," *New Republic*, December 24 and 31, 1977, p. 21.

29. Neil Sheehan and others, *The Pentagon Papers* (New York: Bantam Books, 1971), pp. 264–265.

30. Ibid., pp. 234–270.

31. James McGregor Burns, *Roosevelt: The Soldier of Freedom* (New York: Harcourt Brace Jovanovich, 1970), pp. 139–142.

32. Herbert Agar, *The Price of Union* (Boston: Houghton Mifflin, 1950), pp. 316–317.

33. John J. Nicolay and John Hay, eds., *Complete Works of Abraham Lincoln* (New York: Tandry, 1905), vol. 2, pp. 2–3.

34. Arthur S. Miller, *Presidential Power* (St. Paul, Minn.: West, 1977), p. 135.

35. 299 U.S. 304 (1936).

36. *Panama Refining Co.* v. *Ryan*, 293 U.S. 388 at 415, 430; *Schechter Poultry Corp.* v. *United States*, 295 U.S. 495 (1935).

37. 299 U.S. 304 at 315–316 (1935).

38. Ibid., at 318.

39. Ibid., at 319.

40. Ibid., at 319–320.

41. 301 U.S. 324 (1937).

42. Ibid., at 330–331.

43. Schlesinger, *Imperial Presidency*, pp. 87–88.

44. *New York Times*, December 18, 1978, p. A13; December 19, 1978, p. A1; December 29, 1978, p. A8.

45. Quoted in *The Presidency in Contemporary Context*, Norman C. Thomas ed. (New York: Dodd, Mead, 1975), pp. 238–239.

46. Schlesinger, *Imperial Presidency*, pp. 16, 84.

47. Ibid., p. 157.

48. Taylor Branch, "Profiles in Caution," *Harper's Magazine*, July 1973, p. 69.

49. 418 U.S. 683 (1974).

50. Walter F. Mondale, *The Accountability of Power* (New York: McKay, 1975), pp. 148–151.

51. *New York Times*, June 26, 1974, p. 43.

52. Richard E. Neustadt, *Presidential Power* (New York: Wiley, 1960 and 1976), pp. 115–122.

53. Aaron Wildavsky, "The Two Presidencies," *TransAction*, 4, no. 2 (December 1966), reprinted in *Perspectives on the Presidency*, ed. Aaron Wildavsky (Boston: Little, Brown, 1975), pp. 448–461.

54. Donald A. Peppers, " 'The Two Presidencies': Eight Years Later," in *Perspectives*, ed. Wildavsky, pp. 462–471.

55. *New York Times*, January 8, 1975, p. 1.

56. Ibid., January 8, 1975, p. 1; January 26, 1975, Sec. 4, p. 1.

57. Ibid., February 22, 1975, p. 3.

CHAPTER 8

1. Richard Nixon, Radio Address of September 19, 1968, quoted in Robert Hirschfield, ed., *The Power of the Presidency*, 2nd ed. (Chicago: Aldine, 1973), pp. 165–168.

2. B. W. Headey, "The Role Skills of Cabinet Members," *Political Studies*, 22, no. 1 (March 1974), 66–85.

3. Richard E. Neustadt, "White House and Whitehall," *Public Interest*, Winter 1966, pp. 55–69.

4. Richard F. Fenno, *The President's Cabinet* (Cambridge, Mass.: Harvard University Press, 1959), p. 40.

5. Calvin Coolidge, *Autobiography* (New York: Cosmopolitan, 1929), p. 196.

6. Harry S. Truman, *Memoirs*, vol. 1: *Year of Decision* (New York: Doubleday, 1955), pp. 546, 551.

7. Dean Acheson, "The President and the Secretary of State," in *The Secretary of State*, ed. Don K. Price (Englewood Cliffs, N.J.: Prentice-Hall, 1960), pp. 27–50.

8. Hugh Heclo, *A Government of Strangers* (Washington, D.C.: Brookings Institution, 1977), p. 104.

9. Arthur M. Schlesinger, Jr., *A Thousand Days* (Boston: Houghton Mifflin; London: Andre Deutsch Limited, 1965), pp. 146–155.

10. Richard P. Nathan, *The Plot That Failed: Nixon and the Administrative Presidency* (New York: Wiley, 1975), pp. 49–50.

11. Headey, "Role Skills," pp. 70–71.

12. *Time*, December 4, 1978, p. 34.

13. Nathan, *Plot*, pp. 39–42.

14. Heclo, *Government*, p. 196.

15. Graham K. Wilson, "Are Department Secretaries Really a President's Natural Enemies?" *British Journal of Political Science*, 7, no. 3 (July 1977), 273–299.

16. Nelson W. Polsby, "Presidential Cabinet Making: Lessons for the Political System," *Political Science Quarterly*, 93, no. 1 (Spring 1978), 23.

17. Ibid., p. 20.

18. Stephen Hess, *Organizing the Presidency* (Washington, D.C.: Brookings Institution, 1976), p. 181.

19. Peter Bromhead, *Britain's Developing Constitution* (New York: St. Martin's Press, 1974), p. 51. Emphasis added.

20. Fenno, *President's Cabinet*, p. 18; Leonard D. White, *The Jacksonians* (New York: Macmillan, 1954), p. 93.

21. Truman, *Year of Decision*, p. 546.

22. Emmet John Hughes, *The Ordeal of Power* (New York: Atheneum, 1963), pp. 76–77.

23. Fenno, *President's Cabinet*, p. 138.

24. Arthur S. Link, *Wilson: The New Freedom* (Princeton, N.J.: Princeton University Press, 1956), pp. 74–75.

25. Truman, *Year of Decision*, pp. 55–56.

26. Bromhead, *Constitution*, p. 51.

27. Ibid., pp. 53–55.

28. Cronin, "Everybody Believes in Democracy Until He Gets to the White House," 35 *Law & Contemp. Prob.* 610–617 (1970).

29. 61 Stat. 496 (1947).

30. Nathan, *Plot*, p. 130.

31. *Congressional Quarterly*, October 27, 1973, pp. 2832, 2846.

32. Ibid., p. 2849.

33. Ibid., p. 2831.

34. Edward Weisband and Thomas M. Frank, *Resignation in Protest* (New York: Grossman, 1975), pp. 17–20.

35. *New York Times*, May 7, 1970, p. 18.

36. Merle Miller, *Plain Speaking* (New York: Berkley, 1974), p. 305.

37. Weisband and Frank, *Resignation*, pp. 55–57.

38. Ibid., pp. 59, 147–153.

39. Ibid., pp. 97, 110–112, 165.

40. Ibid., p. 122.

CHAPTER 9

1. President's Committee on Administrative Management, *Report* (Washington, D.C.: U.S. Government Printing Office, 1937), pp. iii–iiv.

2. Ibid., pp. 5–6.

3. Richard E. Neustadt, "Approaches to Staffing the Presidency," *American Political Science Review*, 57, no. 4 (December 1963), 855–863.

4. Ibid., p. 857.

5. Harold Seidman, *Politics, Position, and Power*, 2nd ed. (New York: Oxford University Press, 1975), pp. 76–77.

6. Patrick Anderson, *The Presidents' Men* (New York: Doubleday, Anchor Books, 1969), pp. 10–11.

7. Ibid., pp. 107–133; Stephen Hess, *Organizing the Presidency* (Washington, D.C.: Brookings Institution, 1976), pp. 45–58.

8. Anderson, *Presidents' Men*, pp. 161–222; Hess, *Organizing*, pp. 60–76.

9. Anderson, *Presidents' Men*, pp. 233–317; Hess, *Organizing*, pp. 84–89.

10. Theodore C. Sorenson, *Kennedy* (New York: Harper & Row, 1965), p. 282.

11. Eric F. Goldman, *The Tragedy of Lyndon Johnson* (New York: Knopf, 1969), pp. 24–25.

12. Quoted in Anderson, *Presidents' Men*, pp. 382–383.

13. Goldman, *Tragedy of Lyndon Johnson*, pp. 120–121.

14. Richard P. Nathan, *The Plot That Failed: Nixon and the Administrative Presidency* (New York: Wiley, 1975).

15. *New York Times*, December 19, 1974, p. 53.

16. Ibid., September 3, 1974.

17. Ibid., March 12, 1978, p. 25; April 15, 1978, p. 1; *New Republic*, June 24, 1978, pp. 9–11.

18. George E. Reedy, *The Twilight of the Presidency* (Cleveland: World, 1970), pp. 4, 14–15, 80.

19. Ibid., pp. 88–89.

20. Doris Kearns, *Lyndon Johnson and the American Dream* (New York: Harper & Row, 1976), pp. 6–7.

21. *New York Times*, July 25, 1975, p. 11.

22. Ibid., March 11, 1970, p. 30.

23. Dan Rather and Gary Paul Gates, *The Palace Guard* (New York: Harper & Row, 1974), pp. 124–126.

24. Emmet John Hughes, "A White House Taped," *New York Times Magazine*, June 9, 1974, p. 68.

25. Douglas Hallett, "A Low-Level Memoir of the Nixon White House," *New York Times Magazine*, October 20, 1974, p. 39.

26. *New York Times*, January 24, 1974, p. 16.

27. George C. Homans, *The Human Group* (New York: Harcourt Brace Jovanovich, 1950), p. 113.

28. Glenn Paige, *The Korean Decision* (New York: Free Press, 1968), pp. 273–323.

29. Irving L. Janis, *Victims of Groupthink: A Psychological Study of Foreign-Policy Decisions and Fiascoes*, p 197–8. Copyright © 1972 by Houghton Mifflin Co. Reprinted by permission.

30. Ibid., pp. 13, 205.

31. Ibid., pp. 197–198.

32. *New York Times*, August 18, 1974, sec. 1, p. 34.

33. Ibid., July 10, 1975, p. 14.

34. Ibid., April 16, 1977, p. 11; July 7, 1977, p. 1.

35. Joseph P. Harris, *The Advice and Consent of the Senate* (Berkeley: University of California Press, 1953), p. 391.

36. 118 *Congressional Record* S2510–2512, February 3, 1972.

37. 118 *Congressional Record* S2408, February 2, 1972.

38. 118 *Congressional Record* S2409, February 2, 1972.

39. 1973 *Congressional Quarterly Almanac*, 709; 1974 *Congressional Quarterly Almanac* 670–671.

40. David Halberstam, *The Best and the Brightest* (New York: Random House, 1972), pp. 491–499.

41. Philip Geyelin, *Lyndon B. Johnson and the World* (New York: Praeger, 1966), pp. 170–171.

42. Alexander L. George, "The Case for Multiple Advocacy in Making Foreign Policy," *American Political Science Review*, 66, no. 3 (September 1972), 759.

43. Hess, *Organizing*, pp. 164–165.

44. Reedy, *Twilight*, p. xiii.

CHAPTER 10

1. Richard Nixon, *Public Papers: 1970* (Washington, D.C.: U.S. Government Printing Office, 1971), pp. 308–313, 315–316.

2. Louis Fisher, *Presidential Spending Power* (Princeton, N.J.: Princeton University Press, 1975), p. 29.

3. Ibid., pp. 29–30.

4. Hugh Heclo, *A Government of Strangers* (Washington, D.C.: Brookings Institution, 1977), pp. 36–46.

5. *New York Times*, February 6, 1977.

6. Ibid., January 16, 1974, p. 1; June 10, 1974, p. 1.

7. Ibid., March 10, 1974, sec. 4, p. 4; June 14, 1974, p. 12; August 6, 1974, pp. 11–16; May 20, 1977, p. A16.

8. Quoted in Richard E. Neustadt, *Presidential Power* (New York: Wiley, 1960), p. 50.

9. Quoted in Richard P. Nathan, *The Plot That Failed: Nixon and the Administrative Presidency* (New York: Wiley, 1975), p. 83.

10. Cronin, "Everybody Believes in Democracy Until He Gets to the White House," 35 *Law & Contemp. Prob.* 587 (1970).

11. Quoted in Neustadt, *Presidential Power*, p. 22.

12. Donald R. Matthews, *U.S. Senators and their World* (New York: Random House, Vintage Books, 1960), pp. 103–104.

13. Art. II, Sec. 3.

14. *Kendall v. United States* ex rel. *Stokes*, 12 Pet. 524 at 539–540 (1838).

15. Ibid., at 612–615.

16. *Myers* v. *United States*, 272 U.S. 52 at 134–135 (1926).

17. *Youngstown Sheet & Tube Co.* v. *Sawyer*, 343 U.S. 579 at 587–588 (1952).

18. Fleishman and Afses, "Law and Orders: The Problem of Presidential Legislation," 40 *Law & Contemp. Prob.* 19–20 (1976).

19. Schick, "The Budget Bureau that Was," *Law & Contemporary Problems*, 35 (1970), 519–539; Robert S. Gilmour, "Central Legislative Clearance," *Public Administration Review*, 31, no. 2 (March–April 1971), 150–158.

20. Aaron Wildavsky, *The Politics of the Budgetary Process*, 2nd ed. (Boston: Little, Brown, 1974).

21. A. Lee Fritschler, *Smoking and Politics*, 2nd ed. (Englewood Cliffs, N.J.: Prentice-Hall, 1975).

22. Max Weber, *The Theory of Social and Economic Organization*, trans. A. M. Henderson and Talcott Parsons (New York: Oxford University Press, 1947), p. 338.

23. Herman Finer, "Administrative Responsibility in Democratic Government," *Public Administration Review*, 1, no. 4 (Summer 1941), 335–350; Carl J. Friedrich, "Public Policy and the Nature of Administrative Responsibility," in *Public Policy*, eds. Carl J. Friedrich and Edward S. Mason (Cambridge, Mass.: Harvard University Press, 1940), pp. 15–16.

24. Leonard D. White, *The Federalists* (New York: Macmillan, 1948), pp. 101, 135, 164.

25. Leonard D. White, *The Jacksonians* (New York: Macmillan, 1954), p. 318.

26. Ibid., p. 351.

27. Alexis de Tocqueville, *Democracy in America* (New York: New American Library, 1956), p. 262.

28. Herbert Kaufman, "Emerging Conflicts in the Doctrines of Public Administration," *American Political Science Review*, 50, no. 4 (December 1956), 1060–1062.

29. David Garnham, "Foreign Service Elitism and U.S. Foreign Affairs," *Public Administration Review*, 35, no. 1 (January–February 1975), 44–51.

30. Joel Aberbach and Bert Rockman, "Clashing Beliefs Within the Executive Branch," *American Political Science Review*, 70, no. 2 (June 1976), 456–468.

31. *New York Times*, May 9, 1975, p. 7; July 21, 1975, p. 11; October 12, 1975, sec. 1, p. 60; *Violations and Abuses of Merit Principles in Federal Employment*, Hearings before the Subcommittee on Manpower and Civil Service of the Committee on Post Office and Civil Service, U.S. House of Representatives, 94th Cong., 1st Sess., March 4, 5, April 10, 1975, p. 10.

32. *Myers* v. *United States*, 272 U.S. 52 (1926); *Marbury* v. *Madison*, 1 Cranch 137 at 162.

33. *Myers* v. *United States*, 272 U.S. 52 at 121–122, 133–134, 163–164 (1926).

34. Quoted in Alpheus T. Mason, *Harlan Fiske Stone* (New York: Viking Press, 1956), p. 231.

35. *Humphrey's Executor* v. *United States*, 295 U.S. 602 at 628 (1935).

36. *Washington Star*, December 28, 1977, p. C5.

37. *Congressional Quarterly*, July 30, 1977, pp. 1581–1584.

38. Ibid., April 2, 1977, pp. 615–616.

39. Ibid., October 16, 1976, pp. 3009–3013.

40. Harold Seidman, *Politics, Position, and Power*, 2nd ed. (New York: Oxford University Press, 1975), pp. 116–117, 313.

41. Ibid., pp. 9–10.

42. *New York Times*, January 12, 1978, p. 1.

43. Richard Polenberg, *Reorganizing Roosevelt's Government* (Cambridge, Mass.: Harvard University Press, 1966), p. 8.

44. Arthur M. Schlesinger, Jr., *The Age of Roosevelt*, vol. 3: *The Politics of Upheaval* (Boston: Houghton Mifflin ; London: Andre Deutsch Limited, 1960), pp. 264–270, 343–361.

45. Anthony Downs, *Inside Bureaucracy* (Boston: Little, Brown, 1967), pp. 88–89.

46. Quoted in Seidman, *Politics*, pp. 96–97.

47. Ibid., pp. 226–228.

48. Kaufman, "Emerging Conflicts," 1060–1062.

CHAPTER 11

1. 10 U.S.C.A. § 142.

2. James M. Gavin, *On to Berlin* (New York: Viking Press, 1978), pp. 312–319.

3. Theodore J. Lowi, *The End of Liberalism* (New York: Norton, 1969), p. 159.

4. Ibid., pp. 166–170.

5. Samuel P. Huntington, "Civilian Control and the Military," *American Political Science Review*, 50, no. 3 (September 1956), pp. 677, 680.

6. Ibid., pp. 678, 681.

7. Ibid., pp. 682, 692.

8. Carl Sandburg, *Abraham Lincoln: The War Years* (New York: Harcourt Brace Jovanovich, 1939), vol. 5, pp. 420–421, 497–498, 591.

9. Richard H. Rovere and Arthur M. Schlesinger, Jr., *The MacArthur Controversy* (New York: Noonday Press, 1965), pp. 125–131, 145.

10. Ibid., pp. 156–157, 160–161, 169.

11. Ibid., pp. 171–172.

12. Ibid., p. 173.

13. Merle Miller, *Plain Speaking* (New York: Berkley, 1974), p. 287.

14. Rovere and Schlesinger, *MacArthur*, p. 299.

15. *New York Times*, May 22, 1977, p. 1; June 3, 1978, p. 1; *Albuquerque Journal*, April 29, 1978, p. A6.

16. *New York Times*, May 29, 1977, sec. 4, p. 4; June 3, 1978, p. 8.

17. Arthur M. Schlesinger, Jr., *A Thousand Days* (Boston: Houghton Mifflin; London: Andre Deutsch Limited, 1965), pp. 217–296.

18. Graham Allison, *Essence of Decision* (Boston: Little, Brown, 1971), pp. 118–123.

19. Ibid., 130–132.

20. Doris Kearns, *Lyndon Johnson and the American Dream* (New York: Harper & Row, 1976), pp. 266–273.

21. Ibid., 266–267, 271–272.

22. David M. Shoup, "The New American Militarism," *Atlantic*, April 1969, p. 51.

23. *New York Times*, June 18, 1972, sec. 4, p. 1.

24. Ibid., February 10, 1974, sec. 4, p. 2; February 21, 1974, p. 1; February 22, 1974, p. 1; February 23, 1974, p. 6

25. Dwight D. Eisenhower, *Public Papers: 1960–1961* (Washington, D.C.: U.S. Government Printing Office, 1961), p. 1038.

26. Lloyd S. Etheredge, *A World of Men: The Private Sources of American Foreign Policy* (Cambridge, Mass.: MIT Press, 1978), pp. 26–32.

27. *New Republic*, May 28, 1977, p. 17.

28. Douglas Kinnard, "President Eisenhower and the Defense Budget," *Journal of Politics*, 39, no. 3 (August 1977), 596–623.

29. James Clotfelter, *The Military in American Politics* (New York: Harper & Row, 1973), p. 24.

30. Tad Szulc, "Kennedy's Cold War," *New Republic*, December 24 and 31, 1977, pp. 19–21.

31. David Novick, ed., *Program Budgeting* (Washington, D.C.: U.S. Government Printing Office, 1965), p. 34.

32. David Halberstam, *The Best and the Brightest* (New York: Random House, 1972), p. 217.

33. Paul Y. Hammond, "A Functional Analysis of Defense Department Decision-

Making in the McNamara Administration," *American Political Science Review*, 62, no. 1 (March 1968), 57−69.

34. *New York Times*, October 29, 1977, p. 1; February 6, 1978, p. A17.

35. Theodore H. White, *The Making of the President—1972* (New York: Atheneum, 1973), p. 76.

36. *New York Times*, January 18, 1971, p. 1; December 2, 1974, p. 26; June 11, 1975, p. 19.

37. Ibid., August 25, 1974, Sec. 1, p. 1; *Saturday Review*, March 16, 1968, p. 22.

38. Clotfelter, *Military*, p. 144.

CHAPTER 12

1. *Marbury* v. *Madison*, 1 Cranch 137 at 176.

2. *Luther* v. *Borden*, 7 How. 1 at 47 (1849).

3. *Ex parte Merryman*, 17 Fed. Cas. 144 at 148, 152 (1861).

4. *Ashwander* v. *TVA*, 297 U.S. 288 at 341 (1936).

5. Information on the Marshall period is drawn from Albert J. Beveridge, *The Life of John Marshall* (Boston: Houghton Mifflin, 1919), vol. 3.

6. Art. III, Sec. 3.

7. *Schechter Poultry Corp.* v. *United States*, 295 U.S. 495 (1935); *Louisville Joint Stock Land Bank* v. *Radford*, 295 U.S. 555 (1935); *Humphrey's Executor* v. *United States*, 295 U.S. 602 (1935).

8. Robert H. Jackson, *The Struggle for Judicial Supremacy* (New York: Knopf, 1941), pp. 342−345.

9. Walter F. Murphy, *Congress and the Court*, (Chicago: University of Chicago Press, 1962), p. 59; *West Coast Hotel Company* v. *Parrish*, 300 U.S. 379 (1937).

10. *Tinker* v. *Des Moines*, 393 U.S. 503 (1969); *Gregory* v. *Chicago*, 394 U.S. 111 (1969); *Shuttlesworth* v. *Birmingham*, 394 U.S. 147 (1969); *Street* v. *New York*, 394 U.S. 576 (1969); *Leary* v. *United States*, 395 U.S. 6 (1969); *Brandenburg* v. *Ohio*, 395 U.S. 444 (1969); *Stanley* v. *Georgia*, 394 U.S. 557 (1969); *Shapiro* v. *Thompson*, 394 U.S. 618 (1969).

11. *Chimel* v. *California*, 395 U.S. 752 (1969); *Shipley* v. *California*, 395 U.S. 818 (1969).

12. *Alexander* v. *Holmes*, 396 U.S. 20 (1969).

13. Henry J. Abraham, *Justices and Presidents* (New York: Oxford University Press, 1974), pp. 7, 38.

14. *New York Times* v. *United States*, 403 U.S. 713 (1971); *Swann* v. *Charlotte-Mecklenburg*, 402 U.S. 1 (1971).

15. Abraham, *Justices*, p. 29.

16. *Ex parte McCardle*, 6 Wall. 318 (1868); 7 Wall. 506 (1869); Murphy, *Congress*, pp. 38—40.

17. Ibid., p. 38.

18. Ibid., pp. 154—156.

19. Quoted in Robert Hirschfield, *The Power of the Presidency*, 2nd ed. (Chicago: Aldine, 1973), pp. 71—72.

20. Arthur M. Schlesinger, Jr., *The Age of Roosevelt*, vol. 3: *The Politics of Upheaval* (Boston: Houghton Mifflin ; London: Andre Deutsch Limited,1960), p. 258.

21. *Ex parte Quirin*, 317 U.S. 1 (1942).

22. *Massachusetts v. Laird*, 400 U.S. 886 at 896 (1970).

23. *Luther v. Borden*, 7 How. 1 (1849).

24. *Prize Cases*, 2 Black 635 at 668—670 (1863).

25. *Ex parte Vallandigham*, 1 Wall. 243 (1864).

26. *Ex parte Milligan*, 4 Wall. 2 at 118—119 (1866).

27. Ibid., at 120—121.

28. *Hirabayashi v. United States*, 320 U.S. 81 (1943).

29. *Korematsu v. United States*, 323 U.S. 214 at 223—224 (1944).

30. Ibid., at 225—226.

31. *Duncan v. Kahanamoku*, 327 U.S. 304 (1946).

32. Ibid., at 343.

33. *Korematsu v. United States*, 323 U.S. 214 at 245—246 (1944).

34. *Schechter Poultry Corp. v. United States*, 295 U.S. 495 (1935).

35. *Amalgamated Meat Cutters v. Connally*, 337 F. Supp. 737 (D.D.C. 1971).

36. *Youngstown Sheet & Tube Co. v. Sawyer*, 343 U.S. 579 (1952).

37. Ibid., at 585, 587, 589.

38. Ibid., at 635—638.

39. *New York Times*, June 1, 1979, p. A10.

40. *United States v. United States District Court*, 407 U.S. 297 (1972).

41. Fleishman and Aufses, "Law and Orders: The Problem of Presidential Legislation," 40 *Law & Contemp. Prob.* 16—25 (1976).

42. *United States v. Nixon*, 418 U.S. 683 (1974).

43. *Northern Securities Co. v. United States*, 193 U.S. 197 at 400 (1904).

44. Abraham, *Justices*, pp. 62, 148–149.

45. Ibid., p. 61.

46. Ibid., p. 63.

47. Ibid., pp. 237–238; *Brown* v. *Board of Education*, 347 U.S. 483 (1954).

48. Abraham, *Justices*, p. 246.

49. *New York Times*, July 5, 1978, p. A1.

50. Ibid., May 24, 1977, p. 1.

CHAPTER 13

1. Art. II, Sec. 1.

2. Sec. 1.

3. 1 Stat. 239 (1792).

4. 61 Stat. 380 (1947).

5. Sec. 2.

6. *New York Times*, December 1, 1973, p. 31.

7. Arthur M. Schlesinger, Jr., "On the Presidential Succession," *Political Science Quarterly*, 89, no. 3 (Fall 1974), 478.

8. *Time*, October 15, 1973, p. 14.

9. *New York Times*, January 16, 1974, p. 1.

10. Schlesinger, "Succession," pp. 500–503; *Christian Science Monitor*, November 30, 1973, p. 2.

11. *New York Times*, December 27, 1973, p. 36.

12. Quoted in Philip B. Kurland, *Watergate and the Constitution* (Chicago: University of Chicago Press, 1978), p. 106.

13. *New York Times*, March 1, 1974, p. 13.

14. Ibid., February 22, 1974, p. 14.

15. Ibid., August 26, 1974, pp. 11, 16–18.

16. Raoul Berger, *Impeachment: The Constitutional Process* (Cambridge, Mass.: Harvard University Press, 1973), pp. 74, 86, 89; Kurland, *Watergate*, p. 111; Max Farrand, *Records of the Federal Convention of 1787* (New Haven, Conn.: Yale University Press, 1911), vol. 2, pp. 68–69.

17. U. S. House of Representatives, Committee on the Judiciary, 93rd Cong., 1st Sess. (1973), *Impeachment: Selected Materials*, pp. 10–11.

18. Berger, *Impeachment*, pp. 59–62; Kurland, *Watergate*, p. 109.

19. Berger, *Impeachment*, pp. 56–57; *New York Times*, March 1, 1974, p. 13.

20. Ibid., February 22, 1974, p. 14; March 1, 1974, p. 13.

21. Eric McKitrick, *Andrew Johnson and Reconstruction* (Chicago: University of Chicago Press, 1960), pp. 493–494.

22. *New York Times*, August 26, 1974, p. 12.

23. Ibid., July 11, 1974, p. 17A.

24. Ibid., August 26, 1974, p. 12.

25. Miller, "Cutting the President Down to Size—But Not Too Much," 34 *Geo. Wash. L. Rev.* 413–414 (1975).

26. Koenig, "Recipe for the President's Destruction," ibid., p. 377; Krislov, "A Moderate and Moderately Useful Response to Watergate," ibid., p. 382.

27. Beer, "Votes of Confidence in Britain," ibid., pp. 370–371.

28. Ibid., p. 366.

29. Arthur M. Schlesinger, Jr., "Parliamentary Government," *New Republic*, August 31, 1974, pp. 13–15.

30. William S. Livingston, "Britain and America: The Institutionalization of Accountability," *Journal of Politics*, 38, no. 4 (November 1976), 882.

31. Ibid., pp. 884–885.

32. James L. Sundquist, "Parliamentary Government and Ours," *New Republic*, October 26, 1974, pp. 10–12.

CHAPTER 14

1. Graham T. Allison, *Essence of Decision* (Boston: Little Brown, 1971), pp. 4–7.

2. Arthur M. Schlesinger, Jr., *The Age of Roosevelt*, 3 vols. (Boston: Houghton Mifflin, 1957–1960); *A Thousand Days* (Boston: Houghton Mifflin, 1965).

3. Arthur M. Schlesinger, Jr., *The Imperial Presidency* (Boston: Houghton Mifflin; London: Andre Deutsch Limited, 1973).

4. Ibid., pp. 127, 417.

5. Ibid., pp. 46, 50.

6. Ibid., pp. 170, 210, 212.

7. Ibid., pp. 159, 163.

8. Theodore J. Lowi, "Four Systems of Policy, Politics, and Choice," *Public Administration Review*, 32, no. 4 (July–August 1972), 298–310.

9. Lawrence H. Chamberlain, *The President, Congress and Legislation* (New York: Columbia University Press, 1946).

10. William M. Goldsmith, *The Growth of Presidential Power*, vol. 3: *Triumph and Reappraisal* (New York: Chelsea House, 1974), pp. 1390–1407.

11. George D. Greenberg and others, "Developing Public Policy Theory: Perspectives from Empirical Research," *American Political Science Review*, 71, no. 4 (December 1977), 1534, 1536.

12. Richard I. Hofferbert, *The Study of Public Policy* (Indianapolis: Bobbs-Merrill, 1974), pp. 265–266.

13. Theodore J. Lowi, "American Business, Public Policy, Case-Studies, and Political Theory," *World Politics*, 16, no. 4 (July 1964), 681.

14. Lance T. LeLoup, "Agency Policy Actions: Determinants of Nonincremental Change," in *Policy-Making in the Federal Executive Branch*, eds. Randall B. Ripley and Grace A. Franklin (New York: Free Press, 1975), pp. 65–90.

15. Daniel Patrick Moynihan, *Maximum Feasible Misunderstanding* (New York: Free Press, 1969), p. xiii.

16. Edward R. Tufte, *Political Control of the Economy* (Princeton, N.J.: Princeton University Press, 1978).

17. Ibid., pp. 10, 19–21.

18. The list is borrowed from Robert Dahl, *Polyarchy: Participation and Opposition* (New Haven, Conn.: Yale University Press, 1971).

19. Tufte, *Political Control*, pp. 11, 24–25.

20. Ibid., pp. 43–44.

21. Ibid., pp. 30–37.

22. Ibid., pp. 15–17.

23. Richard M. Nixon, *Six Crises* (New York: Doubleday, 1962), pp. 309–311.

24. Tufte, *Political Control*, pp. 32, 52.

25. U. S. Senate, Select Committee on Presidential Campaign Activities, 93rd Cong., 2nd Sess., *Presidential Campaign Activities of 1972*, bk. 19, 9157–9221 (1974).

26. Tufte, *Political Control*, p. 148.

27. Arthur M. Schlesinger, "Tides of American Politics," *Yale Review*, 29, no. 2 (December 1939), 226.

28. David C. McClelland, *Power: The Inner Experience* (New York: Irvington, 1975).

29. Ibid., pp. 252, 328.

30. Ibid., pp. 315, 326–328, 330–334.

31. Ibid., p. 66.

32. Ibid., pp. 342, 347, 355.

33. McClelland, *Power*, p. 329.

34. R. E. Donley and David G. Winter, "Measuring the Motives of Public Officials at a Distance," *Behavioral Science*, 15, no. 3 (May 1970), 227–236; David G. Winter, "What Makes Candidates Run," *Psychology Today*, 10 (July 1976), 45–49, 92.

INDEX